What some readers have bee
MANUFACTURING V

"This book is dynamite and I can't wait to see the reaction. *Manufacturing Victims* is a sizzling expose of the Psychology Industry. While showing tremendous compassion towards real victims of rape, accidents and torture, Dr. Tana Dineen skillfully takes the Psychology Industry to task for destroying families, promoting hostile views of men and women, promoting distrust and suspicion, and misusing science."

Dr. Elizabeth Loftus, President, American Psychological Society

"*Manufacturing Victims* is a spirited and deeply principled critique of the inanities and abuses of contemporary psychology. Let us hope it serves as a welcome antidote for our society's spreading addiction to toxic therapy."

Theodore Roszak, historian and author,
The Making of a Counter Culture

"A devastating critique of the business of psychotherapy. Well done. Badly needed. Long overdue. It will make a lot of people mad. I hope it makes them take a hard look at the sins of the profession.

Sam Keen, philosopher, author, and former editor of *Psychology Today*

"This penetrating, insightful and carefully documented expose will add depth and power to the national chorus of voices calling for legislative reform of the mental health industry. Dr. Dineen has performed a major service to vulnerable consumers and taxpayers who are too often called upon to bear the burdens of dangerous experimental procedures and other forms of consumer fraud disguised as 'mental health treatment.' "

Dr. Christopher Barden, President, National Association
for Consumer Protection in Mental Health Practices

"As many of us are aware, many clinical psychologists and psychiatrists are 'manufacturing victims,' and living off their creations, who are, sadly, real people. All of us concerned with what is going on can profit greatly from reading this book cover to cover."

Dr. Robyn Dawes, Carnegie Mellon University,
author, *House of Cards: Psychology and Psychotherapy Built on Myth*

Canadian Cataloguing in Publication Data

Dineen, Tana

Manufacturing victims: what the psychology industry is doing to people

2nd ed.
Includes bibliographical references and index.

ISBN 1-55207-012-3

1. Psychotherapist and patient. 2. Psychotherapists - Malpractice.
3. Psychotherapy - Economic aspects. 4. Psychotherapists - Professional
ethics. 1. Title.

R480.8.D56 1998   616.89'14'023   C98-940129-4

The ever-evolving Robert Davies Multimedia Publishing catalogue of fine
books is available on the Internet at:
http://www.rdppub.com
e-mail is received at mail@rdppub.com or rdppub@netcom.ca

Dr. Tana Dineen

Manufacturing Victims

What the Psychology Industry is Doing to People

Second edition

Robert Davies Multimedia Publishing

MONTREAL—TORONTO—PARIS

Copyright ©1996, Tana Dineen
Second edition © 1998, Tana Dineen
ISBN 1-55207-012-3

Robert Davies Multimedia Publishing Inc.,
330-4999 Saint-Catherine Street,
Westmount, Quebec, Canada H3Z 1T3
☎ 1-800-481-2440 / 1-514-481-2440 🖷 1-888-RDAVIES

Distributed in Canada by General Distribution Services
☎ 1-800-387-0141 / 1-800-387-0172 🖷 1-416-445-5967;

in the U.S.A.,
from General Distribution Services,
Suite 202, 85 River Rock Drive, Buffalo, NY 14287
☎ 1-800-805-1083
or from Ingram Book Company

In the U.K. from Lavis Marketing (Oxford)

For all other countries, please order from publisher
e-mail: mail@rdppub.com
Visit our Internet website:
http://www.rdppub.com

The publisher takes this opportunity to thank the Canada Council
and the Ministère de la Culture du Québec (Sodec)
for their continuing support of publishing.

*This book is dedicated to the old woman
with the scar across her face who said:
"Never call me a victim;"
she made her point.*

Table of Contents

ACKNOWLEDGEMENTS

I am indebted to those people throughout my life who have encouraged my will to think and to ask questions. I consider myself lucky to have met, Aldred Neufeldt who, first as a research advisor and later as a friend and colleague, has shown repeatedly how to infuse concepts such as ethics, integrity and tolerance with meaning. I am grateful to him and to "those voices in the wilderness" who remain passionately interested in life's mysteries and who persist in their attempts to uphold the principles of the science of psychology.

I want to express my appreciation especially to George Matheson for making it impossible to avoid writing this book, to Rachel Pollack for never doubting that I could write it, to Alan Gold for his constructive criticism of successive drafts, to Gordon Banta for his helpful suggestions and to Sharon Butala for being the steadfast friend who was always just a phone call away.

As well, I am grateful to have found for a publisher an individual as remarkable and provocative as Robert Davies. And, finally, I would like to express my sincere thanks to Jacques Dumont for his meticulous proof-reading, and to Lucie Lariviere and the resourceful staff at the Greater Victoria Public Library for their assistance with the research.

Preface

One waits in vain for psychologists to state the limits of their knowledge.
Noam Chomsky

I was first drawn to the study of psychology by a fascination with human nature, the complexity of life, the content of consciousness and the richness of symbols. Being both curious and sceptical, I was inclined to ask questions, to look for alternative explanations and to challenge assumptions. While I have enjoyed the research and the clinical work of the past 30 years, I have noted, with increasing distress, a shift within psychology from questions to answers, from curiosity to certainty, from modesty to pretentiousness. Now I find that I am distancing myself from my profession, preferring to use the pronoun *"they"* when referring to psychologists. For me, there can be no pride associated with belonging to a group which is intent on interfering in people's lives as it promotes its own interests under the guise of an established science and the deceptive image of a responsible profession.

Amongst my early teachers were the psychologist, Donald Hebb, and the neurosurgeon, Wilder Penfield. Both taught, by example, the excitement of exploring human mysteries and the importance of maintaining a clear distinction between knowledge and speculation. Despite their accomplishments, reputations, and status, they remained inquisitive, humble and approachable. I can still remember Hebb talking to me about the science of psychology, both its possibilities and its limitations. He was fond of stating that psychology was "more than common sense" and of explaining that he was not implying that psychologists have access to any fund of superior knowledge but rather suggesting that they have an obligation to weigh and examine all issues in a cautious, scientific manner and to remember always that current knowledge is only partial and imperfect.

It was in 1969, while developing a system to monitor and evaluate psychiatric diagnosis and treatment in a general hospital, that I had my first glimpse of psychologists acting as if they had access to some hidden fund of superior knowledge. The extreme confidence of many of the psychiatrists I observed disturbed me. It seemed that there was no room in their minds for doubts and no space for questions. I became wary of the accuracy of their judgments and concerned about the impact of their opinions on people's lives. My research over the next few years looked into how psychiatrists went about deciding what was wrong with their patients and what treatment was needed. When I began systematically to examine their decision making, it became evident that personal beliefs and subjective theories, especially about the causes of problems, influenced their diagnoses and treatments more so than did any available information about individual patients, including observable symptoms and verifiable histories.[1] It was clear that diagnoses were generally more consistent with the psychiatrists' beliefs than with the patients' problems.[2] My findings became part of a growing body of scientific literature which, at that time, was being used to challenge the patriarchal authority of the psychiatric profession.[3]

Later, as I moved into clinical work, first as treatment director in a large psychiatric hospital and later in private practice, I tried to ignore the continual flow of beliefs disguised as findings, the psychological fads promoted as the latest discoveries and the spread of "pop psychology." I concentrated on clinical puzzles ranging from the identification of serious mental illnesses such as schizophrenia to the treatment planning for problems such as developmental disorders to working with people in difficult situations or wanting more out of life. Over the years, I met some very disturbed people who needed help and even protection. However, most of the patients who have come to my office in recent years I would refuse to categorize in this way. I would consider it dishonest to declare them "sick," harmful to label them traumatized or damaged, and disrespectful to treat them as less competent, capable or mature than people I meet in other contexts.

Unfortunately, in the 90's, it has become the accepted role of psychologists to categorize people in these debilitating ways and to turn them into victims and, thus, patients. Adopting the same arrogant tone which so disturbed me back in the 70's, psychologists now translate all of life into a myriad of abuses, addictions and traumas. And they do this not only in psychiatric hospitals and psychology offices but in homes, schools, business settings, media interviews and in courtroom testimony everywhere. It has become the accepted practice to substitute personal belief and theoretical dogma for scientific fact. Psychologists are claiming to know what is "good" and what is "bad," what hurts people and what helps them, and their answers are making people unsure of themselves and suspicious of each other. Psychologists are striving to promote and extend their influence at the expense of creating a society which is self-absorbed and distrustful. By authoritatively defining which human actions and feelings are to be encouraged and which are not to be tolerated, they are dictating how men and women are to live their lives and how society is to function.

I recognize that not all psychologists are allowing themselves to be swept along by seductive theorizing and popular beliefs. However, while continuing to distinguish "fact" from "opinion" and resisting becoming victim-makers themselves, most are hesitating to express their dissenting views. Fearful of jeopardizing their own financial security and reputations, afraid of personal attacks, or concluding that there is nothing they can do, they are choosing to remain silent. Thus, those psychologists who claim to know the answers, are rarely challenged as they go about rewriting private memories, playing on emotions, dictating how events are to be experienced, and casting people into victim roles. Claiming to be helping people, they are making them dependent, propping them up, using them as pawns, and profiting from them.

In the fall of 1993, after spending an afternoon with a colleague reflecting on what was happening in psychology, I asked, half jokingly, whether he thought that psychologists might soon start leaving the profession the way dissenting priests had, some time ago, begun to leave the church. He paused, thought for a moment, and then replied: "Not a chance. There's too much money in it."[4] There was not a hint of humour in his voice; his tone was so serious and his manner so sombre that his words stuck in my head.

Psychology has become big business. It is simply no longer accurate to speak of it as a science and it is unscrupulously misleading to call it a profession. To do so is to maintain the false impression that all psychologists are skillful, dedicated, caring healers, who consistently put their desire to alleviate the suffering of others above their own entrepreneurial interests. It would be too sweeping a generalization to say that there are no psychologists who exhibit these admirable qualities. Such individuals do exist. However, these people are difficult to find amidst the vast workforce which puts hourly rates on compassion and price tags on unsubstantiated beliefs. By and large, psychology is neither a science nor a profession but rather an industry focussed on self-interest and propelled by financial incentives.

This book is about the industry - the business of turning people into victims in need of psychological services. In recent years, I have come to accept an ethical obligation not only to personally dissociate from this business but, also, to speak out and take whatever action I can to curb its influence. I find it no longer possible to ignore the spewing of psychological "facts," "interpretations," and "solutions" and to avoid facing the vast scope of their pernicious influence. In some ways, this book is my apology for decades of "biting my lip." It takes a cold, hard look at the damaging effects which psychologists are having on individuals and on society.

It does not limit its focus to the harm being done by virtue of "the false memories" which some psychologists are now being accused of creating. Rather, it identifies "Recovered Memory Therapy" as only one facet of a business enterprise which relies on the manufacture and maintenance of a continuously expanding variety of "victims." This book broadens the focus to include other facets, critically examining generally accepted beliefs, not only about repressed memories, but also about the effects of traumas, the epidemic of addictions, the prevention of violence, the fragility of women, the vulnerability of children and the ravages of stress. It looks at how psychologists are promoting these beliefs and, at the same time, selling to consumers their own bogus products, calling them "proven effective" treatments and packaging them as solutions to social problems.

Unfortunately this junk has come to predominate applied psychology and, while I admire the efforts of those few colleagues who are trying to re-establish a connection between the science and the practice of psychology, this book is not intended to contribute to any ongoing attempt on their part to save the profession. I wish that I could be more optimistic and support them in their efforts; however, I have little hope that constructive change can come from within the profession. There are too many psychologists in the marketplace scrambling for dollars and the professional organizations, including the American Psychological Association and the state and provincial licensing boards, are too caught up in the business enterprise to be willing (or able) to address the sweeping problems. I believe that it is too late to instill rationality, integrity, or humility into them and, from them, into the practice of psychology.

Given the strong economic and political roots of this industry and the extent to which North Americans have become enamoured of what it sells, I harbour no delusions that this book will "bring down the industry." I am fully aware that many psychologists, and many people who have learned to see themselves as victims and as patients, will not look with favour upon this book. However, it is my hope that it will encourage others to begin looking at psychologists and at the practice of psychology differently. I hope that it will inspire sensible people to reassert their right to think for themselves and stimulate them to question the statements that psychologists make, demanding research in place of rhetoric and logic in place of persuasion. I would like to see people challenge the authority, power and privilege of the purported psychological experts of this era, curb the damages being done by psychologists, diminish the influence of the psychology industry, and take back their own lives.

Endnotes

1. Dineen, Tana. *Diagnostic Decision Making in Psychiatry*. Doctoral Thesis, University of Saskatchewan, Saskatoon, 1975.

2. For instance, one psychiatrist labelled all patients as having a "Depressive Neurosis," claiming that this term was likely to do them the least harm on their medical records; another, refusing to apply any label, attributed all problems to existential conflicts; another, seeing the cause of all symptoms to be metabolic, prescribed niacin therapy for everyone; and another, seeing childhood experiences as the root of all difficulties, sought to identify these.

3. At that time, expertise regarding psychological illness was attributed almost exclusively to medical doctors trained in psychiatry; thus, it was primarily psychiatrists rather than other mental health professional (psychologists, social workers, etc.) whose authority was challenged.

4. This comment was made by Sam Keen, a former editor of *Psychology Today*, who left theology in the 50's and philosophy in the 60's. I have always respected Sam because, in his work and in his life, he has consistently balked at rigidity and continued to wonder about life's mysteries.

Preface to the Second Edition

The first edition of *Manufacturing Victims* drew volatile reactions from within The Psychology Industry. It was instantly dismissed as "a conspiracy book" and later called "The Ripley's Believe It Or Not of Psychology." One psychologist, having read only a brief news report about the book, diagnosed me as suffering from "burnout;" another, having watched me on a national television show, lodged a formal complaint with my licensing board and I and my book are now under investigation in the name of "protecting the television-watching public."

These reactions, as well as the testimony of the "the experts" in courts and "the healers" in their offices, are consistent with the views promoted by The Psychology Industry; that people are incapable of thinking for themselves, taking responsibility for their own actions or living their own lives. Put simply, The Psychology Industry considers and treats people as children who, regardless of age, experience, education or status must be protected, guided, sheltered, excused and disciplined.

I find the prospect of this emerging new paternalistic society in which the "fathers" (the "paters") are the psychologists, whose knowledge is superior and whose power is absolute, to be intolerable. So, I find myself in the role of renegade, openly challenging the authority of my profession.

Many readers of the first edition, including a number of concerned colleagues, have contacted me to let me know how *Manufacturing Victims* has been useful to them in raising questions, challenging "experts," making arguments, winning legal cases and facing moral dilemmas. This second edition includes updated references to research findings being ignored by The Psychology Industry and fresh examples of phoney maladies being marketed, phantom cures being promoted, and self-protective maneuvers being taken. It is my hope that it will provide yet more "meat," and that sensible people will make good use of it in their own efforts to purge the Justice System, Health Care, Education, Religion, and their own personal lives of The Psychology Industry's influence.

Readers are invited to keep me updated and to send information, comments, reactions, questions or criticisms to me directly by visiting the book's frequently updated WEBsite at:

http://scholefieldhouse.com/mv/

Tana Dineen
Victoria, B.C.
January, 1998

INTRODUCTION

Of all the tyrannies a tyranny sincerely exercised for the good of its victims
may be the most oppressive... To be cured against one's will
and of states which we may not regard as disease is to be put on the level with those
who have not yet reached the age of reason or those who never will;
to be classed with infants, imbeciles, and domestic animals.

C.S. Lewis

Psychology presents itself as a concerned and caring profession working for the good of its clients. But in its wake lie damaged people, divided families, distorted justice, destroyed companies, and a weakened nation. Behind the benevolent facade is a voracious self-serving industry that proffers "facts" which are often unfounded, provides "therapy" which can be damaging to its recipients, and exerts influence which is having devastating effects on the social fabric. The foundation of modern psychology, its questioning and critical thinking, if not an illusion from its inception, has at the very least been largely abandoned in favour of power and profit, leaving only the guise of integrity, a show of arrogance and a well-tuned attention to the bottom line. What seemed once a responsible profession is now a big business whose success is directly related to how many people become "users."

No matter where one turns, one find the effects of the psychology industry. Its influence extends across all aspects of life, telling us how to work, how to live, how to love and, even, how to play. We are confronted by psychologists expounding their theories on the endless list of TV talk-shows like Oprah and Larry King, on the TV news journals and in the supermarket tabloids, on subjects as wide-ranging as the "re-caps" of celebrity trials or the epidemic of post traumatic stress disorders after disasters.

Meanwhile, people who are mildly anxious, slightly unhappy or just plain bored are turning more and more to psychology for relief. Some do this through weekly appointments; some do it by frequenting seminars and workshops; some do it by endlessly buying books on "abuse," "adult children," "trauma and stress," and "recovery;" all in the pursuit of an elusive experience held out, like a carrot or a pot of gold, by the Psychology Industry.

It is not news to say that psychology has become an influential force or that society is becoming more and more filled with people who consider themselves victims of one sort or another.

What *is* news is that psychology is itself manufacturing most of these victims, that it is doing this with motives based on power and profit, and that the industry turns people into dependent "users" with no escape from their problems.

The Recovered Memory/False Memory controversy which has raged over the past five years has served as a major stimulus of skepticism in the courts and in the general public regarding psychology. The shock reverberating through the "industry" as more and more accusations are being identified as false and some prominent court decisions are being overturned, suggests that soon, for the first time in history, a psychological product will actually be declared harmful and withdrawn from the therapeutic shelf. "Repressed Memory Therapy" is undeniably under attack as serious damages to individuals, families and the court system are being recognized.[1]

However, the public needs to recognize that what has been exposed is "just the tip of the iceberg" of the problems created by the Psychology Industry. While important in and of itself, remaining focussed on only this particularly untested and unsafe product must not distract attention away from the fact that it is just one example of a much larger, generalized business of manufacturing Fabricated Victims. While people have become used to hearing about all sorts of victims, from those of sexual harassment and verbal abuse, to those of "dysfunctional families," divorce, academic discrimination, even vacation cancellation and home renovation, they have not yet paid attention to the psychological techniques which are being used to create and cater to these "victims." Nor have they noticed how it is the psychologists who are benefitting in the end from this victim-making, as the industry grows in power and affluence, as it creates a market dependent on its services.

Whether psychologists ply their trade in a direct manner by assessing and treating peoples' problems or in an indirect fashion as experts in courts, consultants to government or spokespersons to the media, they foster and promote the positive public image of themselves as caring and powerful. What the Psychology Industry wants people to believe is that it "knows what is best" and that it has special skills which enable it to "know what is true." For example, psychiatrist, Judith Herman, wrote in the popular book *Trauma and Recovery*:

> The therapist becomes the patient's ally, placing all the resources of her knowledge, skill, and experience at the patient's disposal... The patient enters therapy in *need of help and care*. By virtue of this fact, she voluntarily submits herself to an unequal relationship in which the therapist has *superior status and power*.[2]

But who can long remain an ally to a more powerful and more important partner?

The Psychology Industry is not an ally at all; it is a self-serving business determined to extend its influence, expand its markets and increase its overall profits. Motivated by the lust for power and money, the Psychology Industry intends that people accept their need for psychology, assume an inferior and dependent role, and become "users." It is through caring that psychologists create need, and through helping, that they establish dependency.

Consider the following apparently disparate cases:

- A toll free number is promoted nationally for psychological help if people consider themselves "victims of the Oklahoma City Bombing." And psychologists develop a public-education campaign on stress management "to turn this disaster into something productive for survivors so they don't feel their loved ones died in vain."3

- A group of US psychologists train Bosnian and Croatian mental health professionals in a new technique to treat Post Traumatic Stress Disorders in thousands of traumatized war victims.4

- A team of social workers travels to the Middle East to identify and treat the psychological casualties of Operation Desert Storm. They report on the benefits of their work and conclude that "early recognition of the traumatic experiences will assist veterans in seeking treatment sooner and developing an awareness of stress in themselves and family members."5

- The American Psychological Association (APA), using "rape as a barometer of female fear," states that there is "no safe haven" for women, recommends collecting more data on female-directed violence and advocates the development of "more innovative treatment" for both female victims and male perpetrators.6

- The Canadian Register of Health Service Providers in Psychology (CRHSPP) reports on the success of "a cardiovascular marketing project," designed to promote psychology as "an authoritative resource, with knowledge, skills and techniques...integral to the process of CV illness prevention."7

- Psychologists announce that Post Traumatic Stress Disorder is "ambushing many World War II veterans just as they begin to settle into retirement," causing them to require psychological treatment for their repressed stress disorders.8

- A Toronto woman helps to abduct; then, sexually assaults and participates in the murder of two teen-age girls. A psychologist "explains" that her behaviour is due to being a victim of "battered wife syndrome."9

- A doctor in Vermont states that caffeine is "a drug of abuse," pointing out that six million Americans are unable to quit, and suggesting that "the mental health community needs the ability to diagnose caffeine abuse and begin developing treatment services."10

- Social Workers in California refer to predictions that by the year 2000 the depressed elderly will constitute 13% of the US population and suggest ways social work can take an active role in targeting "the large pool of elderly clients" in need of treatment.11

- A man in British Columbia writes to the Prime Minister of Canada demanding "an apology and compensation for his [dead] father's struggle with delayed stress syndrome from the Second World War," which he claims made the family's home life "at times...a living hell."[12]
- A former comedienne completes her Ph.D. dissertation on the deleterious effects of fame on the famous and begins her professional life as an L.A. psychologist specializing in "the anguish of fame."[13]
- Parents are urged to seek counselling for children who are doing well in school because they may be victims of success and suffering from "over-achiever syndrome."

What do all of these situations have in common? Each of these "noble" efforts evokes the image of the world as a dangerous place strewn with psychological casualties, and promotes the seemingly humanitarian idea that more psychological services are needed to reduce "the risks" and tend to "the wounded." In all cases, a psychological formula is being applied defining various groups of people as victims who are in need of psychological help. This is the process involved in the "manufacturing of victims" by the Psychology Industry. These examples illustrate how psychologists are applying their business formula:

PERSON = VICTIM = USER/PATIENT = PROFIT

"Victim," once a term reserved for those who suffered from a calamity of nature, of Fate or of violent crime, now has become psychologized so that it can be applied broadly to anyone and everyone who knowingly, or unknowingly, has been exposed to or experienced stress, distress or trauma. Symptoms such as unhappiness, boredom, anger, sadness, and guilt, can now all

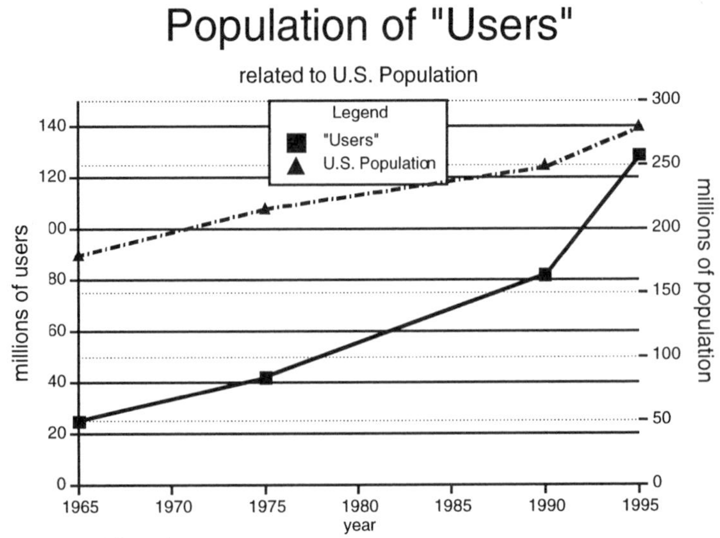

Population of "Users"

related to U.S. Population

Figure 1

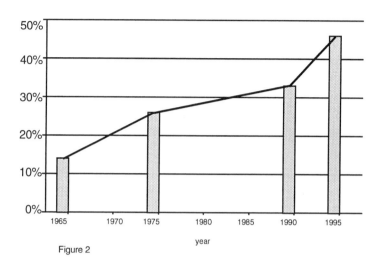

Psychology "Users"
as per cent of U.S" Population

Figure 2

be interpreted as signs of prior trauma, creating victims. Whether these people then pursue treatment, sue their perpetrator, or seek other victims for support, they all become "users" of the Psychology Industry, providing its income and increasing its overall asset worth.

Evidence of the current success and growth of the Psychology Industry can be seen in the number of Americans who have become users. In the early 1960's, 14% of the U.S. population (25 million of a total 180 million) had ever received psychological services. By 1976, that number had risen to 26%.[14] However by 1990, at least 33% (83 million of 250 million) had been psychological users at some point in their lives and in 1995, the American Psychological Association stated that 46% of the US population (128 million) had seen a mental health professional.[15] Some even predict that by the year 2000 users will be the majority — constituting 80% of the population.[16]

With messages about being at risk, upset or wronged, the Psychology Industry lures people into victim roles; then, offers them the opportunity to change from "victim to victor," "survivor to thriver" and, as well, to reap side benefits which seem attractive.

There are many incentives for acquiring, and even for seeking, victim status and, in the short term, there are some pay-offs. The tragedies, the failures, the hardships, the health problems, and the disappointments of life become explained, relieving people of at least three of life's natural burdens: dealing with complexity, facing things beyond their control, and accepting personal responsibility for decisions and actions. The newest psychological technologies promise relief from these and, as well, they give people who have led the dullest of lives, a thread of meaning or a dash of excitement. Lives which seem shamefully ordinary, even boring, take on a melodramatic quality. "Victim" stories flow into conversations, becoming the excuses for the embarrassments, regrets, limitations or failures of people's lives. For some, including many of the "recovery movement" gurus in the industry, victim status itself is the credential which qualifies them as psychologists.[17] For these psychological entrepreneurs and for many others, being a "victim" opens the door to a successful career. And it offers opportunities to place outside oneself the blame for how life has turned out and to express outrage, not only privately, but to attentive audiences and in courts of law.

Near the beginning of the 20th century it was suggested that "Psychologists should ... take the place of doctors, counsellors, fortune tellers, and relatives,"[18] and now, at the dawn of the 21st century, it seems that the Psychology Industry has discovered how to achieve this goal. It is because the current business formula is working so well that there is such an urgency now to expose psychology as the irresponsible and out-of-control industry it has become.

What is referred to in this book as the "*Psychology Industry*" is still thought by the public to be something quite different from other industries, somehow more noble, honest, and less profit driven. When people think of industries, they tend to think of automobiles, computers, cosmetics or entertainment; of easily identifiable products, with price-tags, warranties and trademarks. Such industries are visibly defined by their products and by their boundaries. The Psychology Industry is much harder to pin down; it is much broader than other industries, less defined (or definable). At its core, along with the traditional mental health professions of psychology, psychiatry, psychoanalysis and clinical social work, is a fifth psychological profession: psychotherapy.[19] No longer can clear distinctions be made between them; so, what I call the Psychology Industry comprises all five of these and it encompasses, as well, the ever expanding array of psychotherapists: the counsellors and advisors of all persuasions, whether licensed, credentialed, proclaimed, or self-proclaimed. This view is consistent with that of the American Psychological Association: "The general public often has difficulty in understanding the differences between professional psychologists and *other types of psychologists*, between professional psychologists and psychiatrists, between psychologists and counsellors, or between psychologists and *a variety of other professionals who deal with emotional, health, and behavioral problems*."[20]

As well, this term acknowledges that around the edges of the industry are other individuals whose work, whether it involves writing, consulting, lecturing, or even movie-making, relies on the Psychology Industry which, in turn, benefits from their promotion of all things psychological.

Psychology is not the profession that it claims to be nor is it just a business like other businesses. It is too big and too dangerous now not to be seen, and critiqued, as an industry complete with advertising slogans, sales and marketing programs, research and development, production and assembly lines, and unions. This is the era of licensed, credentialed, certified, and otherwise proclaimed or self-proclaimed "psychologists." With degrees in psychology, medicine, social work, nursing or with no academic qualifications at all, the expanding work force of the Psychology Industry relies for its survival and growth on its ability to manufacture victims. Specializing in trauma, stress and abuse, an increasing number of psychologists are competing for "victim dollars." Few of them ask any questions or show any reservations about their business. Most equate expert status with their own unquestioned and adamant beliefs which, with no pause for critical thought or responsible reflection, they present as "findings" and "facts."

When the term *"psychologist"* (with a small "p") is used in this book, as it is over and over again, it is with reference to this larger and somewhat diffuse group of people. The choice to use the term in this way will surely offend and annoy professional organizations, licensing boards and many of my colleagues who wish to "protect" this title for Licensed Psychologists. It is acknowledged that there are those who have resisted becoming part of the industry and instead continued to take research seriously, admitting the limits of their knowledge, and showing respect for people. But this is not because they have a Ph.D or are licensed; it is because of who they are. Some are attempting to save what remains of the science and of the ethical practice of psychology, but a change of this magnitude can not come from within the professions, the fraternal organizations and the licensing boards which have failed to protect the public and continue to promote the industry.

This business, which presents itself authoritatively in a language which appears to be scientific, has succeeded in turning American society into what Charles Sykes recently termed "a nation of victims."[21] In this regard, another term, *"user,"* is employed throughout this book to identify the broad scope of individuals who either directly or indirectly use the services of the Psychology Industry. It refers not only to those who are clients and patients of psychologists, for some are "users," even though they may never have visited a psychologist, because they adopt and apply psychologized concepts about behaviours, thoughts and feelings. The examples are so plentiful, so pervasive and so much a part of everyday life that they go unrecognized as the products, the end results of the Psychology Industry.

People smile knowingly at cartoons which appear in daily newspapers and magazines. But they miss the point. Taking on a role of victim is no laughing matter.

Virtually everyone who is not already a "user", knows someone who is. The following examples demonstrate the variety of "victims" manufactured, and serviced, by the industry.

A patient I was seeing for the first time in my clinical practice, asked to be hypnotized so that he could discover whatever it was in his past that was making him the way he was now. He had recently watched a television show about satanic ritual abuse which suggested to him that he may be a "victim" and that finding a buried trauma was "the answer."[22] The man, who had a long psychiatric history, reported that on the way to his appointment with me he had resisted the voices in his head telling him to kill the person standing next to him at the bus stop. He described how he "enjoyed" sticking sharp objects up his rectum and produced the bizarre thoughts he had been writing down. His symptoms indicated a biologically based mental illness, schizophrenia. He was told that he would not be hypnotized until it was determined that it was both safe and appropriate. But he believed he had learned of "the answer" to his problems. He refused consent to see his treatment history, and he insisted on an immediate referral to someone he had heard of who was prominent in the area of ritual abuse, a local licensed psychologist. I agreed to call her and after a discussion of the case lasting less than a minute, she stated that the man was a "victim" of satanic ritual abuse and that she could arrange for him to be "treated." She had arrived at her instant diagnosis without asking a single question.[23] Reluctantly, the patient was given the referral he had requested. Very early one morning he called me from a phone booth having been in a hospital emergency department all night receiving thirty stitches, after obeying the voices in his head which had told him to gash himself open with a piece of sharp glass. His psychologist, whom he had been seeing weekly for over a year, had recently informed him that he was not improving because he required two, rather than only one, session per week to deal with the effects of his ritual abuse. He reported that he still couldn't remember having been abused in the ways she described and that he couldn't afford two sessions a week. He asked what to do.

This is but one of many examples in my experience in which psychologists have been bent on applying the formula for profit. The individual becomes "the victim" and thus, "the patient" who needs ongoing (i.e. endless) psychological treatment and, in an enterprising rather than scientific way, the failure to achieve success is explained as indicating the need for more not less.

Examples like this are not found only in clinical practice. For instance, a hairdresser whose warmth and resilience had always impressed me suddenly changed; there was no sparkle and no animated conversation. When asked why, she told of discovering that she was a "victim of incest" and described how memories had begun coming back of how her father had sexually abused her from the time she was six months old. She was in therapy now and that was all she had to talk about.[24] She had lost her vitality and independence, relying on her psychologist to interpret her past, explain her present and predict her future. For the psychologist, a profitable business relationship had been established.

The entrepreneurial strategy can sometimes be quite apparent. For instance, a couple went to a marriage counsellor, who saw each of them separately to begin "the process" of improving their relationship. At the end of the husband's second session, the psychologist informed him that the problems he and his wife were having were due to the "fact" that he was a "victim of a dysfunctional family." He had told her only that his father had often been away from home for work reasons when he was a child and she concluded from this that his father was an alcoholic, which was news to him, and that he should view himself as an "adult child of an alcoholic" needing long-term treatment.[25] His wife had laughed at him when he told her about his session, refusing to believe that the psychologist could have come to this bizarre conclusion. However, when she next saw the psychologist, she was given the same explanation for their problems. Both she and her husband concluded that the psychologist was dangerous and they managed to get away before becoming entangled in her beliefs and trapped in her business.

A young woman told me recently, how she was avoiding phone calls from a friend who had discovered her "wounded inner child" and talked incessantly about "her." The woman's description of her friend's stories, were reminiscent of a John Bradshaw workshop I had attended at which I had been horrified by the cult-like atmosphere and by the required "exercises" which basically dictated to people the scripts of their own childhood.[26] In one of these exercises the participants were told to visualize a playground scene and then told to rescue their child self. They were informed that, if the child resisted, they should drag him or her away from the dark past anyway, kicking and screaming if necessary, into the modern daylight of a therapist's office. An evangelical force had pervaded that room and the standing ovation at the end from the audience of over 1,000, caused me to wonder how many workshops this woman's friend would pay to attend, how many tapes, books, and teddy bears she would buy and whether, in the end, she would have any friends left who would not be avoiding her phone calls.

This example illustrates two effective aspects of the Psychology Industry. Once individuals accept a "victim" label, they become open to a wide variety of psychological services and their lives become centred around them. Like the hairdresser described earlier, being a victim becomes all they have to think, talk or read about. And it becomes the focus of their spending. As well, the entrepreneur, the workshop or seminar leader, the psychological expert, can use victim terminology to promote the industry's view that everyone needs help whether they know it or not. Instead of a light at the end of the tunnel, now there is a psychologist waiting to be paid.

Some time ago, a seventeen year old girl in a small town was hit by a car. The girl was killed and the parents were overwhelmed by what had happened. One of their neighbours suggested that the community take up a collection to pay for a series of grief counselling sessions for the parents. Instantly the surviving parents, rather than the dead girl, had become defined as "the victims." And just as quickly, they were being cast into a "patient" role, becoming part of the market for all of the books, articles and courses about the "normal" stages of grieving which package raw human emotions into sanitized psychological stages.[27] Would it not be better to consider what had happened as a tragic event and what these parents were going through as their own private, and quite inconsolable, feelings of sadness and loss?

Would it not be better to let them turn to God or to each other? But grieving and mourning are no longer within the domain of either family or religion. They have been bought up by the Psychology Industry which markets grieving now as a psychological process to be carried out under supervision and offers gift certificates as substitutes for flowers. How bizarre it is that now anyone who is suffering is viewed as "a victim." And that society has accepted the idea that there must be some psychological solution to all of life's pain and that for a price one can buy it for oneself or even purchase it as a gift.

A newspaper printed a full page article about "Reno Survivors," the growing number of couples who require the help of a licensed psychologist to save their marriages from the fallout from home renovations, including disagreements about paint colours and financial strains. Next to this article about the horrors endured by couples at war over renovations was one in which a psychologist pointed out that home renovations were equally difficult for singles, whose sense of security could be dangerously chipped away in the process.[28] The renovation of a kitchen or bathroom is a battle scene, from which one's emergence as either victim or victor is determined by access to a good psychologist. Had this been in the comic section it might have caused a nervous laugh but, clearly, it was not meant as a joke.

Another article provided a demonstration of how psychologists are applying the formula to manufacture victims by targeting the veterans of real wars; giving suggestions about unresolved traumas and how they can be triggered. It spoke of how, a half century after the end of the Second World War, the aging veterans were having their traumatic memories triggered by anniversary celebrations. As an example, it gave a 72-year-old veteran, recently diagnosed as suffering from "post-traumatic stress disorder," describing his nightmares and the guilt he was feeling over having killed a young German soldier by slashing his throat with a bayonet. "Now a half century later only one of them can rest in peace..." Why call the surviving war veteran "a victim"? Why turn his moral turmoil into a psychological illness? Could it be that the Psychology Industry sees a potential market here, that with Veteran's Administration (VA) funding drying up for psychologists, there is a need to create some new demand for services? Could it be that the toll free number at the end of the article which "veterans experiencing sleeplessness, anxiety, crying spells, flashbacks, depression or heavy drinking" were invited to call, is part of a marketing scheme?[29] It may sound cynical but remember that the Psychology Industry needs "users."

Much as the marketing of Rolex watches or Gucci bags has led to the emergence of frauds and counterfeits, the psychological mass marketing of the "victim" has been so successful that it has its own counterfeits. For example, a bank teller described the problems she was having with her daughter. The girl, who was seeing a social worker because she was flagrantly disobeying the rules at home and at school, had threatened to make up a story about how her new step-father was sexually abusing her. Unless her mother agreed to let her stay out as late as she liked, buy anything she wanted and do anything she pleased, she would tell her social worker the story. The recently remarried mother was horrified and her new husband was terrified. They had both read too many newspaper reports about people being criminally charged on the basis of such stories and they were trying to find a way to deal with being held hostage under this threat of "crying victim."

The word "victim" used to evoke images of blood and torn limbs on a battlefield, naked bodies thrown into a mass grave, scenes of torture, terrible accidents, brutal murders and violent rapes. These harsh images, which defined the word, have now been fused with fuzzy images of people grieving, expressing regrets, hugging teddy bears, making threats or rushing to a psychologist in the midst of an argument over home improvements. Certainly there are people today who can be recognized in terms of the harsh, rather than the fuzzy, images; such as the three described in these news reports:

> The body of a six year old girl, no part of which was not cut or bruised, was buried in Cyprus Hills Cemetery in New York. Before Elisa's mother had smashed her against a concrete wall, she had repeatedly sexually assaulted her daughter with a toothbrush and a hairbrush, had forced her to eat her own feces, and had used her head as a mop to clean the floor. Elisa had stopped attending school; neighbours had listened to her scream and moan and plead with her mother to stop; her mother had phoned the police and told them what she was doing; and, social workers had known she was "at risk" from the day she was born to a homeless crack addict.[30]

★ ★ ★

> The old man's head moved and his eyes opened as the body collectors threw him into the truckload of corpses Wednesday.
>
> "He's alive! That man's alive!" shouted a photographer.
>
> The Zairians loading the bodies were unmoved. "He may be alive now, but he's dying and we're not going to be coming back this way today," said the man in charge. However he yielded to journalists' begging to retrieve the man, who likely died later by the roadside.[31]

★ ★ ★

> A Manhattan woman on her way to work with her infant daughter in her arms was shot to death Saturday when she was used as a human shield in what police say was a drug dispute.
>
> Flower-seller, Cynthia Diaz Roanova, 18, had just left her apartment, carrying her 10-month-old daughter, when one of two men arguing on the street outside the building pulled a gun...Three shots were fired, one hitting the victim in the face...[32]

These people are victims. And everyone has known authentic victims. One who comes quickly to my mind is a little boy in Truillo, Peru. He walked up to me one sunny day as I was sitting on a bench in the town square. He glanced with curiosity at my Spanish dictionary and pointed to my shoes, wanting to shine them for what would have amounted to a few pennies. Wanting to learn something about his life, I asked him, in Spanish, to sit for a minute and talk with me. He told me that he was eight years old, had no idea who his parents were, and lived "on the streets" in the slum area; he couldn't write his name and he had no address. He pointed to a man watching us from across the square, saying that he was the boss to whom he and the other kids like him reported. He explained that by shining enough shoes during the day he could earn something to eat at night. He said that often he didn't earn enough, sometimes going several days with nothing to eat. He showed me the scars and fresh burn marks on his hands and arms, saying that he'd have more of these if he didn't get back to work. He smiled and waved good-bye as he ran off across the square seeking another customer. That was his life; every day he struggled to survive. But that little boy was alert to what was going on around him and he was very much alive.

I think of him often and, sometimes, I wonder what happened to him and whether, by some miracle, he managed to escape. In many years of clinical practice, I have seen a number of patients who are authentic survivors, many of accidents, some of crimes, and a few of situations a bit similar to his.

Some time ago, a young woman came to my office with a specific request. She was a Christian Iranian, who had grown up in Teheran, where she had married and had a child, a daughter. Her husband, university educated, had worked for a small newspaper. One day, the Iranian police had come to her parents' home, where the young couple lived, and arrested both of them as traitors of the government. She was taken to a prison where she was kept for eight months, repeatedly being interrogated about her husband's activities. While in prison, she heard of her husband's torture and execution. Eventually, she was released and, with her parents' help, escaped with her daughter, arriving in Canada as a political refugee. She held little hope that she would ever again see her family, her friends, or anything of the life that had been familiar to her. Despite the vivid experiences she described of brutality, torture, cruelty and murder, and in spite of the fear, nightmares, loneliness and loss that she experienced, she spoke with a thread of life running through her words. This, all of it, was her life. Even while in prison, she had humorous moments and lighter times. Now she had learned a new language, succeeded in being accepted into university, and what she wanted from me was some help to develop ways to control feelings of panic that intruded from time to time, interfering with her concentration. She made it clear that she wanted to create a new life for herself, far different from what she had imagined, but still a life. She was "a survivor" already; so, why call her "a victim"? To insist that she needed to explore her past trauma and deal with it in some psychologically approved manner would be to ignore her own resilience and to undermine what she had accomplished already on her own. Responding to her request meant expressing respect and admiration for how well she had done and showing her some simple ways to put the feelings of panic aside whenever they began to interfere with her studying. The last time we met she talked about how well she was doing in her course work and what plans she had for the next school year. One can only hope that over the years, during some moment of uncertainty, she will not become the prey of a psychologist who, with the arrogance which has come to replace judgement, makes her a victim by convincing her to go back.

Given the determination she displayed from the first, it is reasonably likely that she would have the strength to resist such a sales pitch. It is possible that, although everyone has moments of weakness, those who have survived experiences such as this young woman did, are actually better able than most to resist psychological influence. While occasionally they make big news, authentic victims are not "big business." They tend not to be good raw material for the type of victim-making profitable to psychologists.

In the Psychology Industry, it is generally recognized that there is not much money to be made, nor glory to be gained, by working with readily identifiable victims. As a recent humorous article pointed out, it is difficult to get the dead to pay for psychotherapy.[33] And the poor, the homeless, and those working and struggling either to survive, like the Peruvian boy, or to go on with life, like the Iranian woman, are unlikely to have the money or the time to indulge in "recovery." So, as far as the Psychology Industry goes, unless there is some funding source to tap, some money to be made, most authentic victims/survivors might as well be dead.

It is the fabricated victims rather than the real ones who are big news and big business. Granted, stories of authentic victims tend to preface the scripts of those being cultivated as "users," causing the various new forms of "victims" to seem "just the same." But the word "victim" has a new, diluted meaning. Drawing its thrust from association with actual atrocities such as those committed during the Holocaust, the word is now closely connected to the popular psychologized versions of emotional "trauma." "Victim," as used by psychologists, frequently refers to someone who is momentarily upset or generally less satisfied, less happy, less successful or less fulfilled than they believe they should be and who attributes that feeling to an event which was done to them, supposedly done to them, or merely witnessed or worried about. The image it evokes is likely to be of one of the fabricated victims, someone "in process," trying to become "a survivor" and eventually "a thriver" or someone in pursuit of retribution and compensation for damages visible only to a psychologist.

Virtually any event can now qualify a person as a victim. There are the dramatic varieties such as the alleged victims of satanic ritual abuse or of UFO abductions.[34] Then there are the more everyday varieties such as victims of shopping addictions[35] and home renovation. To be declared a victim of sexual assault can now mean anything from having been abducted and repeatedly raped at knife point to having had an affair with a professor which ended with a grade that wasn't the expected "A," having got drunk one night and gone to bed with a date who looked less appealing in the sober morning light, or even having been whistled at.[36] To be declared a victim of violence can mean anything from having been dragged into a dark lane and beaten to death to having been slapped during a quarrel or even to having imagined the experience of being hurt in a subway accident or in a scene from a movie.[37] Psychologists say that whatever happened, "the experience," which they translate into psychological effects, can be equally devastating.

The following quote provides an illustration:

> Every victim of personal crime is confronted with a brutal reality: the deliberate violation of one human being by another. The crime may be a murder or a rape, a robbery or a burglary, the theft of an automobile, a pocket picking or a purse snatching— but *the essential internal injury is the same.* Victims have been assaulted emotionally and sometimes physically by a predator who *has shaken their world to its foundations.* [38]

Stereotyping of this magnitude is offensive not only because it overlooks human strength, courage and resilience, ignores those who might be capable of dealing with the theft of a wallet, and insults the authentic victims who have endured what most of us cannot even imagine, but also because it misuses science, misleads the public and eludes basic common sense. That such statements, when made by psychologists, are taken seriously and that such ideas now pervade our culture, threatening to make victims of us all, is astounding and it demonstrates the power of psychological marketing.

A popular bumper sticker used to read "Trust Me, I'm a Doctor." Recently the psychological equivalent was expressed on a national news program but this time with all seriousness: "He has to know; after all he is a psychologist!" The medical version long ago became a joke. But the radio announcer wasn't laughing when she referred to the psychologist in this same naive way. She seemed actually to believe that anyone who calls themselves a psychologist has insight, special knowledge and understanding and that anyone who is a member of the profession has an unswerving allegiance to truth. The image she held in her mind was the prevailing one of psychology as "a caring profession." That image needs to be challenged.

This book intends to shatter it and to expose psychology as an industry out to sell services, gain influence and make money at the expense of both the authentic victims, which it fails to respect or to protect, and of the Fabricated Victims manufactured by it. The Psychology Industry is a North American invention whose influence has spread rapidly across the United States and Canada. Thus, most examples are drawn from this region of the world. However, it should be noted that, like many industries which trace their origin to the U.S., the Psychology Industry has been spreading its influence beyond North America. To date, its damaging effects are being felt primarily in Western Europe, especially in Britain[39] and the Netherlands,[40] and in Australia and New Zealand.[41] (The case examples have been taken from the author's own clinical files, provided by colleagues, found in court transcripts, magazines, newspapers and in the writings of psychologists, whose credentials span the entire gamut from those with Ph.D.s, M.D.s, M.S.W.s, licensed by their professional boards, to those with certificates in various types of psychotherapy and counselling, to those self-proclaimed as "healers" and "therapists.")

Chapter One outlines the psychological techniques employed in "victim-making" and illustrates how conclusions, which rely on these techniques and on flaws in psychological thinking, have led to a wide acceptance of erroneous beliefs about "the typical victim." It concludes with a description of the stereotypical image which serves as a mould for making the Fabricated Victims. Chapter Two looks at three types of Fabricated Victims: 1) *synthetic victims,* who are being cast in a variety of victim roles by procedures which influence their memories of the past, experiences of the present and expectations of the future, 2) *contrived victims,* who become caught up in popularized ideas about the psychological causes and consequences of medical conditions such as cancer and heart disease; and 3) *counterfeit victims,* who turn to psychology for validation of their self-determined victim states. It describes the manufacturing process and discusses the short term gains which Fabricated victims enjoy and the eventual harm they incur.

The remainder of the book is about the industry which manufactures them. Chapter Three provides a brief look at the business history of the Industry, showing that psychology, while claiming to be an objective science, has from its inception had its eye on money and power, as it responded to economic factors and forces in society. It describes how it has become an integral part of the industrial free-enterprise society and, amidst the economic recession and depressive mood of the Eighties, shifted its efforts into the manufacture of victims. Chapter Four challenges the public image of psychology as a profession based on an objective science, illustrating the industry's misuse and abuse of science and its tendency to ignore studies which undermine its claims of efficacy and even suggest negative effects on individuals and on society. Chapter Five looks at how the Psychology Industry accomplishes its business goals by turning life into a series of problems needing treatment, impressing society with a plethora of specialties and credentials, making its services both accessible and essential, and attempting to control competition and criticism. Chapter Six shows that, since the goal of the Psychology Industry is to broaden its market, increase its sales and raise its income, there has been a trend towards mechanization. It identifies the industrial, and often unskilled aspects, from the simplistic generalizations found in "processes" such as "healthy grieving" and "Recovery," through the "one-concept-fits-all" approach of abuse and addiction counselling, to the franchising and supervising activities of some psychologists.

Chapter Seven takes a final look at the long shadow which the Psychology Industry has cast over human life and human relationships. It suggests that people be on guard against solutions offered from within the industry, especially by the professional organizations which have so clearly demonstrated their intent on self-protection, self-preservation and self-interest. As short term initiatives, it suggests: making psychologists legally responsible for their actions; cutting insurance coverage for psychology; ceasing to recognize psychologists as experts in court; stopping the public sanctioning of the Psychology Industry; and demanding "truth" in advertising. In the long-term it suggests, not only curbing the influence by carrying through on these initiatives but, also, dismantling the Psychology Industry so that people can, with responsibility, take back their own private lives.

Endnotes

1. For an excellent review of the exposure of this particular form of therapy and of the shifting trends regarding accusations and the handling of court cases see: *Smiling Through Tears*, by Pamela Freyd & Eleanor Goldstein. (Boca Raton, FL: Upton Books, 1997.)

2. Herman, Judith Lewis. *Trauma and Recovery*. New York: Basic Books, 1992. p.134-5.

3. "Responding to Oklahoma City's needs." *The APA Monitor*. Washington, D.C.: American Psychological Association, June, 1995.

4. "Team works to quell stress in Bosnia." *The APA Monitor*, August 1995. p.8.

5. West, Lola et al. "Operation Desert Storm: The Response of a Social Work Outreach Team." *Social Work in Health Care*, 1993, 19(2), pp.81-98.

6. "Women's safety illusory when males turn violent." *The APA Monitor*, February 1994.

7. "McBain Conference a Major Success." *Rapport*, 2, April 1994.

8. "Haunting memories of war a lifetime ago." Associated Press, as reported by the *Seattle Times*, August 13, 1995. p. A.3.

9. "Expert: Battered Women Can Kill." The Canadian Press, August 4, 1995.

10. "Abuse widespread, researchers show." *The APA Monitor*, February 1994. p.17.

11. Dorfman, Rachelle A. et al. "Screening for Depression among a Well Elderly Population." *Social Work*, 40(3), May 1995.

12. "Compensation due for dead dad— son." *Times Colonist*, June 10, 1995. B1.

13. "Pamela's Ph.D. in fame." *The Daily Telegraph.*, December 12, 1995. p.17.

14. VandenBos, Gary R., Cummings, Nicholas A. and DeLeon, Patrick H. "A century of Psychotherapy: Economic and environmental influences." In *The History of Psychotherapy: A Century of Change*. Freedheim, Donald K. (ed.), Washington, D.C.: American Psychological Association, 1992.

15. The 1995 phone survey reported in *The APA Monitor*, June 1995.

16. The following quote provides one example: "...the prediction that by the year 2000 eight out of ten people in the United States will have been exposed to some type of psychotherapeutic experience is not unrealistic. Psychotherapy, once reserved for special cases and now in vogue for everyone, looks more and more like the thing to do." (Kalellin, Peter M. *Pick Up Your Couch and Walk!* New York: Crossroad, 1993.)

17. Many high profile "therapists," including John Bradshaw, claim victim status and many now see victim status as the most important credential for offering psychotherapy. One popular book of the recovery movement which argues against academic credentials and for victim ones is *Beyond Therapy, Beyond Science* by Anne Wilson Schaef. (San Francisco: Harper, 1992.)

18. Fischer, A., "Der praktische Psychologe"— ein neuer Beruf," *Der Kunstwart and Kulturwart*, 1913, 26, pp.313. Cited in Geuter, Ulfried. *The Professionalization of Psychology in Nazi Germany*. London: Cambridge University Press, 1992.

19. Henry, William E., Sims, John H., and Spray, S. Lee. *The Fifth Profession: Becoming a Psychotherapist*. San Francisco: Jossey Bass Behavioral Science Series, 1971.

20. Fox, Ronald E. (past president of the APA) "Training professional psychologists for the twenty-first century." *American Psychologist*. 1994, 49(3).

21. Sykes, Charles. *A Nation of Victims: The Decay of the American Society*. New York: St. Martin's Press, 1992.

22. One of the many books which contains messages of the type this man reported hearing on television is *Ritual Abuse: What it is, why it happens, how to help*, by Margaret Smith. (San Francisco:

Harper, 1993.) Another which looks at this from a sociological perspective is *Satanic Panic: The Creation of a Contemporary Legend*, by Jeffrey S. Victor (Chicago: Open Court Publishing Co., 1993.)

23.The therapist called had been in practise over 20 years and was a recognized "expert" in the area of satanic ritual abuse, having presented papers on the topic at several professional conferences.

24. Among the bestsellers of the incest-recovery movement is *The Courage to Heal*, by Ellen Bass & Laura Davis. (New York: HarperCollins, 1988.) For a critique of this book and others see Carol Tavris' "Beware the Incest-Survivor Machine." *New York Times Book Review*. (January 3, 1993.)

25. Two of the books which popularized the idea of the "adult child" are Charles Whitfield's *Healing the Child Within*. (Deerfield Beach, Florida: Health Communications, Inc., 1987) and John Bradshaw's *Bradshaw On: The Family*. (Deerfield Beach, Florida: Health Communications, Inc., 1988.) For a critique of the concept see Wendy Kaminer's *I'm Dysfunctional, You're Dysfunctional*. (New York: Vintage Books/Random House, 1993.)

26. John Bradshaw is an ex-priest and recovered alcoholic. Among his bestsellers are *Bradshaw On: The Family* and *Homecoming*. The workshop attended was held at the Regal Constellation Hotel, Toronto, July 4-7, 1990.

27. The now massive literature on grieving followed from Elizabeth Kubler-Ross's bestseller *On Death and Dying*. (New York: Macmillan, 1969). The stages of grieving one's own impending death, identified on basis of interviews with terminally ill patients, have now been termed "normal" and are used to describe the process of adjustment not only to death but to all forms of loss from the death of a loved one, the end of a marriage or of "a dream." See, for example, *Healing Grief*, by Barbara Ward (London: Random House, 1993).

28. The articles entitled: "Reno Wars" and "Singles have it tough as nails" appeared in the *Times-Colonist*, Saturday, August 13, 1994. C1.

29. The article entitled "Haunting memories of war a lifetime ago" was by Mitchell Landsber of the Associated Press (Montrose, N.Y.), August 13, 1995. Recent publications from American Psychological Association indicate a concern that VA funding for psychologists may be diminishing.

30. "Abandoned to her fate." *Time*, December 11, 1995. pp.38-42.

31. "Dead or barely alive, it means little to body collectors" Associated Press: Goma, Zaire, July 28, 1994.

33. "Teen mom grabbed as shield dies." New York, Reuter, August 22, 1994.

33. Menahem, Samuel E. "Psychotherapy of the dead." In *Oral Sadism and the Vegetarian Personality: Readings from the Journal of Polymorphous Perversity*. Glenn C. Ellenbogen (ed.) New York: Ballantine Books, 1987. pp.14-21.

34. A recent book on victims of UFO abductions, written by the prominent Harvard University psychiatrist John Mack, is *Abductions: Human Encounters with Aliens*. New York: Macmillan, 1994.

35. A book focussed exclusively on victims of shopping addiction is: Mohr, Elen; Sonenberg, Nina & Sonenberg, Catalano. *Consuming Passions: Help for Compulsive Shoppers*. Oakland, CA: New Harbinger Publications, 1993. An article entitled ""Shopping until you drop" can be a serious addiction" (London: The Guardian News Service, October 4, 1994) announced the launching by British psychologists of a major study, stemming from a U.S. suggestion that 6% of shoppers could be addicts.

36. Books about sexual assault have flooded the pop psychology market. Among the very few books which challenge any of the new definitions of "rape' is Katie Roiphe's, *The Morning After: Sex, Fear and Feminism on Campus* (Boston: Little, Brown and Co., 1993).

37. Among the books which provide a broad sweep of the definition of "violence," linking it with psychological trauma, is Judith Lewis Herman's *Trauma Recovery: The Aftermath of Violence— From Domestic Abuse to Political Terror*. (New York: HarperCollins, 1992.)

38. Bard, Morton & Sangrey, Dawn. *The Crime Victim's Book*. New York: Basic Books, 1979.

39. Lady Diana's various well publicized psychological problems and visits to therapists made her one of the world's most prominent "users" and one the more influential of the celebrity promoters, especially of "bulimia." A number of British authors, for example David Smail, in his book *Taking Care: An Alternative to Therapy.*(London: J.M. Dent & Sons Ltd., 1987), have focussed on the influence of beliefs imported from America on psychology in Great Britain.

40. One of the earliest cases of alleged satanic ritual abuse brought to the author's attention was that of a woman who had returned to a small town in New York State, accompanied by a support worker from the Netherlands, for the explicit purpose of convincing the police to lay charges against her father and other members of the community.

41. Psychologists in Australia and New Zealand have come to follow the lead of the U.S., with their professional organizations adopting the same "ethical codes" and victim-making stances. See Felicity Goodyear-Smith's book: *First Do No Harm: The Sexual Abuse Industry.* (Auckland, New Zealand: Benton-Gay Publishing, 1993.)

Chapter 1

Victim-Making

The therapists transformed age-old human dilemmas into psychological problems and claimed that they (and they alone) had the treatment... The result was an explosion of inadequacy.

Charles Sykes

Often I have the feeling of being on the other side of "the looking glass;" like Alice, I am trying to make sense of distortions, exaggerations, and deceptions. We live in a world of illusion, where our grasp on reality is often tenuous. Wedding cakes that look real are artificial; actors posing as doctors prescribe the latest cough remedies; old movies are colorized; special effects appear believable; and the world of "virtual reality" becomes our new reality. Victim-making is part of this world of fabrications and illusions.

With today's distortion of the term "victim" and the endless proliferation of pretenders, it may seem impossible to distinguish the real victims from the fabricated: the synthetic, the contrived and the counterfeit varieties. But if one makes an effort to flee the psychological domain with all its misleading statements, misinformation and outright lies about what it means to be a victim, it is possible to know the difference.

From ancient times to today's newspaper, Fate and cruelty have affected humanity; victims with shocking stories have existed. Reports of the earthquake in Kobe, Japan, the bombing in Oklahoma City, or the atrocities committed by Jeffery Dahmer or Paul Bernardo, are reminders of a cruel and terrifying side of nature and of human nature which cannot be controlled or eliminated. They are incontrovertible evidence of our vulnerability and they cause naive notions of limitless security or power to crumble. The experiences of real victims, as well as creating discomfort, bring into question the psychological practice of victim-making; they bring us back from a psychological "virtual reality" to the tangible reality in which we actually live out our lives.

The situations in which people become victims span the whole gamut from local tragedies to global genocides. Consider the following three stories; one, a rape victim, the second, a holocaust survivor, and the third, a man whose life was shattered by a car accident. Each experienced directly and very forcefully the cruel side of human nature.

In July 1992, the news media reported the mysterious disappearance of a young woman. On July 12, 1992 screams led police to the place where she was found, tied and bound. For nine days she had been held captive, the victim of a rapist-killer.

It had all begun when, at the end of her shift, right outside the store where she worked, she was abducted at gunpoint. A man forced her to go to a makeshift camp in a wooded area where he tied her ankles, bound her hands behind her back, and shoved a piece of torn blanket into her mouth. When she slept, she did so tied up in a cramped position on the hard ground; when he left her alone she was hog-tied in such a way that her muscles were painfully stretched. He fed her sporadically and occasionally took her for short walks. He held her there, unable to move and naked for most of the time, forcing her to perform whatever sexual acts he demanded. As she later described it:

> The most common and most painful position was with me on my hands and knees, my face pushed right into the ground and him raping me from behind. This resulted in unbelievable pain in my lower back. The best way I can explain it is to imagine someone taking two bones in your back and rubbing them together with extreme pressure. At one point, he continued to rape me for, I believe, 90 minutes.
>
> Another part of my body that David Snow injured was my breasts. From pulling and twisting, he gave me painful swollen nipples and bruises on my chest and breasts.
>
> My jaw was also very sore for about a month from a combination of him hitting me in the face and forcing me to perform oral sex on him.[1]

In her "victim impact statement," she referred to the discomfort and pain at the time and described bruises and injuries which eventually healed and the ache in her lower back which persisted. She spoke of simple movements like tying her shoes, sitting down and picking things off the floor as being continuing reminders of what she had endured. She spoke, as well, of her inability to "put into words how terrifying it feels to have someone take control of your life."[2]

The holocaust survivor and Nobel Prize winner Elie Wiesel, is someone who knows well how difficult it is to try to put such experiences into words and how easily those words can be twisted and misunderstood. His first book, *Night*, is a thin volume which relates his memories from before his arrest at age fourteen to his release from Buchenwald at the end of the war. Wiesel describes a reality which "he saw and touched and tasted directly."[3] He records how he and his family were marched from the ghetto to the train station, where they were loaded into a cattle car — eighty people to each car. When the train arrived at Birkenau, the reception centre for Auschwitz, he watched as his mother and his young sister were forced to walk "to the right;" while, he and his father were ordered to walk the other direction. His mother and sister were burned in the crematory; he and his father watched the flames and the smoke. Three weeks later they were transferred to Buna where the notorious Dr. Mengele carried out his "selections" as prisoners were ordered to strip naked and run in front of him so that he could "examine" them, selecting those whose physical condition was more suited for execution than continued labour. Below is a description of just one event which was part of his life at that time:

> Akiba Drumer left us, a victim of the selection. Lately he had wandered among us, his eyes glazed. It was impossible to raise his morale...
> As soon as he felt the first cracks forming in his faith, he had lost his reason for struggling and had begun to die...when the selection came he was condemned in advance, offering his own neck to the executioner. All he asked of us was:
> "In three days I shall no longer be here...Say the Kaddish for me."
> We promised him...
> Then he went off toward the hospital, his step steadier, not looking back. An ambulance was waiting to take him to Birkenau.
> These were terrible days. We received more blows than food; we were crushed with work. And three days after he had gone we forgot to say the Kaddish.[4]

Later Wiesel was in an infirmary bed with an injured foot when the rumour spread that the camp was to be evacuated. It was assumed that the SS guards would execute all those who were unable to walk; so he got up and marched with the others out the gates of the camp. The wind was icy. It snowed relentlessly. The SS had orders to shoot anyone who could not keep up. Near him men, collapsing in the dirty snow, were being shot. He kept repeating to himself: "Don't think. Don't stop. Run." [5]

He describes how he kept going and how that night a boy from Warsaw played "a final concert" in the snow:

> I shall never forget Juliek. How could I forget that concert, given to an audience of dying and dead men! To this day, whenever I hear Beethoven played my eyes close and out of the dark rises the sad, pale face of my Polish friend, as he said farewell on his violin to an audience of dying men.
> I do not know for how long he played. I was overcome by sleep. When I awoke, in the daylight, I could see Juliek, opposite me, slumped over dead.[6]

After a train ride, during which those already dead and those about to die were periodically thrown from the car to reduce the stench, Wiesel and his father arrived at Buchenwald. His father, his only reason throughout the entire ordeal to "keep going," had been struck down with dysentery. On January 28, the boy climbed into his bunk above his father and in the morning:

I awoke on January 29 at dawn. In my father's place lay another invalid. They must have taken him away before dawn and carried him to the crematory. He may still have been breathing.[7]

The third, an accident victim, consulted me on the first anniversary of the event which had shattered his life. What he described was not, like the holocaust, a part of history; it was not even the type of event which gets into the newspaper. He was a middle aged Italian immigrant who had worked hard as a truck driver for twenty years before finally getting a job in a packing plant. In tearful, broken English, he described what had happened to him. He had been alone in his car, driving home, when he saw the lights of a transport truck coming at him. The truck hit him head on, totally demolishing his car, crashing his head into the windshield, and smashing his right arm. He was unconscious when he arrived at the emergency room. The arm was not set properly and had not healed; no-one seemed concerned about his head injury. His arm remained visibly deformed and a bone literally stuck out from his wrist. He described the pain, the dizziness and the flashes of light inside his head that kept him awake through the night, how he was unable to do anything he used to do, such as shovel snow, drive a car, remember an appointment, or even follow a conversation. He spoke of how he avoided going to visit friends or even talking with his family because he had no memory of what they had just said and he feared "looking stupid." People had kept telling him that he would get better; he was beginning to doubt that he ever would.

This man, the young woman and Elie Wiesel, are victims. Each of them has experienced something out of the ordinary; each of them speaks of what happened in the past, putting into words his or her own thoughts, feelings and reactions so that those who want to understand what it means to be a victim can learn by listening to them. Hearing what they say about their own experiences and about their own lives involves respecting victims as individuals.

But the Psychology Industry uses and abuses the experiences of people such as these, in order to further its own business interests. In order to thrive, the Psychology Industry requires an ever expanding number of fabricated victims. The three principles on which the modern day mass production of victims relies are:

PSYCHOLOGIZING — using psychological constructs to reduce real experiences to theories, thus making the external world a figment of an unconscious and highly subjective inner realm. The Psychology Industry pretends to understand the unconscious, to know people better than they know themselves and, thus, to be able to accurately interpret their experiences.

PATHOLOGIZING — turning, with psychological arrogance, ordinary (and extraordinary) people in abnormal (seemingly unbearable) situations into "abnormal" people, labelling all victims "damaged," "wounded," "abused," "traumatized," incapable of dealing with it, getting over it or going on with life. The Psychology Industry claims the authority to deduce psychological illness and harm, to cut through to uncertainties, vulnerabilities and regrets, and to diagnose, categorize and label human experience.

GENERALIZING — equating the exceptional and the brutal with the ordinary and the mundane; thus ignoring the differences which set victims apart in an insulting effort to extend and blur them with the more common experiences of a lifetime. The Psychology Industry assumes the capacity to psychologize the mundane, using metaphor to create an absurd realm of similarities, equating the thought with the deed, the dream with the fact, and the illusion with the reality.

Through these simplistic techniques, the Psychology Industry reduces the complex fabric of life to a single thread, turning the whole gamut of human qualities into psychologically defined mechanical "processes." All of this psychologizing, pathologizing, and generalizing is done for the purpose of victim-making, patient-making — user making.

Psychologizing

Sometimes a cigar is just a cigar.[8]

Treating the medical metaphors of modern psychiatry as literal reflects and reinforces our modern aversion to moral conflict, human tragedy, and plain language.[9]

Psychologizing is one of the three major ways by which victims are manufactured by and for the Psychology Industry. It turns what individual victims say about events and their effects into ideas which are very different and even disconnected from the victims' descriptions. Presenting these ideas as facts, psychologists can then apply them to other peoples' lives transforming virtually anyone into a victim. Psychologizing assumes as its basis an interior world in which an Unconscious has profound influence and power, a place where things are different from what they seem on the outside and can only be discovered, understood, explained, and changed with the help and direction of psychologists. And it relies on the belief that, like guides familiar with the terrain, psychologists can see what is hidden there : what is not known (about the past), what can't be seen (in the present), and what must be discovered (to achieve a better future).

Psychologizing involves:
1) constructing a theory about victimization,
2) applying that theory to individuals,
3) turning personal events into psychological symbols, which are expressed in psychological language,
4) creating the need for psychologists who can interpret the symbols.

Psychology has created numerous theories in an attempt to explain both the similarities and the differences in peoples' actions and reactions. In the past, psychological theories were developed by researchers who, through scientific methods, addressed issues of perception (such as the ability to see differences in colours) or of behaviour (such as the use of rewards or reinforcement to change reactions). Today, the theories of the Psychology Industry are more likely to be developed by practitioners on the basis of their experience with patients and to be accepted despite being untested by any scientific means. It is these clinical theories which are presented as the latest, the most up-to-date, explanations of the cause of problems and which serve to demonstrate the need for "healing" and "recovery."

It is these theories, which are applied either directly to individuals through psychological consultations when unwitting patients are lead to believe that they have experienced trauma "but don't know it yet," or indirectly by experts who speak of "hypothetical cases." For instance, in the case of Paul Bernardo, charged with the abduction, repeated rape and gruesome murder of two teenage girls, psychologist experts applied their theories as they testified. Two psychologists testified about "battered wife syndrome" as it might hypothetically apply to Bernardo's ex-wife's involvement and complicity in the case. The theory was introduced in an effort to cast Karla Holmolka as a psychological victim rather than an accomplice. As is usual in courts, the supposed victim of this hypothetical syndrome was never interviewed or even seen by the experts. Rather, the psychologists applied the syndrome as a template in an attempt to explain the behaviours of a woman they had never met.

Through the application of their theories, psychologists turn the concrete events, feelings and thoughts of peoples' lives into psychological symbols and esoteric language. As Martin Gross notes,[10] America has become a *"Psychological Society"* in which psychologists are allowed, even expected, to interpret what people say, feel and do, and to explain what their words, moods, and actions really mean at some "deeper unconscious level" which is accessible only to them. It has come to be accepted that what happens to people on the "outside" has an effect on the "inside" and that it is what happens on the "inside" that determines what then happens in their lives. This psychological concept holds remarkable similarity to the astrological idea that what happens in the sky determines what happens in peoples' lives. Both rely on the assumed ability of trained, gifted or selected people who can see either what is written in the sky or what is hidden in the unconscious. The practitioners of both speak and act as if they are members of a secret society in which they have been taught to see and hear at a deeper (more real than real) level. They translate external events into their own esoteric language and attribute profound influences to them. And in doing so they cause themselves to be held in awe and their services to be in demand.

Just as *glossolalia* (speaking in tongues) of the early Christian Church created the need for those with the "gift of interpretation," the esoteric psychological jargon creates the need for psychologists who can explain and cure the problems. Calling it their "expertise," psychologists claim an ability to see the inner worlds of other people. Focussing on what they believe is happening on the inside and ignoring, or minimizing, the importance of what is happening on the outside, psychologists say with assumed confidence: "*I know* how you really feel;" "*I know* what you're really saying;" "*I know* how badly you've been hurt;" "*I know* what really happened to you." Their interpretations are hard to refute. And the uninitiated consumer, hesitates to ask: "How do you know?" or to say: "You're wrong." So, psychologists get away with applying their theories, with their psychologizing and with their victim-making.

PSYCHOLOGIZING

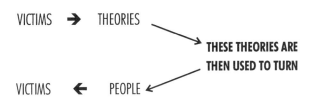

Consider again the example from the Introduction in which the psychologist instantly, and quite magically, determined that a man had been tortured by Satanists. The only information given her was that the man looked anxious, claimed to hear voices, reported having done some bizarre things to himself and had watched a television show about ritual abuse. He had no memory of any "Satanic Ritual Abuse" (SRA). The psychologist had never seen the man and likely the only satanic rituals she had witnessed were movie versions. But she claimed that *she knew* what had happened to him; *she knew* that he was an SRA victim. She described in amazing detail how "they" had tortured him. Without hesitation and without asking a single question, she claimed *to know* what had happened and declared that he needed help to recover these memories and be cured; help that she, and those trained by her, could offer. This psychologist demonstrated none of the finely tuned skills in listening and in understanding on which the popular acceptance of psychologists' power has tended to be based. Instead of asking about his life and making some effort to understand what was happening to this particular man, she presumed a psychologized theory of SRA. There was no way to challenge what she, so authoritatively, claimed to know. Instead of listening to him, she was only listening for what she already assumed to be fact. Knowing nothing of his external life, she claimed intimate knowledge of this man's inner world and it was this which she intended to help him uncover. (It was later learned that, through months of therapy, she had made no effort to confirm even the man's name, let alone, what, if anything, had ever happened to him.) She had simply listened for what she believed his history to be, considering all of his current life and his current suffering to be the result of what she presumed had happened in his past. She, and the young man who became her patient, demonstrate how dangerous the psychologizing of "the victim experience" can be in the hands of the Psychology Industry where it is used as a technology to manufacture and service victims and to promote the importance and power of psychologists.

Psychologist, Judith Herman, wrote in *Trauma and Recovery*:

> The ordinary response to atrocities is to banish them from consciousness... Atrocities, however, refuse to be buried. Equally as powerful as the desire to deny atrocities is *the conviction that denial does not work*... Remembering and telling the truth about terrible events *are prerequisites* both for the restoration of the social order and for the healing of individual victims.[11]

Few people recognize the subtle but profound effect of psychologizing inherent in statements like these. In these excerpts, which are consistent with the theme of the book, Herman expresses her conviction (theory) that terrible events (specifically sexual and domestic violence) cannot be forgotten, must be remembered and talked about, and that society as well as the individual, depends on this for health.

Psychologizing is not a process exclusive to victims of abuse or violence nor did it originate in the current Psychology Industry. In fact, William James, the psychologist, as early as 1900, expressed concern in this regard:

> I hope that Freud and his pupils will push their ideas to their utmost limits, so that we may learn what they are. They can't fail to throw light on human nature, but I confess that he made on me personally the impression of a man *obsessed with fixed ideas*. I can make nothing in my own case with his dream theories, and obviously *"symbolism is a most dangerous method."*[12]

What concerned James was that Freud and his followers would forget that their ideas were theories and instead, would **listen for** material from patients that would support their psychologizing, ignoring any conflicting data. He feared that with their "obsessed thinking," they would apply fixed and predetermined ideas about people and change their words into a symbolic language understood only by psychologists. The danger that James foresaw was that they would hear only what they wanted or expected to hear and that they would turn the experiences of individuals into a general experience; thus, a patient would become equated with all other patients with "similar" problems.

This process of applying a theory to turn what people say into a "deeper," psychologized meaning, from the individual words into general experience through the use of abstract concepts, has been pushed to the limits in the interpretation of the experiences of victims, both real and fabricated. The danger which James detected in the psychologists' "fixed ideas" and "symbolism" has infiltrated and contaminated the study of "victims."

An example of this process, and only one of many possible examples, involves the work of Robert Lifton. A psychiatrist with a psychoanalytic bent, Lifton is a pioneer and major contributor to the study of victims. He describes himself as a "psychiatric investigator" who has examined the lives of those who survived the Nazi death camps, the bombing of Hiroshima and the Vietnam War. He sees his work as *"a form of re-creation."*[13] He listens but, by his own admirably honest admission, he does so believing that "in contrast to the more immediate involvement of other animals, human beings experience their world by *symbolizing;"*[14] thus, he listens for the psychologically symbolic. He further says that "as human beings we know our bodies and our minds *only through what we can imagine*"[15] and that "to grasp our humanity *we need to structure these images into metaphors and models*... In other words, psychologists do not simply interpret or analyze; we also construct; we engage in our own struggles around form. We are much concerned with narrative, and we inevitably contribute to the narrative of whatever life we examine."[16]

Lifton approached these victims with a specific interest; that of death, the effect of seeing death (psychic numbing) and of surviving when others died (death guilt). Thus, by his own forthright acknowledgment, he was not an unbiased, open listener but rather someone who listened for specific ideas and images. And from this, he constructed psychologized theories to describe what he thought went on inside peoples' minds, in their unconscious, when they survived the horror.

When his interpretation is placed along side the words of victims, including Hiroshima survivors or Elie Wiesel, the filtering and distorting effects of psychologizing become apparent. Consider the following description of a man's own experience of the bombing of Hiroshima, as it was told to Lifton; the second is Lifton's interpretation. In his own words, the man describes:

> I went to look for my family. I became a pitiless person, because if I had pity, I would not have been able to walk through the city, to walk over those dead bodies. The most impressive thing was the expression in people's eyes — bodies badly injured which had turned black — their eyes looking for someone to come and help them. They looked at me and knew that I was stronger than they... I was looking for my family and looking carefully at everyone I met to see if he or she was a family member — but the eyes — the emptiness — the helpless expression — were something I will never forget... I saw disappointment in their eyes. They looked at me with great expectation, staring right through me. It was very hard to be stared at by those eyes...[17]

Now, compare that to Lifton's commentary, noting his jargon, and remembering his psychological world-view and what he is **listening for:**

> *In other words*, he felt accused by the eyes of the anonymous dead and dying of wrongdoing and transgression (a sense of guilt), for not helping them, for letting them die, for selfishly remaining alive and strong; and exposed and seen through by the same eyes for these identical failings (a sense of shame). Psychic closing-off was thus broken through by feelings of self-condemnation, by death guilt. And this psychic opening-up exposed him to various forms of delayed guilt over having been so pitiless a person while his feelings were numbed.[18]

And again, listen to Robert Lifton interpret Wiesel's experiences as described in *Night*, translating the author's words into terms which fit his psychologized "survivor syndrome" and theory of "death guilt:"

> The survivor of Nazi concentration camps moreover, like the survivor of Hiroshima, carried the burden not only of what he did but what he felt. Thus, Wiesel tells how, as a fifteen year old

boy, he took tender care of his sick father under the most extreme conditions en route to and within Auschwitz, Buna, and Buchenwald. But when temporarily separated from him he was suddenly horrified at his wish that he not be able to find him: "If only I could get rid of the dead weight, so that I could use all my strength to struggle for my own survival, and only worry about myself." And when his father died, he perceived "in the recess of my weakened conscience," a feeling close to "free at last!" He describes feeling both guilty and "ashamed of myself, ashamed forever;" and the indelibility of the imprint of these events is more forcefully conveyed when he recalls how, shortly after being liberated (and following a severe illness of his own), he looked into a mirror and "a corpse gazed back at me. The look in his eyes, as they stared into mine, has never left me."[19]

But does this psychological re-creation (i.e. psychologizing) make Wiesel's actual experience truly more understandable? Years after his ordeal, having returned to Birkenau and Auschwitz, Wiesel spoke of what had happened there not merely in terms of what was going on inside his head but, also, in terms of what was happening all around him. Remembering his father, he said:

> The Russian soldiers could have saved him. But they arrived too late, too late — for us. We had already been marched off to Gleiwitz, and from there, in open cattle cars, to Buchenwald. We were surrounded by corpses; we no longer knew who was alive and who was not. I remember a man — my father — murmuring to himself, or to the icy wind that lashed his face: "What a pity, what a pity..."[20]

Lifton takes these immediate and personal experiences, and "re-creates" them according to his abstract psychological theories. For instance, in support of his idea of "death guilt"[21] as part of the victim experience, he writes:

> Sometimes the delayed guilt takes the form of remembered voices of those left to die while one was oneself being rescued — as described by the elderly widow, who was carried to safety in a wheelbarrow by her son and daughter-in-law: "I heard many voices calling for help, voices calling their father, voices of women and children... Even now I wonder what has happened to those people... I couldn't move my body very well, and my son had six children to take care of in addition to me, so, well, we just didn't help people... I felt it was a wrong thing not to help them, but we were so much occupied by running away ourselves that we left them... Even now I still hear their voices..."[22]

Lifton again *speaks for* a victim, interpreting this woman's experience also in terms of "death guilt:"

> The unspoken self-accusation here is that her life was saved at the expense of many others.[23]

Here we see a theorist filtering out the personal and emotional aspects of the accounts as he listens for specific psychologized themes. Apparently unaware of this at a conscious level, Lifton writes:

> ...what impressed me throughout the work was *the vividness of recall*, the sense conveyed that the bomb was falling right here in my office.

But then he displays a detached analytic attitude when he continues:

> ...a vividness which seems to reflect both the indelible imprint of the event and its endlessly reverberating psychological repercussions.[24]

Why would one who is earnestly interested in understanding victims, reconstruct their experiences filtering out the personal vividness? One explanation may be found in Lifton's writing about his interviews with Hiroshima survivors.

> I was confronted with the brutal details... I noticed that my reactions were changing. I was listening to descriptions of the same horrors, but their effect on me lessened. *I concentrated upon recurrent patterns...* The experience was an unforgettable demonstration of the psychic closing-off we shall see to be characteristic of all aspects of atomic bomb exposure, even of this kind of exposure to the exposed. It also taught me *the importance of making sense of the event*, of calling upon one's personal and professional resources to give it form, *as means of coping with it.*[25]

Listening to authentic victims has an effect on the listener, an effect which may make listening difficult and create the need to change the experiences into something, into a pattern, a theory that seems to make sense and that is manageable; something with which the theorist or psychologist can cope.

It is appropriate for Lifton, as a researcher, to search for psychological patterns in the ways authentic victims handle their experiences. This is the task of an investigator. However, it becomes "a most dangerous method," to quote James, when this search for patterns involves ignoring the actual words spoken and assuming that the pattern fits *all* victims. Lifton did this when he wrote:

> *The survivor is one* who has come into contact with death in some bodily or psychic fashion and has remained alive. There are five characteristic themes in the survivor: the death imprint, death guilt, psychic numbing, conflicts around nurturing and contagion, and struggles with meaning or formulation.[26]

With this psychologized and simplified theory it can be easily seen how such investigative work can be taken by the Psychology Industry and turned into the rationale and procedures of psychological treatment. To the psychologist, a person's lack of emotions or questions about the purpose of life or a sense of grief, all become signs that the individual is or has been a victim. Each person ostensibly is someone whose inner world must be explored in expectation of confirming theories about "the victim experience." Listening for themes and patterns, psychologists find them.

Psychoanalysis is not the only arena in which psychologizing occurs. Elizabeth Kubler-Ross[27] studied a number of terminally ill patients and, through her observation and interviewing, she developed a theory about the psychological stages that people go through in preparing to die: Denial, Anger, Bargaining, Depression, Acceptance, and Hope. It was to be a psychological model of the dying process that would give some descriptive understanding of the experience. However, the Psychology Industry has turned around this theory, like those of Lifton and others, describing the steps as psychological necessities.

Thus, psychological theories which are initially intended to expand the understanding of victims, survivors and the dying, can be made useful to enterprising psychologists. The theories which describe the experience become the basis for determining who is a victim. For example, anyone who claims to be "out of touch with their feelings" is said to be numbed and, therefore, to be a victim. The same theories also become the basis for establishing the proper treatment procedure, such as, in the case of someone "numbed," removing the blocks to intense emotions through uncovering repressed memories. Some theorists make this turn about easier by being dogmatic, ignoring the victims' actual words in favour of their own theories; others do it by employing apparently magical powers, reading the victim's unconscious, creating and interpreting symbolism.

An unfortunate result of psychologizing is that the personal experiences of victims become the clinical theories through which others are assessed and treated as if they are victims; psychologizing sustains victim-making.

Pathologizing

> *I think we should **stop divinizing psychiatry** and **start humanizing it**. To begin with, we must learn to differentiate between what is human in man and what is pathological in him... Sigmund Freud, it is true, once wrote that "The moment one inquires about the sense or value of life, one is sick," but I rather think that one thereby manifests one's humanness.*[28]

Psychologizing is not the sole means by which true victims are shown disrespect or through which fabricated victims are made. It is also done by looking for and emphasizing the negative, pointing to the wounds suffered, the scars left, the weaknesses and the lasting effects. Pathologizing the experiences of victims turns their normal feelings into abnormal states and their normal reactions into emotional problems.

Some time after the young woman, described in the Introduction, was abducted and held captive, a newspaper article was written by a reporter who felt that, since the term "sexual assault" is repeated so often and with such a wide range of relatively trivial meanings, the public needed to be reminded that the term could refer to a violent rape. So, in her article, she highlighted the brutality of the woman's experience.[29]

The woman quickly wrote a response to the newspaper, expressing her own views as to why these graphic and extremely personal details should not have been made available "for public consumption." For her, she said, the ordeal was essentially over; she no longer wanted to be "the victim." Like the ordeal, being a victim was part of her past; she wanted to live in the present and get on with her life. She pointed out that, as well as ignoring how the article could harm her, the reporter had failed to take a constructive angle to her story;

> For example, why not explore the circumstances that kept the victim alive: How she dealt with the offender and how she kept her will to live in a traumatic situation beyond her control and conception of reality?[30]

We have become so accustomed in our psychologized world to thinking of victims in terms of trauma and destruction that it is very difficult to bring ourselves to consider survivors as anything other than the psychologically damaged. To do as this woman suggests would be to emphasize her strength over her helplessness. And this is not the way that the Psychology Industry wants people to think.

Wiesel offers another example of this inclination toward pathologizing in a chapter he wrote entitled "Trivializing Memory":

> As for philosophers and psychiatrists, some of them have long been *intrigued by simplistic theories*... In the course of scholarly colloquia, one sometimes hears more about the guilt of the victims and the psychological problems of the survivors than about the crimes of the killers. Didn't an American novelist recently suggest that the suicide of my friend Primo Levi was nothing but *a bout of depression* that good psychoanalytic treatment could have cured. Thus is the tragedy of a great writer, a man who never ceased to battle the black angel of Auschwitz, reduced to *a banal nervous breakdown*.[31]

Whether it is to ignore the personal strengths of the individual or the appropriate reactions to the reality of the experience itself, the Psychology Industry tends to turn authentic victims into damaged people. As one psychologist said about "the camp experience:" "To one degree or another they (the prisoners) *all stifled* their true feelings, they *all denied* the dictates of conscience and social feeling in hope of survival, and they were *all warped and distorted* as a result."[32]

Psychologists automatically assume that victims are psychologically damaged; that somehow their abnormal experiences have made them abnormal people. We can wonder why this belief exists, or as Des Pres puts it: "Why... do we insist that survivors did not really survive: that ... their spirit was destroyed beyond salvaging?" [33]

The answer to this lies, at least in part, in the writings of those who claim to understand "the victim experience" on the basis of their own experience of some traumatic event and/or having studied victims.

One of the most influential is Bruno Bettelheim. His opinions pervade today's psychological approach to victims. His concept of "survivorship" consists of the classic traumatic cause and pathological effect:
(1) the original trauma which, in the context of the Holocaust, is *"the personality-disintegrating impact* of being imprisoned in a German concentration camp which completely destroyed one's social existence by depriving one of all previous support systems such as family, friends, position in life, while at the same time subjecting one to utter terrorization and degradation through the severest mistreatment and omnipresent, inescapable, immediate threat to one's life;" and
(2) "the *life-long aftereffects* of such trauma, which seem to require very special forms of mastery if one is not to succumb to them."[34]

Claiming to have been trained as a psychologist in Vienna, Bettelheim derived much of his authority on his limited experience as a prisoner in Dachau and Buchenwald early in the war (1938/39). Released before these camps became the scenes of torture and mass extermination, which Wiesel and others lived to describe, Bettelheim moved to America, where he wrote an academic article in which he presented his "clinical observations" of his fellow prisoners. Published in 1943, it gave Bettelheim an early position of authority on victims, a position enhanced by his public image as both a psychologist and a survivor.[35] It is clear from this article and his subsequent writings that, even while a prisoner, he assumed the role of a psychologist looking for and finding pathology in others.

While other survivors talked of keeping the rituals of their Jewish religion or of the importance of family and relationships to their survival, Bettelheim described himself as "a student of psychoanalysis and a follower of Freud" who had his own "idiosyncratic" way of surviving by falling back on his "faith" in psychoanalysis.[36]

From the outset, Bettelheim saw his fellow prisoners as abnormal people. In his initial 1943 paper, he wrote with intolerance of them, distancing himself from them by referring to himself as "the author," "the observer," "the thinker," even the "normal one":

> The author saw his fellow prisoners acting in most peculiar ways, although he had every reason to assume that they, too, had been normal persons before being imprisoned: Now they suddenly appeared to be *pathological* liars, to be unable to restrain their emotional outbursts, be they of anger or despair, to be unable to make objective evaluations...[37]

As Bettelheim proceeded to develop his theories, he did so by psychologizing and pathologizing survivors. For instance, he suggested three alternative responses to being a victim:

> The most destructive of these three possible responses was to unconsciously conclude that the reintegration of one's personality was impossible, pointless, or both...Their state of mind is similar to that of an individual *suffering from a depressive or paranoid psychiatric disturbance...*[38]

There were other survivors — and they may well be the majority — ... Survivors who deny that their camp experience has demolished their integration, who *repress guilt* and sense that they ought to live up to some special obligation, often do quite well in life, as far as appearances go. But emotionally they are depleted because much of their vital energy goes into *keeping denial and repression going*, and because they can no longer trust their inner integration to offer them security, should it again be put to the test for it failed once before. So, while these survivors are relatively symptom free, their life is in some essential respects, deep down, full of inner insecurity...[39]

Finally, there is the group of survivors who concluded from their experience that only a better integration would permit them to live as well as they could with the aftereffects of their concentration camp experience... *A precondition for a new integration is acceptance of how severely one has been traumatized, and of what the nature of the trauma has been.*[40]

Thus, Bettelheim managed to make even those who neither reported nor demonstrated any pathology look sick; to ignore what the majority of victims were saying, and to conclude that:

(1) All victims are psychologically damaged.

(2) All survivors need psychological treatment.

These conclusions turned all victims into potential psychotherapy patients. Now popularized, the Psychology Industry and the public have come to know and accept Bettelheim's conclusions as "clinical truths." While his ideas are not always attributed to him, "His version is **the** version"[41] not only for interpreting the experiences of concentration camp survivors but in recent years, for describing the experiences of other survivors. The concept of "survivorship," which is his invention, has been extrapolated to fit any and all victims, including the manufactured ones.

PATHOLOGIZING

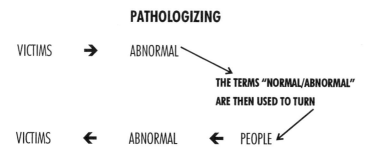

As Bettelheim, with an air of psychological superiority, viewed all of his fellow prisoners as psychologically damaged, suffering "life-long aftereffects;" so too does the Psychology Industry now view all people who have experienced any "traumatic event" (real or imaginary) as suffering long term psychopathology. Just as he considered the options for concentration camp survivors to be either a lifetime of denial, repression, and underlying insecurity or possible new integration through psychotherapy; so too do psychologists present these two options to "victims": to be "in denial" or be "in therapy." For Bettelheim, the preferable solution was a process of "working through," beginning with an acceptance of the trauma and its terrible impact; for psychologists, it is a similar process of confronting the memory and understanding its devastating effects. But the Psychology Industry doesn't stop at assessing pathology in all victims. It goes further by identifying pathology in everyone, making everyone a victim. To do this it plays with the notion of "normal."

One of the first activities of psychological research was to measure peoples' abilities, behaviors and skills. Measurement of human qualities was the original basis on which psychology became distinct from both philosophy and medicine and came to be recognized as a science. And, as will be shown later, it grew as a profession as its measuring devices were applied in education, industry and the military. Its tests assessed the normal range of intelligence (statistically defined as being the range from 80 to 120 on an intelligence test); measured the normal abilities for workers in factories and offices; and determined the normal personality for admission into the armed services.

To create these tests, psychologists determined what normal was by measuring the intelligence, or ablities or personality characteristics of thousands of people and then calculating an average and a normal range. In the same way that a normal range of temperature or rainfall can be calculated, so a normal range of intelligence, ability or behavior could be established.

But psychologists have now twisted this concept of "normal;" when they speak it means something quite different. Instead of referring to something quantitative and objective, they are referring to something qualitative and subjective. To them, it means how they think we should behave, how we ought to be living our lives, how we ought to feel. Anxiety, apprehension and doubt are all aspects of the life experience. Some feel anxious when they fly in a plane; others when they see a snake or when they give a speech. These may be annoying emotions, disturbing feelings, even something which, for the moment, disrupt living. But for a psychologist they are more. Being anxious means "having anxiety" which in turn translates into "being an anxious person" or having "an anxiety disorder." Where being anxious used to be an annoying aspect of normal life, now it is considered abnormal, a form of pathology, a psychological disorder requiring professional treatment.

Feeling anxious or depressed is something that we can be aware of, and it may at times be so severe that some form of treatment (rest, relaxation, escape, or medication) is needed. But psychologists have gone beyond diagnosing and treating feelings of anxiety, boredom and sadness. They have gone beyond determining what are normal (pleasant) and abnormal (unpleasant) feelings, to determining what are abnormal families (ie. "dysfunctional"), abnormal conversations (eg. "harrassment") and abnormal arguments (eg. "verbal abuse").

The original concept of "normal" as average has been replaced by the psychological one involving pathology. No longer does "normal" have to do with the common experience of people, for psychologists have made normal such a narrow range that most people today are, by some definition or another, abnormal. Today "normal" is how psychologists think the world should be: how families should function, how couples ought to "enjoy intimacy," how one ought to "resolve conflicts." It portrays the psychological image of a utopian world and defines all those without perfect lives as "victims." For if they are not "normal" by psychology's standard, then something is wrong; they have pathology and, according to the Psychology Industry, pathology is most likely the result of having been a victim. Those who grew up in "dysfunctional families" become "adult children of alcoholics;" those who have less than ideal marriages evidence past "abuse;" those who have less than ideal lives must find "the hidden cause."

One can then better understand the protest of the young woman when she challenges the reporter who failed to say anything about her strengths, her skills, her ability to survive. In this pathologizing world in which she is trying to "get on with her life," only her negative feelings, her weaknesses and her problems were seen to count; "once a victim, always a victim."

Bettelheim is largely responsible for this tendency to pathologize the victim experience. Throughout his writings:

1)   Bettelheim exhibited a paternalistic concern for his companion prisoners, observing them from a personally distanced and psychoanalytically detached perspective. In describing his early experience at Dachau, he wrote: "While swapping tales that morning, it suddenly flashed through my mind, this is driving me crazy, and I felt that if I were to go on that way, I would in fact end up crazy. That was when I decided that rather than be taken in by such rumours I would try to understand what was psychologically behind them... While some prisoners were reticent, most were more than willing to talk about themselves, because to find someone interested in them and their problems *helped their badly shaken self esteem.*"[42]

2)   Bettelheim based his conclusions on his own concentration camp experience which, unpleasant as it may have been, was very limited compared to what Wiesel and others went through and can hardly be considered as "typical." In doing so, he assumed a paradoxical approach, distancing himself from the other *prisoners* (they were abnormal, he was normal) but then equating all other *survivors* to himself when he spoke of the need to engage in a life-long psychological struggle to cope.

3)   Bettelheim infantilized victims, seeing them as "incompetent children," incapable of doing things for themselves and viewing the guards as harsh father figures. For examples, he wrote: "prisoners were often mistreated in ways that a cruel and domineering father might use against helpless children."[43]

4)   Bettelheim thought that the trauma made it impossible to have healthy personal and social relationships. In contrast to other survivors' reports, he stated that they "were not real friends; they were companions at work, and more often in misery. But while misery loves company, it does not make for friendship. Genuine attachments just do not grow in a barren field of experience nourished only by emotions of frustration and despair..."[44]

5)   Bettelheim denied the psychologically strong coping behaviours of some prisoners such as those who worked in the underground while in

camps, and he described all prisoners in negative ("sick") terms. He ignored the possibility that some survivors may be able to deal with their experiences and live a healthy life.

6) Bettelheim considered *all* survivors to have been psychologically damaged and to be in need of help in their long term struggle to deal with their problems. Not only did Bettelheim see the need for psychotherapy; he saw that "the survivor's new integration will be ... more meaningful than that of many a person who has been spared subjection to an extreme experience."[45] Thus he was one of the first of the modern day breed of psychologist to make the "victim's" experience seem special, bestowing on victims a sense of importance, and describing psychotherapy as a "heroic journey."

These flaws, respectively:

* **assuming a paternalistic attitude,**
* **using their own limited and sometimes unrelated experience,**
* **treating other people as "children,"**
* **pathologizing relationships,**
* **ignoring personal strengths of individuals,**
* **identifying the need for psychological treatment.**

characterize the approach of the Psychology Industry as it manufactures victims.

As have many psychologists since, Bettelheim created a psychologized and pathologized theory about victims and survivors. But he didn't stop there; he took pathologizing a step further into abstraction by arguing that verbal threats in the concentration camps were *more* damaging than the physical torture and extermination that was carried out. He wrote:

> Even the cruelest parent threatens physical punishment much more often than he actually inflicts it, so childlike feelings of helplessness were created much more effectively by the constant threat of beatings than by actual torture. During a real beating one could, for example, take some pride in suffering manfully, in not giving the foreman or guard the satisfaction of grovelling before him, etc. No such emotional protection was possible against the mere threat.[46]

Thus the thought becomes more powerful than the act; the word more damaging than the deed; the fantasy more real than the fact. Such was the personal philosophy of Bettelheim. As Richard Pollak writes in his recent devastating biography,[47] Bettelheim embraced a philosophy that "held, generally, that because life had no real purpose it was made livable only by pretending through fictions that it did." His own life, on examination, is an example of such a work of fiction. He was never trained as a psychologist or a psychoanalyst; he exaggerated his "studies" of concentration-camp life; and his "cures" of autistic children were not verifiable. As Lehman-Haupt writes: "Bettelheim seems to have re-enacted the archetypal American success story of inventing a false past, concocting a new formula for snake oil, and selling it to the public with flummery."[48]

Despite the exposed fraud, the Psychology Industry still accepts his approach by which all victims become patients; the stage remains set for "all the world to become a victim."

Generalizing: The Dangerous "Slippery Slope"

A trauma is a trauma is a trauma[49]

During the Iran Hostage crisis of the late 70's, a group of mental health professionals met regularly to plan the best way to offer the psychological help which, it was assumed, the hostages would need once they were released. From the start, the members of the group admitted to having a problem. As hard as they tried, they found it difficult to put themselves into the hostages" place — "to feel deep in our guts, what their experience of captivity might actually be like." One member of the group describes how they managed to solve this problem prior to meeting any of these victims:

> Then one day a member of our group asked us to think: Were our lives really so far removed from those of the hostages? How many of us had cause to *regard ourselves as victims*?
> As it turned out, nearly all of us had recently *felt threatened or exploited*. The actual episodes reported by the group members differed widely. One social worker had been the *victim of a break-in*. A psychologist *had lost* his younger sister to leukemia. And a psychiatrist had learned of his wife's *plans to leave* him. The result of our collective realization was dramatic. We felt *a powerful surge of empathy* toward the 52 captives, held for over a year, whom we would soon be welcoming back.[50]

Notice the ease with which the group slipped and slid from grappling with the complex question they raised to accepting the simplistic solution that they all knew how the hostages felt because they had felt that way too. Having accepted the suggestion that they could regard themselves as victims, they began to slide into generalizations. They searched inside themselves for feelings of threat and exploitation, slipping into their own experiences and losing sight of those of the hostages. Quickly, they became involved in their own issues, talking excitedly about their own experiences of break-ins, death and divorce. Eventually, drawing "dramatic" comparisons between their lives and those of the hostages, they concluded that they could empathize and understand, that they shared the experience and the effects.

Now what they did may sound ridiculous. It is! But it demonstrates a bizarre form of "psycho-thinking" which can be called *"slippery slope logic."* On this slippery slope, people, like those in the group, begin with a rational thought and then, in gradual stages, slide or drift into irrational conclusions, always believing that each thought along the way makes sense, with the result that the end and the beginning are seen as comparable. In what seems like a tobogan ride of logic, they slide down backwards, not noticing their rapid descent or bothering to compare where they land at the bottom of the hill with where they began at the top.

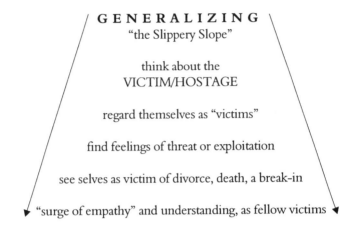

GENERALIZING
"the Slippery Slope"

think about the
VICTIM/HOSTAGE

regard themselves as "victims"

find feelings of threat or exploitation

see selves as victim of divorce, death, a break-in

"surge of empathy" and understanding, as fellow victims

A group of respected, highly paid professionals sitting in a board room managed to conclude that they knew how captives being held in a prison in Iran would feel once they were released. They reached this point by thinking about how they might see themselves as victims. Not one individual, it seems, questioned whether they could, in fact, legitimately regard themselves as victims. In the spirit of generalizing, they convinced themselves that they too were victims and placed themselves, along with the hostages, in a general survivor category. They ceased grappling with the insurmountable challenge of putting "themselves into the hostages' place." Sitting in a comfortable room, exchanging stories from their own lives, they began to imagine deep in their guts what it felt like to be a victim and then imagined that it was the same as being held captive in an Iranian prison.

Could they have managed as easily to identify with Holocaust or Hiroshima survivors? Probably. Consider this example, taken from Lifton's writings:

> It is precisely this kind of death guilt, rather than external events in themselves, which survivors of Nazi camps and Hiroshima refer to when they speak of their "living hell." And from these extreme experiences we come to realize that no one's emotions about death and survival are ever experienced entirely as individual matters; that images of dying are bound up with inner questions about who and what will survive, and images of surviving with who (and what) has died in one's place.

> Analogous patterns of guilt over survival priority have been observed in lesser disasters, and in relationship to dying patients. Again, the doctor attending these patients experiences the emotions of a survivor and "must contend with the guilt evoked by the questioning glance of the dying, with the unspoken question, "Why should I die while you live? "[51]

In this case, on the slope made slippery through the psychologized concept of death guilt, Lifton begins with the experience of a prisoner watching another die and ends up equating that with a physician attending a dying patient.

With this logic, one could continue the slide into the conclusion that all physicians experience a form of the "Survivor Syndrome", and thus, are handicapped in some way by it. In fact, to take this a step, or rather, a slide further, anyone and everyone who has ever seen anyone die or known anyone who has died, might then wonder about death and survival. Ipso facto, all adults do, or one day will, suffer from the "survivor syndrome."

With Lifton, the possibility for "Slippery Slope Logic" can be seen in the slide from

> surviving the Holocaust
>> to
>>> surviving while others were victims
>>>> to
>>>>> surviving while patients die
>>>>>> to
>>>>>>> surviving while anyone dies.

Thus, all of us have something in common with death camp survivors; we have all survived someone else's death.

Lifton himself doesn't take it quite this far but he does begin the descent. And others do slide all the way to the bottom. They begin with the concept of victim which, in the context of external events, does have real meaning and they accept the psychologized, pathologized understanding which makes it an idea, an image, a stereotype. Then they slide backwards into other popularized words and ideas, such as "stress" and "grief," and end up at the bottom of the slope, with everything meaning "victim," and "victim" not meaning anything at all.

Along with psychologizing and pathologizing, "generalizing," as promoted and practiced by the Psychology Industry, becomes another means of manufacturing victims, as the following chapter will show by describing the various models of "victims" produced by the industry.

In the Introduction, a psychologist was quoted as saying that whether the crime was murder or rape, or a purse snatched or pocket picked, the internal psychological injury was the same. Below, two of the "victims" cited in his book describe their experiences:

> You feel stripped naked. You feel as if someone has exposed you totally...You're powerless...You're powerless. Violation is an

adult way to explain that, but it isn't an adult response. It's reminiscent of the kind of helplessness that goes back to early childhood. And I think that's what makes it so crucially painful. Because you can't fight back.[52]

and

I just hate to think of myself as a victim. It's like when I lost my job — I hadn't done anything wrong, but it was so embarrassing to have to tell people that I had lost my job. And when this happened, I felt the same way. It was a guilty secret. I didn't want to talk about it.[53]

The first presents the thoughts of a "victim of a purse snatching," the second, a "victim of a robbery." Both demonstrate "generalizing" from one event to another and both are clear examples of how people come to experience events when they follow the scripts provided by the Psychology Industry.

Instances of generalizing can be found everywhere; new "victims" and new categories of "victims" are continually being created. A recent report by a group of psychologists from a major U.S. university declared a new category of victim: "Victims of Television Violence." They began with the assumption that witnessing actual violence is traumatic. Then they moved on to make the point that everyone who has seen violence on TV, has felt "the trauma," and consciously or unconsciously been upset by it. Therefore, they concluded that watching television violence is *as traumatic* as being part of it in real life and can lead to a form of Post Traumatic Stress Disorder. Taking their conclusion seriously one would then have to assume that, since "the average hourly rate (is) 15 scenes of violence per channel,"[54] that all TV viewers are "victims" and suffer from this psychological disorder.

Through this process of mental gymnastics, psychologists take events or situations which at first are not similar and twist them until they can be viewed as identical. They search for what they consider to be a common element, a feeling or a term, and then, ignoring the differences and the dimensions, they equate the experiences. Thus, television violence becomes as traumatic as real violence, a pocket picked becomes as emotionally injurious as a rape, angry words become as abusive as a physical attack. Psychologists define the psychological importance of events ("it's just as bad as...") and ignore the nature of the external events. Years ago, children used to have a playground chant: "Sticks and stones may break my bones but names'll never hurt me." They knew the differences between insults and assaults. But today the Psychology Industry is telling everyone that an angry word hurts like a bullet and that being whistled at is like being raped. With psychologists' help, everyone can share the experiences of victims and by so doing, can come to see themselves as victims of one sort or another.

A Victim Does Not a Patient Make

Attempts to interpret the survivors' experience — to see it in terms other than its own — have done more harm than good.[55]

Julius Segal, a psychologist who has worked with returned prisoners of war, hostages, Holocaust survivors, refugees, and others who have experienced extreme traumas, provided the example above of the group preparing to treat the hostages. As he stated:

... according to popular expectations, (the hostages) should have become victims of lifelong emotional problems. For months prior to (their) release, pundits and professionals alike offered dire predictions of the outcome of our captives in Teheran. Unhealable scars would blemish their psyches, we were told, and they would remain emotional and physical wrecks for the rest of their lives. One psychologist announced her mournful prognoses on national television: "... permanent problems in interpersonal relationships... permanent coordination difficulties... permanent damage to memory."[56]

Bettelheim made similar predictions for survivors of the Nazi extermination camps:

... the assumption that these prisoners developed states of mind similar to those observed in psychotic persons seems borne out by the behavior of former prisoners of extermination camps after their liberation. In some persons the symptoms appeared more severe, in others less so; some showed that their symptoms were reversible, others not... Some were still suffering from delusions of persecution, others suffered from delusions of grandeur. The latter were the counterpart of guilt feelings for having been spared while parents or siblings had all perished. They were trying to justify and explain their own survival by delusionally inflating their importance. It also enabled them to compensate for the extreme damage done to their narcissism by the experience they had undergone.[57]

These expectations, and similarly negative ones, exist for all victims no matter what the traumatic event is that they experienced. It would seem that "a victim does a patient make." However, Segal continued on from the paragraph above by stating:

No such forecasts have been realized...the hostages emerged to freedom *without lingering symptoms*: no disabling anxiety or depression, no lacerating guilt, no insuperable problems readapting to the world.[58]

So, despite being victims of brutal interrogations, isolation, threats of execution, and suffering from malnutrition and dysentery, most of them were able to resume normal living without the anticipated psychological problems. Again, as Segal wrote:

This case is not unique. For over thirty years, I have studied victims of overwhelming stress... repeatedly, I have been inspired by the countless cases that run counter to "experts" predictions. Instead of patterns of deficit and defeat, there is one of coping and conquest.[59]

There are, in fact, a number of studies which show that many survivors have adapted well in the subsequent years. For example, one study of Holocaust survivors drew attention to what the authors described as "the magnificent ability of human beings to rebuild shattered lives, careers, and families, even as they wrestle with the bitterest of memories."[60] In another, Antonovsky, studying concentration camp survivors, wrote of his fascination that "a not-inconsiderable number of concentration camp survivors were found to be well-adapted... what, we must ask, has given these women the strength, despite their experiences, to maintain what would seem to be the capacity not only to function well, but even to be happy."[61]

When such studies or interviews are conducted by people other than psychologists, there are few abstractions found to support themes such as Lifton's "death guilt" or Bettelheim's pathologized view of survivors. For instance, Sylvia Rothchild, after listening to hundreds of interviews with survivors, commented: "Expecting them to be sad, even morbid, I wasn't prepared for the flashes of exhilaration, for the strength and pride of life-obsessed people who had lived through the worst of times..."[62] She noted that when asked how they have lived **after** their experiences, the responses were richly varied but specific and concrete:

A survivor from Sobibor says he lives but has no appetite for life: "I have deep feelings for other survivors but basically I believe most people are rotten." A woman who escaped with him has another nature. "I'm happy and content," she says. "I like my life and my self..." Survivors respond differently to violence. "If somebody hits you with a rock," says Elizabeth Mermelstein, "throw him back a piece of bread." A survivor of Sobibor says: "Only fighting back can give you honour and respect."[63]

So how is it that the popular belief is one of deep damage and long-term distress? Why do we believe that victims are weakened by their experience and that they can never recover unless they cease to deny the devastating effects of "the trauma," uncover it, face it, confront it and go through the required psychological process, changing themselves from "victim" to "survivor" and, finally, to victorious "thriver." Later chapters will show that it is in a large part due to the Psychology Industry which has so much to benefit from this prediction and from this never ending need for services. As psychologist Norman Garmezy, from the University of Minnesota, said: "our mental health practitioners and researchers are predisposed by interest, investment, and training in seeing deviance, psychopathology, and weakness wherever they look"[64] and what better place to find it than in those who have obviously undergone stress.

The horrific suffering that some victims bear cannot be trivialized or denied, nor can it be implied that people never carry with them the scars of such misfortune or maltreatment. There are authentic victims and some of these people do have trouble coping with life because of what happened to them. It must be fully acknowledged that some victims need help in living with the effects of their experience, and as Bettelheim says, "some will get better and some will not." What is questionable is the stereotyping of all victims into a common patient image and the use of that image for purposes which have direct benefit to the Psychology Industry.

As Segal found out, and as astute observers discover over and over, people have surprising strength and resilience to overcome the difficulties in life. The Psychology Industry, its beliefs and practices, have been, in a large part, responsible for the self-denigrating and self-defeating tendency to deny these strengths and to create a world in which people live in fear of crisis, afraid that they will crumble. It repeatedly confirms the fear which most have when listening to the story of someone like Wiesel or the young rape victim that: "If that happened to me I couldn't cope" and it encourages the response: "I can't get over it." even to events which pale in comparison to these.

"Being a victim" and "being a patient" have been wrongly associated.

VICTIM =/= PATIENT

The idea has been planted in the heads of most people that if they falter at all, doubt themselves at all, ever fear or ever fail, they lack "the inner strength," "the self-esteem," "the power" to deal with their own lives. They believe that their "egos have been tattered," their "energy has been depleted;" they see themselves as "victims" and they become "users" of the Psychology Industry.

Endnotes

1. "Not for the timid: Details of sex assaults show true savagery." *Vancouver Sun,* March 27, 1993. p.B10-11.

2. Ibid. pp.B10-11.

3. This quote is from Robert McAfee Brown's preface (p.vi) to the 1986 Bantam edition of *Night* which was first published in 1960.

4. Wiesel, Elie. *Night.* New York: Bantam Books, 1960. pp.72-73.

5. Ibid. p.81.

6. Ibid. pp.90-91.

7. Ibid. p.106.

8. Attributed to Sigmund Freud.

9. Szasz, Thomas. *The Myth of Psychotherapy: Mental Healing as Religion, Rhetoric and Repression.* Garden City, N.Y.: Anchor Press/Doubleday, 1978. p.205

10. Gross Martin L. *The Psychological Society: The impact and the failure of psychiatry, psychotherapy, psychoanalysis and the psychological revolution.* New York: Random House, 1978.

11. Herman, Judith. *Trauma and Recovery.* New York: Basic Books, 1992. p.1. (italics added)

12. In a letter from Williams James to Theodore Fournoy, dated September 28, 1909. (italics added)

13. Lifton, Robert Jay. *Death in Life: Survivors of Hiroshima.* New York: Random House, 1967. p.1. (italics added)

14. Lifton, Robert Jay. *The Broken Connexion: On death and the continuity of life*. New York: Simon & Schuster, 1979. p.179. (italics added)

15. Lifton. *The Broken Connection*. p.3. (italics added)

16. Ibid. *The Broken Connection*. p.3. (italics added)

17. Lifton. *Death in Life*. p.36.

18. Ibid. p.36. (the parenthetical comments are in the original text, italics are added)

19. Ibid. p.491.

20.Wiesel, Elie. *From the Kingdom of Memory: Reminiscences*. New York: Summit Books, 1990. p.120-121.

21. Lifton uses the term "death guilt" throughout his work and associates this victim characteristic with the guilt (often accompanied by shame) experienced in living when others died.

22. Lifton. *Death in Life*. p.36.

23. Ibid. p.36.

24. Ibid. p.9-10.

25. Ibid. p.10. (italics added)

26. Lifton. *The Broken Connection*. p.169.

27. Kubler-Ross, Elisabeth. *On Death and Dying: What the dying have to teach doctors, nurses, clergy and their own families*. New York: Collier Books, Macmillan Publishing Co., 1969.

28. Frankl, Victor E. *The Unheard Cry for Meaning*. New York: Simon & Schuster, 1978. p.87.

29."Not for the timid: Details of sex assaults show true savagery." *Vancouver Sun*, March 27, 1993. pp.B10-B11.

30. "Not for public consumption." *Vancouver Sun*, May 29, 1993.

31. Wiesel. *From the Kingdom of Memory*. pp.170-171. (italics added)

32. Hoppe, Klaus D. "The psychodynamics of concentration camp victims," *The Psychoanalytic Forum*, 1966, 1 (1), pp.76-85. Cited by Des Pres in *The Survivor*, p.155. (italics added)

33. Des Pres, Terrence. *The Survivor*. New York: Oxford University Press, 1976. p.155.

34. Bettelheim, Bruno. *Surviving and Other Essays*. New York: Vintage Books/Random House, 1980. pp.24-25. (italics added)

35. Bettelheim's paper entitled "Individual and Mass Behaviour in Extreme Situations" was turned down many times before being published in *"The Journal of Abnormal and Social Psychology*, Vol.38 (October, 1943), pp.417-452.

36. Bettelheim. *Surviving*. p.36.

37. Bettelheim, Bruno.*The Informed Heart: Autonomy in a Mass Age*. New York: The Free Press, 1960. p.114.

38. Bettelheim. *Surviving*. pp.28-29.

39. Ibid. pp.31-33.

40. Ibid. pp.34-35. (italics added)

41. Des Pres. *The Survivor*. p.158.

42. Bettelheim. *The Informed Heart*. pp.111-112 and 116. (italics added)

43. Ibid. p.131.

44. Ibid. p.231.

45. Bettelheim. *Surviving*. p.35.

46. Bettelheim. *The Informed Heart*. p.131.

47. Pollak, Richard. *The Creation of Dr. B.: A Biography of Bruno Bettelheim*. New York: Simon and Schuster, 1996.

48. Lehman-Haupt, Christopher. "Psychologist an 'empty fortress' in unsparing new biography." *New York Times (*reprinted in *The Globe and Mail*, January 18, 1997.)

49. A section title in *Aftershock: Surviving the Delayed Effects of Trauma, Crisis and Loss* by Andrew E. Slaby (New York: Villard Books, 1989.)

50. Segal, Julius. *Winning Life's Toughest Battles*. New York: McGraw-Hill Books, 1986. (italics added)

51. Lifton. *Death in Life*. pp. 491-492 .

52. Bard, Morton and Sangrey, Don. *The Crime Victim's Book*. New York: Basic Books, 1979. p.10.

53. Ibid. p.76.

54. Lichter, S. Robert and Amundson, Daniel. *A Day of TV Violence; 1992 vs 1994*. Washington, D.C.: Center for Media and Public Affairs, Aug.1, 1994. p.2.

55. Des Pres. *The Survivor*. p.157.

56. Segal. *Winning Life's Toughest Battles*. p. 2.

57. Bettelheim. *The Informed Heart*. p.251.

58. Segal. *Winning Life's Toughest Battles*. p.2. (italics added)

59. Ibid. pp.2-3.

60. Weinfeld, M., Sigal, J.J., and Eaton, W.W. "Long-term effects of the holocaust on selected social attitudes and behaviours of survivors: A cautionary note." *Social Forces*, 60, September 1981, 1-19.

61. This study by Antonovsky, Moaz, Dowty, & Wijsnbeek (1971) was cited by Des Pres in *The Survivor*. See also: Antonovsky, Anton. *Health, Stress, and Coping*. New York: Jossey-Bass, 1979.

62. Rothchild, Sylvia (ed.) *Voices from the Holocaust*. New York: New American Library, p.7.

63. Ibid. p.313.

64. Garmezy, Norman. "Forward." In Werner, E., and Smith, R.S. *Vulnerable but invincible*. New York: McGraw-Hill, 1982, xiii-xix.

FABRICATED VICTIMS

As our 15th-century forebears were obsessed with the creation of saints and our 19th-century ancestors with the creation of heroes, from Christopher Columbus to George Washington, so are we with the recognition, praise and, when necessary, the manufacture of victims... Never before in human history were so many acronyms pursuing identity. It's as though all human encounter were one big sore spot...

Robert Hughes
The Culture of Complaint

The young woman abducted and raped, the accident victim whose life was shattered, Elie Wiesel, the Iranian student, the hostages – not one of these people would have chosen to have happen to them what happened. As Des Pres has pointed out "survivors do not choose their fate and would escape if they could."[1] So, why, when authentic victims would escape if they could, are people today allowing themselves to be categorized as victims?

No one wants to be in a car crash, to be raped, assaulted or tortured. Deciding to become a real victim involves choosing pain, injury, helplessness and loss. In contrast, becoming a Fabricated Victim entails none of these obvious costs. Rather, it amounts to being reassured that the worst thing that can happen has already happened and that help, support and protection are on the way. The Psychology Industry sells the idea that once one is identified as a victim, one can anticipate relief and healing; "take control of the situation," "reclaim one's life," and make of it something better.

Belief in the progression from victim to victor is encouraged in "happily-ever-after" endings such as the one told by a woman who identified herself as an Adult Child of an Alcoholic and a victim of abuse:

Friends often ask me what keeps me from giving up... Most of all, I now believe it is possible to change if you choose a positive, realistic goal and ask the right people for help.

My life is my own example. From a destitute addict to a healthy, happy participant in life, I have found my Prince Charming, and maybe someday we'll even have a castle. It isn't always easy but, with support, I've at least gained the courage to try. Every fairy tale I ever read as a kid had a happy ending, and I'll be damned if mine doesn't too.[2]

Having a psychologist find "the sore spot," "put a finger on it," and label "what went wrong," provides the opening scene in the Psychology Industry's popularized version of the heroic journey, the modern day quest for innocence and fulfillment. Being recognized as a victim of incest, verbal abuse, a shopping addiction..., as suffering from flashbacks, blocked feelings, low self esteem..., as needing to trust someone, remember something, understand what happened..., provides the starting point; it identifies the client as the central character in a drama and the psychologist as the guide equipped to show the way. Becoming a Fabricated Victim isn't about endings and losses so much as it is about beginnings and gains.

What all Fabricated Victims have in common is not some extraordinary experience but rather this expectation of a future made brighter by virtue of victim status. Fabricated Victims are given permission to lead psychologized lives; while people who fail to qualify are left to deal with life as it is, complete with disappointments, failures, self-doubts, embarrassing moments, regrets, sicknesses, debts, and even sins to be confessed and crimes to be punished. Those left unidentified and undiagnosed by the Psychology Industry must go on with their lives; while, the Fabricated Victims step into another, psychologized and pathologized reality where guilt and shame are banished and responsibilities are diminished.

People choose to step into this other reality for a variety of reasons. First, there are the *synthetic victims*, the ordinary, often quite normal, people who are brought under the Psychology Industry's pervasive influence. Receptive, suggestible or, momentarily vulnerable, these are the people who come to believe in what the industry sells and to accept as factual some revised, reinterpreted or fictionalized version of their own lives. In their efforts to become genuine, they become phoney and, in their efforts to speak the truth, they become liars.

Aside from the synthetics, there is another large group of fabricated victims. These are the *contrived victims*, the people who have been diagnosed with some genuine medical problem to which the Psychology Industry attributes a psychological cause, solution or need. Sick, suffering and often quite desperate, these people are easily swayed by misinformation.

Then, there are the *counterfeit victims*, those who turn to the Psychology Industry for a victim identity which they know to be false but which achieves for them some specific purpose. These are the people who intentionally lie and for whom psychologists are paid accomplices. They knowingly make up stories, feign symptoms, play sick or injured or damaged in order to escape the blame, avoid the punishment, find an excuse, get even with someone, extort money, join a group or seem less boring.

The Psychology Industry would prefer that the Synthetic Victims go on believing, that the Contrived Victims continue to look beyond medicine for support, and that the Counterfeit Victims go undetected .

SYNTHETIC VICTIMS

Victimism debilitates its practitioners by trapping them in a world of oppressive demons that they cannot, by definition, control.[3]

"They tell you that everything you knew for twenty, thirty, forty years was wrong. Your parents, whom you trusted, the values they instilled in you as a child. You're told they are all garbage... Anything you say can be and will be misinterpreted. There is no way around it. This is costing people their lives." [4]

This is how Lynn Gondolf describes the Psychology Industry as it turns ordinary, often quite normal, people into victims. She had entered therapy, hoping to find a solution to her chronic binge-and-purge eating disorder. At the beginning, she told her psychologist about her memories of being raped by an uncle, between the ages of 5 and 13, claiming that she had always remembered clearly what had happened; "...that wasn't anything I'd forgotten or ever would forget." And she told him that she could understand that her eating disorder may have been connected to these experiences, for her uncle had always given her a dollar for candy after each incident. But the psychologist was not satisfied that she was expressing "enough" emotion and insisted that there must be more buried somewhere deep in her unconscious.

He explained her dreams and interpreted her drawings, and had her do automatic writing during hypnosis, as he led her to search for hidden signs that other members of her family had abused her as well. He also insisted that she attend a group in which ten women met in a small room for the purpose of remembering more about what had been done to them. "They wanted us to talk about experiences very explicitly in front of the others and get into a rage" she later described the experience. "It gets contagious. This one says she remembers something, then this one, then this one. The stories got grosser and grosser and you had a tiny roomful of girls screaming and raging and bawling. If you didn't have memories, you didn't get any attention. I can dream stuff up, sure..." Eventually, when Gondolf began to "remember" episodes of her father raping her, the psychologist called in her brother and sisters, and told them that she'd probably kill herself unless they supported her in these allegations.

A year after beginning treatment, Gondolf had accused her father of sexually abusing her, been diagnosed with a variety of depressive disorders, gone from taking no medication to using a mixture of eight different drugs, lost her job, and become entirely dependent on her psychologist. By the time her insurance money ran out, she had hit "rock bottom." When she had no more money to pay for therapy, her psychologist decided to end treatment, attributing her failure to improve to her resistance and noncompliance. Declaring her a danger to herself, he tried to have her committed to a state institution. Instead, she went to a treatment centre to withdraw from the medication and "slowly began to learn how to live again, how to work things out by myself." She came to realize that her father "hadn't done a thing."

It took two years for Gondolf to begin to function normally again, for, as she described it, "I'd believed all this stuff... and you suffer all the psychological trauma as if it all really had gone on." Gondolf publicly stated that her father was innocent of all the allegations she had made and she became one of the first synthetic victims to talk openly about the devastating effects which the Psychology Industry can have on people.

With the current controversy over "false memories" sparked by such statements, the idea of a false or fabricated victim is most likely to bring to mind the image of someone who has discovered that their memories of being abused or assaulted are false; a Lynn Gondolf, or Laura Pasley, or Melody Gavigan. For there is a growing number of individuals who claim that they were persuaded by psychologists into accepting they were victims of trauma, only later to discover that what they had come to believe in therapy was not true. They are the ones who have left or escaped the Psychology Industry and begun to speak and write openly about how they were led/misled into having false memories. With their stories appearing in places like *Mother Jones, Macleans* and *Time*, they have drawn the public's attention to the Psychology Industry's business of manufacturing "Synthetic Victims.'

> **Synthetic**: *(adj), [Gk synthetikos, of composition] 1. produced artificially, man-made; 2. devised, arranged, or fabricated for special situations to imitate or replace usual realities.*
>
> Webster's Dictionary

While cases like that of Gondolf may be the best known, the term has a much broader scope, identifying not only those people turned into *"false memory"* victims by therapies intent on recovering memories but also those who have been turned into other types of synthetic victims through the widespread Psychology Industry tactics which include

"false interpreting" – the application of specific theories and particular therapies,

"false naming' – the fraudulent assignment of diagnoses, labels and explanatory terms,

and **"false remembering'** – the search for traumatic events, their deeper meaning, and their causal nature.

Two basic and recurrent themes on which these tactics rely for their success are:

> *Trauma* : the notion that for every current problem there must be a dramatic cause; that some event(s) in the past, even as far

back in time as childhood or infancy, was so disturbing that it continues to affect the way the individual thinks, feels and acts.

and

Addiction: the idea that bad or undesirable behaviours are due to something beyond control. The traditional model is alcoholism as a "disease," but numerous variations have been developed, often with some attribution to current stress or early trauma.

Whichever theme, or combination of these themes, is applied, the effect is to suggest a lack of personal control, an external cause on which to place responsibility and blame, and damaging effects which are internal, personal, and subjective. And these three characteristics make the person appear like a victim.

FALSE INTERPRETING

Alice laughed. "There's no use trying," she said: "One can't believe impossible things."

"I dare say you haven't had much practice," said the Queen.

"When I was your age, I always did it for half-an-hour a day.

Why, sometimes I believed as many as six impossible things before breakfast."[5]

The capacity to believe impossible things stems largely from a predominant human tendency to favour proving something true over demonstrating it to be false. Consider the following scenario, which demonstrates how this tendency can lead to false interpreting.[6]

Someone tells a neighbour about experiencing a few recent dizzy spells and the neighbour mentions that dizziness might result from a brain tumour. Worried now, the person begins to read about brain tumours and locates an article in which 250 hospitalized neurology patients were classified as follows:

	BRAIN TUMOUR Present	Absent
Present	160	40
Dizziness		
Absent	40	10

Figure 1

Would looking at this table suggest to the person that being dizzy is connected with having a brain tumour? Probably. Because most people, looking at it, are drawn to the largest number and think only about the finding that 160 people in the study had a brain tumour and experienced dizziness; thus, they connect brain tumours with dizziness. They latch onto the finding that a lot more of the people who had brain tumours were dizzy. What they fail to take into account is the information provided by looking at the other numbers. If they looked at the other column, the 50 hospitalized neurology patients who do not have brain tumours and noticed the 40 who had brain tumours but were not dizzy, they would see that most of the people got dizzy (ie. that 4 out of every 5 people who were hospitalized neurology patients, whether they had a brain tumour or not, got dizzy.) Thus, the study does not support the suggestion that dizziness is a symptom of a brain tumour; what most people who read this study would conclude is a false interpretation.[7]

Now, the Psychology Industry thrives on just this kind of false interpretation. Substituting Tumours with terms stemming from the concepts of "trauma" and "addiction" and replacing Dizziness with symptoms of its own defining, it presents endless variations on this table, connecting, for example, bedwetting with having been abused, or even, disliking tapioca pudding with repressed memories of childhood sexual abuse.[8]

Consider, for example, this message:

> Symptoms and problems whose roots were traced to past lives cover a broad spectrum. For example, I now find that almost all patients with chronic weight excess of ten pounds or more have had a lifetime in which they either starved to death or suffered food deprivation for long periods... Many of my patients have discovered that the causes of their phobias, fears, and even aversions were rooted in some traumatic event of a previous lifetime.[9]

Just as dizziness can incorrectly come to be seen as a symptom of a brain tumour; being overweight or afraid of something can be seen as signifying something that happened in a past life. And of the thousands who read Edith Fiore's bestseller *You Have Been Here Before*, which was deemed to be full of challenging evidence to support a revolutionary new approach, many began to connect their problems to past life experiences and seek out "past-life" therapists.

Favouring confirmation over denial, support over doubt, certainty over questioning, contributes to the acceptance of causal connections between whatever problem a person has and whatever cause might be suggested. As far-fetched as some Psychology Industry explanations sound, there are thousands of people who have become convinced of past life experiences and, more recently, of UFO abductions and encounters with Satanists. The tendency to make, and to accept, causal connections lies at the base of the Psychology Industry's manufacturing of victims through "false interpretations," with these interpretations ranging all the way from the absurd to the seemingly reasonable. Psychologists' belief in the importance of any given symptom or theory can be so strong that it leads to "illusionary correlations" in which connections are perceived or imagined where there are none, simply because they correspond to the psychologists' own preconceptions. What they think they know is often only a partial or fabricated truth based on their perceptions. And what they call reality is a simple interpretation maintained and reinforced by further misperceptions and by talking to others who share their view of reality.

False interpreting, the result of drawing false correlations, is the essential ingredient in the manufacture and maintenance of all synthetic victims. It involves placing the psychologist's own ideas and beliefs above the individual client's problems. For the client, this leads to getting "the therapist's particular brand of psychotherapy, addressing the problem areas that the therapist finds significant. The form of treatment, then, is determined by the therapist's habitual approach and not by the nature of the problem that the patient brings in."[10] The psychologist sees everything from one, and only one, perspective, and makes each and every client conform to this distorted reality.

While the more bizarre of these, such as past-lives, UFO encounters and Devil worshippers, are being looked upon with progressively more scepticism, those which seem to have a somewhat more realistic basis remain largely unquestioned. For instance, Schaef holds a perspective which she believes and claims is "beyond therapy, beyond science." She states: "Many of the categories found in the *DSM-III* fit much more readily under the rubric of addiction and codependence, and working with them with the tools of the Twelve-Step program and "the deep process work" (the name for her version of therapy) not only was cheaper and easier, it was more effective."[11] In other words, most if not all problems fit her beliefs and therapy. Or consider Bass and Davis, who believe that almost one quarter of all children are sexually abused before they turn eighteen, and state: "The long-term effects of child sexual abuse can be so pervasive that it's sometimes hard to pinpoint exactly how the abuse affected you. It permeates everything: your sense of self, your intimate relationships, your sexuality, your parenting, your work life, even your sanity."[12]

False interpretations have their most profound effect when they are expressed subtly as indirect suggestions originating in the psychologist's own beliefs and values. Pittman confesses that while psychologists "are trained to pretend that we have no value systems at all," in fact, "psychotherapy involves applying the value system of the therapist to the dilemmas of the clients."[13] While clients are being warned to avoid therapists who make blatant value-laden statements, these same people who issue the warnings are often the ones who couch their interpretations in subtler forms that suggest specific possibilities and imply likelihoods. Gondolf's therapist gained her trust by just listening, never doubting her, never challenging her, but always implying that there was more to be found.

These values which lie at the core of most of the false interpretations can be seen in the statements of psychologists who seem highly professional, respectable and even rational. For instance:

We all suffer from "aftershock," maybe less violently but still at a price we shouldn't have to pay. In fact, aftershock is the disease of today.[14]

Among women, incest is so common as to be an epidemic. Incest is easily the greatest single underlying reason why women seek therapy and other treatment.[15]

More than half of all women are survivors of childhood sexual trauma... it does not have to involve touch... Incest can occur through words, sounds, or even exposure of the child to sights or acts that are sexual but do not involve her.[16]

Most individuals have many Co-existing Dependencies.[17]

Leavetaking is the universal experience. From birth to death we face a continuum of partings...The trauma associated with leave-taking takes various forms. The individual may become mildly or deeply neurotic or even psychotic. There may be depression (sometimes interspersed with euphoria), anger, anxiety, guilt. A person scarred by a parting may drink heavily, worry in excess, become promiscuous. There are other effects: for example, a mother may get fat after her children leave home. Her obesity is an attempt to deny the fact of leavetaking.[18]

Just as in ancient times when all roads led to Rome, now all interpretive paths lead to the same core cause; that is, the person is not in control, is damaged internally and has someone else to blame. For instance, Laura Pasley, a woman who, like Gondolf, entered therapy because of an eating disorder, has described how her psychologist (Steve), based on his own brand of false interpretations, had her believing a long list of "impossible things" including that her own mother had been trying to kill her for years:

I was bulimic. If Mama bought us groceries and any of them were easily ingested "binge foods," Steve said it was to kill me. At one point, I took some badly needed groceries back to her, threw the bag and asked if she was trying to kill me because there were some cookies and chips in the bag... I suspected her every move, her every motive.[19]

Virtually anything that anyone does or any experience can be manipulated to fit a trauma or addiction theme, and virtually any attempt a person makes to refute or question false interpretations meets with resistance. For example, Fiore, the past lives psychologist, describes the case of a young woman who had sought help to overcome a snake phobia.

After combing back through her life under hypnosis and finding nothing to explain her fears, I tried a hunch. I asked her if she had had an encounter with snakes before she was born. She saw herself as a fifteen year old Aztec girl in front of a pyramid watching priests dancing with poisonous snakes in their mouths. She trembled with emotion and reported the bizarre rites in vivid detail.

When the woman returned to the present and, after puzzling over what she had just experienced became quite distressed and said: "I don't believe all that stuff," Fiore's conclusion was "Here is a person who definitely rejected reincarnation, but who had just relived a lifetime that took place four hundred years ago."[20]

Another psychologist, with an equally strong propensity for false interpretation, in this instance involving multiple personalities rather than past lives, was confronted by an angry former patient: "Don't you think it is odd that no one is getting better and that everyone wants to cut and kill themselves after they get into therapy with you?" He responded by asking: "Which personality am I talking to now?"

And consider one other, Peter Rutter, author of *Sex in the Forbidden Zone*, who believes that any woman who has been seduced by (or who has seduced) a man "in power" (e.g. her therapist, doctor, minister, teacher, lawyer, etc.) is a victim. He has such a firm and "crystal clear" understanding of this form of "abuse" that when his interpretation is challenged by a woman's contradictory personal experience, he is quite prepared to handle it. In speaking about his lectures, he says, "Sometimes people in the audience, courageous souls, stand up and say: 'It happened to me and I feel fine.' or 'It was wonderful.' or 'I had an affair with my therapist and not only was I not damaged, I feel that it healed me.' " When that happens, Rutter reasons that: "You can't tell that person 'No. You're wrong;' so, I respond by saying: 'That's fine. Good for you. But can I give you my 747 analogy and that is: You're in the waiting lounge waiting to board a Boeing 747 with 360 other people and they call the flight and they say we're ready for boarding and we just want to tell you one thing – this plane is going to crash and everyone will be killed except two of you. We can't tell you who but two of you will walk away unscathed. And the question is: Would you get on that plane... It's the same with all trauma. There are people who come out of trauma as far as we know unscathed.' "[22]

These responses to direct questions and confrontations illustrate the more obvious attempts to support false interpretation. But psychologists all over the country, not only in therapy sessions and pop psychology books but, also, in professional journals and conferences, on television shows and in courtrooms, are giving false interpretations, based on false beliefs, and supported by false assumptions and connections. When they sound reasonable and are presented in a "caring and professional" way, complete with caution and concern, people accept them, incorporate them in their thinking and apply them to their own lives. The false interpretions of the Psychology Industry which are most dangerous are those which have gone "mainstream," influencing the way people who would not consider themselves "users" come to interpret situations and understand their own feelings. Below is a sampling of the everyday, "garden variety," authoritative Psychology Industry suggestions which are so familiar and so universally accepted that they are leading not only individuals but society to false conclusions:

- People often overeat because they're unhappy. What are you unhappy about?

- Sleeping problems are indicative of depression. They can be a sign of an undiagnosed, treatable condition.
- Some relationships are toxic and, like anything harmful, must be ended. You owe it to yourself to look critically at the people in your life and weed out the toxic ones.
- Every time he yells at you, it hurts. It's just as if he had hit you.
- Spanking a child is like teaching someone that assault is O.K.
- Low self esteem can make a person so needy that it can lead to shopping binges and an entire loss of control over spending.

FALSE REMEMBERING

Repressed memories of sexual abuse and satanic abuse
are the favorites among therapists. All the elements
of a good soap opera are there – sex, drama and money.[23]

Cases, like that of Gondolf or Pasley, which involve the rewriting of personal histories in such a way that events which never happened come to be accepted as historical facts, are among the clearest examples of the pernicious and perverted influence of the Psychology Industry. Called by some "the quackery of the 20th century"[24] and "the black eye of psychology,"[25] Repressed Memory Therapy (RMT) is the segment of the Psychology Industry which has already come under public, (and professional) scrutiny.

RMT, or "memory work" as it is often called, is a particularly popular approach to psychotherapy based on the fixed belief that psychological problems are caused by traumas, most likely sexual and most often experienced in childhood, and that any inability to fully remember them is due to "denial" and "repression." While some memories are completely hidden in this way, it is believed that others are only partially remembered, and lack either the essential detail or the appropriate emotions. Either way, the Psychology Industry contends that the key to eliminating the ongoing impact lies in recovering and re-experiencing the memories of what happened. "The patient must reconstruct not only what happened but also what she felt" states Herman, "the recitation of facts without the accompanying emotions is a sterile exercise, without therapeutic effect."[26]

Most people assume that events are either remembered or forgotten and find it difficult to understand how memories can exist in this netherland of "repression." To explain this point of view, Alice Miller, in describing the effects of child abuse, writes that the children "will not remember the torments to which they were exposed, because those torments, together with the needs related to them, have all been repressed: that is, completely banished from consciousness... And later, as adults, they have forgotten such experiences, or at least the memory (is) not vivid enough to cause them to speak of them."[27]

Proponents of this approach rely on false interpretations, along with leading suggestions, and supportive encouragement, to convince people that there may be things in their past which they have forgotten and that these "repressed memories" are the cause of their problems. Since virtually everyone has a time span they can't remember clearly and most people remember relatively little, and often only snippets, from when they were very young, a psychologist probing these "gaps" and connecting them with the possibility of some hidden trauma can make people receptive to the idea. "If you can't remember what happened that summer, perhaps something happened that you don't want to remember" or "If you can't remember precisely how it all happened, perhaps we need to go over it in your mind until it becomes clear." Even people who previously had no idea that they might have been a victim can begin to think that it may be possible. When the psychologist explains what is being proposed, it can seem so technical, so mechanical, that it may even seem to make sense: "You have a problem which you have described to me but you can look at it only on the surface. I can help you look at it below the surface and lead you to find the source of what is wrong. Then we can fix it."

Once people are convinced of the possible existence of such hidden memories, they can accept that the goal of therapy is to uncover them, often through hypnosis or guided imagery sessions in which possible scenarios are suggested or in which they are led into imagining certain events. At other times, psychologists rely on dreams, drawings or family photographs to stimulate ideas and thoughts which can then be rehearsed and repeated over and over again until they become accepted as memories. In other cases, when memories already exist, the goal becomes one of reviewing and *revising the memories* until they are experienced with stronger emotion and new meaning.

Psychiatrist and hypnotist Herbert Spiegel once gave a live demonstration designed to show how easily such false memories can be implanted by hypnotic suggestion. In 1968, in front of his colleagues and television cameras, he hypnotized a man and told him that Communists intended to take over radio and television stations. He gave no details but did suggest to the man that later he would remember specific information. When the hypnosis session ended, the subject began to talk about the plot, providing an elaborate story complete with minor details such as a description of the furnishings in the room where he first heard about the planned takeover. He also accepted and encorporated further suggestions given to him by the people he talked to, even though he was no longer in hypnosis. He was subsequently rehypnotized and the suggestions about the plot were "removed." Once out of hypnosis, he was shown the videotape of the whole event, and reacted with shock and surprise.

Twelve years later, Spiegel wrote about the episode: "During the experiment, in response to the hypnotic signal, the subject created a totally false story to rationalize his compliance. He sincerely believed it to be true. Since he was locked into the hypnotic bind, he suspended his own critical judgment. He lied but did not actually know he was lying. At the time, he was in effect *an honest liar.*"[28]

Despite Spiegel's demonstration, hundreds of other experiments that show peoples' memories can be influenced and changed with and without hypnosis, and a growing number of individuals who are recanting and admitting that memories uncovered in therapy are false, the Psychology Industry goes on encouraging new memories and revising existing ones, and in the process creating new Synthetic Victims and strengthening the "honest lies" of others. Psychologists, convinced of the clinical utility of memory work, use these memories in therapy regardless of their accuracy. Fiore, in her book on past life therapy, writes that "whether the former lifetimes that are "lived" are fantasies or actual experiences lived in a bygone era does not matter to me as a therapist – getting results is important."[29] Another psychologist, with a more traditional approach to psychotherapy, stated to her colleagues, "the retrieval of true, distorted or false memories of abuse can lead to an individual's improvement in therapy. A patient might need to have his/her memories *validated* for therapeutic gains even if these memories are "false," but as long as no harmful steps ensue."[30] Apparently the Psychology Industry sees no harm in lying to a patient if it is "in their own good" despite the potential harm that can come from later discovering the memories to be false, hurting others by virtue of believing them or one day being exposed as liars.

Addressing an audience of psychologists, who practiced hypnosis, a lawyer pointed out that "You can misuse hypnosis in the way you ask questions but you can misuse the way you ask questions without hypnosis. All lawyers know that. The idea of lawyering is not to hear what the witness says but to put the words in the witness's mouth so they come out like a ventriloquist." He went on to suggest that if psychologists can create false memories, as has been demonstrated, their ethical (and legal) responsibility lies not in ceasing to do so but rather in ensuring that the false memories they create are "good memories," those which are therapeutically helpful to the client. [31]

Psychologists involved in memory work hold the belief that what they are doing is for the good of their patient, even if "the work" involves the patient "reliving" terrifying experiences, akin to nighmares or horror movies. The following case illustrates how people can allow themselves to be subjected to such experiences and to accept them as actual historical memories.

A young woman, hospitalized because of continued hemorrhaging after a miscarriage, became upset and asked to be seen by a psychiatrist. When he arrived, she told him that, having been moved into the hospital ward where her mother had died earlier of cancer and fearing that she might be dying too, she had panicked. She had already been moved to another ward and, after describing what had happened, she smiled slightly and supposed that she'd survive. When he returned the next day, she still seemed distressed and, when he encouraged her to tell him what was troubling her, she talked about a bad dream she had had a week before: "I dreamed that I had an itchy place on my hand... And when I scratched it, all these bugs came out of where I was scratching it! Little spiders, just pouring out of the skin on my hand. It was just – I can't even tell you how it was. It was so terrible." The psychiatrist saw the dream as "blatantly symbolic" and suggested that "What we need to do is find out what the dream is revealing from the inside."

In that visit and the half dozen that followed, the woman did not want to explore the terrible dream; so, he listened as she talked. Eventually she said that there was something she wanted to tell him but didn't know what it was. Over the many sessions that followed, he encouraged her to talk. "Let it come, as much as you can. Don't judge it, if you can help it. Don't try to make it anything but what it was. Just let it be what it was. Just let yourself go." Screaming in terror, the woman began to "relive memories." "It's... it's... it's all black," she began, eventually describing in detail how at the age of five she had been tortured for months in satanic rituals, in which her mother had taken part, and which included being forced to watch cult members nail babies to crosses, stab a dead baby with a crucifix, and eat the ashes of a dead woman. After months of such experiences, the little girl lay "all a mess, her stomach swollen with malnutrition, her flesh flaccid, her eyes vacant, with blood all over. Then, Satan himself appeared." As these "memories" kept coming, the woman asked her psychiatrist, whether she might not be making all this up. He reassured her that he believed her. "After eight months of therapy, aside from his reassurance, the only 'proof' she had of her ordeal were body memories," such as "whenever she relived the moments when Satan had his burning tail wrapped around her neck, a sharply defined rash appeared in the shape of the spade-like tip of his tail."[32]

There are, also, many instances of, not only adults becoming caught up in reliving such memories from the distant past but, of children being influenced to talk about things in the recent past as if they were real. Entire communities have become caught up in seemingly benevolent efforts to protect these children from abuses which they come to suspect are committed by their neighbors. What follows is a very brief glimpse of the influence of a psychologist on one such child in one of these communities.

Nine months after law-enforcement and social service workers in a quiet North Carolina town attended a conference and were briefed on the dangers of child molesters in day-care centres, charges of sexual abuse were laid against the owners of a local day-care. As rumours and panic spread, new meaning was read into children's bruises, tantrums, fears, and stories. At least seventy children, most between the ages of three and five, were sent to four state recommended therapists. According to court records, one of the therapists, who was the head of the counselling group which had sponsored the conference, showed a five year old girl drawings of satanic symbols, which included a horned mask and inverted crosses, in an effort to uncover instances of devil worship. According to her notes, when the child looked at the mask, she claimed that the day-care owner had worn "one of those." Initially having reported only to have been spanked by this man, after bi-weekly sessions for six months, the girl was remembering "oral penetration by a penis, vaginal penetration by a brown felt-tipped marker and witnessing the murder of human babies." The psychologist explained the delay in getting to this material by describing how children can be terrified into silence.[33]

Another example, illustrating the combined effect of victim-group dynamics and a psychologist's influence, involves a woman who was fifty pounds overweight, in "a destructive relationship" and generally unhappy with her life. She sought help and was placed in a group because she had, according to the psychologist, "as many emotional problems as the other members."

She had, according to the psychologist's descriptions, "a sugar coated view of her family;" "there had been no violence, alcoholism, divorce, neglect or abuse." The life histories of the other group members sounded very different and, initially she sat apart, listened and saw no similarities. However, when some of the others in the group began to talk about incidents of sexual abuse, she started to have trouble sleeping. One morning, having been unable to sleep all night, she called the psychologist in a panic. When she arrived at the office she looked, according to the psychologist, "exhausted and seemed more vulnerable than I had ever seen her." She directed her to go over her memories and gradually revise the way she remembered her relationship with her father so that eventually she experienced those memories as incidents of sexual abuse. The patient was asked to pretend that she was talking to her father, first as a two year old; then as a five year old, and so on through the years. At age 13, she recalled having asked her father to "leave me alone!" The psychologist asked her what she meant and, according to records, the rest of the session was spent with this woman recalling memories of her father's obsession with her body. She recounted, for example, a day when he took pictures of her while she was sunning in a bikini, remembering how she felt ashamed when he had the picture enlarged and hung in the den. Upset by it, she had taken it down, but her father told her that she had a lovely body and should be proud of it.

The psychologist, who interpreted the father's actions as "emotional incest," considered this a breakthrough: "Coming to the group sessions and hearing the other women's candid remarks about their families had gradually uprooted these memories, which were in such marked contrast to her idealized view of her family that she had been filled with anxiety. The sleep deprivation crumbled the last of her resistance. Finally she was open to a flood of memories."

This "memory work," the revising of a formerly not very disturbing memory, into a traumatic one, caused the patient to "understand" her being fat in terms of "a desire to be invisible" and thus protected from her father's "obsession." From that point on, all of the times when her father either looked at her or didn't, became "proof" that she was an incest victim. As evidence of the diagnosis' effectiveness, the woman is quoted as saying: "My life is much less of a puzzle now. I see myself with such clarity."[34]

When personal histories are revised in such a way that people begin to suspect their families, their friends, and their neigbours of evil intentions or evil deeds, the world can seem to be inhabited by monsters. In the case of this overweight woman, the shattering of an "illusion" of a happy childhood and a normal family, was considered essential from the perspective of this psychologist with her particular approach. Based on preconceived assumptions, the psychologist provided an answer to her client's problems by transforming her father into a sexual predator; the effects of that transformation on the woman's relationship with her father was not of concern.

Unfortunately, what people come to believe through revising existing memories or uncovering new ones, can lead to dramatic changes in the way they relate to others in their lives. And, too often, they lead to accusations which have devastating effects. The following illustrates what can and does happen to innocent people, caught up in the results of memory work.

You are under arrest and you are charged with sexual assault, rape, gross indecency and uttering a death threat.

Thus began a man's year-long ordeal, as his car was surrounded by police cars on a public street, while video cameras rolled. For Harold Levy, this day in May 1993, was the beginning, but in fact, things had been happening for months and months making ready for this moment.

Years earlier, a young woman known to Levy and his family, had entered into treatment for an eating disorder. The psychologist came to the early conclusion that the problem was "due to sexual abuse" and referred her to therapists, unlicensed social workers who specialized in this area. One thing led to the other, resulting in "a chain of horrors" as Levy now describes it. Once the young woman was persuaded of the allegations, the police became involved. Without any further investigation beyond that of the statement of the accuser, as suppported by her therapists, they proceeded to lay charges.

Levy, a prominent lawyer-journalist-law professor, had no idea that anything was going on; he remained completely unaware of any allegations until "this day in May." After that, his home was searched and police reported finding pornographic tapes. Ironically, the videotapes were of television shows about accused people whose cases had raised questions about prosecutions; material for a book Levy was writing on the miscarriage of justice.

Almost a year later, in April 1994, the woman recanted the allegations that Levy had, using knives and beer bottles, sexually assaulted her over many years. Apparently, facing the pending trial and finally seeing the gravity of the situation, she had received independent psychological assistance and counsel, and had come to realize that a group of biased and overzealous therapists had strongly influenced her. These people she blamed for encouraging her to dredge up false memories of the alleged abuses. Nothing was true. The charges were dropped.

In an interview with Levy,[35] he spoke of the effect on himself and his family. "You know how they talk of a nuclear family, well it was like the bomb exploded. There was no doubt in anyone that the charges were untrue but it caused enormous amounts of pain in everyone." When asked to speculate on what gives psychologists such power to take someone like this young woman and change her mind so that she would come out with both these false allegations and a false image of a man whom she had known for years, he replied:

I think its a mixture of several things. They deal with people who are very vulnerable and weak and in crisis and they give them something to latch on to. And these people know how to hand out the victim roles and all the things that go with them: the compassion, the simple explanation of what's wrong with them, what ails them, what troubles them and takes away their peace of mind. I think that they are skilled and have all the psychological tools that they need to do this. They provide them support; they have networks and safe houses. They keep them away... don't want them to talk to people who might be able to help. They isolate their clients from them. So they have a whole structure of control and influence. And for some reason the public has been hooked in to this and judges listen to them and accept their tyranny because, if you don't go along with them, you are branded.

Speaking of the police and prosecution, Levy's lawyer, Alan Gold, a prominent defense attorney in Canada, specializing in the area of false allegations arising from psychological treatment, said:

Their critical faculties are totally suspended when they receive the wildest allegations of sexual abuse. It is just assumed they must be true. You cannot ignore the presumption of innocence and expect not to cause miscarriages of justice. This case always depended on the word of a person who clearly had some emotional problems.[36]

Gold places the responsibility for synthetic victims squarely on the shoulders of psychologists and their professional organizations. In an interview,[37] he described how, over the past decade, a belief system has grown up and become an ideology in which scepticism and questioning are not tolerated. Initially, in the mid-eighties, no one questioned the allegations, as psychologists assured the public that they were true with statements such as "no one would lie about something like that." Once an uncritical foundation was set, not only did unwitting clients come under the influence of these psychologists but they also began to influence the courts and politicians. As Gold said: " the same psychologist that testifies in court today, conducted the seminar that taught the police how to investigate the case last weekend." Identifying it as a "self-contained belief system," he described how police, prosecutors, patients, and the public have all been brought under the influence of these "purveyors of quackery" who "want to cripple the whole adult population." Gold pointed the finger of responsibility directly at the psychology organizations which, for years have held a blind eye to these practices, refusing to challenge their members with the scientific data which contradicts their claims. In many ways, psychologists had, and still have, a free hand to "pour into their suggestible clients" whatever belief they wanted whether it was UFO abduction, past lives, or sexual abuse. "Nobody stood up for the truth" until the early 90's "when some top scientists began to speak out on their own independent of their professional organizations which continued their conspiracy of silence."

FALSE NAMING

The traumatized person is often relieved simply to learn the true name of her condition. By ascertaining her diagnosis, she begins the process of recovery.[38]

Traditionally, in medicine, diagnosing or naming a condition has been a source of hope to patients. The label implies that the physician knows what is wrong, what to do and what the outcome is likely to be. For example, a severe pain in the lower right quadrant of the body along with an elevated temperature, is indicative of appendicitis, which to both the doctor and the patient means surgery and a good recovery.

However, naming or diagnosing "diseases" in the pseudo-medical field of the Psychology Industry is mostly fictional in nature. While some forms of mental illness have sufficient physiological factors to be consistently identified (e.g. Alzheimer's or Parkinson's Disease), most of the disorders treated by the Psychology Industry are merely psychological or social terms reflecting cultural influences and moral positions. What is considered a "psychological illness" in one culture or at one time in history, may be seen in another culture as appropriate, eccentric, criminal, or spiritual. A case of Multiple Personality might be seen as a psychological illness, a weird aspect of a non-conforming person, or a spirit possession; just as excessive alcohol consumption might be viewed as an addiction, a cultural trait, a quality of the flamboyant artistic personality, or a criminal act.

Frank and Frank have identified three factors which affect "naming;" the moral, the theoretical and the entrepreneurial. All are independent of the traditional etiological, therapeutic and prognostic aspects of diagnosis.[39]

It has been argued that the diagnoses of the Psychology Industry, which are revised frequently, are actually culturally influencing moral judgments which convert the person's behaviour into "pathology" and make the psychologist an enforcer (or reinforcer) of changing societal values.[40] For instance, the Psychology Industry may assess pejoratively as "a perpetrator," the construction worker whose whistle at a passing woman is interpreted as harassing and assaultive; while the Psychology Industry may be more forgiving of behaviours such as alcoholism, drug abuse and eating disorders, seeing them as "addictive diseases."

Secondly, a diagnosis may be the product of a theory; for "variants of normal behaviour and ordinary unhappiness become illnesses amenable to psychotherapy when a theory exists to explain them as such."[41] Just as homosexuality was once a psychological diagnosis because psychoanalytic theory offered a pathological explanation for the behaviour, so have high levels of heterosexual activity become "sexual addiction" a theoretical disease of the Psychology Industry. As Schofield stated thirty years ago: "Case finding tends frequently to result in case making..." While he argued that "the individual who is dissatisfied with his work, unhappy in his social relationships, lacking in recreational skills... is not helped by sensitization to the notion that he is 'sick,'"[42] the Fabricated Victim of today is told that he can benefit from such a label.

Finally, the entrepreneurial factor plays a dramatic role in current diagnostics. Just as "therapeutic schools unwittingly foster the phenomena which they cure"[43] so too do the larger number of treatment centres, foster the frequency of diagnosis of the problems they treat. For example, profit-oriented residential treatment centres for addictions increased by 350% and their caseloads by 400% between 1978 and 1984.[44] Unlike Victor Borge's despondent uncle, who worried about "discovering a cure for which there is no disease," the Psychology Industry does not need to worry, for there is a disease, or at least a diagnosis, for every imaginable treatment.

Whichever the reason underlying the diagnosis, be it social control, theoretical musing or economic greed, "naming" serves a purpose. While it may give comfort and hope through the implied understanding on the part of the psychologist, it also provides a new identity for the client: "I am a victim." Unlike medicine, where an incorrect diagnosis can result in death, no such embarrassing risk exists for the Psychology Industry; clients may get worse, a few may even commit suicide but these can in retrospect be seen as "untreatable," while most just languish in their victim-status. Meanwhile, as these Synthetic Victims remain in treatment, not yet recovered, psychologists continue to collect their salaries and fees.

Showalter, professor of English at Princeton University, in her 1997 book, *Hystories: Hysterical Epidemics and Modern Media,* points out that these Epidemics require at least three ingredients: physician enthusiasts and theorists; unhappy, vulnerable patients; and supportive cultural environments. A doctor or other authority figure must first define, name, and publicize the disorder and then attract patients into its community.[45]

The Psychology Industry relies on the *Diagnostic and Statistical Manual*, (the *DSM-IV*) of the American Psychiatric Association,[46] for many of the names and labels it uses. The original 1954 version of this manual was influenced by Kraepelin's 1883 classification system[47] which had served to crystallize the nineteenth century belief that mental illnesses were biologically based and thus similar to physical diseases. But, unlike medical diagnoses which convey a probable cause, appropriate treatment and likely prognosis, the disorders listed in the *DSM-IV* are terms designed to be useful for communicating information, conducting research, providing treatment and *doing billing.* Unlike physical illnesses, such as pneumonia or tuberculosis, they do not indicate an etiology, specific treatment or prognosis. The terms listed in the *DSM-IV* are not diseases but rather disorders which, for the most part, are simply labels determined by sets of criteria.

The Psychology Industry has taken these descriptive terms and, using them in a new way, often changing the names, implied a known cause, an available psychological treatment and an optimistic prognosis. For instance:

DSM Term	Psychology Industry derivative labels

Post Traumatic Stress Disorder (PTSD)	Rape Trauma Syndrome
	Battered Wife Syndrome
	Legal Abuse Syndrome
	Lottery Stress Disorder
	Sequelae of emotional incest,
	  car accident, childbirth, alien abduction,
	  Satanic Ritual Abuse, etc.

Substance Abuse/Dependency (referring to alcohol & drugs)	Love and Sex addiction Co-Dependency Gambling & Stock Market addictions Internet & Star Trek addictions Adult Children of alcoholics, workaholics, etc. Religious addictions

The brief history of PTSD, one of the Psychology Industry's favourite terms, illustrates this process of evolving labels. PTSD initially appeared in the *DSM* in 1980, legitimizing "the relentless suffering of Vietnam veterans" and lifting it "out of the realm of psychopathology into the realm of *fundable* war casualty." It quickly became a buzzword going far beyond its original patient population "bringing added support to thousands of rape victims seeking respect and protection within the legal system."[48] In the hands of the Psychology Industry it lead to the battlefield being seen as "a microcosm of trauma,"[49] resulting in virtually any scene from everyday life having the potential to be seen as a battlefield. With PTSD as a diagnostic starting point, women could be labelled as "the casualties of the war of the sexes;"[50] verbal insults could be equated with bullets and hurt feelings could be seen as wounds. Twisting the term, and using any tragic or disturbing occurrence as a cause of PTSD and any problem as the beginning point for seeking out the trauma at its source, the Psychology Industry could justify intruding into, and judging, people's lives.

In London, England, a headmaster was stabbed to death when he went to the rescue of a 13 year old student being attacked by a teenage gang. The next day, Cardinal Basil Hume prayed with the 440 children and staff for both the man and his killer. After suggesting how they should be inspired by the headmaster's noble act and reminding them that he was a friend of the pupils and that they were his friends, he said: "It is right that we should cry. We have to mourn, we have to grieve. It's part of human living. I believe every teacher in this school would have done what Philip Lawrence did." As well, he urged the killer to contact the police, saying that the young man "who did this terrible crime has to acknowledge it, he has to be punished for it, he has to pay his debt" and "we have to try hard in our hearts to forgive."[51]

While the Cardinal remained focussed on *the man as a victim*, a good person, and a friend, a leading psychiatrist was identifying *the students as victims* of trauma. Professor Isaac Marks declared them to be at risk of Post Traumatic Stress Disorders and recommended immediate counselling. He warned that the children who had seen the attack or held the dying man in their arms "would suffer a range of feelings varying from detachment to disbelief, mood swings, flashbacks and nightmares." He suggested that "some may develop hyper-vigilance, where sufferers constantly worry about their safety," and stated that "in the coming days and weeks, many youngsters would feel a sense of guilt or reponsibility." He predicted that "the few who carry the effects for years may find they underperform at school, or become over-protective towards their loved ones in adulthood."[52] Thus, he ignored an authentic victim and used *DSM* terminology to turn a group of mourning friends into a pool of potential synthetic victims.

False naming sometimes involves "diagnosing" people who have experienced a tragedy but, often, it involves turning confused or unhappy people into victims of one sort or another. One example is the case of a forty year old free-lance photographer who was upset after his wife left him. Wondering why this had happened and frustrated that all of his attempts to have another relationship had failed, he saw a psychologist. At the end of the initial interview, the therapist diagnosed him as a "love and sex addict," dependent on feeling loved and having sex, "just like alcoholics need alcohol." The psychologist concluded that he was experiencing "withdrawal effects." Based on this label, the psychologist prescribed individual therapy to help him "uncover the early childhood events which caused him to confuse love and sex" and which made him "crave" affection. As well, he was referred to a "love and sex addicts anonymous" group based on the 12-Step approach of AA.

The man was told that this disorder required that he question why sex had become so important to him and to search his memory for times in his childhood when he had been so deprived of unconditional love that he had become "lovesick." To this end, he sought the help of a hypnotherapist to "take him back" in his memories to get to the root of his problem. In therapy, he became persuaded that he had never learned to love himself. The psychologist helped him to analyze every relationship, past and present, discovering that he was prone to falling in love and becoming sexually obsessed with partners who couldn't love him back. In the group, he found friendly supportive people, and he broke the rules and developed a friendship with one woman. But when their friendship eventually became sexual, he and the woman immediately felt so guilty that they stopped seeing each other.

Because of diagnostic blinders, at no time did this man consider what he might be doing to turn women off, or consider the reasons for his wife's infidelity, nor was he able to see what was good in the new relationship. Since he was labelled an addict, all relationships involving sex, including this latter one, were interpreted as expressions of his addiction. He was caught in a "psychological catch-22.'

When ordinary people become falsely labelled in this way, they often go on for some time not realizing it. Sometimes it costs them money; sometimes their insurance pays. The Psychology Industry, while it does have an interest in attracting and serving self-paying clients, generally finds that those with insurance coverage are easier to attract and maintain. But to the dismay of the Psychology Industry insurance companies are becoming wary of the diagnostic process and beginning to ask questions about labels applied. One dramatic example involved a large number of people who were diagnosed with one of the more serious *DSM-IV* disorders, a "Major Depression." They came to be diagnosed after responding to an advertising campaign urging people from across America to telephone a toll-free number if they felt "tired and sad." When they called, they were connected to high pressure sales personnel who convinced them that they were so seriously depressed that they required emergency admission to a special treatment program. Told that it would cost them nothing because a free return airline ticket would be provided and their medical insurance would cover the rest, people arrived at psychiatric hospitals in California where, whatever their symptoms or problems might be, they were admitted, diagnosed and given "treatment," ranging from spa baths to outings to Disneyland. For patients who had second thoughts, leaving was not an option because free plane tickets home would not be provided until they had completed the programme. The insurance company which was billed for these services eventually filed a multimillion dollar lawsuit alleging widespread fraud. As expected, other insurance companies and affected patients are filing similar suits claiming that healthy people have been lured into mental hospitals, given "bogus diagnoses" of conditions typically covered by health insurance and treated until their insurance money runs out.[53] In a recent case, "Tenet Healthcare Corp. agreed to pay about $100 million to former patients, who allege that the company and its doctors illegally imprisoned them in psychiatric hospitals to bilk insurance benefits. Pete Alexis, a regional officer who oversaw the corporation's Texas psychiatric hospitals, admitted conspiring to pay from $20 million to $40 million in bribes to psychiatrists, psychologists, and others in exchange for patient referrals."[54]

CONTRIVED VICTIMS

contrive: (vb) [ME controven] 1. to form or create in an artistic or creative manner; 2. to bring about by stratagem or with difficulty.

Webster's Dictionary

Everyone who is born holds dual citizenship, in the kingdom of the well and in the kingdom of the sick.

Susan Sontag
Illness As Metaphor

Just as much a product of the Psychology Industry as the Synthetic Victims are the many seriously ill medical patients convinced to turn to psychologists for help. The method, while not immediately apparent, is actually relatively straightforward. It involves reshaping their understanding of their medical diagnosis so as to make it appear that, in one way or another, their diseases are the result of psychological factors and that their survival depends on identifying and controlling these hidden causes. Well publicized beliefs, along with a longstanding tendency to view these people as victims, makes it relatively easy for the Psychology Industry to successfully convert them.

Continuous reference to people with heart-disease, cancer, AIDS, and so on, as victims, has caused society to become accustomed to thinking about them as unfortunate victims involved in a losing war going on within their own bodies. For centuries people believed that such conditions were the result of humor, phlegm and bile within the body which needed to be drawn out through bleeding, purging and blistering. At the turn of the century, the rise of the "germ theory," which was so effective at identifying and controlling diseases, gave strength to this image of an internal war in which those who died were victims. This pursuit of identifiable physical causes, such as germs and genes, tended to minimize the role of psychological agents which were less easily seen and quantified.

However, beginning in the 1950's, the work of Selye and others drew attention to the idea that other factors, particularly those that were psychological and social, can affect health, sparking a resurgence of interest in the area of psychosomatic medicine. From this has emerged a component of the Psychology Industry which gives the impression that the age old mystery of the mind-body connection has been solved and invites people to take refuge "in a fairyland populated with such fuzzy concepts as "stress."[55] As the Psychology Industry enthusiastically packages its own modern equivalents of snake oils, it ignores serious researchers who realize that:

> Disease is not only a matter of a disturbance of the self-regulatory mechanisms within cells, or of any one simple factor such as infection, nutritional deprivation, or the psychology of the diseased person.[56]

Instead it endorses the notion that psychological factors such as stress, anger, and depression, whether they be linked to a type of relationship, an event or a life style, make people vulnerable to disease and can, through the tools and techniques of the Psychology Industry, be avoided or reversed. For example:

> Stress has been called the silent killer, attacking those who had no previous warning... I tell my patients to imagine stress as a heavy knapsack that has some of its compartments filled with sand. It makes your trip difficult and more burdensome than necessary, especially if you are carrying 75 or 100 pounds of the stuff. It puts tremendous strain on your heart, which often responds as if it were carrying this load physically. My work demonstrates that there are as many as 40 different compartments for the sand, but you can't tell which ones are filled when it's all a lump on your back. The Quality of Life Index used in our program will help you find the compartments with sand, dump them, and go on your way with a much lighter load."[57]

Anger kills. We're speaking here not about the anger that drives people to shoot, stab, or otherwise wreak havoc on their fellow humans. We mean instead the everyday sort of anger, annoyance, and irritation that courses through the minds and bodies of many perfectly normal people.[58]

In response to these notions, millions of dollars are spent each year by people trying either to avoid illness or to recover from a disease. Best-selling books rise to the top of the charts, purporting to reveal how to reduce stress and to prevent or treat illnesses ranging from ulcers to heart attacks to cancer, from asthma to allergies to AIDS.[59] At the same time, workshops, seminars and treatment programs developed by the Psychology Industry sell the idea that the manipulation of a single psychological factor can be effective in avoiding or resolving illness. Based on anecdotes and case studies in which people got better after treatment, the Psychology Industry makes claims about how laughter works as a remedy, how curbing anger can save your life, how optimism cures. Claiming to have discovered the psychological equivalent of penicillin but entirely unable to demonstrate comparable shifts in disease and death rates, the Psychology Industry continues to applaud itself for its essential contribution to health care.

Often combined with the Psychology Industry's success stories are references to research data showing that psychological procedures can affect specific physiological measures. What is missing is any evidence to show that these alterations lead to changes in the actual disease. For instance, it has been shown that stress produces changes in the body's immune system, not a surprising finding by any means but one which the Psychology Industry views as highly significant. Presuming these changes to be extremely important, it presents them as a cause of later disease, an outright unsupported assumption. And it goes on to turn this unsubstantiated cause into a cure, presenting as fact the unfounded notion that if these effects could be avoided or reversed, illness could be averted.

The Psychology Industry offers its wares to frightened, vulnerable, medically ill people. In its marketing it claims that between "40 to 60% of visits to physicians stem from psychological problems"[60] and that "psychologists are extremely well-suited to contribute to the care of these patients."[61] It employs the image of the psychologist as "doctor," "healer," "compassionate listener," along with the language of science, to achieve its objective. It convinces patients that psychological factors played a role in their getting sick and that conversely they can, with the help of the Psychology Industry, control these factors and overcome their disease. People are told that they can "control their stress," "enhance their positive emotions," "boost their immunity," "fight their cancer cells" and "get well again." Instead of being medical patients with a biological disease, they are manufactured into Contrived Victims of a psychological disorder.

The best known and most effective money-makers in this system have been the relaxation procedures, based on the concept of "relaxation response," which deal with cardio-vascular diseases; and the "mind-body" techniques for fighting immune disorders such as cancer and AIDS.

Early studies showed that individuals who are aggressive, competitive, work-oriented and with a constant sense of urgency had a greater risk of a heart attack. Those who suffered a heart attack were often told that their life style and Type A behaviour was the cause, and that they needed to change and develop a more relaxed "relaxation response." However this fascinating finding and the many programs that have been developed and marketed to either change personality patterns or to teach relaxation skills have proven of little clinical value.[62] Yet the idea continues to be promoted as a significant contribution of the Psychology Industry.

Becoming popular around the same time, and probably of greater overall commercial effect, is the plethora of "mind-body" programmes offered to help often terminally ill people "fight" their disease. In the mid 70's, Carl and Stephanie Simonton attracted public attention with their book *Getting Well Again*.[63] In it, they presented a psychological programme, described as "an important weapon in the 'war on cancer,' " which they claimed could help people overcome their disease and survive. They explained how people's reactions to stressful events in their lives could contribute to the onset of cancer and how their reactions could reverse the disease's progress. These people were, in theory, declared victims of past events in their lives, just like their cousins, the Synthetic Victims. But in addition, they were told that they had been "participants in their own getting sick;" they were, also, their own victims.

Psychologists argued that, if these Contrived Victims could make themselves ill, they could also make themselves well through techniques for learning positive attitudes, relaxation, visualization, goal setting, managing pain, exercise, and building an emotional support system. They were lead to believe, based on the simplistic interpretation of very complex psychosomatic research data, that, although they suffered from an identifiable biological disease, the answer, at least in part, was psychological.

The industry prospered and grew by offering help through workshops, tapes, books and treatment centres; all for a price, endorsed by famous people and supported by the popular anecdotal data. Many sick people, desperate for a cure, readily accepted their role as victims of stresses and traumas in their lives and became "users" of the Psychology Industry. For as the Simontons wrote:

> It is a good idea to seek aid and support of a trained counsellor or therapist. Many times, just asking for help is the first step in breaking a rule one learned in early childhood and establishing a more healthy way of responding to stress. Unfortunately, many of us grew up in a culturally induced reluctance to seek help for emotional problems. Yet if we are diagnosed with a severe illness, we do not feel embarrassed or ashamed to seek the help of a physician who has spent many years learning about the body. Neither should we feel embarrassed about enlisting the help of a professional to learn the ways in which stress has played a role in our illness.[64]

People who may have been emotionally strong and capable throughout most of their lives and who were now facing possible death from cancer, were being told that they were:

- Not as strong as they thought.
- Succumbing to the stresses of the years preceding the onset of the disease.
- Partially to blame for the cancer.
- Needing psychological help to deal with their emotions and to fight the disease.

On such person, a man in his early sixties, a member of the underground in Europe during the Second World War and subsequently, a very successful lawyer, was diagnosed with advanced lung cancer. He was angry that he had survived the war "only to die of cancer;" he was sad that he might not see his grandchildren grow up; and he was desperate to live longer. But his oncologist honestly offered him little hope; so, the man reluctantly sought psychological help. He acquiesced to the urgings of the psychologist to reconsider his self-image and modify his life-style, reducing the amount of work. Instead of spending time continuing to engage in the work he loved, he devoted his energy to identifying recent stresses in his life which he had ignored and accepting responsibility for his irresponsibility to himself in the way he reacted to them. He admitted that he was not as strong or as capable as he had thought. And he began a series of sessions to learn to visualize his cancer cells and imagine fighting them. (He was good at this given his wartime experience.) He spent the last few months of his life as a contrived victim and a user of the Psychology Industry, hopelessly struggling to get well again.[65]

While the treatment programs for Contrived Victims claim to be "well supported by scientific data," they have failed to deliver the cures initially promised and today they are more likely to hedge their bets with statements such as: "even if the disease cannot be slowed down, living life in a fulfilling fashion, feeling good about yourself, and leaving your body in a peaceful way are worthwhile goals...."

Combining the earlier methods popularized with cancer patients, with approaches from other areas of victim-making, psychologists no longer try to tailor the method to the diagnosis. Instead, they tend to either fall back on the false naming strategy used with other Synthetic Victims, labelling people with diseases or at risk as suffering from Post Traumatic Stress Disorder. Or they offer what could be termed "treatment collages" [66] in which unrelated techniques are drawn from the Psychology Industry's assortment of explanations and answers. For example, Mikluscak-Cooper and Miller[67] offer those people "at risk or infected with HIV" a collage which they describe as a twelve-step program. It is an assembly of diverse fragments drawn from the authors' "personal experience with themselves, their patients and their friends" including:

- "Positive self-talk – using affirmations to stay in the moment," such as "I can be calm and serene," very similar to Coueism, the old form of "auto-suggestion," best known for "Every day and in every way I am getting better and better."
- "Stages of acceptance" – remarkably similar to Kubler-Ross' "stages of dying," these six stages outline the process of psychologically accepting a positive HIV test result or a diagnosis of AIDS.
- Promoting oneself from victim to survivor status.
- A support group in which to discuss and share deep thoughts and feelings. "Through this common bond (they) can assist and nurture each other."
- Meditation and "self-healing imagery" to "help the immune system," similar in method to that of the Simontons.
- "Touching the Source" – explained as "experience and research show that you do have a Power or Inner Healer available to you that you can tap into any time you desire."
- Conduct a "life review" to identify behaviour patterns and responses that "may be contributing to the disease or the risk of getting the disease."
- Dealing with dysfunction and abuse – "Many of us grew up in dysfunctional families: families with alcoholism, drug addiction, or physical, mental, emotional spiritual, or sexual abuse. If we don't deal with these issues we unconsciously allow the abusers to continue abusing us in our later lives... your self-esteem was damaged. You no doubt have difficulty in relationships, with trust and abandonment issues... beat your mattress, feel your anger and grief... write a letter to your inner child..."
- Identify codependency – Here the authors provide a long list of family factors which lead to codependency (eg. addictions, a parent with a chronic illness, abuse), and they add; "on the other hand, people from homes where there were none of these problems can also develop strong codependency traits."
- Counselling – "We suggest that individuals receive counselling in addition to using this book."

These are only some of the elements found in this program and in many others offered by psychologists to those "at risk" or with serious medical illnesses who can be persuaded that they are victims not only of disease but also of negative psychological factors. While it would be absurd to deny that a connection exists between the mind and the body or that people with serious illnesses deserve support and compassion, there is no basis on which to assume that the Psychology Industry holds the key to the mystery or the monopoly on caring.

COUNTERFEIT VICTIMS

Lest men suspect your tale to be untrue,
Keep probability – some say – in view...
Sigh then, or frown, but leave (as in despair)
Motive and end and moral, in the air;
Nice contradiction between fact and fact
Will make the whole read human and exact.

Robert Graves,
The Devil's Advice to Story Tellers (1938)

"He 'put the screwdriver in my vagina, the handle, and then he put the other one in my rectum' and then he 'moved both the screwdrivers at the same time while they were inside of me.' He said 'Just lay there like a good little girl,' as he 'took the screwdrivers out of my vagina and rectum' and eventually 'pushed his penis into my vagina...' " [68]

This statement to the police launched a man-hunt for a violent rapist who had abducted the woman at gun-point, and taken her to an underground garage where he raped and sodomized her. She provided a full description of the man including a gold signet ring on his right ring finger. The woman was referred to a "women's sexual assault centre" where she began to receive support and counselling. A door-to-door campaign was launched by the police to alert the public and a search was begun for clues. In a further statement, the young woman reported that the assault took place in a dark park area, and later she disclosed that she had the name and address of the man.

When he was arrested, the shocked young man said that he had met the woman at a bar and had invited her back to his small apartment where they had consensual sex. He pointed out that they were not alone in the house and, in fact, when his landlady had intruded on them at one point, the young woman had made no effort to protest or seek help. In his mind, she had been fully willing, and, feeling somewhat lucky, he had even given his name and address to her, hopeful that they might meet again. After his arrest and statement, the woman changed her story, saying that she had been picked up in the bar and gone home with this man, where they had, what he was quite likely to have perceived as, consensual sex.

With this and other information gathered by the police, it became clear that no attack had taken place. The woman had lied about the event. Having expended over $300,000 on an investigation based on fabricated facts, the police charged her with Public Mischief, to which she responded : "How can you charge me, you can't prove I consented to the sex."

Meanwhile, she continued to receive counselling at a sexual assault centre, where she was seen by a social worker and a psychiatrist. At the trial, the psychiatrist testified that, regardless of the facts, the woman was suffering from Post Traumatic Stress Disorder due to the trauma of rape. She claimed that it is typical in these types of cases that the women are confused and unable to remember the events clearly, a result of what she called "Rape Trauma

Syndrome." And she interpreted the event the woman had reported to the police as a case of "Date Rape."

In addition, the psychiatrist claimed, that the woman had actually been raped before, when she was 12 years old and was now confusing that event with the more recent sexual experience; thus, she was not guilty of having intentionally misled the police. Although there was nothing to corroborate the claim of an earlier assault and the woman could not even recall it clearly, the psychiatrist went on record saying: "give me ten years with this woman and I will help her remember that she was raped."

Despite acknowledging the lies and attempts to mislead the police, resulting in the arrest of an innocent man, and saying that the woman "seemed to be parroting explanations, words and ideas given to her by others," on the basis that she may have been "suffering from some sort of stress disorder," the judge acquitted the woman. Her claim to be a victim, albeit not a real victim but a counterfeit one, achieved her release but it left her bound to looking and acting like a victim.

Why would she choose such a role? In conversations with the police she revealed several possible motives for making up the story. She had a boyfriend who was not at the time paying much attention to her. Perhaps, the rape story was intended to rekindle his interest, or get even with him for neglecting her. Or, since she was staying at his place she may have needed an alibi for coming in late that evening or just an excuse for having had a sexual encounter she wished, in reflection, had not occurred

Counterfeit Victims often invent their stories "in the heat of the moment" or as a way to cope with some pressure or situation. The Psychology Industry provides the themes, the encouragement, the support and, often, the validation. Assault, rape, and harassment, being highly publicized and emotionally charged issues, are some of the more popular themes. In some circles, such as the sexual assault centre to which this woman was sent, it is considered quite improper to suggest that any story told could be untrue. But Psychology Industry inspired fictional tales are told. This is only one of many reported to police, university administrations, employers, and the media. One recent study[69] conducted in a small metropolitan area in the midwestern United States, looked at the excuses given by women who, having taken their stories to the police, later admitted that no rape had occurred. The reasons given generally fell into three categories:

(1) creating an alibi,
(2) seeking revenge following rejection or disappointment,
(3) wanting attention or sympathy.

The following three examples[70] are "prototypical" cases of each:

- A married 30-year old female reported that she had been raped in her apartment complex. During the polygraph examination, she admitted that she was a willing partner. She reported that she had been raped because her partner did not stop before ejaculation, as he had agreed, and she was afraid she was pregnant. Her husband was overseas.

- A 16 year-old reported she was raped and her boyfriend was charged. She later admitted that she was "mad at him" because he was seeing another girl, and she "wanted to get him into trouble."
- An unmarried female, age 41, was in post-divorce counselling, and she wanted more attention and sympathy from her counsellor because she "liked him." She fabricated a rape episode, and he took her to the police station and assisted her in making the charge. She could not back out since she would have to admit lying to him.

When such stories fail to be refuted and end up being told convincingly in court or in the press, innocent people can be convicted and sent to prison, or lose their jobs and reputations. Sometimes, when a story fails to hold up under an investigation, the complainant, instead, is charged and put on trial. The young woman above is one example, another was a 27 year old Indian woman who had made several of these false sexual assault complaints, including one of being gang raped on Halloween by five leather-clad men. When charged with Public Mischief, she pleaded guilty, claimed past abuse as an excuse and asked to be sent to a jail for alcohol treatment. The judge, in granting her request, may actually have provided this woman, who could not otherwise afford or qualify for such a program, with something she wanted; food, housing, and the attention and sympathy of caring psychologists.[71]

The model of the counterfeit victim is neither complicated nor foreign. Like the child saying "he made me do it," it is something that is familiar to everyone. It begins with being "in a jam," needing an excuse for having done something, wanting attention or affection, or venting anger and seeking revenge. Rather than dealing directly with the situation through an honest admission, requesting attention or being angry, the person avoids taking adult responsibility or initiative and fabricates a story which points the finger at someone else. The story and the associated victim-status is then used to achieve the initial goal.

The stories range from themes of domestic dissatisfaction and disputes to fraudulent claims and vicious crimes. They may involve a woman lying to a spouse she is afraid of losing, a person wanting more devotion from a friend, or an employee angry at the boss. Or they may involve someone suing a manufacturer over faulty equipment used improperly, or a serial murderer concocting a defense. Often only thinly masked, they serve a purpose for the Counterfeit Victim. And while apparent to the general public, the psychologist who is in the business of manufacturing and serving victims can remain oblivious to these ploys.

A convenient way to avoid potential conflict over disinterest and boredom with sex, the stories are finding their way into bedrooms across America. For instance, a woman referring to her husband said: "I did not mind doing whatever he wanted done to him but I did not want him to try and make me come." And she went on to say that he pressured her to let him touch her, try to please her, do things that might make sex less one-sided. "And so I made up a lie to make him stop trying to make love to me – I said I had been raped and this is why sex is a problem for me." Seeing her as a victim, suffering from what the Psychology Industry defined as Rape Trauma Syndrome, her husband, a physician, stopped pressuring her for sex. But eventually, extremely dissatisfied with his own sex life, he made an appointment for his wife with a psychologist who specialized in dealing with the trauma associated with rape. Cornered now and unsure of her ability to fake the syndrome, session after session, she had a problem. What she did was send a FAX to the psychologist admitting her lie and saying: "I almost wish it was true, at least I would have an explanation for my behavior and the fabrication I have presented to my husband..." Unprepared to have her story and her feelings probed, this woman relinquished the excuse which had served to keep her husband from making love to her. She is an example of a Counterfeit Victim who employed a ready-made Psychology Industry excuse, without having thought through what might be required to make it work. Exposed as a fake, she was then faced with the choice of either dealing with the anger her husband was likely to direct at her or adopting another Psychology Industry excuse, which might serve to prolong, prop up and reduce the demands of her marriage. When she finally admitted the lie to her husband, she left out the fact that she had enjoyed sex with other men but never with him. She didn't tell him that he "had never turned her on" and that she had faked sexual interest and orgasm from the beginning of their relationship. Interestingly, similar to the public mischief case, this woman eventually claimed in therapy that, although the rape was a lie, she had actually been assaulted by a friend of the family when she was much younger. This claim, which could neither be proven or disproven, gained for her once again, the sympathy and support of her spouse.[72]

Another person who faked being a victim without having thought it through was Roseanne Barr. This outspoken comedienne, whose volatile relationship with her husband, Tom Arnold, became as public as their television shows, presented herself for a time as a battered wife, describing how Arnold had "pushed, pummelled and pinched her." But four days after making-up with him and dropping divorce proceedings, she withdrew the charges that he had physically abused her, saying: "I signed an uncorrected, unread copy of a letter from my divorce lawyer in anger and haste... He never beat me. He never abused me. Although it's a titillating story to many out there, it is untrue and insults women who really are battered."[73]

Barr's allegations of abuse, which some suspected were born out of a desire for revenge connected to her jealousy over Arnold's relationship with his slim, 24 year old assistant, disappeared as quickly as they had surfaced. There was little evidence of damage to either the accused or the accusor.

But, not all Counterfeit Victims, find it so easy, or painless, to change a story. And certainly it is not always possible to shrug off the lies, and their effects. Katie Roife described how Mindy, a student at Princeton who had fabricated a rape story, was forced to publicly admit her lie.

> Her story went like this: a boy who had "started hitting on me in a way that made me feel particularly uncomfortable," followed her home and "dragged" her back to his room. The entire campus, as she described it, was indifferent: "Although I

screamed the entire time, no one called for help, no one even looked out the window to see if the person screaming was in danger." He carried her to his room "and, while he shouted the most degrading obscenities imaginable, raped me." He told her that "his father buys him cheap girls like me to use up and throw away." And then he banged her head against the metal bedpost until she was unconscious. She then explained that he was forced to leave campus for a year and now he was back. "Because I see this person every day," she claimed, "my rape remains a constant daily reality for me." Now, she said, she was on the road to recovery, and "there are some nights when I sleep soundly and there are even some mornings when I look in the mirror and I like what I see. I may be a victim, but now I am also a survivor." Mindy's story, which was part of a speak-out associated with a Take Back the Night rally, was printed in the student newspaper, allowing "the facts" to be checked out.

She claimed she had reported a rape, and she hadn't.... She told people that a certain male undergraduate was the rapist, and he complained to the administration. Mindy responded to administrative pressure by printing an apology in the student newspaper, explaining the motivation as political: "I made my statements in the *Daily Princeton* and at the Take Back the Night March in order to raise awareness for the plight of the campus rape victims" and describing how she had "in several personal conversations and especially at the Take Back the Night March, (been) overcome by emotion..."[74]

While these cases and thousands like them gain little public notice, they affect tens of thousands of people who are mislead or falsely accused. Sometimes these people are cleared though many, in the interim, incur huge legal costs and suffer damage to their families and their reputations, and sometimes they are convicted and forced to serve sentences for acts they never committed. These allegations are usually based on options both offered and supported by the Psychology Industry. Rape Trauma, Battered-Wife Syndrome, Abuse, Incest: a whole range of possibilities exist for people to tailor to their own particular needs. And most of the accusers are women for whom the topics are especially tailored and who have traditionally been the major consumers of the Psychology Industry.

The options are packaged to appear anti-patriarchal, pro-feminist and especially applicable to women's issues and are presented in popular magazines, TV talk shows, movies and sit-coms. Roseanne Barr may have picked up the idea for her accusation, as she claimed, from her lawyer or, possibly, she read it in a script for one of her own shows. Whatever her source, women are constantly being presented with such ideas, whether in the front cover portrayals of celebrity victims, ranging from Loni Anderson[75] to Lady Di[76], or announcements of newly discovered possibilities for claiming victim status.

The *Ladies Home Journal* recently printed an article on "Stress Sex"[77], telling women:

We all know that stress can make us do crazy things. Now, according to a ground-breaking theory, it may be the reason more and more wives are cheating on their husbands. How stressed-out – and vulnerable to infidelity – are *you*?

The article stated that "as many as 55% of wives eventually cheat on their husbands" and described, what used to be called "adultery" or simply "having an affair," as "stress-induced-straying." No longer can a woman participate and even enjoy succumbing to passion, seducing a man or being seduced. "Although a woman who's stressed may well be aware of just how tired or angry she is, or how little the reality of her life matches what she thought it would be, she may *not* be conscious of how much she longs for the recreation, emotional connection and sexual passion she no longer enjoys. But below the surface, the longing is there, and it makes her uniquely vulnerable to an extramarital fling." No longer does she need to entertain responsibility or guilt for an affair, for the Psychology Industry has borrowed from Flip Wilson "The Devil made me do it!" and rewritten it as: "Stress made me do it."

The Psychology Industry extends the excuses, including this one, beyond the relatively trivial misbehaviour of an extramarital fling all the way to murder. For example, after launching the police on a lengthy search for a black man who had stolen her car and driven off with her children, and after appearing repeatedly on television begging the public for help, Susan Smith changed her story, admitting to having drowned her sons, by buckling them in their safety seats and sending the car rolling into murky water. On the day she was arrested for the murder of her two young sons, the experts began to discuss how "a stress pileup can lead to murder."[78] Psychologists and others who had studied women who kill their children, reported that "severe depression or an unbearable "pileup of stresses" may trigger latent emotional or mental illness." Citing other cases, a University of New Hampshire psychologist stated that those who kill are "sometimes women who have very low self-esteem, or women who feel that they have the possibility of a relationship and the man doesn't want the responsibility of kids."[79] The trial of this mother, who had already pleaded guilty, was described by one reporter as a "contest of victim vs. beast;"[80] if the victim image failed to hold up she could be sentenced to death in the electric chair. Her lawyers aggressively attempted to depict her as "the victim of destructive relationships," pointing to abuses in her past, an ongoing divorce from the father of the children, and the rejection of a man "she loved" who came from a wealthy family and was trying to break off "their relationship." Her life rested on being viewed as having suffered too much already.[81] So, day after day Susan Smith sat in a South Carolina courtroom, looking pale, listless and dumpy, as others sought to portray her as a victim.

At the same time, in a Toronto court-room, another woman was playing a victim role, following a quite different "love at all costs" script. Karla Holmolka, having managed a "sweetheart deal" plea bargain,[82] was testifying against her ex-husband, Paul Bernardo, who was being tried for the murders of two teenaged girls, both of whom had been held captive, repeatedly raped, sodomized, beaten and eventually strangled. Video tapes, obtained by the police just after Homolka's immunity was arranged, showed both Bernardo and Homolka sexually and physically assaulting the two girls.[83]

In court, appearing self-assured, attractive, and very stylish, Homolka attempted to portray herself as a victim of "battered wife syndrome." Talking about how much "in love" she had been at first with Bernardo, she testified that he regularly beat her during their five year relationship, and forced her to marry him and take part in the abductions and sexual assaults. She claimed to be controlled by him, "trapped in the relationship," with no way to stop the violence. In a statement which resembled a quote from a psychology text, she claimed to have totally repressed the memory of one of the assaults. Two psychologists testified as experts in "the battered wife syndrome." Neither had seen this woman, but they stated that the kind of abuse Homolka claimed to have suffered indicated an extreme form of the syndrome; that "a woman being abused is basically living a lie;" and that a batterer who abuses and manipulates a woman into utter dependence "can get someone to do the most heinous crimes that have been reported." Ultimately, whether the girls were murdered by Homolka, Bernardo or both is something which likely will never be known but, regardless of the facts, two psychologist were willing to support Homolka's claim as a victim, and her excuse.[84]

Holmolka, who had begun taking university courses in sociology and psychology in preparation for "a new life," which she has suggested may include working with abused women,[85] was to become eligible for parole in 1997; Bernardo was sentenced to 25 years without parole and later declared "a violent offender" extending his jail term to "life."[86] While Bernardo's lawyer made no attempt to cast him in a victim image in court, there are some well publicized cases in which men have used Psychology Industry defenses for similar crimes with the support of psychologists.

Perhaps the best known of these Counterfeit Victims is "The Hillside Strangler," Kenneth Bianchi, who, along with his cousin Angelo Buono, abducted and strangled ten young women in Los Angeles. He was eventually arrested in Bellingham, Washington for the strangulation deaths of two other young women. The LA women were stripped naked, and raped and sodomized by the men before (and in some cases while) being killed; the two Bellingham women were strangled immediately, with Bianchi masturbating over their clothed, dead bodies. These crimes, committed in LA between October 1977 and February 1978 and in Bellingham on January 11, 1979, led to what was at that time the longest running criminal trial in U.S. history. A total of eight psychologists became involved at various stages of the case, most supporting and professionally validating Bianchi's Psychology Industry inspired story/alibi.[87]

Bianchi, who had a large library of psychology books and had even impersonated a psychologist in a weight reduction counselling practice,[88] was better prepared than most to successfully employ a Counterfeit Victim defense. When arrested, the evidence against him was strong; he was likely to be convicted and executed. Bianchi looked to the Psychology Industry for an excuse. Claiming that he could remember nothing about the night of

January 11 beyond having gone for a drive, he began to draw psychologists, their method and their beliefs, into his defence. The first to become involved was a psychiatric social worker who, after seeing him for several weeks, hinted to Bianchi that MPD might be the explanation for his *amnesia*. The second, a forensic psychiatrist, did not pick up on the MPD idea, but did recommend hypnosis as a means to uncover the repressed memories. The third, Jack Watkins, a psychologist who specialized in hypnosis and had a strong interest in MPD, believed that the amnesia was an indicator of MPD.[89] In the first "successful" hypnosis session, Watkins began to explore the possibility of MPD by suggesting that there was another part to Bianchi and inviting that part to speak. At that point a part named "Steve" spoke and remembered the murders, describing in detail the Los Angeles cases, and implicating his cousin. Watkins became convinced that only Steve (and not Ken) was guilty of the murders. Bianchi, with this psychologically derived alibi, then agreed to testify against his cousin in California, as part of a plea bargain which would help him avoid the death penalty in Washington and prevent him from being tried for the California murders.

While it did save Bianchi's life by virtue of the plea bargain, the alibi did eventually fall apart when one of the psychologists hired by the prosecution, Martin Orne, demonstrated that Bianchi was faking hypnosis. He argued convincingly that, based on Bianchi's history of lying, and his knowledge of psychology (including hypnosis and MPD), Bianchi was conning "the experts."[90]

While some of the psychologists, "the true believers," never ceased, regardless of the facts, to support Bianchi's claim to be a MPD victim, the courts ultimately did not accept it. Later it was revealed that Bianchi had watched Sybil, a movie about a woman with many personalities, twice during his first few months in jail. As well, he had kept a diary for as long as it was useful to support his Psychology Industry excuse, but abandoned it once the excuse began to fail. Watkins, when asked some time later by a BBC producer whether Bianchi could possibly have known enough to fake it, replied that he would have had to have had "several years of study in Rorschach [tests] and graduate study in psychology for him to be able to do that."[91]

Cases such as Bianchi, Holmolka and Smith, while they receive media attention are not the typical Counterfeit Victims. In many ways they serve as an embarrassment to the Psychology Industry, as psychologists are drawn into supporting their fallacious causes, later to be publicly embarrassed as they are exposed as fakes. It is, rather, the countless other liars who are never exposed or whose lies have become so commonplace that they are merely shrugged off, who serve the industry much better. These are the more common pretenders, who fabricate stories and feign symptoms based on themes provided by the Psychology Industry.

Medicine has long been aware of a small proportion of patients who pretend to be suffering from a particular physical illness for no apparent reason other than attention.[92] In its most extreme form, *Munchausen Syndrome*, individuals consent to undergo extremely painful tests and major surgery, and may even bleed, poison, and mutilate themselves in order to appear sick.[93] Until recently the faking of psychological symptoms has been considered even more rare than the feigning of physical symptoms. But the growth of the victim-making industry, with the proliferation of information about psychological conditions and the growth of services to cater to them, may be leading to an epidemic, not of MPD or violence, but rather of "playing sick." Some people, like Mindy, fake symptoms and make up stories because they want to belong to a group, receive attention, and gain support. But such individuals are only one segment of a much larger group of Counterfeit Victims who take on a wide variety of roles, for reasons ranging from getting their way at work, home or in court, to defrauding insurance companies, to establishing alibis for murder.

One of the jurors in the O.J. Simpson trial, was released from duty because she had earlier reported to the police that she had been a victim of domestic violence. Subsequently, on national television, Jeanette Harris admitted that the accusations of battering and marital rape were false stating: "I have never ever been a victim of domestic abuse." When asked why she had made the claims when she knew them to be untrue, she replied: "It was just a part of a custody dispute; nobody believed that." It has become a common practice, with 25 to 30% of custody cases now involving accusations of spousal or child abuse, to incorporate such claims in an effort to gain an upper-hand in disputes whether or not the allegations are true. These Counterfeit Victims are so prevalent that they have moved out of the reach not only of punishment but also of shame, and can freely announce what they have done even on national television.

Physical injuries have, for a long time, been a common basis for insurance claims and civil law suits. However, the victim-making capacity of the Psychology Industry has facilitated the rapidly growing business of financial claims based on psychological injuries. Like the "soft-tissue damage" claims, some real and some feigned, which can never be seen on X-rays or lab tests, psychological damages are invisible and only established through the statements of the victims. Some appear in workers compensation claims,[94] some are in victim claims after motor vehicle or personal injury accidents. Others appear in personal law suits in which the victims claim psychological damages, sometimes from child abuse or date-rape, or from a sexually harassing look at the office, or from verbally abusive comments about one's weight.

Consider the following:

> $65,000 has been paid in compensation and rehabilitation to a public servant and his wife because he claimed he was stressed by a toy - a 15 cm stuffed penis resembling a sock with eyes... The toy penis was kept on the desk and later the bookshelf of a public servant who had a desk adjoining the man's desk.
>
> The man had been paid $45,000 in sickness benefits because he claimed he was stressed by the toy... The Commonwealth Department (in Adelaide, South Australia) spent $19,000 trying to rehabilitate the woman, including money for psychological counselling, gym membership and an interior decorating course.

The woman sued for further compensation. At the hearing, "a psychiatrist for the appellant told the tribunal the woman would not be fit to work until six to 12 months after her case was finalised." Her claim and subsequent appeal were eventually rejected; the Tribunal finding that the woman "had invented her claim that she was offended... after other avenues of seeking compensation were exhausted." But $65,000 had already been paid by South Australia's tax-payers.[95]

When accompanied by the supportive report of a psychologist and a confirming diagnosis, the insurance payoffs can range from time off work to a compensation package, and civil lawsuits can yield payments for specific damages (the trouble sleeping, the nightmares, the fatigue), general damages (the loss of "enjoyment of life" or "ability to enjoy sex") and punitive damages (to punish the accused for whatever it is claimed he, or she, has done.)

All of this has become so routine that virtually no-one questions the role psychologists are playing in these scams; often insurance claims are simply processed and lawsuits are settled out of court. Whereas, psychologists, at one time, were expected to investigate injury claims and to make an effort to detect malingerers, even to the point of challenging people on their motives, the Psychology Industry today, when it comes to assessing psychological damages, tends toward a nod of approval. What the patient says, whether based on fact or revenge, financial gain or some other motive, and often regardless of conflicting information, is assumed and accepted as true. Whether it is out of naivete, fear of reprimand[96] or basic self-interest, psychologists seem disinclined or dumb to the notion of questioning the client and, on occasion, uncovering the Counterfeit Victim.[97]

However, on occasions when psychologists are confronted with the counterfeit nature of a victim, a tendency exists to re-interpret the individual's problems resulting in the manufacturing of a synthetic victim. A recent case in Massachusetts provides such an example.[98] It involved a fifteen-year-old girl whose problems dated back to elementary school where she had been considered a pathological liar.[99] She displayed some self mutilation behaviour and once falsely blamed her father for burning her with cigarettes. During one hospital admission, she described four personalities, in addition to her own; three girls, aged 4, 8, and 12, and a 10-year-old boy. Later, two other alters emerged: another boy and a 78-year-old woman. She was diagnosed as having MPD and referred for both in-patient and out-patient therapy. Instead of confronting her immediately when it began to be a bit too obvious that this was a hoax, her therapy was continued and it was learned that she had learned all she could about sexual abuse and read *Sybil*, seen the movie, and even copied some of the sketches Sybil drew. Eventually, another personality, this one a paraplegic, arrived at the therapist's office, crawled inside and presented a journal the girl had been keeping, entries of which intimated that she had been feigning MPD. When confronted, the girl seemed relieved that the deception was finally over. However, instead of therapy being terminated immediately, she began to be seen as a case of *factitious disorder*[100] and received a further year of treatment until she showed no signs of MPD.

In talking about the various forms of therapy that exist, Kottler concluded that the overall goal of psychological treatment is "satisfied clients."[101] It would seem, with regards to Counterfeit Victims, that the Psychology Industry is so dedicated to this principle of customer satisfaction that it welcomes liars, encourages lying and provides endless opportunities for the support of all victims, including the counterfeits.

THE COST OF FABRICATED VICTIMHOOD

And this is the way the world will end
And this is the way the world will end
Not with a bang, but a whimper.

T.S. Eliot

In pursuit of its "satisfied customers," the Psychology Industry ignores its ethical and professional responsibility to consider the long-term effects of its activities on individuals and on society.

First and foremost, in regards to the individual damages, is the harm being done to authentic victims. When so many "cry victim" it becomes almost impossible to know what is true and what is false. As Charles Sykes has pointed out: *"When everyone is a victim, then no one is."*[102]

While the Psychology Industry incessantly promotes its efforts to decrease violence and injustice in society, and to protect and help victims, its primary effect is to divert attention and resources into its own psychologized concepts of violence and trauma and its bogus solutions. It has encouraged whining and blaming to the point where the demands of its users are drowning out the cries of real victims. When one examines the actual effects of the industry's efforts with the victims of brutal crimes, wars, and local tragedies, one finds these individuals often mythologized, ignored, or left to their own fate. Through influencing the legal system to be sensitive to "subtle cues" of abuse, intolerant of acts which only by its own definitions could be considered crimes, and validating the accusations, excuses, and claims of both honest and intentional liars, it is fostering a backlash against authentic victims. The search for "truth" amidst the psychologizing, pathologizing, and generalizing of the Psychology Industry is wreaking such havoc on American society that "crying victim" (even if the assault or rape, abuse or battering is "for real') will soon inspire dispassion and disbelief.

As well, Fabricated Victims of all types run the risk of becoming trapped and tangled up in their identity as victims, and in various ways coming to see themselves, and to be seen, as "wounded." Unsure of their ability to take care of themselves, they become dependent, immature, and helpless; needing protection, support, and "nurturance." By surrendering their autonomy, self-determination and personal power, they come to be identified as helpless individuals, lacking the ability to think clearly and make their own decisions.

"Protected" from situations which test or demand their abilities to deal with conflict, they resign themselves to the unreal compassion and soothing of therapeutic, self-help and support group relationships. Cutting themselves off from family members and friends who may challenge and confront their beliefs, they lose their roots both in their personal histories and in their communities. Tied only to psychologists who remain "allies" as long as funds last and fees are paid, they enter a "freefall" into eventual self-destruction.

The Counterfeit Victims, even those whose initial lie may have been said in "the heat of the moment," find that, with each modification, elaboration or "validation" of their story, it becomes more and more difficult to take back the lie, which may become the central, enduring theme of their lives. Synthetic Victims too can become trapped, as they become accustomed to feeling, appearing, sounding and behaving like victims, incorporating whatever suggestions are offered by the Psychology Industry into their new understanding of themselves and their lives. For the Contrived Victims, their acceptance of Psychology Industry explanations and proffered hope can often mean that they spend their last months with therapists and counsellors, instead of with friends and family. Ignoring Fritz Perls' declaration: "I don't want to be saved, I want to be spent," they lose their last few months or years trying to be saved rather than spending it fully, remembering and savouring the past and fully enjoying the present.

As well, Fabricated Victims, especially those who accuse others of crimes and evil acts, run the increasing risk of eventually experiencing guilt and shame, and possible humiliation and blame. While initially supported in their beliefs, many Synthetic Victims will at some time in the future begin to realize the destructive effects that their accusations have had on others and feel personal responsibility and profound embarrassment. While some psychologists may also come to see their complicity and have to admit their own responsibility, it is unlikely that the Psychology Industry will be there at that time to help either these psychologists or these Fabricated Victims. Similarly, while some Counterfeits, aware of their lying and feeling no remorse, may get away with it and enjoy the profits of their deception; others, in increasing numbers, will face the possibility of being exposed. As several examples in the previous section illustrate, Counterfeits can be exposed, and run the increasing risk of public humiliation and criminal prosecution. And to some extent, Synthetic Victims run the same risk. Their lies, too, can be exposed and, as society becomes more aware of these deceptions, it will become both less believing and less tolerant of those who claim to be victims. It will quit trying to tell the difference between the "honest" and the intentional liar, and judge all of them the same, demanding "the truth" and punishing the liars. It is conceivable, as well, that those falsely and unfairly accused will stop thinking kindly of naive Synthetic Victims, and that even "recanters" will begin to face law suits and find themselves unable to hold psychologists responsible for the actions they have taken based on false interpretations and memories.

The Psychology Industry is separating people from their families, promoting stereotypic and hostile views of men and women, degrading friendship, and generally promoting distrust and suspicion. While no one would condone severe abuse, the Psychology Industry interprets vague recollections to make minor events sinister. And while no-one would excuse domestic violence, the Psychology Industry blurs the concept and ignores the context. The Psychology Industry promotes fear and inequality, treating all interpersonal relationships as potentially threatening. It is teaching people to see others as potential enemies, to be monitored, scrutinized and accused. In so doing, it is squelching the human character of people to trust, to flirt, to seduce, to argue and yell, to assume responsibility, to be cautious, to take risks, to be passionate, to make the right choices and to make mistakes. It has created a sense of distance between people, so that the only ones to be trusted are the psychologists and other users who relate in regulated, constricted, artificial and time-limited ways.

And, in so doing, society and the country as a whole, suffer. "Justice" is elevated over health, education, family and friendship. As funds become diverted from health into law and order, the overall health of the country deteriorates and, with that, the eventual health of every citizen. Similarly, education suffers both through reduced funding and through the emphasis on psychological notions instead of academic needs. Schools are told to foster self-esteem rather than academic excellence.[103] Teachers become afraid of helping pupils for fear that their intentions will be misinterpreted. Tears rather than sweat become the way to get rich as law suits fostered by "liability science" bankrupt individuals, institutions and large corporations. And the American economy, which once was the strongest in the world, is weakened as citizen blames citizen, and child sues parent. The threat of the nuclear "bang" has been replaced by that of the victim's "whimper."

Endnotes

1. Des Pres, Terrence. *The Survivor.* New York: Oxford University Press, 1976. p.13.

2. Hayes, Nelson. *Adult Children of Alcoholics Remember.* New York: Ballantine, 1989. pp.242-243.

3. Sykes, Charles J. *A Nation of Victims: The Decay of the American Character.* New York: St. Martin's Press. 1992. p.18.

4. Gondolf, Lynn. In "Doors of Memory" by Ethan Watters, *Mother Jones,* January 1993, p.26.

5. Carroll, Lewis. *Through the Looking Glass.*

6. Plous, Scott. *Psychology of Judgement and Decision Making.* New York: McGraw, 1993. pp.162-164.

7. Someone might claim that it is still a cause for worry because if four out of five people on a neurology ward are dizzy it might mean that dizziness is associated with some neurological problem but, to draw that conclusion, one would need to look at the frequency of dizziness of people hospitalized for other reasons or not hospitalized.

8. Marie, Jan. "31 symptoms of physical, emotional, and sexual trauma." Cited by Susan F. Smith, "Body memories: And other pseudo-scientific notions of 'survivor psychology.'" *Issues in Child Abuse Accusations,* 5(4), 1993, pp.22-234.

9. Fiore, Edith. *You Have Been Here Before: A Psychologist Looks at Past Lives.* New York: Ballantine Books, 1978, pp.6-7. Fiore's book, which by 1987 was into it's 9th printing, was heralded as a revolutionary approach to psychology, ie. state of the art technology, and deemed full of challenging *evidence.*

10. Williams, M. H. "The bait-and-switch tactic in psychotherapy." *Psychotherapy*. 1985, 22, 110-113. p.111.

11. Schaef, Anne W. *Beyond Therapy, Beyond Science: A New Model for Healing the Whole Person.* San Francisco: Harper San Francisco, 1992. p.94.

12. Bass, Ellen and Davis, Laura *The Courage to Heal: A Guide for Women Survivors of Child Sexual Abuse.* New York: Harper & Row (3rd revised edition Harper Perennial, 1994). pp.24 and 37.

13. Pittman,Frank, III "A Buyer's guide to psychotherapy." *Psychology Today*, 1994 (Jan/Feb) p.52-53.

14. Slaby. *Aftershock.* p.4-5.

15. Blume, Sue E. *Secret Survivors: Uncovering Incest and Its Aftereffects in Women.* New York: John Wiley & Sons, 1989. p.xiii.

16. Ibid. pp. xiv and 5.

17. Wegscheider-Cruse, Sharon, and Cruse, Joseph. *Understanding Codependency.* Deerfield Beach, Florida: Health Communications, Inc., 1990. p.17

18. Feinberg, Mortimer R., Feinberg, Gloria & Tarrant, John J. *Leavetaking.* New York: Simon & Schuster, 1978. pp.9-12.

19. Pasley, Laura. "Misplaced Trust." *Skeptical Inquirer*, 1994, p.65.

20. Fiore, Edith. *You Have Been Here Before: A Psychologist Looks at Past Lives.* New York: Ballantine Books, 1978. pp.5-6.

21. From an interview on the television program "The Fifth Estate." Cited in Ofshe, Richard and Watters, Ethan. *Making Monsters: False Memories, Psychotherapy, and Sexual Hysteria.* New York: Charles Scribner's Sons, 1994. p.223.

22. From a personal interview with Dr. Rutter in November, 1995.

23. Gondlof, Lynn. Cited in *Survivor Psychology: The dark side of a mental health mission* by Susan Smith. Boca Raton, Fl: Upton Books, 1995. p.22.

24. Statement made by Richard Ofshe on the Dennis Prager TV show, June 1995.

25. Attributed to APA past-president, Ronald Fox in "Fox identifies top threats to professional psychology" by Sara Martin, *The APA Monitor,* March, 1995. p.44.

26. Herman. *Trauma and Recovery.* p.177.

27. Miller, Alice. *Banished Knowledge.* New York: Doubleday, 1990. pp. 2 and 4.

28. Spiegel, H. "Hypnosis and evidence: Help or hindrance?" *Annals of the New York Academy of Science*, 1980, 347, p.78.

29. Fiore. *You Have Been Here Before.* p.6.

30. Cote, Isabelle. "Adult recollections of childhood trauma." A paper presented to the 74th Annual Meeting of the Ontario Psychiatric Association, Toronto, January, 1994. p.15.

31. Sheflin, Alan. Address on "False Memory Syndrome" presented at the Federation of Canadian Societies of Clinical Hypnosis, Banff, Alberta, May, 1995.

32. Michelle Smith's story as told in the bestseller *Michelle Remembers,* co-authored by Michelle and her psychiatrist, Lawrence Pazder (New York: Congdon & Lattes, 1980), was the first satanic-cult survivor story to become a bestseller. Billed as a "true story," similar memories came to be recovered in therapy sessions across America and, often by people who had read this book. Some have recently described it as a fabricated hoax.

33. Robert Kelly, the owner of The Little Rascals daycare in Edenton, North Carolina was convicted in 1993 of sexually abusing 12 children and sentenced to 12 consecutive life terms. Dawn Wilson, the Center's cook, was also convicted and sentenced to a life term. In May of 1995 these conviction were overturned by the state Court of Appeals. Two years later, in May 1997, prosecutors dropped 99 pending charges against Kelly and seven charges against Wilson, as well as all charges against the remaining defendants. Assistant District Attorney Nancy Lamb said the decision to end the Little Rascals case was made to "allow wounds to heal," and that the decision did not mean that the state had a weak case against Kelly and Wilson.
Cases such as this one have been reported in the popular media (see 'The Demons of Edenton' in Elle, Nov., 1993, pp.139-142 & 'Unspeakable Acts' in *Good Housekeeping*, October, 1995,

p.204) and critiqued in academic books such as Ceci, Stephen J. and Bruck, Margaret. *Jeopardy in the Courtroom: A Scientific Analysis of Children's Testimony.* Washington, D.C.: American Psychological Association, 1995. Referred to now as "witch hunts," similar scenarios have occurred across America, from Bakersfield, to Martensvillle, to Wenatchee.

34. This case was described by Patricia Love in her book *The Emotional Incest Syndrome.* (New York: Bantam. 1990), pp.134-136.

35. Quotations are from an interview with Harold Levy conducted on November 3, 1995.

36. Cited from an article by Kirk Makin. "Crown's "reluctance" to drop case enrages defence" *The Globe and Mail,* April 30, 1994. p.A3.

37. Quotations are from an interview with Alan Gold conducted on November 7, 1995.

38. Herman. *Trauma and Recovery.* p.158.

39. Frank, J.D. and Frank, J. B. *Persuasion and Healing: A Comparative Study of Psychotherapy.* (3rd ed.) Baltimore: John Hopkins, 1991. pp.8-9.

40. Kleinman, A. *Rethinking Psychiatry: From Cultural Category to Personal Experience.* New York: Free Press, 1988.

41. Frank and Frank. *Persuasion and Healing.* p.9.

42. Schofield, W. *Psychotherapy, The Purchase of Friendship.* Englewood Cliffs, N.J.: Spectrum Books, Prentice-Hall, 1964. p.27.

43. Jasper, K. *The Nature of Psychotherapy: A Critical Appraisal.* J. Hoenig and M.W. Hamilton (trans.) Chicago: Phoenix Books, University of Chicago Press, 1964. p.8.

44. Peele, Stanton. *Diseasing America: Addiction Treatment Out of Control.* Lexington, Mass.: Lexington Books, 1989. p.49. (Citing R. Longabaugh, Evaluating recovery out-comes, presented as a conference, *Program on Alcohol Issues,* University of California, San Diego, February 4-6, 1988.)

45. As examples of "hystories" (her term), Showalter addresses: alien abduction, chronic fatigue syndrome, satanic ritual abuse, recovered memory, Gulf War syndrome, and multiple personality syndrome. Showalter, Elaine. *Hystories: Hysterical Epidemics and Modern Media.* New York: Columbia University Press, 1997. p.17.

46. American Psychiatric Association. *Diagnostic and Statistical Manual (DSM-IV).* Washington, D.C.: American Psychiatric Association, 1994.

47. Emil Kraepelin's *Textbook of Psychiatry* first published in 1883 soon became the standard text of a newly recognized area of medicine which he was determined to make strictly scientific, following the methods of biological sciences.

48. Peebles, Mary Jo. "Posttraumatic Stress Disorder: A historical perspective on diagnosis and treatment." Topeka, KS: The Menninger Foundation, 1989, pp. 274-286.

49. Scrignar, C.B. *Post Traumatic Stress Disorder: Diagnosis, treatment and legal issues.* Westport, Conn.: Praeger, 1984. p.2.

50. "There is a war between the sexes. Rape victims, battered women, and sexually abused children are its casualties." Herman. *Trauma and Recovery.* p.32.

51. "Cardinal Hume urges killer to give himself up to police." *The London Times,* December 12, 1995, p.5.

52. "Pupils who saw murder "face years of trauma.'" *The London Evening Standard,* December 11, 1995, p.6.

53. "Hospitals 'faked mental illness in healthy patients.'" News of the lawsuit filed in Los Angeles reached as far as London when it was printed in *The Daily Telegraph,* December 12, 1995, p.12.

54. Zuñiga, Jo Ann "Tenet agrees to $100 million settlement: Firm accused of imprisoning patients." *Houston Chronicle,* July 30,1997.

55. Dantzer, Robert. *The Psychosomatic Delusion: Why the mind is NOT the source of all our ills.* New York: The Free Press, 1993. p.i.

56. Weiner, Herbert. *Psychobiology and Human Disease.* New York: Elsevier, 1977. p.xii.

57. Eliot, Robert S. *From Stress to Strength.* New York: Bantam Books, 1994. p.6.

58. Williams, Redford & Williams, Virginia. *Anger Kills*. New York: Random House, 1993. p.xii.

59. Elliott, Glen. Stress and illness. In Stanley Cheron (ed.) *Psychosomatic Medicine: Theory, Physiology and Practice. Vol. 1.* Madison, Conn: International Universities Press, Inc, 1989. pp.45-90.

60. Pack Stroup, Heather and Herndon, Paul L. "Asserting a greater role towards health: expanding visions of psychology practice." *Practitioner*, Vol 8, #1, February 1995, p.22.

61. Ibid. p.22

62. Bruce Charash, in his book *Heart Myths* (New York: Viking Press, 1991) listed the cardiac prone personality as a popularized myth, presenting just some of the research that exposes the foundation of these programs to be incorrect and indicates that "Type A" is not an established risk factor for premature heart attacks and cardiac deaths.

63. Simonton, O. Carl, Matthews-Simonton, Stephanie, and Creighton, James L. *Getting Well Again: The new best-seller about the Simontons' revolutionary life-saving self-awareness techniques.* New York: Bantam Books, 1981 (originally published by J. P. Tarcher in 1978).

64. Simonton et al. *Getting Well Again.* p.105.

65. This case summary was provided by a psychologist who treated the patient.

66. A "collage" is defined as "a presentation showing disparate scenes in rapid succession without transition."

67. Mikluscak-Cooper, Cindy, and Miller, Emmett E. *Living in Hope: A 12-Step Approach for Persons at Risk or Infected with HIV.* Berkeley, CA: Celestial Arts, 1991.

68. The case of "Public Mischief" against the accused, Kari Ann Size (*R. v Size*), took place in Toronto, Canada; the Judge's report was released on Feb. 27, 1991.

69. Kanin, Eugene J. "False Rape Allegations." *Archives of Sexual Behavior*, 23 (1), 1994.

70. Ibid. pp.86-87.

71. "Cried wolf about rape, woman jailed to help kick alcohol habit." *Times-Colonist*, Aug. 26, 1994.

72. This case example was provided by a colleague. In addition to eventually claiming to have been sexually abused as a child, she also claimed to have been sexually assaulted as an adult.

73. "Raging Bulls: Tom & Roseanne" was a feature story in *People Magazine*, May 2, 1994, pp.34-58. Roseanne's retraction of the charges, made in late April, was reported in news services across America (eg. *Times-Colonist*, Tuesday, April 26, 1994).

74. This example and quotations are taken from Katie Roife's book *The Morning After: Sex, Fear and Feminism on Campus.* Boston: Little, Brown and Co., 1993. pp.39-41.

75. The cover story of *Good Housekeeping* (November, 1995), pp.116-119 & 210-213 entitled "Beyond Burt" presented Loni Anderson as a recovered abused wife, showed how she "learned to trust again" and featured her new book *My Life in High Heels* (New York: Morrow, 1995) which "finally tells the shocking story of the addictions, the abuse, and the infidelity that destroyed her marriage," lashes out at Burt Reynolds and celebrates Loni's own love of clothes and shoes.

76. Over the many years of media coverage of Lady Diana, there have been many explanations of her behaviours in Psychology Industry terms. For example when she was suspected of phone harassment, she hit the cover of *People* magazine (September 5, 1994), which printed a story entitled "A Princess in Peril" (pp.68-77) in which one psychiatrist was cited as supporting the idea that "such compulsiveness - in bending the truth, in binge eating, in making anonymous calls - is a sign of feeling 'helpless and hopeless' " and then quoted *The Sun* as saying that she "seems to have convinced herself... that she did not make [the] anonymous calls. In psychiatric jargon, this is the "denial phase of a distressed mind. In plain English, it is lying."

77. "Stress Sex" by Carol Lynn Mithers was in the September 1993 issue of *Ladies Home Journal*, pp.62-72.

78. "Stress pileup can lead to murder, say experts" *The Associated Press* (Union, South Carolina), November 5, 1994.

79. Glenys Kaufman-Kantor of the Family Research Lab at the University of New Hampshire cited in "Stress pileup can lead to murder, say experts."

80. "Contest of victim vs beast." *The New York Times*, July 9, 1995.

81. Susan Smith did not receive the death penalty. Many men (especially poor, blacks) on death row had suffered documented abuses and "stresses" far exceeding anything Smith could claim, yet they were held responsible and sentenced to death. The major difference: gender. For a review of these cases see *It's All the Rage* by Wendy Kaminer (New York: Addison-Wesley, 1995).

82. Mary Garofalo did the "Current Affair" broadcast which was blacked out in Canada due to a publication ban. A report on the show was done by The Canadian Press in Ottawa, July 28, 1994.

83. The nude body of one of the girls was found in a ditch; the body parts of the other were retrieved from a nearby lake, encased in cement. And some of the more horrific segments of the girls' experiences in captivity had been video taped. It was just one day before the tapes of not only Bernardo's but also Homolka's participation in these activities found their way into police hands that Homolka made her deal. She pleaded guilty to manslaughter in both cases and was granted immunity on all other possible charges, including the rape and murder of another girl, her own younger sister.

84. Karla Holmolka's testimony was highlighted in the Canadian press for several weeks (see, for example "Holmolka: I felt totally trapped" by Tom Blackwell of The Canadian Press, June 21, 1995) and the testimony of the psychologists (one from Ontario and one from California) was highlighted in a Canadian Press article entitled "Expert: Battered women can kill," August 4, 1995 and a *Globe & Mail* (August 4, 1995) article by Kirk Makin entitled "Judge says Bernardo trial straying from main issue."

85. The cover story of *Mclean's* magazine (June 26, 1995, pp.32-35) entitled "The Holmolka Enigma" told Karla's story, citing letters she had written from prison as one source.

86. "Bernardo handed indefinite jail term" by Tom Blackwell, The Canadian Press, November 4, 1995.

87. While Bianchi did not admit to posing as a Counterfeit Victim, the evidence that he did so was compelling. One recounting of the story, based on court reports and interviews with the police investigators involved in the case, is Darcy O'Brien's book *Two of a Kind: The Hillside Stranglers*. (New York: New American Library, 1985).

88. He had rented his office from a licensed psychologist in North Hollywood who had been impressed by his sincerity.

89. Watkins held the opinion that the most frequent misdiagnosis of this condition was "Antisocial Personality Disorder." He quickly eliminated the possibility that he was being conned by a sociopath, finding in Bianchi's history insufficient indications (i.e. "school reports did not stress lying," "he avoided fights"), and seeing the young Ken instead as "an abused, neurotic child" whose "lying would be a normal defense...to cope with smothering, cruel punishment, and pressures..." from his mother.

90. Orne concluded that Bianchi was faking MPD and made the diagnosis of Antisocial Personality Disorder with Sexual Sadism. The argument is summarized in an article entitled "On the differential diagnosis of multiple personality in the forensic context" by Orne, Martin T., Dinges, David F. & Orne, Emily Carota in *The International Journal of Clinical and Experimental Hypnosis*, 1984, XXXII (2), pp.118-169.

91. Cited in O'Brien, Darcy. *Two of a Kind: The Hillside Stranglers*. Scarborough, Ont.: New American Library, 1985. p.274.

92. *Patient or Pretender* by Marc D. Feldman, Charles V. Ford and Toni Reinhold (New York: Wiley, 1985. p.274) provides an overview of this condition, including both physical and psychological examples.

93. Those knowledgeable about medical conditions, especially nurses, have been considered particularly prone to this condition. With the advent of support groups, it has been discovered

that conditions such as terminal cancer have been faked, for the purpose of gaining, along with sympathy from friends, admission to such services.

94. For instance, the Workers Compensation Board in Ontario Canada recognizes both work-related stress and critical incident stress as insured disabilities.

95. *The Adelaide Advertiser*, April 30, 1991, p. 13.

96. In many segments of the industry questioning the truth of a client's claim has become unacceptable and posing it seriously is greeted with accusations of insensitivity. Recently a psychologist was found guilty of misconduct, suspended from practising, and ordered to attend specified courses aimed at increasing his sensitivity to patients who were [or claimed to be] survivors of sexual abuse. The primary allegation was that he had confronted a patient on the possibility of that she was attempting to use her "sexual abuse to scam the insurance at work." (Disciplinary Hearing in *The Bulletin of the College of Psychologists of Ontario*, Vol.21, No.2, November 1994, pp.7-9.)

97. One of the experts in the Bianchi case later became a prison psychiatrist and came to realize that prisoners do tend to lie. "That was a shock to me because I had been used to believing what my patients told me..." he said. Cited in Darcy O'Brien. *Two of a Kind*. p.354.

98. This case, which was reported in *Psychotherapy* (Summer, 1991), was discussed in *Patient or Pretender* by Marc D. Feldman, Charles V. Ford and Toni Reinhold (New York: John Wiley & Sons, 1994), pp.139-140.

99. It is often argued that people who suffer from MPD are likely to have a history of being accused of lying because one personality doesn't know what another personality has done and also because one personality may be inclined to lie as a way to trap or embarrass another. The psychologists who diagnosed Bianchi, whose mother reportedly recognized him as a compulsive liar from the moment he could talk, also used this rationale.

100. *A factitious disorder* refers to the intentional production or feigning of physical or psychological signs, the motivation for which is to assume the sick role, with external incentives, such as economic gain, revenge, or avoiding responsibly being absent. (DSM-IV) Because, in the case of this young girl, attention seemed to be what she wanted, this alternate diagnosis could be applied.

101. Kottler, Jeffrey A. *The Compleat Therapist*. San Francisco: Jossey-Bass Publ., 1991. p.12.

102. Sykes. *A Nation of Victims*. p.18.

103. Sykes, Charles J. *Dumbing Down Our Kids: Why American children feel good about themselves but can't read, write or add*. New York: St. Martin's Press, 1995.

Chapter 3

The Growth of the Psychology Industry

*We must admit that the rapid growth of psychology in America has been
due to conditions of the soil as well as the vitality of the germ.*

J. M. Cattell, Presidential Address to the
American Psychological Association, 1895

The growth of psychology as an industry is conveniently ignored or overlooked in most records of the history of psychology.[1] While it is true that, as
a discipline, psychology has a rich philosophical and scholarly heritage, it is
also true that a parallel history exists involving deceptions to mislead consumers, economic associations to advance the profession, and biased attention to whatever pays.

Throughout the history of civilization, the inquiring mind has been
intrigued by its own workings and fascinated by its own behaviours, and it
was to this that psychology responded initially. However, this genuine
inquisitiveness, along with objectivity and integrity, has succumbed to exaggerated claims, unsupported "expert opinions," sweeping public statements
based on minimal or questionable data, broad generalizations about psychological damages, fad treatments and trendy interest areas.

"How did this happen?" How did psychology reach this dubious point of
becoming both an enormous industry within, and a product of, the society
that it had promised to change?

To begin to understand this "other history," one must consider the subtle
but profound effects that nationalism, consumerism, feminism, genderism,
professionalism and capitalism have had on what had begun as the science
of psychology; how psychological "facts" were created or distorted to prove
a biased view or to support a political or financial interest. Rather than the
scientific approach of psychology being the correcting force, the Psychology
Industry with its business plans, personal goals and social agendas has become
the determining force shaping the profession. Although the academic discipline and the practice of psychology have had, until recently, quite separate
and distinct histories, most people now use the terms synonymously, believ-

ing that they mean the same thing. They view psychology as both a science that determines the "facts" that are cited by psychologists and the media, and a practice which involves the skillful and objective application of psychological knowledge. What virtually no one realizes is the extent to which the former has given way to the latter and, by aligning with other more powerful forces in society, fostered the growth of psychology into a major industry; thus sacrificing its soul (psyche) and its science (-ology).

Shaping and Being Shaped

Most people assume that the sciences are objective; concerned with fact and truth and not susceptible to the broader influences of society. But the sciences are as much *shaped* by the society in which they exist as they are *shapers* of that society. History is full of occasions when new discoveries were rejected because of the dogma of the times; when great men were laughed at (or burned at the stake) because their world wasn't ready for them. As Schultz[2] notes "even the greatest of minds (perhaps especially the greatest of minds) have often been constrained by what has been called the 'Zeitgeist,' " that is, the general intellectual, moral, and cultural climate of the era.

Similarly, most people, including most psychologists, assume that psychology serves society as a shaper. They fail to see that it has allowed itself to be shaped; to be influenced, restricted and directed by other forces in society in order to achieve its own prominence.

Regrettably, with what Rollo May[3] calls "the anti-historical tendency of psychology," psychologists fail to acknowledge the relationship between their own aspirations for influence and affluence, and the effects of the political and social climate in which they work. Practicing and writing as if psychology has experienced a recent "virgin birth," they tend to deny that their current theories and practices contain influences from the past and are the result of the interweaving of many historical, cultural and political factors which stretch well beyond the limited scope of psychology. With this arrogance ("what we 'know' now is better than what they knew then") and denial ("what others think does not need to influence what we 'know' "), psychologists ignore the past, placing the emphasis on what they call their "new findings" and "recent research." In so doing, they expose the dimensions of their ignorance. By disregarding history, they fail to see their transitory position in the greater history of civilization. They do not wonder why it is that now, in the 20th century Western world, they are achieving recognition, when medicine and law have existed for millennia. They have not questioned their position in an industrial and capitalistic culture, nor their assumption that this society would provide the resources and the climate for a Psychology Industry to prosper. And until recently, they presumed that the power and policies of the United States would always favourably influence the international order, and that their place in the social fabric was secure. Like most in the Western world, they have grasped hold of an optimistic and opportunistic world view that considers "progress" to be onwards and upwards, "bigger and better," and they have scorned the dire forecast of the sociologist, Max Weber: "Not summer's bloom lies ahead of us but rather a polar night of icy darkness and hardship" and the warning of Nisbet who wrote "how crucial it was for the rulers of Orwell's society in *1984* to blot out or else remake the past. Without the past as represented by rituals, traditions, and memory there can be no roots; and without roots, human beings are condemned to a form of isolation in time that easily becomes self-destructive."[4]

Despite their extravagant claims to understand people, they have, and continue, to manifest immense naiveté about society which can only have profound implications for the nature of their theories of human behaviour. As Sarason writes: "every psychologist has a picture of what man is or should be, of what society is or should be, and this picture infiltrates (indeed, is in part the basis of) his or her theories, along with the psychologist's way of thinking about theory and practice."[5] Thus, what psychologists discover, promote or practice is also a product of their own wishes, goals and aspirations. They become agents of social influence and through their theories, expert opinions and work, they not only create a niche for themselves , they also advance their elitist, western image of the world which has shaped them.

If to be prominent is to be sensitive and responsive to the tides and whims of society then, to be successful is to merge one's personal goals with these larger social factors; to be a shaper and allow oneself to be shaped at the same time.

Looking Back at the Past

Prior to the mid 1800's, psychology had been the province of philosophers and theologians, carried out through speculation and inference, intuition and generalization. However, by mid-century, the scientific method, which had shown modest gains in the understanding of physical nature, began to be applied to human nature. Even at this early stage, the foundation for a consumer-based psychology began to be laid. Two interesting examples can be found in the area of intelligence testing, one of the first entrepreneurial activities of psychologists. The first provides an example of the misuse of science to support a psychologist's political beliefs; the second, perhaps more subtle in nature and profound in its eventual effect, demonstrates the susceptibility of a psychologist to the dominant values inherent in his society.

Sir Francis Galton, well known in the history of psychology and a cousin of Charles Darwin, sought to apply the theory of evolution to that of intellectual capacity. In 1869, he published *Hereditary Genius* which held that eminent men have eminent sons; that is, that intellectual greatness is inherited.[6] To "prove" his assumptions, Galton studied the ancestries of famous scientists, jurists, physicians, and the like; individuals of genius and all members of the aristocracy. His ultimate goal was to encourage the production of the more eminent or mentally fit and to discourage the birthrate of those he thought to be unfit; to promote eugenics. Galton had not only wanted to understand the inherited quality of greatness; he also wanted to use psychology to protect and maintain the power of his social class which was under threat of change.[7, 8] The British Empire was collapsing. England's status as a world power was crumbling and the dominant aristocratic class was being threatened and replaced by a rising class of unsophisticated but wealthy financiers and industrial barons.[9] Under the guise of protecting and improving society, he established the Eugenics Laboratory[10] and founded an organization to promote ideas of racial improvement and the supremacy of the gifted (of which he was fortunately one.)

From the vantage point of the mid 1990's, with the intervening history of the Holocaust, Stalinism, and the repeated reports of cultural and racial "cleansing," one would wonder how this attitude could have been held by one as prominent and respected as Galton. However, his work bore the imprint of his social class and in the end it "proved" what he and they wanted to believe: that intelligence was genetically inherited and that psychological technology must be employed to protect and improve it. And this view was not restricted to England. As Herrnstein and Murray noted: "The first wave of public controversy occurred during the first decades of the century, when a few testing enthusiasts proposed using the results of mental tests to support outrageous racial policies. Sterilization laws were passed in sixteen American states between 1907 and 1917, with the elimination of mental retardation being one of the prime targets of the public policy. "Three generations of imbeciles are enough," Justice Oliver Wendell Holmes declared in an opinion upholding the constitutionality of such a law. It was a statement made possible, perhaps encouraged, by the new enthusiasm for mental testing.[11]

In the same time period, but in a different country which had undergone social changes for a hundred years, Alfred Binet, a French psychologist was studying the intellectual development of children. Unlike Galton who viewed formal schooling as a waste of time and money because intelligence was inherited, Binet believed that education appropriate to ability could prepare children for the emerging industrial society. To help reform the public school system, he developed a scale to measure "intelligence,"[12] a concept which he interpreted as the ability to solve certain types of logical problems. It was this definition of intelligence, influenced by the attitudes and needs of an industrialized society, that lead Sarason to comment about Binet: "his world view prevented him from recognizing that his concept of intelligence was an invention and, like all inventions, as revealing of the inventor's society as of the inventor."[13]

This scale may have been the first successful product of the Psychology Industry as it merged the needs of an industrializing society with the aspirations of the psychologist; and, it marked the beginning of the phenomenal growth of mental testing in schools and industry. Binet's scale and the whole concept of mental testing was quickly seized upon and applied with eagerness particularly by American psychologists who saw it as a way to establish the importance of psychology. American society wanted a practical, down-to-earth form of psychology, and mental testing provided the first of many ways that psychology could be used in a bold and direct American way.[14] As well as assisting the government in making political and racial decisions, such as the barring of "defective aliens," it provided industry with a means to select and train workers. Like Binet, these early entrepreneurial psychologists failed to consider, or refused to acknowledge, that their definition of intelligence really expressed the values of their affluent social class; one being that intelligent people make better citizens and better workers.

These and the many other examples like them are not intended to suggest or prove that any malevolence or sinister conspiracy existed. Rather, what they serve to demonstrate is that, from the beginning, psychology has furthered its own interests by yielding objectivity and responding to the demands and beliefs of its own social world, often failing to go far enough in its thinking and questioning. "The inability of these psychologists to ask and pursue questions insured that their theories and research would play into and reinforce the prejudiced attitudes of the dominant groups in society, groups to which these psychologists belonged;"[15] a characteristic evident now in the Psychology Industry.

Following Medicine's Example

Psychology was neither alone nor the first to exploit social opportunities to advance its own interests. Medicine had chosen the same route and led the way both in professionalization, which restricted the competition and established control over the market, and in developing a mutual beneficial working relationship with business and industry. Medicine became the model that the Psychology Industry followed in building itself into a competitive business.

Prior to the mid 1800's, the state of medicine, as practiced by pharmacists, homeopaths, osteopaths, herbalists, local shamans, and by some regular doctors with "medical training," was so abysmal that patients with cholera were given an even chance of being done in by the disease or by the doctor.[16] However in the latter half of the century, American medicine began to adopt a scientific approach, as it studied the body, created esoteric diagnoses and developed technical treatments. For a society oriented around and excited by production, progress and profit, scientific medicine offered the promise of healthier and more efficient bodies which could be controlled and maintained like machines; it opened the possibility of reducing the toll of disease on industry's human resources. Industrialists were particularly enthusiastic and financially supportive of this scientific form of medicine, which attempted to analyze and control the parts of the body in much the same way as their industries managed and controlled production. Promoting what came to be known as the "germ theory," scientific medicine made it possible to identify specific causes of disease and reduce the effects on industry's work force. The germ theory, as well, drew attention to the individual's body and distracted attention away from the social or environmental causes of illness such as the polluted factories, hazardous working conditions or overcrowded and industrialized cities.

Scientific medicine served the needs of the financiers and industrialists; it was politically and economically useful to the affluent, capitalist class. To ensure its viability, a number of wealthy industrialists, lead by Carnegie and Rockefeller, developed a form of philanthropy that built and endowed medical schools which agreed to technically train and properly socialize their students. In turn, this benefitted the doctors who, rewarded with the professional prestige and influence, gained control over their competition. Through the joint efforts of the American Medical Association and industry, laws came to be enacted that restricted medical licensing to scientifically trained practitioners and penalties were established for even fraternizing with the unlicensed.

This self-serving relationship, which allowed business interests to determine how doctors should think, and who and what they should treat, not only shaped the practice of medicine, but eventually the practice of psychology for it was from within medicine that the current practice of the Psychology Industry emerged.

Medical Psychology

The medical literature of the 1800's abounded with descriptions of neurasthenia, hysteria, and hypochondriasis, as well as lunacy and insanity. The psychological symptoms they presented could be detected in people's mood and behaviours. These conditions were spoken of as "shattered nerves,"[17] a term reflecting the belief that they were due to physical problems in the nervous system. The most severe instances were treated by "mad doctors" who worked behind high walls in insane asylums. However, as cases were identified amongst members of the wealthier upper class who desired to avoid the embarrassment of incarcerating a family member, a new designation of medical specialist developed, the "alienists." Their title arising from the phrase "alienation of the mind," these doctors focussed on a broader range of problems which fell under the title of "mental pathology" or "medical psychology."

It was from this that Sigmund Freud, a neurologist by training, developed the field of psychoanalysis. Among Freud's notable contributions was his description of the Unconscious, a concept of which many, including the hypnotists, were already aware[18] and his explanation of the dynamic of family relationships including the contentious theory of infantile sexuality which still plays a role in the internal disputes of the Psychology Industry. Freud saw psychoanalysis as a means of describing and understanding the "dark side" of human nature and he believed that increased understanding by the individual could lead to greater acceptance of one's self and to a reduction in anxiety, considered to be the result of unconsciously trying to hide these less flattering, darker aspects.

Although the medical establishment in Europe was sceptical and resistant, psychoanalysis was quickly and eagerly picked up and Americanized by the fledgling psychiatric profession in the U.S. who saw it as a means to mould or adapt the individual to the changing world. G. Stanley Hall, the host for his 1909 visit to America, told Freud that he had come at a good "psychological moment,"[19] a time when, "with mobility of place, profession and status, and a new instability of values, old ways of looking at the world no longer applied. The individual is thrown back on himself and is more receptive to theories such as psychoanalysis which search for meaning in his dreams, wishes, fears, and confusion."[20] By acquiring psychoanalysis, watering it down and sweetening it to their taste, American psychiatrists brought "Freudianism in line with American beliefs about the virtue and necessity of an optimistic approach... and promised that self-improvement was possible without calling society into question."[21] In a manner consistent with the medical germ theory, Americanized psychoanalysis defined psychological problems as being specific to the individual, reducing any broader social context such as alienation, poverty or industrialization. Now, eighty years later, American psychology has a similar character, emphasizing individual and interior issues and ignoring the larger social and external context as it manufactures victims.

Transformed into a formal American institution, psychoanalysis served the mutual interests of the individual, society and medicine. For the person experiencing the instability of an external world in which the old way did not apply, it offered a way to search for personal meaning in dreams, fantasies, fears and anxiety. For the industrialized society, it taught people that problems and solutions were to be found inside one's self and not in the external world. And for psychiatrists, who imported the theory and protected its esoteric language (eg. catharsis, Id, abreaction), it provided both the theory and procedures that made them distinct from, but acceptable to, their medical colleagues. As well, the decision of the American Psychoanalytic Association, in 1927, to limit the practice of psychoanalysis to medical doctors, served to further its medicalization, its professionalization and the elite status of its members as psychological specialists. By maintaining their medical identity, analysts adopted a pseudo-scientific stance and generally ignored the metaphorical, poetic and "magical" aspects that were inherent in its nature when Freud and Jung first conceived it.

The American version of psychoanalysis became preoccupied with a picture of the psyche which emphasized the "ego" and its healthy ability to control and master the conflicts and urges within the person. Basically it supported and promoted the optimistic American dream of health, wealth and happiness. The French analyst, Jacques Lacan, described the American psychoanalytic movement as offering "to the Americans to guide them towards happiness, without upsetting the autonomies, egotistical or otherwise, that pave with their non-conflictual spheres, the American Way of getting there."[22] Psychoanalysis had secured a place for itself in American culture, appearing to meet the demands for therapeutic and medical precision, to give meaning and hope for change, and to do it without challenging or upsetting the social order.

Just as psychoanalysis sought to maintain its connections with scientific medicine, psychology claimed the nature and measurement of behaviour as its domain of scientific expertise. This approach provided a subject amenable to laboratory study and of interest to business and industry. The gain for medicine and psychology was not only professional status, but social prestige, a monopoly on practice and increased affluence. What aspects of these relationships were conscious and what were unconscious is not the issue here. What is, is that both groups had aligned with dominant forces (i.e. the shapers) existing in their world and in so doing, had opened themselves to the influence of these powers (to be 'shaped).' As Brown writes: "the obvious advantages to the profession(s) notwithstanding, scientific medicine (and one can add psychology) contained within it the seeds of ultimate destruction for the profession."[23]

Fertile Soil

"We must admit that the rapid growth of psychology in America has been due to conditions of the soil as well as the vitality of the germ," said J. M. Cattell in his 1895 presidential address to the American Psychological Association.[24]

What was this ripeness? Why was the U.S. so ready to accept psychology? There were a number of factors of social, national and international dimensions. In part, America was "ripe" for all sciences whether they were natural (such as physics or biology) or social (such as psychology or political science). As Kurt Koffka observed; "Americans possessed a very high regard for science, 'accurate and earthbound' science, which produced in them, an aversion, sometimes bordering on contempt, for metaphysics that tries to escape from the welter of mere facts into a loftier realm of ideas and ideals."[25]

In the academic world, psychology had won its independence from philosophy and was becoming identified as the source of new behavioural techniques which would lead society "on its onward and upward course to human betterment." [26] By 1895, the number of psychology laboratories had grown to 24 from none in 1880, which were often funded, like medical schools, through the "wholesale philanthropy" of prominent industrialists.

Meanwhile the advent of monopolistic capitalism in which large industries swallowed up the smaller, was resulting in fewer but larger groups of workers. These employees now had the ability and the strength to object to their conditions of work, to disrupt production and cause industrial unrest. It was to psychology that industry appealed for solutions.

By the turn of the century, the dramatic increase in factory mechanisation, deplorable working conditions, and pressures to boost productivity (and thereby profit) resulted in a labour force in militant conflict with business. Initial attempts to control this situation through force (using Pinkerton police, imported strikebreakers, State militia, etc.) were generally unsuccessful and employers felt the need for more effective ways to control workers and their productivity; strategies that would come to form the specialty of "industrial psychology" (to be distinguished from the later Psychology Industry).

The first psychological strategy, and perhaps the one with the most lasting influence, was Taylorism, developed by Frederick Winslow Taylor. Taylor recognized that even "unskilled" work required specific knowledge and skill not possessed by management, thus giving employees power to control and limit production. Taylor proposed that "management remove all discretion in the work process from the workers. Under Taylorism, management divided skilled work into its elementary component parts and redistributed it among a number of less skilled workers, each of whom performed only limited tasks in ways rigidly defined by management (or indirectly defined by controls built into the machines they operate)."[27] This is perhaps most evident in the assembly line technology developed by Henry Ford.

Taylorism offered a number of advantages to business: 1) it increased the dependence of workers and the power of management, preventing workers from leaving the company and going into business for themselves, 2) it lowered the cost of labour because unskilled people could be easily trained, replacing more expensive skilled workers, 3) it allowed for easy replacement of "trouble-makers, thus weakening labour's bargaining power, and 4) it removed workers' freedom to influence production, making each worker, in Taylor's own words, "a mere automaton, a wooden man." [28] The relevance of Taylorism to the Psychology Industry is not only the forged links between psychology and industry but also the early model for the assembly-line approach to manufacturing and servicing victims which now characterizes the Psychology Industry itself.

Psychology and the Military

In the years leading up to the first World War, the procedures of psychological measurement, begun in the perception labs of Weber, Wundt and Helmholz in Germany, as well as by Galton and Binet, flourished. Psychologists, such as Cattell, began to measure all sorts of abilities and functions in order to determine human capacity and to identify individuals with disabilities. So apparently successful was the venture that both government and industry expressed interest, encouragement and funding for the development of psychological tests for military and vocational selection. Whether it was to produce good soldiers or good workers, the intention was the same: to develop the means through which the "human machine" could be made to function most efficiently. Such requests provided psychologists with a further opportunity to promote their profession and to increase their social prestige and affluence. Such opportunistic intentions are evident in the vote of the Council of the American Psychological Association, in 1917, to instruct their president

> To appoint committees from the membership of the American Psychological Association to render to the government of the United States all possible assistance with psychological problems arising from the present military emergency... American psychologists can substantially serve the government under the medical corps of the Army and Navy by examining recruits with respect especially to intellectual deficiency, psychopathic tendencies, nervous instability and inadequate self-control...[29]

Psychologists, while appearing to respond to a call for patriotism, were moving to assert themselves as essential to their society. By assuming the role of identifying and weeding out mental incompetents and disruptive individuals, psychologists were allying themselves with the stronger forces of government, industry and medicine. Walter Lippman expressed his concern at the time when he wrote of the power-hungry intelligence testers who yearned to "occupy a position of power which no intellectual has held since the collapse of theocracy;"[30] but no one heeded the threat.

For the first time, the government became actively involved in applying psychology on a mass basis to the armed forces.[31] Such an opportunity provided psychology with "an ideal laboratory" in which to study large numbers of people in a controlled environment and to develop techniques which would later prove useful to, and be used extensively by, industry. Interestingly it was from this experience, and with these tools, that the Psychological Corporation was started in 1921 by Cattell, funded by $10 shares bought by American Psychological Association members, for the purpose of promoting the application of psychology.[32]

With the shift away from the exploration of consciousness to the measurement of ability, it was a natural next step to begin to study the behaviour that was being observed and measured. E. L. Thorndike's work[33] demonstrates this shift for, although he described his efforts as the study of "animal intelligence" (adopting the popular psychological terminology of his time), he was actually introducing the study of animal behaviour.[34] In many ways what he proved through experimentation was already well known in the classical laws of association; that was that behaviour is more likely to be repeated if it leads to a positive effect or feeling (i.e. "satisfaction"). His work, however, served to demonstrate that psychology could have a focus suitable to study in a laboratory, thus giving strength to its cultural image as a science. But Thorndike did not limit his contribution to the research laboratory; he saw its application and importance "in the entire history of the management of human affairs."[35]

Despite his confident prediction of his own importance, Thorndike's work was quickly overshadowed by that of John B. Watson, often called the Father of Behaviourism.[36] Almost everyone has heard of Ivan Pavlov, the Russian physiologist, and his dogs.[37] Pavlov demonstrated that since dogs would quite naturally begin to salivate if shown food, if a bell was rung when the food was given, the sound of the bell could cause the dogs to produce saliva even when there was no food. In Pavlov's thinking, this "conditioned reflex" was the result of a physiological connection (an "arc") inside the brain. Watson, an American, unconcerned with such physiological explanations, insisted that psychology address only "the prediction and control of observable behaviour," abandoning any and all interests in mental and body states, instincts, introspection or any other "ghosts in the machine" as he called them. In contrast to the earlier focus of psychology on abilities and traits, Behaviourism saw all behaviours (which Watson called "Responses") as a result of outside "Stimuli" and therefore, susceptible to being developed, managed and controlled by external forces.[38] Watson urged psychologists to focus on "the problems of living... and to deal with matters of practical consequence, e.g. the psychology of advertising , and of testing..."[39]

When Watson experienced a sudden fall from grace in the academic community because of a sensationalized divorce, he quickly found his place in a receptive advertising industry where he remained, with success, until his retirement. "In this pursuit he had the company of A.A. Brill, who used his psychological expertise to develop advertising that encouraged women to smoke. Psychology was used by business to ensure that consumption kept pace with production."[40] It also developed a wider political affect as it became a means to influence and control various groups in society. For example, Watson applied his laboratory findings and his popular fame to such social topics as child-rearing, writing that children could be conditioned for either genius and success, or "doltishness" and failure. In contrast to the permissive, developmental approach of the psychoanalysts, he believed that it was the parents' responsibility to provide the appropriate conditions to ensure the proper upbringing [41] and, with this, anything was possible.

Behaviourism was not restricted to advertising and child care. It, and its psychologist proponents, were welcomed into the industrial scene which, after WWI, was again experiencing unprecedented labour problems. Needing to develop techniques to control this unrest, government and business looked with hope to psychology and generously funded industrial psychology programmes. Although some initial attempts focused on providing services to treat the pathology of "problem workers," they proved to be inadequate to control the situation and new approaches began to focus on ways to alter behaviour and to develop productive employee responses.

Notable amongst these was the work of Elton (George) Mayo, an Australian psychologist, brought to the U.S. by the Rockefeller Foundation. His well known research[42] at the Hawthorne Plant of the Western Electric Company, although severely flawed and later judged to be invalid, had a profound and lasting effect on industry and on the whole of applied psychology. His conclusion was that workers have an "eager desire for cooperative activity" and function better in groups, rather than as isolated individuals.[43] He believed that the "Hawthorne Effect," as it came to be known, provided conclusive evidence that "friendly supervision" led to greater productivity and less unrest without the employer having to concede any costly improvements in wages or working conditions. As a result, Mayo claimed to have discovered a new method of human control: "the power of human relations."[44]

Despite the shoddy research,[45, 46, 47] Mayo's work had two profound effects which would later spread from industry to the psychotherapeutic community; the invention of the "non-directive interviewing technique" and the genesis of the "human relations movement." Mayo taught interviewers to listen attentively without interrupting, focussing on the workers' personal situations rather than on their work grievances. This non-directive style served as a powerful "emotional release" of resentment. As well, it implied that the company had concern for the workers' feelings, and fostered a "rapport" or cooperative relationship between the workers and the company.

Although termed as "non-directive," it was blatantly controlling as it defined workers' problems as originating within themselves rather than from any common workplace issues.[48] Such an inner-directed approach was enthusiastically adopted[49] by industry and the Rockefeller and Ford Foundations generously funded Carl Rogers to refine this human relations technique, which would later, through similar use with university students, emerge as Rogerian psychotherapy.

In spite of the lack of any valid or reliable scientific basis, the philosophy of Mayo and his associates became the foundation of the "human relations movement" that would dominate industry through the 40's and 50's. In a peculiarly American way, it held the optimistic view that individuals were naturally energetic, industrious and achievement oriented. Those workers who failed to produce or who disrupted the "friendly relationship" were judged as having a unique personal problem (a psychological equivalent of the "germ theory.") It emphasised structured counselling techniques to develop positive mental attitudes rather than to solve the practical external problems, an approach that would become the basis for the humanistic psychotherapy movement of the 60's and 70's. And it created a new occupational category: interviewer/counsellor, which would, in time, lead to the growth of non-professional counsellors and psychotherapists.

Like World War I, World War II posed major problems for the U.S. and its allies who needed both to produce and maintain strong soldiers and strong workers, and to influence public opinion. Again psychology responded, not only with the traditional massive screening programs to select personnel, but also with services which relied on its experience in advertising: attitude formation, propaganda techniques and analysis, and counter intelligence. As well, it began to do something with which it was totally unfamiliar and inexperienced, to treat psychological casualties. As members of the military, psychologists studied the behaviour of soldiers under varying degrees of stress and their findings led to treatment innovations including group therapy, brief therapy, hypnosis and stress management techniques, all aimed at improving the efficiency of normal people under stress and getting soldiers back into conflict. Since these services were provided through the assistance of the National Committee for Mental Hygiene[50, 51] (funded jointly by the government and industrial foundations), many of these techniques were applied to similar problems at home among civilians and workers in industry.

A significant shift was taking place. Psychologists were beginning to treat "normal people with problems" and not just those with identifiable mental illness. The market for their services expanded significantly as they defined a much larger group as being in need of treatment. Through the efforts of William C. Menninger, a prominent industrial psychiatrist[52] and the director of the U.S. Army psychiatric program, the first version of the *Diagnostic and Statistical Manual(DSM)* was created which gave far more recognition and emphasis to the "neuroses" and behavioral problems which plagued both business and the military. By classifying problems in this way, the *DSM* further established them as being the appropriate concern and territory for the Psychology Industry.[53] It was clear that psychologists viewed therapy as a legitimate aspect of their professional role, second only to assessment.[54]

By the end of the war in 1945, psychology had become well established in identifying and treating those individuals who either failed to conform or to be productive according to the capitalistic American model. Psychologists were convinced that they had much to contribute in building the postwar world, through policy and research and through training others in applied psychology. Psychology was clearly accepting and promoting its double identity as a science and as a technological means to better the world which saw itself emerging into a victorious and optimistic future.

The Promise of Psychology

The post-war growth of psychology was comparable only to the optimistic and excited reception it received from all aspects of society. The scientism of psychology made grand promises: solutions to societal and international problems, understanding and change of individual and social behaviour, and the creation of a safer and better world by eliminating the destructive forces that had brought about the war so that war would have no place again. "If the weltanschauung of psychology changed in the two decades after World War II, it was in the strengthening of the axiom that the social world is knowable, predictable, and controllable and in the related axiom that breakthroughs in understanding the individual human mind would be basic building blocks for a better society."[55] Applied programmes of psychology were started in universities, clinical departments were created in hospitals, research funds were poured into the social sciences and government agencies were established to study mental health (e.g. the National Institute of Mental Health).[56] "The purists were a minority. Here and there they were able to keep their enclaves pure, but overall the integration between the hard- and the soft-headed came about... by the pressure of external society and fatefully, federal money. Psychology as a science and practice were married."[57] And the disparate parts of psychology began to merge and form the Psychology Industry.

Probably the most prominent aspect of post-war psychology and the most relevant to the developing Psychology Industry was the revision of behaviourial psychology by B. F. Skinner.[58] His was an exclusively descriptive form of behavioursim that was devoted to the study of observable, measurable responses and devoid of any theoretical stance. His interest was to describe and predict behaviour, not to explain it with what he called "spurious physiologizing." He had no interest in exploring the attitudes and beliefs, the dreams and fears inside the person. The individual came to be considered as an "empty-organism" or a "Black Box," of interest only for what external behaviourial responses it emitted.[59]

However, unlike Watson who thought of behaviour as being due to, and controlled by, something preceding it which caused or stimulated it, Skinner believed that behaviour was more directly related to the outcome or the effect it produced; the "Reinforcement" as he termed it. And like Thorndike, a half century earlier, he believed that those behaviours which led to satisfaction (ie. positive reinforcement) would increase in probability.

Known as "operant conditioning," Skinner's concepts became widely popular appearing in education (teacher training methods), psychiatric treatment (token economies), therapy (desensitization and behaviourial modification), and business (reinforcement scheduling). The popularity of psychoanalytic treatment evident immediately after the war, was subsumed by the behaviourists who promised quicker and surer change, regardless of personality characteristics or family upbringing.

Behaviour Modification, the applied product of behavioural psychology, created a technological foundation for a mass effect in industry and in therapy. It assumed that people can and should be made to adapt to a relatively unalterable world. Whether as children, patients or employees, they were rewarded or reinforced for behaviours which were considered to be appropriate by the teacher, psychologist, or employer. Behaviour modification seemed to be a godsend. It was cheaper, faster and more reliable in moulding new behaviour. It was easy to teach so "behaviour therapists" could be produced quickly from the pool of untrained personnel. It required no trust or rapport, or "friendliness." And it made "obedience" or "conformity" its goal, not the "insight" of psychoanalysis or the "happiness" of human relations. It was ideal for the school, the factory, the home; for the whole of a controlling society. Its popularity grew[60] and with it, grew the Psychology Industry.

Psychology was in its "hay day." Funding was generous and seemingly bottomless, training facilities were flourishing and the profession was enjoying a previously unexperienced popularity. In 1955, Fillmore Sanford, the Executive Secretary of the American Psychological Association told a Congressional commerce committee: "If the present rate of growth continues, we will have, by simple arithmetic, 60 million members (of the association) 100 years from now; and in 200 years, if we continue to grow, membership in the association will coincide exactly with membership in the human race." The prediction was wrong, but maybe not by much considering the current cultural susceptibility to psychological ideas.

If one looks solely at the rampant excitement and optimism of psychology and the generous funds flowing into the social sciences both from public and private sectors, one would assume that this was a rosy period of world order. But such was not the case. The world was caught in a terrifying "cold war" with atomic bomb testing and threatened nuclear war. There were armed hostilities in Greece, Korea and China, and a Berlin, and then a Cuban, blockade creating international concern. At home things were no happier. There were intense labour struggles, urban ghetto problems, de-segregation fights, and the tyranny of Senator Joseph McCarthy. This was, as W. H. Auden had identified it, "The Age of Anxiety" and the culture was eager for relief. Psychology responded and convinced itself and others that it held the ultimate, if not yet available, answers to peace, security, and eventual prosperity.

Curiously, however, it was from this point in time that psychology, as a science focussed on experimental research, began a rapid decline while schools of clinical and applied psychology virtually exploded. Psychology as a Science was being replaced by Psychology as an Industry. Psychologists were discovering that they could earn far more, in prestige and money, through business than they could in the university. The results of research now became the fodder for therapeutic theories and health promotion programmes.

This was already evident in the Behaviourism movement for, with the growing interest, attention and money given to it by government and industry, Behaviourism began to gain popularity within the therapy business. The empirical approach of the laboratory flowed into the consulting room where psychologists offered "scientific" treatment approaches based on the principles of classical (Pavlovian) and operant (Skinnerian) conditioning with such labels as "behaviour modification," "systematic desensitization" and "behaviour therapy."[61] Rapid and effective treatment was promised for the "anxiety neuroses" of the day which had replaced the "repressive disorders" prominent in Victorian society at the beginning of the century and central to Freud's psychoanalytic theory. Psychological treatment was now available without need for medical diagnoses ("the symptom is the disease") or stigma. As well, new and "want-to-be" psychologists were able to learn and dispense concrete and easily understandable concepts without the requirement for extensive professional training. With this new category of "behavioural therapist" a form of psychological Taylorism was beginning which would grow in the decades to come. By the middle of the 60's, the behaviourial orientation had gained wide acceptance with "scientifically-proven" results and was being promoted to mental health workers, educators and physicians. It was even suggested that the blessings of behavioural technology "may be the elimination of mental illness, crime and even war."[62]

The latter part of the 60's marked a radical change in psychology and in the nature of the Psychology Industry, in part due to economic factors and, in part, to the social and political climate. It was becoming clear that the long-term viability of the industry rested on third party recognition of psychologists as reimbursable providers of "medical" services. Through the organized lobbying activities of the professional associations, the public gained greater access to psychologists and their services.[63] Socially, the physical sciences and technology had created a more comfortable, if not happier, world to live in and had contributed a plethora of "time-saving" and "leisure-enjoying" devices. Society enjoyed wealth in leisure and money beyond anything previously experienced. However it failed to achieve the emotional and social benefits of peace, security and safety. Internationally, the threat of a nuclear holocaust hovered as the war in Vietnam demonstrated technological disregard for human life (both friend and foe). Domestically, a sense existed that people had lost any control of corporations and that these giants now controlled American society.

Just as the sudden and tragic end of the mythical Kennedy Camelot and the growing malaise of the mid-60's with the Vietnam conflict led to the emergence of the "counter-culture" of the Hippies, so a growing disappointment with traditional psychology and the tension between the theoretical and applied aspects of the profession led to a counter movement within psychology. The 50's had been a time of empire building as the social sciences held forth utopian ideals (including Skinner's own novel, *Walden Two*). The failure to meet these expectations and deal with the pervasive anxiety, and the pressure of emerging social problems created a demand for psychology to address larger social issues which it was neither prepared nor qualified to meet. Its continued fixation on a psychology of the individual meant it could not offer any effective solutions to these larger social issues.

From this discontent, a significant and vocal minority, the Hippies, emerged with their "counter culture." They challenged the values and benefits of the technological society. As Roszak stated then: "from my point of view, the counter culture, far more than merely "meriting" attention, desperately requires it, since I am at a loss to know where, besides among these dissenting young people and their heirs of the next few generations, the radical discontent and innovation can be found that might transform this disoriented civilization of ours into something a human being can identify as home."[64] The call of technology "to know" was challenged by the anthem of the hippies, "to live." For them, "the primary purpose of human existence (was) not to devise ways of piling up ever greater heaps of knowledge, but to discover ways to live from day to day that integrated the whole of our nature by way of yielding nobility of conduct, honest fellowship, and joy." [65]

A vocal therapist of this time and one who provided impetus both to the "counter culture" and to this pop philosophy of psychotherapy, was Fritz Perls. A physician and psychologist, Perls introduced Gestalt therapy to the human potential enthusiasts of the late 60's. His work positioned him at the core of the "personal growth" movement, which was by then the public outgrowth of industry's human potential movement. It was Perls who coined the Hippie term "mind fucking" to describe what he perceived as the controlling nature of psychoanalysis and other verbal therapies. Blatantly romantic, Gestalt therapy promoted the belief that within everyone is the potential for emotional stability and happiness, achievable through gestalt therapy. Optimism was for sale.

In retrospect, it is clearly evident that the machinery of technology, embedded in science and industry, was unaffected by these expressions of idealism and dissent, while the Psychology Industry responded to this as an opportunity for innovation and expansion. Three main "happenings" occurred in the psychology business at this time: 1) the technical definitions of psychology and psychotherapy were expanded to include a variety of unusual and quasi-therapeutic techniques, 2) the criteria of technical respectability was broadened so that what constituted "good" psychology became a more open question, and 3) the nature of training and certification became more vague and diffuse so that who was a "qualified" psychologist became a less legitimate question, and the therapeutic marketplace, despite licensing and certification laws, became more competitive than ever before.[66] No longer did professional psychology and psychiatry have a hold on the Psychology Industry and throughout the 70's the market became flooded with techniques ranging from Transactional Analysis, hypnosis, existential analysis,

Rolfing and Primal Therapy, to re-evaluation therapy, est, Reichian sensitiv-ity, actualization, job therapy, Esalen love massage, bioenergetics and jour-neys into consciousness.

In a move to detach and distinguish itself from its conservative and conforming scientific predecessors, psychology now promoted "growth" rather than "cure" as the ideal goal. As psychologists grasped the vast opportunities before them, they began to echo the words of Erving and Miriam Polster: "Therapy is too good to be limited to the sick." It was readily accepted, bought and paid for by "an educated public eager for some easy form of psychological salvation in which you didn't have to be sick in order to get well."[67] Gone (temporarily) was the medical view of therapy and in its place, a populist version arose in which "being in therapy" was something about which to be proud and public. As well, traditional training in psychol-ogy was no longer a prerequisite for the successful development of a psychotherapy practice. In fact, some began to argue that formal training might actually impair an individual's natural abilities for helping [68] and that it was easier and better to train therapists without worrying about their knowledge of medicine, psychology, social work or counselling. As London commented,[69] all one really needed to "establish one's own (psychology) business, and bona fides, (was) the right blend of nerve and entrepreneurial skill." Relevant personal experience ("you have to have been there yourself to help others") also became an important quality of the "good" psychologist; a belief that would spawn the growth of the self-help movement in the 80's and became an apparent requirement of the recovery therapists of the 90's.

While group treatment had existed for as long as individual psychotherapy (e.g. Mesmer's magnetic treatment of groups around a bacquette), its eco-nomic benefits (i.e. one psychologist and more patients, paying less fees per person) became obvious with the growth in demand for psychological services. Within the hippie/humanitarian concept of fellowship, the psy-chologist became "the first among equals" and enjoyed a larger income while serving more people. It was not a big step from this happy juncture of profit and productivity to the Marathon or "group intensive" which functioned as "pressure cookers" to force regression which appeared as irrational expres-sions of emotions.[70] And from this, the approach expanded to the weekend experience and the therapeutic workshops and seminars of the 80's and 90's in which a short piece of work could result in an even larger net profit for the therapist.

Like medical clinics, "growth centres" began to pop up all over the country, functioning as "the department stores of self-actualization,"[71] pro-viding therapy for the healthy. They offered one stop shopping for a variety of therapies all based on the maxim: "let it all hang out."

This "me first" form of psychotherapy was not restricted to the Left wing and Hippie groups. An establishment version of encounter group and marathon was developed and provided by psychologists employed by indus-try. Reminiscent of Mayo's human relations movement, Sensitivity or T-Groups as they were known, promoted "closeness, trust, authenticity and confrontation," with the expressed aim that "healthier executives" made better managers who could better achieve the corporate goals. All aspects of business, including education, health, the private sector and government bought into this new form of human relations. Between 1968 and 1970, the U.S. Department of Labor alone spent $1.44 million dollars to teach sensitivity to its supervisors.

It would be incorrect to assume that all of the psychology vendors at this time were frauds or charlatans or that all of the customers were gullible or naive. What is accurate is that both were willing parties, invested in their own self-interests and each seeing the other as a means to achieve these goals. The customers pursued their mythical American goals of "love," "self-actualization," "awareness" and "higher consciousness;" while the Psychology Industry built its therapeutic metropoles and merchandised "growth services."

At the 1949 Boulder Conference on Graduate Education in Clinical Psychology, Victor Raimy is quoted as having said: "Psychotherapy is an undefined technique applied to unspecified cases with unpredictable results. For this technique, rigorous training is required." [72] By the end of the 70's not much had changed when Herink reported that the number of name brands of psychotherapy exceeded 250 [73] and generally the best evidence of their effectiveness lay in what Strupp identified as "our deep conviction that a sizable number of patients have benefitted." [74]

These subjective, sometimes poorly articulated and generally nonestablishment forms of psychology might have continued for generations were it not for changes occurring in the psychology world and within its larger social context. As predicted by the American Psychological Association in the 50's, the general popularity of psychology had grown exponentially so that psychotherapies and psychotherapists had begun to aggressively compete for market share. No longer was there any shortage of psychologists. They existed in every flavour and size, in all of the affluent geographical areas. At the same time, significant economic changes were occurring in society. Politically, the 60's boom in health care and social welfare spending came to an end as medical costs began to exceed all budgets. In Canada, a universal health care system had been introduced in the 60's and the U.S. government had begun to explore creation of its own National Health Insurance program. The inflation of the 70's had lead to wage and price controls and the eventual restructuring and down-sizing of many aspects of industry in what would come to be called the "post-industrial society."

With the growth of private health insurance coverage and with possible national health insurance inclusion for out-patient psychotherapy, the insurers and the legislators sought greater assurance that their dollars were being, or would be, well spent. They wanted to know that the right problems and the right patients were being treated by the right therapies for the right outcomes. And it was perfectly understandable that, as practitioners and business people, psychologists wanted to be included in any and all the insurance schemes. In this merging of economic interests, private business interests and the government, [75] they began to play a powerful role in the shaping of the future of the Psychology Industry in the United States and Canada.

Four important trends developed that contributed to the "retooling" of psychology into what would become the "victim industry:"
1) Responsibility to ensure efficiency and effectiveness of services.
2) Move towards "remedicalization."
3) Promotion of certification and licensing programs.
4) Consumer driven economy.

Each of these had significant influence on the restructuring of the Psychology Industry in the late 80's and 90's, as briefly described below and addressed in more detail in the following chapters.

Demonstrated Effectiveness

Initially, private health insurance plans and health maintenance organizations (HMOs) did not include benefits for psychological care and most purveyors of psychological services in the 50's and 60's either worked for an institutional salary or on a direct fee-for-service basis. However, the HMO Act of 1973 specifically required and provided funds for mental health services including out-patient and substance abuse treatment. Intended to control spiralling health costs, the HMO's were able to slow down the inflationary increases of medicine and surgery. However, mental health costs went out of control, with in-patient costs accelerating at three times the inflation rate of medical and surgical costs.[76] The response of the proprietary managed health organizations has been to impose requirements on psychologists to be accountable for their treatment and for demonstrable cost effectiveness.

This demand has had several effects. It re-emphasized the need for clinical research, and it created two sectors within the Psychology Industry; those who accept the concept of managed care (of people outside of the profession telling them what they could and could not do), and those who oppose being managed by a third party and consequently seek alternative income sources.

The immediate problem facing psychotherapy researchers was that most of the problems being presented to psychologists, and many of the outcomes expected, did not fit any current psychological classification that could be measured. "Problems" included existential issues such as the lack of meaning in life, disaffection with life circumstances, or general unhappiness, while others, free of symptoms, had recreational, educational or religious goals of self-development. As Morris Parloff of the National Institute of Mental Health noted in a report to the Society of Psychotherapy Research:

> The psychotherapist's classical efforts to aid the disturbed, the disturbing and the vulnerable (poor, young, aged, and oppressed) have been extended to include the mildly disturbed or the frankly undisturbed. The goal of "normalizing" has merged with the aim of "optimizing." The potential consumer is not dissuaded from the expectation of self-actualization, growth, and an ever-closer approximation of self-perfection.[77]

With this wide range of potential goals, research had to rely on the therapies not only to provide the treatment but also to define the desired

CALVIN AND HOBBES

outcome, and a psychological treatment was considered effective if it achieved its own specific goals. But how should these goals be determined? As Strupp and Hadley identified, different parts of society have differing views of the desired outcome of therapy even when it is addressing generally accepted psychological problems.[78] First, the individual client "wishes first and foremost to be happy, to feel content"[79] and thus defines goals in terms of highly subjective feelings of well-being. Psychotherapists, on the other hand, working within a specific theoretical framework, refer to some model of a "healthy" personality (eg. one who expresses emotions "openly," or has "rational" thoughts) to determine and defend their desired outcomes. A third interested party, the general society including family, friends, colleagues and the insurers, on the other hand, define their desired outcome "in terms of behaviourial stability, predictability, and conformity to the social code"[80] and are concerned with prevailing standards of sanctioned behaviour.

Despite such divergent reference points and such vested interests, outcome evaluation and cost-benefit studies were conducted leading to the general conclusion that psychotherapy was somewhat effective with some of the clients some of the time. For instance, Bergin reported that in a study of nearly 1000 therapy cases, 65% of those in therapy were improved compared to 40% who never saw a therapist, while 10% in treatment deteriorated as compared to only 5% of those not treated.[81] Parloff reported that nearly 500 rigorously controlled studies showed that "all forms of psychological treatment ... are comparably effective in producing therapeutic benefits with particular disorders (such as anxiety, fears, sexual problems, reactions to life crises and problems of everyday life)."[82]

These and other studies lead Parloff to comment that "the research evidence ... has not met the needs of the policy makers and does not greatly enhance the credibility of the field of psychotherapy."[83] Research had failed to show that psychotherapy was effective and safe, and of significant benefit to its consumers. Subsequent attempts to demonstrate the effectiveness of specific therapies with selected problems (known as "prescriptionism," differential therapeutics or treatment matching) have been similarly unsuccessful.[84]

In order to justify the continuing practice of psychotherapy in light of these discouraging results, the Psychology Industry has averted attention to the therapeutic alliance and the role (and power) of the psychologist as being the crucial determinants of effectiveness. Rather than emphasizing the theoretical approach or technique, the psychologist/patient relationship and interaction are being described as central to positive change, leading to the conclusion, yet unsupported, that either some psychologists are more powerful than others (i.e. better able to sell change) or that a psychologist/patient match-making ought to occur so that psychologists select the patients with whom they are better suited to work[85] (i.e. those that will buy what they say).

Remedicalization

An alternative way to stem the criticism and gain the needed credibility was "to scramble for protection under the powerful umbrella of medicine."[86] Insurance carriers had the tradition of basing reimbursement decisions on the advice, pronouncements, and testimony of the professions regarding what was considered "reasonable, necessary and standard" clinical practice. Psychology hoped that, if it could associate itself with the strong and established profession of medicine, it could, by alliance or by default, gain the credibility it could not gather through research.

This movement was most evident in the re-acquisition of medical concepts and terminology, the attempt to redefine physical illnesses in emotional and psychological language, and the attempt to have psychologists either defined as "physicians" by such regulations as the Medicare Statute or as providing "equivalent services" as physicians.[87]

In contrast to the anti-medical stance of the 60's and early 70's, the Psychology Industry began to model itself along the lines of traditional medicine. Problems became "psychopathology" or diseases (eg. the "epidemic of depression"), difficulties became "disorders" or "syndromes," individuals again became "patients," assessments became "diagnoses," and outcomes were now "prognoses." A significant contribution to this movement was the official introduction in 1980 of *DSM-III*, which the American Journal of Psychiatry described as having served to augment the "general trend toward the remedicalization of the phenomena of psychiatry." In an editorial in the issue discussing the *DSM-III* and psychotherapy, Chodoff[88] concluded by acknowledging "the other purposes (beyond diagnosis) the diagnostic manual serves (are) to provide labels for hospital, third party, and other records, and to supply data for research into the prevalence and outcome of psychiatric conditions no matter how they are treated." However, studies in the mid-70's [89] showed the overall unreliability of these psychiatric labels, a conclusion that was supported by Chodoff when he noted that "treatment tends to give rise to a personality diagnosis." Thus, if the *DSM* is unreliable and diagnostically imprecise, it can only be concluded that the major effect of *DSM-III* was its provision of billing codes and the consequent absorption of mental health problems into the medical health care (and insurance) system.

Not only did psychology adopt medical terminology, it also tried to co-opt medical patients and their business, with political statements such as "60% or more of the physician visits are made by patients who demonstrate an emotional, rather than an organic, etiology for their physical symptoms."[90]

Based on a modified Cartesian Mind/Body view, psychology held that not only was the mind involved in "functional" conditions, that is, those that served a useful purpose in the person's psychological life and were not caused by physiological alterations, but that the mind or psyche was somewhat responsible for, and thus able to affect, organic illnesses. This approach not only engendered "health psychology" departments in hospitals but generated an abundant array of entrepreneurial psychotherapy ventures to treat cancer, heart disease, orthopaedic disorders, PMS, etc. Nicholas Cummings, an American Psychological Association president, stated, without providing supporting evidence, that "psychotherapy is a viable form of intervention that can alleviate problems in living and lessen disease, and it belongs in any comprehensive health system." [91]

This view of psychology as an essential health service was not unanimously supported and a debate developed within the ranks of psychology as well as with third-party insurers and the government, over whether a National Health Insurance scheme in the United States or, alternatively, managed health care organizations could afford to include out-patient psychotherapy. Prominent psychologists lined up on both sides with the delineating factor being whether or not they were clinicians with a vested interest. Those who were opposed[92] based their argument on the lack of sufficient research data to show the effectiveness of psychotherapy, the lack of financial controls and monitoring, the consequent subsidizing of the rich (the majority of out-patient psychotherapy users) at the expense of the poorer tax payers, and the overall doubtful value of it to the health of the nation.[93]

Body oriented medicine and mind oriented psychology made "strange bed-fellows" and, by and large, this relationship didn't work. As the monies for health care became less available, the fight for the dollars increased, facilities began to turn towards "essential" medical and psychiatric services and psychologists failed to get the endorsement and the open access to funds which they sought. Some psychologists, often the more junior or less qualified, have accepted the move to managed care, while the Psychology Industry as a whole has opposed it. Despite arguments about patients' needs and professional control, the underlying issues are ones of power, control and money, and the Psychology Industry in response to the "health care crisis" is actively seeking alternative sources of funding within the legal profession, the justice system and with the always desirable, first party (patient) payments.

Certification and Regulation

To compete in these arenas, psychologists need credentials. Whether it is to convince a lawyer, a court, a business or the public that they are qualified, or to compete against each other for private patients, psychologists need, and thus have created, a plethora of systems to certify and licence themselves and each other.

Historically, licensing of professionals, such as physicians, accountants and lawyers, was instituted out of concern for public interest to assure minimal competence in the profession. The degrees, licences or credentials basically said that the individuals could be trusted to approach their professional work with intelligence, integrity, and skill, whatever they did. These certificates distinguished those individuals that the profession thought to be capable, from the untrained or unethical practitioners and quacks, and gave them respectability. At the same time, certification served to promote the services of the members, the authorized providers.

Physicians and licensed psychologists already had this distinction. But how were those outside of these professions, to gain recognition if they couldn't fit under one of these "umbrellas"? One way was to establish their own qualifying boards and credential their own members, thus distinguishing themselves from those outside of their orientation or theoretical approach. The 80's saw a boom in these programs which, under the guise of protecting the public, served the economic interests of the Psychology Industry. With them, not only did the individual practitioner receive some credential that suggested, though certainly did not ensure, competence, but also those who were more experienced in these therapies now had a second source of income: the training and supervision of candidates. Not all of these programmes were scams for some provided extensive training as an alternative to the "dead" academic training programs existing within many of the universities. However, this credentialing movement did spawn a large number of "diploma-by-mail" and "pay-me-and-I'll-say-you're-good" schemes.

If alternative therapies and psychology in general could not achieve public insurance subsidy, then at least they could give themselves the appearance of being professional. The use of specific terms such as: "Doctor," "Certified," "Board Approved," and "Registered," gave the impression to potential consumers and the public that the individuals were highly qualified, "government-approved" experts in their fields, thereby improving their position in the private business sector. Some associations were even able to persuade private insurers to recognize their members as "health care providers," opening the avenue to insured out-patient psychology services.

Consumerism

The 80's began with a time of affluence in that segment of society most amenable to psychological services. The conservative, Right-facing, individualistic form of Reaganomics provided the social climate for strident patriotic and tribal values, for the repression of open questioning, and for individual and national isolation and self-interest. "A civilization (existed) in which, as never before, man (was) preoccupied with Self."[94] The right to moral equality promoted in the 60's had been transformed by that generation, now in their 40's, into a philosophy of individual achievement and acquisition, and any failure to achieve and acquire was interpreted as having a psychological cause. As the decade progressed, the economy faltered, unemployment increased, the national debt became a public burden and, for the first time in the country's history, a generation existed which would experience a lower standard of living than its parents. People, optimistically expecting prosperity and happiness, became poorer and dissatisfied. They were angry at previous generations and authorities that had overspent and overused resources resulting in depletion, pollution and higher costs. It seemed as if all the problems were due to what others had done in the past. Present disappointments and hardships were the result of others' past actions. People wanted to be cured of their individual unhappiness and to be assured of their "right" to wealth and success. And people began to see themselves as victims.

To coin Cattell's words from almost a hundred years earlier, America was ripe for a new psychology. And the Psychology Industry, as always reactive to "the noisy yammering of the secular world,"[95] saw this as a business opportunity, and it responded by refocussing its attention and retooling its technology. It began to see people as victims experiencing the consequences of past events rather than as individuals struggling with intrapsychic impulses, or striving to develop positive attitudes. It reinterpreted illness as the result of traumatic events rather than of negative thoughts and behaviours. It defined "regression" (going back into the past) and "recovery" as the primary tools of the new technology.

Among the early contributors to this were Alice Miller[96] and Jeffrey Masson.[97] Miller, a Swiss psychoanalytic psychiatrist, argued in a series of publications, that adult problems of self-preoccupation (narcissism) and immoral behaviour (psychopathic personality; her example being Adolf Hitler) were the results of actual child-rearing practices. Unlike Freud, who basically considered memories of early childhood to be a mixture of fact and fantasy, she argued that those things that patients reported as early memories were real events and exterior to the child; that they were due to things the mother (and father) actually had done. (She later presented her own "uncovered" experience of early sexual abuse as support for this belief, consistent with the "you have to have been there to know what we mean" form of therapist training found in recovery therapies.) Masson, entrusted with the Freud archives, broke the trust and wrote that Freud had developed the theory of infantile sexual fantasy solely as a means to defend his colleague and long-time friend, Wilhelm Fliess, from charges of sexually abusing a young girl. These authors and others[98] gave rise to the popular and eagerly accepted concept of the "Inner Child," an intrapsychic individual who had been "injured" by early childhood trauma which was repressed from memory.

This concept of trauma and repression and its adaptations served to meet the pressing needs of society and thus, indirectly, of the Psychology Industry. It provided a simple and sellable explanation as to "why" people were unhappy or unsuccessful, and it placed the responsibility (the blame) for this outside of the individuals and upon others: those who generally appeared happier, wealthier, or in a better life position. Through this belief, a broad new market for the Psychology Industry was created, one which could be generalized to explain most "problems" in life and which could be easily marketed and sold to society.

Even as Miller and Masson were publishing their books, various forms of victim-making therapies began to appear. Probably the first significant one involved the diagnosis and treatment of Multiple Personality Disorders (MPD), later expanded and relabelled Dissociative Identity Disorder (DID). Although as a psychological concept, MPD had existed for many years, the frequency of its occurrence in its true form, was considered to be rare.[99] In the 1970's, the first reports connecting MPD to childhood trauma began to appear in single case histories. "Among the first and best-known was the case of Sybil, treated by Cornelia Wilbur and dramatized by Schrieber"[100] in her book *Sybil*. The *New York Times* ranked *Sybil* among the ten best-selling nonfiction books of the year and it was quickly turned into a Hollywood movie. Schrieber was deluged with letters from women thanking her for helping them understand that they were "multiples." It was not long before psychologists, in what Spiegel referred to as "a whole new cult, a whole new wave of hysteria,"[101] began finding cases of multiple personality among their patients.[102] Quickly, psychologists began to report higher and higher frequencies of this diagnosis, eventually claiming occurrences of one person in every hundred in the general population with much higher incidence rates in groups such as sexual abuse survivors, hospital in-patients and chemically dependent individuals.[103] They attributed the cause to early childhood trauma, usually sexual in nature, and "repressed" from memory. Quickly MPD became accepted as the explanation for many unusual or unacceptable behaviours or for the feelings of disorientation or being out of sorts (eg. "it's just not like me to..."). And it emerged as a legal defense against criminal charges.[104] It provided a simple and novel explanation, an exciting and different story. And because its supporters included physicians and psychologists, the public assumed it must be true.

This new "epidemic" of MPD gave rise to a host of new treatments and services which involved the acceptance of the psychologist's diagnosis[105] and the psychological "uncovering" of these repressed memories of trauma. In addition to providing direct service to individuals, it introduced psychologists into the legal arena in a way that had never been experienced before as clients began to report being *victims of* child abuse, sexual abuse, cult abuse and even ritual satanic abuse. Psychology was finally gaining the exposure and status that it had been seeking, but it was gaining this in association with the legal profession rather than medicine. Whereas the medical profession had been unwilling to acknowledge the expertise of non-medical and untrained psychologists, lawyers were eager to find "experts" who could be employed to support their clients' cases.

But MPD was not the only victim-making technology of this retooled Psychology Industry. Other formats quickly emerged in the latter part of the 80's, but all with the underlying framework which defined the patient as "Good" but damaged by past trauma and therefore a victim in need of the psychologist's nurturing help, and someone else as "Bad," a perpetrator, an enemy. Whether it was an alcoholic parent, an abusive spouse, a perverted teacher or doctor, a rude store clerk or an annoying or harassing colleague, the patient was always the innocent victim; the Other, the malevolent cause.

And with the proliferation of untrained and poorly educated members of the Psychology Industry, the victim-making approach gained popularity. It was simple to understand, easy to sell and similar personal experience provided the needed qualification. By aligning with the victims, accepting their reports as true and not confronting or identifying anything negative in them, victim-making psychologists became popular. Not only did they explain patients' behaviours and feelings, they supported them and defended their right to compensation in court by providing "expert opinion" based on their clinical experience and subjective beliefs. Psychologists appeared on television and in the media to explain social phenomena, political events and criminal behaviours. Using the *DSM III* diagnoses such as Post Traumatic Stress Disorder, they recast "acts of God" (eg. hurricanes and floods), acts of war (eg. WWII and Bosnia) and acts of foolishness as psychological events, creating victims of trauma in need of the services of the Psychology Industry.

In looking back over the past 100 years, one finds cause to wonder how the psychology of William James, rich with a sense of "soul," and that of Freud and Jung with its wealth of internal life, could end up in what one American Psychological Association president called the psychological version of the fast food industry with its simplistic, mechanistic view of life. One is reminded of Saul Bellow's comic novel, *Herzog*, in which an academic, realizing the ridiculousness of his efforts to find meaning in his life after his wife leaves him for another man, writes: "What this country needs is a good five-cent synthesis."

This is what the Psychology Industry now offers to the public. In striving to secure status and position in society, psychology has surrendered its inquisitiveness, its complexity and its integrity, as well as its soul, in exchange for a simplistic, but more easily marketable, "five-cent synthesis." In doing so it has stolen from, but tossed aside, the contextual wealth of the works of Freud and Jung, of Watson and Skinner, and of many other pioneers of the profession.

Starting with Watson and early Behaviourism, the Psychology Industry has taken the idea that for every effect there is a stimulus and for every problem there must be a cause outside of the person. But, discarding their caution about the subjectivity of looking inside the Black Box, it claims to know what is inside the person's mind. Calling the Black Box the "unconscious," and defining the unconscious as the receptacle of traumatic memories and the continuing stimulus or cause of problems, it claims access to both the problem and the solution. To paraphrase Freud, the damaged child becomes the father of the dysfunctional man (or, more often, the dysfunctional woman). Thus, the Psychology Industry's manufacturing process involves looking for the earlier traumatic events which have resulted in a malfunctioning unconscious (or damaged Inner Child) which is the cause of whatever problems people have or think they have and which must be uncovered in order for them to recover — to survive, thrive, and have it all.

It is important to note that the Psychology Industry chooses to ignore Freud's unconscious and Skinner's operant conditioning. It refuses to acknowledge that the unconscious is far more complicated than just a mental container full of horrible memories, as it handles and manages wishes and fantasies, dreams and nightmares; for the unconscious deals in the imaginary as much as the real. In doing this, the Psychology Industry holds a blind eye to the fact that everyone constructs his or her own individual and subjective perspective on life and that "the clinical reconstruction of early childhood experience deals with the subject's present view *about* his past, and not with the discovery of archeological artifacts that have been buried."[106]

As well, the Psychology Industry disregards the behavioural principle that events have reinforcements as well as stimuli. It neglects to consider the variety of possible rewards that may foster and encourage victim thinking and victim acting on the part of the person, and victim-making on the part of the psychologist. To ignore these reinforcers may be advantageous and profitable to psychologists as it maintains the person as victim, but it defeats the supposed intention of psychology, that is for people to change, becoming more (rather than less) independent and functional.

If these shocking presumptions were not an actual description of the current state of the Psychology Industry, they might be laughable. But regrettably, this is the simplistic theory applied by thousands of therapists and accepted by tens of thousands of unhappy people who naively trust psychology to be scientific and objective, to be optimistic and positive, and to be caring and other-oriented.

★ ★ ★

Reviewing the parallel history in this way is not meant to imply the existence of an evil conspiracy or to suggest that psychology has been consciously designed to serve business interests and to control the minds of the public. Nor does it suggest that it is inherently wrong to desire money, or to seek affluence, prestige and social status. However, as history demonstrates, psychologists, in the pursuit of their own goals of happiness and success, have done so at great expense to society and through the denial of their own profession's scientific foundation. Torrey once described psychology as "the world's second oldest profession, remarkably similar to the first. Both involve a contract (implicit or explicit) between a specialist and a client for a service, and for this service a fee is paid."[107] Both professions shape themselves and their services to fit the wishes and feelings of their clients, to make them feel better in body or in mind, but the underlying goal is to do what ever has to be done in order to make a living. "Give the customer what he wants" is the motto, whether it is the pleasure of sex, the benefits of strong workers and soldiers, the thrill of self-actualization, or the blamelessness of victimhood. In this liaison, American society has abandoned its moral and cultural tradition while psychology has lost its soul and neglected, even scorned, its own scientific foundation. Psychology has failed to see how it changes itself in response to the wishes and fantasies of its client. Psychologists have overlooked the influence of social and financial rewards on their own thinking and actions and failed to notice that, in pursuing their own goals, they have conformed to the common ideology, the Zeitgeist.

Endnotes

1. One exception worth reading is: Herman, Ellen. *The Romance of American Psychology: Political Culture in the Age of Experts.* Berkeley, CA: University of California Press, 1995.

2. Schultz, Duane P. *A History of Modern Psychology.* New York: Academic Press, 1969. p. 10.

3. "Social responsibilities of psychologists" in May, Rollo. *Psychology and the Human Dilemma* New York: Norton, 1967.

4. Nisbet, Robert. *History of The Idea of Progress.* New York: Basic Books, 1979. p.323.

5. Sarason, Seymour B. *Psychology Misdirected.* New York: The Free Press, 1981. p.154.

6. Galton, Francis. *Hereditary Genius.* London: Macmillan, 1869.

7. Galton was especially disparaging of Jews, calling them "specialized for a parasitical existence upon other nations" and questioning whether "they are capable of fulfilling the varied duties of a civilized nation by themselves." Torrey, E. Fuller. *Freudian Fraud: The malignant effect of Freud's theory on American thought and culture.* New York: HarperCollins, 1993. p.42.

8. The hereditarians' belief that genes are the crucial determinants of human behaviour had been connected to a belief in the inequality of humankind. This included political inequity, a conclusion that Galton himself had clearly expressed. "The average citizen is too base for the everyday work of modern civilization" and all citizens are therefore not "equally capable of voting." The inequality also carried with it social consequences which Galton made explicit: Lower class citizens should be treated with kindness only "so long as they maintained celibacy," but if they "continued to procreate children, inferior in moral, intellectual and physical qualities, it is easy to believe that the time may come when such persons would be considered as enemies to the State and to have forfeited all claims to kindness." Torrey, 1993. p. 56.

9. See Peter Gay, *The Bourgeois Experience, Victoria to Freud.* New York: W. W. Norton, 1993.

10. Which is still in operation as the Galton Laboratory, University College, Wolfson House, 4 Stephenson Way, London, NW1 2HE.

11. Herrnstein, Richard J. and Murray, Charles. *The Bell Curve: Intelligence and Class Structure in American Life.* New York: The Free Press, 1994. p. 5 (Holmes quote: *Buck v. Bell*, 1927).

12. Binet's work, along with Theodore Simon, led to the construction of the first intelligence scale, the precursor of the Stanford-Binet Intelligence Scale, the best known and most researched individual intelligence test.

13. Sarason. *Psychology Misdirected.* p.74.

14. Herrnstein and Murray wrote: "... the use of tests endured and grew because society's largest institutions — schools, military forces, industries, governments — depend significantly on measurable individual differences." p.6.

15. Sarason. *Psychology Misdirected.* p.84.

16. Brown, E. Richard. *Rockefeller Medicine Men: Medicine & Capitalism in America.* Berkeley, CA: University of California Press, 1979. p.62-63.

17. See for example Oppenheim, Janet. *"Shattered Nerves": Doctors, Patients, and Depression in Victorian England.* Oxford: Oxford University Press, 1991.

18. Frederick Nietzsche had written "every extension of knowledge arises from making conscious the unconscious."

19. G. Stanley Hall to Sigmund Freud, October 7, 1909, Clark University Papers. Cited in Turkle, Sherry. *Psychoanalytic Politics: Freud's French Revolution* New York: Basic Books, 1978. p.30

20. Turkle. *Psychoanalytic Politics.* p.31.

21. Ibid. p.7.

22. Jacques Lacan, "The Direction of the Treatment," in *Ecrits: A Selection*, Alan Sheridan (trans.), New York: W.W. Norton and Co., 1977. p.231.

23. Brown. *Rockefeller Medecine Men,* p.73.

24. Ironically, an APA Award for lifetime scientific contribution to be given to Cattell in 1997 was withdrawn after attention was drawn to his racist and antisemitic writings notably in the

1930's, which accepted and endorsed eugenics. With an arrogant prejudice, the presumed ability to judge 'good' from 'bad', the Psychology Industry now condemns that which it once espoused.

25. Koffka, Kurt. *Principles of Gestalt Psychology*. New York: Harcourt, Brace, Jovanovich, 1935. p.18.

26. In Germany, "there is scarcely an engineering college... without its elaborately equipped psychotechnical laboratory. Governmental agencies have been active. The tramway companies, the state railways, the great steel works, the dye industries and many factories have their own psychological laboratories..." Bingham, W.V. "Management's concern with research in industrial psychology." *Harvard Business Review*, 1931,10(1), p.52.

27. Ralph, Diana. *Work and Madness: The Rise of Community Psychiatry*. Montreal: Black Rose Books, 1983. p. 63.

28. Taylor, F. W. *The Principles of Scientific Management*. New York: W.W. Norton, 1967. p.125.

29. R. M. Yerkes. "Psychology in relation to the war." In E. R. Hilgard (ed.) *American Psychology in Historical Perspective*. It is interesting to note that Yerkes, the American Psychological Association president at that time, was a major in the Sanitary Corp, as the Medical Corp was restricted to medical personnel only.

30. Lippmann, Walter. "A future for the tests." *New Republic*. November 29, 1922. p.10.

31. Giberson, L.G. "Industrial psychiatry: A wartime survey." *The Medical Clinics of North America,* 1942, 26. p.1088.

32. The Psychological Corporation continues to this day as one of the largest providers of psychological tests for use in industry, education and clinical treatment.

33. Thorndike, Edward Lee. *Animal Intelligence: Experimental Studies*. New York: Macmillan, 1911.

34. Despite his interest in animal behaviour, he continued his interest in mental measurement; *Introduction to the Theory of Mental and Social Measurement* (1904) and *The Measurement of Intelligence* (1927), and he applied his work with animals to the human educational experience; *Educational Psychology* (1903).

35. Thorndike. *Animal Intelligence: Experimental Studies*. p.244. See also *Human Nature and the Social Order*. New York: Macmillan, 1940.

36. *Behaviorism* (Chicago: University of Chicago Press, 1925, revised 1930), was written for the popular market after Watson was forced to leave Johns Hopkins University.

37. Pavlov, Ivan. *Conditioned Reflexes: An Investigation of the Physiological activity of the Cerebral Cortex*. New York: Dover Press. (English translation, 1927.)

38. *Psychology From the Standpoint of a Behaviourist* (1919) explained how the principles of behaviour derived from animal studies could be applied to man.

39. Reisman, J. *A History of Clinical Psychology*. New York: Irvington, 1976. p. 134.

40. Cushman, Philip. "Psychotherapy to 1992: A historically situated interpretation." In *History of Psychotherapy: A Century of Change*. Donald K. Freedheim (ed.) Washington, D.C.: American Psychological Association, 1992.

41. *Psychological Care of the Infant and Child* (1928) "There is a sensible way of treating children: treat them as though they were young adults. Never hug or kiss them, never let them sit on your lap. If you must, kiss them once on the forehead when they say good-night. Shake hands with them in the morning. Let them learn to overcome difficulties from the moment of birth."

42. *The Human Problems of an Industrial Civilization* (1933) and *The Social Problems of an Industrial Civilization* (1945).

43. Other conclusions of his were that work is group activity, and that a sense of belongingness is more important in determining morale than are physical conditions.

44. See Roesthlisberger, F.J. *Management and Morale*. Cambridge, Mass: Harvard University Press, 1941. p.16.

45. Data which supposedly demonstrated the Hawthorne effect were based on an unrepresentative sample of only five workers, and two of those were replaced eight months into the experiment, when their productivity failed to increase, by workers whose productivity was from

the start (before any exposure to "friendly supervision") much higher than any of the remaining subjects. See: Ralph. *Work and Madness.* p. 76.

46. Carey, A. "The Hawthorne studies: A radical criticism." *American Sociological Review,* 1967, 32(3). pp.403-416; Landsberger, H.A. *Hawthorne Revisited.* Ithaca, N.Y.: Cornell University Press, 1958; Sykes, A.J.M. "Economics interests and the Hawthornes researches." *Human Relations.* 1965, 18. pp.253-263.

47. Reanalysis of Mayo's own data actually indicated that the " 'friendliness' of the supervision... was probably as much an effect as a cause of increased productivity" and the greatest increases in productivity occurred in response to pay incentives. Ralph, *Work and Madness.* p.77, citing Bramel, D. and Friend, R. "Human Relations in Industry: The Famous Hawthorne Experiments." Unpublished paper, State University of New York at Stony Brook, 1978.

48. This co-opting power is illustrated by Marcuse from an example of Mayo's associates: "A worker 'B' makes the general statement that the piece rates on his job are too low. The interview reveals that his wife is in hospital and that he is worried about the doctor bills he has incurred. In this case the latent content of the complaint consists of the fact that B's present earnings, due to his wife's illness, are insufficient to meet his current financial obligations." Roethlisberger, F.J. and Dickson, W.J. *Management and the Worker: An Account of a Research Program Conducted by the Western Electric Company, Hawthorne Works, Chicago.* Cambridge, Mass: Harvard University Press, 1939, p.267.

49. "Mayo and his associates organized a massive 'personnel counselling' program at the Hawthorne plant which interviewed 20,000 employees in the first two years alone of its 14 year operation." Ralph. *Work and Madness.* p.78.

50. The National Committee for Mental Hygiene began as a low budget lobby group for preventive psychiatry and reform of insane asylums. However, with spreading industrial strikes during WWI private philanthropies, including the Rockefeller Foundation, began providing large funding to it and it leapt in prominence and influence. A spokesman for the national Committee explained its philosophy: "Industrial unrest to a large degree means bad mental hygiene... mental hygiene has a message also for those who consider themselves quite normal, for by its aims, the man who is fifty per cent efficient can make himself seventy per cent efficient." Bromberg, W. *The Mind of Man.* New York: Harper and Brothers, 1937, p.217. And during WWII, it worked with government agencies to set up services to promote "citizen morale" and to treat civilian employees. See Ralph. *Work and Madness.* p.88.

51. The National Committee for Mental Hygiene officially founded on February 19, 1909, amalgamated Freud's theory of human behaviour with ideals of social reform and functioned as a major vehicle for the synthesis of the two in America. Torrey, E. Fuller. *Freudian Fraud: The malignant effect of Freud's theory on American thought and culture.* New York: HarperCollins, 1993. p. 21.

52. Management began hiring psychiatrists in industry as early as 1915 specifically to control "these grudge-bearers, agitators, drinkers, fighters and lazy persons" who threatened profits. Southard, E.E. "The modern specialist in unrest: A place for the psychiatrist." *Mental Hygiene,* 1920(A), 4, 557.

53. As Menninger (1963) noted, the history of psychiatry is largely a history of "the urge to classify," an "urge" exemplified by his 70 page appendix of classification systems proposed in the interval from 2600 B.C. to 1959 A.D.) Despite critical data and damning comments to the contrary, by the early 60's this diagnostic system had been generally accepted in mental health practice and journals were filled with articles discussing personality traits, biochemical characteristics and treatment responses of people described in these terms. (C. T. Dineen, "A Study of Diagnostic Decision Making in Psychiatry," Unpublished Doctoral Dissertation, University of Saskatchewan, 1975, p.4.)

54. Hutt, M.T. and Milton, E.O. "An analysis of duties performed by clinical psychologists in the army." *American Psychologist,* 1947, 2, pp.52-56.

55. Kessen, W. "The American Child and Other Cultural Inventions." *American Psychologist,* 34(10), 1979, p. 820.

56. "Industrial and military influence dominated the formation of the NIMH, ...and both business and government invested heavily in research to develop methods to treat large masses of people cheaply... Between 1948 and 1960, NIMH's budget increased almost 15-fold, from $4.5 million to $67.4 million." Ralph. *Work and Madness* p.96 and 101.

57. Sarason. *Psychology Misdirected.* p.34.

58. The writings of B. F. Skinner include: *Walden Two*. New York: Macmillan, 1948; *Science and Human Behavior*. New York: Macmillan, 1953; *Beyond Freedom and Dignity*, New York: Alfred A. Knopf, 1971; *Cumulative Record: A Selection of Papers*. New York: Appleton-Century-Crofts, 1972; and *Reflections on Behaviorism and Society*. Engelewood Cliffs, NJ: Prentice-Hall, 1978.

59. "Black Box" is a term derived from physics where it was used to stand for a model of the functioning of any complex system based on the hypothesizing of constructs, mechanisms and procedures internal to the system. The basic notion is that when one cannot know precisely what is inside a system causing it to function in the way it does, one treats it as though it were an impenetrable "black box" and makes inductive interpretations about its internal properties. The black box then becomes a model of the system and a representation of it that can, in theory, account for how the system functions given the various inputs to it and the observed outputs from it. The black box is never considered to be empty; it is populated, often richly, with structures, constructs, operations and the like. Behaviourists , with an aversion to hypothesized internal mechanisms, misuse the original meaning of this term. (Reker, Arthur. *Dictionary of Psychology*. New York: Penguin, 1985)

60. In 1957, the NIMH committed 8% of its "psychosocial" treatment research to behaviour modification, but by 1973 that share had grown to 55% (over half of the whole budget). Segal, J. (ed.) *Research in the Service of Mental Health*. Rockville, MD: National Institute of Mental Health, 1975. p.329.

61. Such as Joseph Wolpe's *Psychotherapy by Reciprocal Inhibition* (1958) and Hans Eysenck's *Behaviour Therapy and the Neuroses* (1960).

62. London, Perry. *Behaviour Control* (2nd edit.). New York: New American Library, 1977. p.5.

63. VandenBos, Gary R., Cummings, Nicholas A. and DeLeon, Patrick H. A century of psychotherapy: Economic and environmental influences. In *History of Psychotherapy: A Century of Change*. p.90.

64. Roszak, Theodore. *The Making of a Counter Culture; Reflections on the Technocratic Society and its Youthful Opposition*. Garden City, NY: Anchor Books, 1969. p.xii-xiii.

65. Ibid. p.233.

66. London, Perry. "The Psychotherapy Boom; From the Long Couch for the Sick to the Push Button for the Bored." *Psychology Today*, June 1974, p.63-68.

67. Ibid. p.64.

68. Carkhuff, Robert R. *Helping and Human Relations: A Primer for Lay and Professional Helpers.* (Vol. 1 and 2.) New York: Holt, Rinehart and Winston, 1969.

69. London, "The Psychotherapy Boom," p.64.

70. Marathons originated with the work of George Bach and Frederick Stoller, and were shown to produce short-lived effects of good feelings.

71. Gross, Martin L. *The Psychological Society: The impact -and the failure - of psychiatry, psychotherapy, psychoanalysis and the psychological revolution*. New York: Random House, 1978. p.299.

72. Cited in London, Perry, and Klerman, Gerald L. Evaluating Psychotherapy. *American Journal of Psychiatry*, 139:6, June 1982, p.709.

73. Herink, R.(ed) *The Psychotherapy Handbook: The A to Z Guide to More than 250 Different Therapies in Use Today*. New York: New American Library (Meridian), 1980.

74. Strupp, Hans H., "Is the medical model appropriate for psychoanalysis?" *Journal of the American Academy of Psychoanalysis*, 10(1), 1982, p.124.

75. Specifically, the U.S. Senate Finance Committee.

76. VandenBos, Gary R., Cummings, Nicholas A. and DeLeon, Patrick H. "A Century of Psychotherapy: Economic and environmental influences." In Freedheim, Donald K. (ed.). *History of Psychotherapy.* Washington, D.C.: American Psychological Association, 1992. p.92.

77. Parloff, Morris B., "Psychotherapy Research Evidence and Reimbursement Decisions: Bambi meets Godzilla." *American Journal of Psychiatry*, 139(6), June 1982, p. 719.

78. Strupp, Hans H. and Hadley, Suzanne W. "A tripartite model of mental health and therapeutic outcome: With special reference to negative effects in psychotherapy." *American Psychologist*, March 1977, pp.187-196.

79. Ibid. p.188.

80. Ibid. p.188.

81. Bergin, Allen F. "Psychotherapy Can Be Dangerous." *Psychology Today*, Nov. 1975, pp.96-104.

82. Parloff. *Psychotherapy Research Evidence.* p.720.

83. Ibid. p.721.

84. For example, Lambert, M.J., Shapiro, D.A., and Bergin, A.E. "The effectiveness of psychotherapy." In S.L. Garfield and A.E. Bergin (Eds.) *Handbook of Psychotherapy and Behavioral Change* 3rd ed.. New York: Wiley, 1986.; and Parloff, M.B., and Elkin, I. "The NIMH treatment of depression collaborative research program." In D.K. Freedheim (ed.) *History of Psychotherapy: A Century of Change.*

85. Talley, P.F., Strupp, H.H., and Morey, L.C. "Matchmaking in psychotherapy: Patient-therapist dimensions and their impact on outcome." *Journal of Consulting and Clinical Psychology*, 1990, 58, pp.182-188.

86. Strupp, Hans H., "Is the medical model appropriate for psychoanalysis?" *Journal of the American Academy of Psychoanalysis*, 10(1), p.124.

87. *Physicians Payment Review Commission: Annual Report to Congress 1989.* Washington, DC, 1990.

88. Chodoff, Paul. "DSM-III and Psychotherapy." *American Journal of Psychiatry*, 1986, 143(2), pp.201-203.

89. Dineen, Tana. *A Study of Diagnostic Decision Making in Psychiatry.* Doctoral Thesis, University of Saskatchewan, Saskatoon, 1975.

90. Cummings, Nicholas A. "The Anatomy of Psychotherapy Under National Health Insurance." *American Psychologist*, September, 1977, 711-721. p.711.

91. Ibid. p.713.

92. For example Albee, G. W. "To thine own self be true. Comments on 'Insurance reimbursement.' " *American Psychologist*, 1975, 30, pp.1156-1158.

93. It is interesting to note the irrational Canadian "solution" to this dispute whereby medical practitioners became insured delivers of psychotherapy, while other psychotherapists were left outside of the insurance system. Thus, from the Canadian viewpoint, psychotherapy was "effective and efficient" and worthy of tax payers' money if provided by a physician, however trained or untrained, but not if done by a psychologist, social worker or any other type of psychotherapist. Although initial attempts to change this arrangement to expand coverage seemed hopeful, increasing medical costs and diminishing health care dollars removed any possibility and lead to the closure of many publicly funded health psychology and psychotherapy services in Canada.

94. Gross, Martin L. *The Psychological Society: The impact -and the failure - of psychiatry, psychotherapy, psychoanalysis and the psychological revolution.* New York: Random House, 1978. p.4.

95. Parloff, M.B. "Can psychotherapy research guide the policymaker? A little knowledge may be a dangerous thing." *American Psychologist*, 1979, 34, pp.296-306.

96. Miller, Alice. *The Drama of the Gifted Child: The Search for the True Self.* New York: Basic Books, 1990. (Previously published as *Prisoner of Childhood*, 1981; translated from the German *Das Drama des begabten Kindes*, by Ruth Ward).

97. Masson, Jeffrey Moussaieff. *Against Therapy: Emotional Tyranny and the Myth of Psychological Healing.* New York: Atheneum, 1988.

98. For example: John Bradshaw *Bradshaw on The Family: A Revolutionary Way of Self-Discovery*. (Deerfield Beach, Florida: Health Communications, 1988); and Charles L. Whitfield, *Healing The Child Within: Discovery and Recovery for Adult Children of Dysfunctional Families*. (Deerfield Beach, FL, Health Communications, 1989.)

99. Thigpen, Corbett H. and Cleckley, Hervey M. "On the incidence of Multiple Personality Disorder: A Brief Communication." *International Journal of Clinical and Experimental Hypnosis*, 1984, XXXII (2), pp.63-66.

100. Putnam, Frank W. *Diagnosis and Treatment of Multiple Personality Disorder*. Guilford Press, 1989. p.47.

101. Borch-Jacobsen, Mikkel. "Sybil - The making of a disease: An interview with Dr. Herbert Spiegel." *The New York Review*, 24, 1997. p.60. Spiegel, who had done hypnosis with Sybil, questioned the diagnosis: "Sybil told me that she had read *The Three Faces of Eve*, Thigpen and Cleckley's book on a case of multiple personality. She was very impressed with that book. One outstanding feature of highly hypnotizable subjects is their histrionic way of making statements. I have the impression that Sybil learned from reading this book that she could express her agonies and her stresses in life through the histrionic display of multiple personalities, especially if it were encouraged by the therapist." p. 62.

102. Ibid. p.60.

103. For example; Rivera, Margo, *Multiple Personality: An Outcome of Child Abuse*. Toronto: The Ontario Institute for Studies in Education, 1991; C. A. Ross, C. Norton, and K. Wozney. "Multiple Personality Disorder: An analysis of 236 cases." *Canadian Journal of Psychiatry*, 1989, 34(5), pp.413-418.

104. Accused of a series of murders in which the bodies of the victims were left on the hillside, Bianco claimed in his defence that he was suffering from multiple personality disorder and that another of his personalities was responsible for the killings, although this diagnosis was supported by experts including Jack Watkins, a psychologist, the Court was convinced by other experts that the accused was fabricating this diagnosis.

105. The expectation (or demand) that patients accept the judgment of their doctors has been a primary standard of professions for a long time. In 1888, the American Medical Association commanded patients to trust their doctors: "The obedience of a patient to the prescriptions of his doctor should be prompt and implicit. The patient should never permit his own crude opinions as to their fitness to influence his attention to them." *The Three Ethical Codes*. Detroit: Illustrated Medical Journal Co., 1888.

106. Wolf, Peter H. "Psychoanalytic Research and Infantile Sexuality." *International Journal of Psychiatry*, 1967, 4(1), p.61-64.

107. Torrey, E. Fuller. *Witchdoctors and Psychiatrists*. New York: Harper and Row, 1986. p.1.

Chapter 4

Selling Psychology as Science

There are in fact two things, science and opinion;
the former begets knowledge, the latter ignorance.

Hippocrates, Law, Bk. 1

N orth American society is easily convinced of the value of anything characterised as science or scientific. In a truly gullible way, people believe that a product is better if it is described as "proven effective" or "scientifically developed" whether it is a tooth paste, a new drug, a hair-loss treatment, a government "study" or a therapy.

Whatever the product being promoted, the term science is there to influence the consumer; to create the impression that the product is better, safer, efficient or effective. This strategy works because American society tends to be impressed, and even intimidated, by science, believing that it holds the promise of better things. For example, some years ago, a leading drug manufacturer convinced millions of people to buy its aspirin, by declaring that "in a scientific comparison test of five brands of aspirin, its was the most effective;" a persuasive claim unless one knew that all five brands were equal in results and therefore all five could claim the same position as "most effective." Advertisers have found that consumers will believe that something is good and safe if it is called "scientific," even if science has become confused with surveys, opinion polls, celebrity expert statements, advertising slogans and journalistic hype.

So it is hardly surprising that "Science" has become the Gucci label of the Psychology Industry, enhancing, even if falsely, its credibility by implying quality, reliability and excellence. It goes without questioning that what is being sold is "safe and effective." But are the "facts" given by the Psychology Industry sound and scientific? Can they be relied on when making decisions or creating policies? Are the services and treatments of the Psychology Industry safe? Are they effective? Is psychology a science? Or is it just using "science" to sell itself?

In an attempt to answer these questions, one must look at whether the Psychology Industry acts like a science in regards to what it studies and what it does. One must ask whether the studies it refers to are really scientific, whether the terms and concepts it uses are valid, and whether the data it produces and cites are reliable? And one must look at whether psychology subjects itself to the same scientific evaluation and responds to the results?

One hundred years ago, William James wrote, "I wish by treating Psychology like a natural science, to help her become one."[1] During the first half of this century, psychology did grow as a science, fostered in part by academic research and, in part, by industrial, political and social forces. The science was most evident in areas of physiological, behavioural and cognitive psychology, which arguably were the most amenable to scientific rigor. The other "softer" areas, including personality, social, educational and clinical psychology, acquired some aspects of the scientific approach but were greatly influenced by the demands from within the profession and without, to provide society with immediately useful applications and solutions. This pressure to be practical and effective and the associated incentives of prestige and profit worked to the detriment of psychology as a science. As Allan Bloom wrote:

> Psychology is mysteriously disappearing from the social sciences. Its unheard-of success in the real world may have tempted it to give up the theoretical life. As the psychotherapist has taken his place alongside the family doctor, perhaps his education now belongs to something more akin to the medical school than to the sciences, and the research relevant for him is more directed to treatment of specific problems of patients than to the founding of a theory of the psyche...This leaves open the question of what the solid ground is on which therapy stands, and where its newer ideas come from.[2]

For the most part, psychology, which abandoned philosophy in the 1890's, has, in the 1990's, abandoned science. As a philosophy, it had a soul, a legitimate territory of study and a theoretical style of thinking. As a science, it had a mind, a recognized focus of enquiry and an empirical approach to data.[3] What is now called "psychology" is, to use Huber's term, "junk science" rooted in neither, with no soul or science, no boundaries and no method; swept along by the shifting ground of popular belief and the ephemeral demands for expert opinion. There is little, if any, similarity between this pseudoscience and the real science on which traditional psychology was founded.

Science functions on the basic principle that for something to be more than subjective opinion or personal belief, it has to be objectively demonstrated to the satisfaction of colleagues. Although this would seem to be simple, experimental bias (i.e. the belief that the theory is right) can have a profound effect not only in the interpretation of the results but on the actual data. For example, one study showed that if school teachers are told that their pupils are very bright, the class will perform significantly better than if the students are described as slow and below average in ability.

Although these fundamentals of peer validation and objectivity are widely accepted by all of the mature sciences, the Psychology Industry often fails to practice them. The vast majority of psychologists either see no need to support or justify their claims or they present fraudulent or misleading "data." While they argue that their methods are effective, they rely on "clinical experience," "trained intuition," "case studies" or the "subjective evaluation" of clients as evidence, which allows them to rise above and ignore these principles, effectively ruling out any external verification. As disquieting as this may be, in the Psychology Industry scientific principles are violated, research is ignored, and, in some cases, data is misinterpreted or even fabricated to fit the need.

FAKED AND FISHY DATA

> *Man's major foe is deep within him. But the enemy is no longer the same. Formerly it was ignorance; today it is falsehood.*
>
> Jean-Francois Revel[4]

A major North American breast-cancer study[5] recently concluded that removing a cancerous lump was just as effective a surgical treatment as removal of the entire breast; a finding which lead many women to have lumpectomies rather than mastectomies. It was subsequently uncovered that at least one contributor to the study, an eminent Montreal physician and university professor, had submitted falsified, "fishy" data.[6] This not only shook the scientific community and the funding institutions, it shocked the medical profession and the thousands of female patients who had based their treatment decisions on the preliminary findings of this study.

Such flagrant dishonesty is seldom uncovered in medical research but in psychology it may actually be quite prevalent. One of the best known cases is that of Sir Cyril Burt. Burt, who began his career as a school psychologist in England, believed in eugenics and the intellectual superiority of his Nordic race.[7] By 1943 he had published his first study supporting the claim that intelligence is an inherited trait.[8] In this study, he reported assessing 15 pairs of identical twins who had been raised apart in different environments from birth. The number of paired subjects gradually grew over time to a total of 53 reported in 1966. As well, Burt and his associate, Howard, reported intelligence measures on 963 parent-child pairs, 321 grandparent-grandchild matchings and 375 uncle-nephew groupings.[9] In all of these studies, and many others, the results strongly supported the "genetic inheritance" theory and, "for many years, the central evidence cited to support the claims that IQ is a highly heritable trait was the massive life's work of the late Sir Cyril Burt."[10] Curiously, the correlation showing the relationship of the scores between child and relative remained the same to the third decimal ($r=0.771$).

In the early 1970's, contradictions, ambiguities and absurdities began to be noticed in Burt's writings, raising questions and reservations about his data. Then, in 1976, Oliver Gillie, the medical correspondent for the London Sunday Times, wrote a front-page article stating that Burt was guilty of major scientific fraud. In his research, Gillie had attempted to locate Burt's two associates, Misses Howard and Conway who, according to Burt, had done the IQ testing and had published papers with him and on their own in the journal that he edited. There was no evidence anywhere of these two research associates. Burt's colleagues had never seen them, neither had secretaries, students or other staff at University College, London. They could not be found. Neither could any of the identical twins that they had supposedly tested. Apparently they had never existed. A subsequent biography[11] clearly showed that Burt had collected no data at all during the last thirty years of his life, those years in which he published the definitive studies on intelligence.[12]

This would have been merely an embarrassment to psychology and to the many believers and supporters of Burt, were it not for the breadth of influence his claims have had. As a result of his enthusiastic and aggressive arguments, England established the policy that an IQ test be given to all children in their eleventh year, to measure their "innate intelligence." The results were used to stream the children into one of three separate and very unequal school systems. Similar but less rigid approaches were established in both the US and Canada. If one accepts that education has an affect on children's futures in terms of employment, earning power, status, etc., then the implementation of Burt's fraudulent findings has damaged whole generations in England and North America.

The "sin" of both the breast study physician and Sir Cyril Burt was that they provided fake or "fishy" data which, on the basis of their professional status, others accepted and trusted, and upon which policies were established and decisions made. Although the exposure of such overt fraud is rare, it is not unusual for statistics to be presented, articles and books to be published, and conclusions to be drawn in the absence of any reasonable supporting data or evidence.

Consider the following excerpts:

> By age twenty-five, 95% of people have experienced negative, guilt-inducing, or traumatic incidents. These involve a range of experiences including the family losing their house, divorce, having a depressed or phobic parent, a best friend killed in a car accident. ... The most traumatic incidents, however, involved physical, sexual, and emotional abuse. When perpetrated by a trusted person and/or force is involved, the trauma is even more devastating. [13]

> Spouse and child abuse occurs in 50-60% of families, at least on an occasional basis...This can occur twice a month, every three months or once a year. [14]

> The majority of people and groups are good, but there are 10-15% of people and groups who have negative motivations and cause major problems. [15]

> According to Wegscheider-Cruse, 83% of all nurses are firstborn children of alcoholics and therefore codependents by definition.[16]

In fact, I was toying with the idea that many of the categories found in the DSM-III fit much more readily under the rubric of addiction and codependence, and working with them with the tools of the Twelve-Step programme and the deep process work not only was cheaper and easier, it was more effective. [17]

A jury awarded $1 million to a man who said he was fired by an auto parts store because he weighed 400 pounds. A key expert testified that obesity is 80 per cent genetic and 20 per cent environmental.[18]

A recent newspaper article about the effectiveness of NLP (NeuroLinguistic Programming) techniques to treat asthma, carried the statement of two practitioners that a client doesn't "have to believe it will work for it to work" They claimed "a 99 per cent success rate with one-time treatments of about 75 minutes that cost $70.[19]

In each and all of these cases, which appear to present scientific data, implying that the statements are based on some research, no documentation or reference was provided to support the claim. And in each, a written request for further information, references or supporting data, either received no response or a reply stating that the statistics were based on experience and professional opinion, rather than any scientific study. For example, in writing to the two NLP practitioners about their asthma treatment claims, some scepticism was expressed and a request was made to look at the data, with an offer of collaboration to "demonstrate the effectiveness of this treatment." Their response avoided either confirming or denying their publicized state- ment but placed the responsibility for the claims on the journalist who was "doing her best — but in the process of going from word of mouth to printer, there (was) inevitably some misinterpretation." They continued: "The facts are: when a client knows specifically what the allergens are and can find three appropriate counter examples, the odds for success are very high. There are a few other factors that need to be considered, one being their willingness to let go of any "secondary gain" and another being their ability to focus their attention." Apparently no data existed to support the claims of success and no study was ever conducted. As well, several "factors" were presented in the response which never appeared in the article, all of which place the reason for failure squarely on the shoulders of the client despite the claim that they didn't even have to believe in it for it to work. (The letter continued with a further description of the other services that they offer and testimonials from several "satisfied customers.")

In all of the above examples, the numbers supported the author's point of view or bias and served to endorse the service or technique promoted by the author. They constitute only as a small sample of this common fraud in which the appeearence of "science" is being used to sell psychology.

ABUSE OF NUMBERS

You know what they say about smoking;
its one of the leading causes of — statistics.

Arthur Black[20]

It has often been said that numbers don't lie; people lie. But numbers certainly help people to lie more convincingly. Consider the recently reported study that "linked hot dogs to a risk of developing leukaemia." The data suggested that the risk was five times greater for a male child who eats more than 12 hot dogs a month and whose father has a history of eating more than 12 hot dogs each month.[21] Although the researchers reportedly had no theory to explain this "link," it was concluded that hot dogs were a causal factor in the development of this disease. Supposedly, this research provided the proof. But there are many other ways that this data could be explained. One is that, if children and their parents eat that many hot dogs each month, the results may be an effect of poor overall nutrition, of poor health generally, or of living in or near poverty. It is equally possible that this was a fluke of the numbers and, that if the study was repeated, new data would not show this connection. Scientific conclusions such as this can not be drawn from a single isolated study, especially in the absence of any explanatory theory. (It is interesting to note that apparently all the hypotheses tested in this study failed to be proven and this anomaly was the only "significant" result the researchers had for all their work.) Statisticians call this approach "data dredging,"[22] looking for anything in the mass of numbers that will either support one's ideas or that will justify having spent all the time and money on the study and support requests for future funding.

Although this "hot dog causes leukaemia" conclusion seems already to be forgotten, many faulty psychology studies with poor design and questionable results are accepted and reported, and their "findings" perpetuated, influencing public opinion and policy, and giving birth to new theories and therapies. The Mayo study of the "Hawthorne effect" is an example of inappropriate, inadequate and shoddy research. The sample on which its conclusions were drawn that industrial productivity increased with friendly supervision and employee involvement in groups within the factory, was not representative of the 20,000 or more employees of Western Electric. The data was not based on a comprehensive study of hundreds of employees, not even dozens. It was based on only five workers, and two of these people whose output failed to increase were replaced eight months into the experiment by workers whose productivity was from the start much higher than that of any of the other subjects.[23] As well, subsequent reviews of the data have actually indicated that "friendly supervision" had a negligible effect on productivity and that the real factor influencing productivity was pay incentives. But, despite the invalid nature of the results, the fraudulently drawn conclusions based on numbers were accepted by business and affected two decades or more of industrial psychology.

Both the Hawthorne and the "hot dog" study demonstrate that the results of a research study can be affected or manipulated by such factors as "who is asked" and "what is measured." However, when the conclusions are reported, these details are seldom mentioned because the funding agencies, the news reporters and the talk show hosts are not researchers, they want simple absolute statements, not complex and qualified ones. It is assumed that the researchers followed the basic rules of science and that the findings mean what they say. This push of the positive and simple is not restricted to the popular media; it occurs in professional literature as well. A recent study by Statistics Canada, relevant to the manufacturing of victims, provides just such an example. In November, 1993, media sources in the U.S. and Canada carried the results of a Canadian government study that found:

- 98% of Canadian women have personally experienced sexual violation,
- 51% of women (16 and over) have been the victims of rape or attempted rape, and
- 40% of women reported at least one experience of rape.

The CBC national news carried the headline: "Two out of three Canadian women have been sexually assaulted" [24] Could this be true? Are more than half of Canadian males really violent criminals? Is Canada one of the most violent nations in the world, far worse than most third world countries? Or is this, as John Fekete claimed in his analysis of the study,[25] a case of "data rape"?

The real question to be asked is whether these findings were based on science or pseudoscience (with an unhealthy dash of political agenda). And the answer can be found in looking carefully at the mis/use of numbers in the study: The Women's Safety Project (Project),[26] which was first presented as part of the Final Report of the Canadian Panel on Violence Against Women (Report).[27]

The value or credibility of a research project basically depends on having a representative sample (who is asked), using a structured interview (what is asked) and following a standard procedure (how it is asked). If these simple benchmarks are applied to this study does one find science which informs or numbers which mislead?

To determine whether the metaphorical conclusion of a "national epidemic" is accurate or not, one must first consider the group of women on which this study was based; that is 420 women in one city (Toronto). A sample from one city can not be considered to be representative of women across the whole of the country; that is, one can not say that "as with 420 women in Toronto, so with 12 million in Canada." To even approximate a representation of women nationally, the survey would need to be conducted in different cities and towns (and rural areas) across the country; an approach often followed in applied medical research (e.g. drug and surgery studies) to neutralize any bias. Without this, it is grossly inappropriate to extrapolate the data from one small group to describe women in general. As well, the "background information" provided about this group of women raises question as to whether the sample is even representative of Toronto. For example, the Project provides the age distribution of the women in groupings from 15 - 64 years and the respondents' academic background.[28](Figures 1 and 2 show these numbers in comparison to over-all Canadian demographics.)

If this was a truly representative sample of Canadian women, why is it that no women over 64 years of age were included in the study, when the most recent census indicates that 12% of Toronto females (and 13.3 % in Canada) are 65 or older (Fig. 1).[29] This leads one to wonder if they were omitted from the study by the researchers because other studies have shown that older women report sexual violence *significantly less frequently* than

Age distribution in Canada & Project
percentage of women 15 years and older

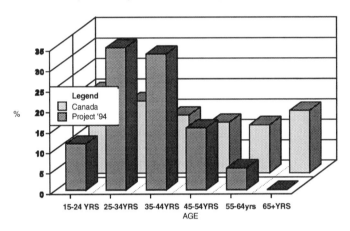

Figure 1

Educational background
as per cent of population sample

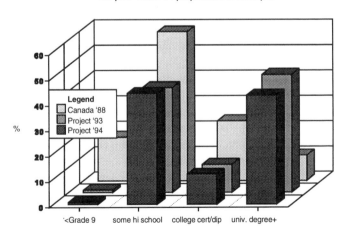

Figure 2

younger women? Similarly, one must question the claim that the group of subjects were "randomly" selected if 46.5 % of the group had a university degree when only 7.8 % of Canadian women have such a degree.[30](Fig. 2)

It must be concluded that this is not a scientifically random sample, and that, in some way, this atypical group was created by the procedures through which the subjects were gathered, that is, through "passive volunteering." A large group of households (n=673) were contacted and asked to participate. 37.8% refused or declined for various reasons; the remaining women became the subject group. Any survey method has its difficulties and a one third refusal rate is apparently not unusual in this area of study.[31] However, it introduces a very strong bias into the research when one considers not only the possible reasons some might have to decline but also the reasons others would have to take the time to particpate, particularly when the interview(s) could amount to many hours. As the Report acknowledges, the study relied on "their (the respondents) generosity and courage in taking the time to reveal and discuss very intimate, and often deeply painful material from their personal histories."[32] What would motivate someone to do this? What do members of this group have in common? The apparent answer is that they have "upsetting" or "abusive" personal experiences to talk about and/or that they have a political agenda consistent with that of the study, and/or that they liked the attention derived from participating in the study.

In this era when research is expected to be "politically correct," it is considered unwise to suggest that political agendas can influence research.[33] But, since the times of Galton, the intention of researchers has affected where they place their attention; that is, they see what they want, they get what they ask for, and they can use numbers to "prove" their beliefs; thus, their opinions are presented gift wrapped in numbers. In this case, the Women's Safety Project and the Final Report had an expressed intention (or bias) which was stated in their words: to "confirm" (i.e. the results were decided before the study was run) as seen through "a feminist lens" (i.e. with a feminist bias) that sexual violence directly touches the majority of women. Although the protocol or outline of the introductory interview was not obtainable, the Report indicates that the women were told before the study that it focussed on "the broad range of experiences of sexual violence which violate women's safety. This includes the many experiences perpetrated within personal relationships."[34] The bias and expectations of the researchers were communicated to the women prior to their answering any questions, potentially influencing their responses and contaminating the data.

Scientific research expects that all subjects will be interviewed in the same way so that the results can be compared. But in this study, the lack of standardization is immediately evident in the length of the interviews which ranged from 45 minutes to 25 hours, averaging about two hours. It would seem, if the roles of interviewer and therapist are compared (trusting, sensitive, attentive), that the longer interviews had more in common with therapy than with any scientific research.[35]

To fully address the issues that arise from this one example would require a document as long or longer than the original report.[36] However, a cursory look at a few of the findings regarding sleeping difficulties provides some immediately obvious examples of an abuse of numbers. The "Number of Women *Experiencing* Difficulty Sleeping due to Fear" was given as 238 or 56.7% of the women asked. However the question that lead to this result was *"Was there ever a time* in your life when you had trouble sleeping, or staying asleep at night, because you were nervous about or afraid for your personal safety?"[37] This question relates to the whole life period of the woman (including childhood), and enquires about any instance, past or present. The data shows that for 100 of these women, the fear lasted for "up to one month" (the shortest category available in the interview) which would include cases when it was felt on only one occasion. A further 74 women could not even remember how long they felt that way. No apparent attempt was made to discern whether this "difficulty" was in any way related to medical problems or other causes of sleep disturbance, which reportedly affect a significant proportion of the adult population. Thus, the conclusion about "women experiencing difficulty" is clearly misleading. The report continues that "31.8% of women indicated that it was a general fear for their safety which kept them awake and afraid. ...This fear speaks to the social impact, as it is lived on a very intimate and personal level, of living in a society where women are routinely sexually attacked and murdered."[38] This conclusion clearly displays the political bias of the researchers with its suggestion of "routine murder" when Canada has a homicide rate of 0.002%, including male and female victims,[39] and its inattention to the fact that more women fear "break-ins," a non-sexual crime. Finally, it is interesting to note that this study reported that 52% of women attributed their decreased sense of safety to media reports of violence, of which this report was a major contributor.[40] Thus, this report by its own efforts became part of the cause for women's fear of violence, part of the Victim-Making industry.

While this study serves as an example of the misuse of data and statistics to support a strong bias and a political cause, it is by no means alone in doing this.[41] Gilbert refers to such estimates and "data" as "advocacy numbers, figures that embody less an effort at scientific understanding than an attempt to persuade the public that a problem is vastly larger than commonly recognized. Advocacy numbers are derived not through outright deceit but through a more subtle process of distortion. Under the veil of social science, rigorous research methods are employed to measure a problem defined so broadly that it forms a vessel into which almost any human difficulty can be poured."[42] Research findings, just because they appear in journals, have lots of numbers, receive government support or are reported in the media, are not necessarily scientific. The Psychology Industry is very effective in misusing its numbers to support its views and to sell itself.

ABUSE OF CONCEPTS

Means not, but blunders round about a meaning;
And he whose fustian's so sublimely bad,
It is not poetry, but prose run mad.

Alexander Pope,
Prologue to Imitations of Horace, l.186

Whether it is "Post Traumatic Stress Disorder" which can be used to describe a Viet Nam veteran's reaction to napalm attacks or a UFO abduction, "sexual abuse" which can apply to anything from forced rape to a whistle, or "addiction" which can refer to a dependence on heroin or a desire to spend money shopping; terms that previously had substance and meaning are now being abused by the Psychology Industry to create an appearance of scientific credibility. The practitioners of pseudoscience have discovered that if they couch their fictions in professional terms, their ideas take on the air of "scientific evidence," sounding more believable. By appropriating someone else's asset of credibility they bolster their own appearance of scientific validity.

One example of the many cases of such illusory associations between scientific concepts and pseudoscience fiction is that of "Learned Helplessness." Because it is a well researched behavioural paradigm which describes how people are affected by one situation so that they act helpless in another, it is often abused by the victim-making Psychology Industry. "Learned Helplessness" was first identified by Steven Maier and Martin Seligman in 1964 in the animal learning laboratory of Richard Solomon. In research designed to study avoidance behaviour, dogs were subjected to electric shocks from the floor of their cages and then tested to see if they could learn new behaviours to escape or avoid the shock. Seligman and Maier discovered that when the shock was uncontrollable, that is there was nothing the dogs could do to stop it, they became passive so that later when avoidance was possible they failed to act. They had learned to act helpless.

Learned Helplessness came to be understood as consisting of three essential characteristics:

1) the animal or person has to display inappropriate helplessness in which they fail, through the lack of action (i.e. passivity), to deal with the demands of a situation in which effective coping is possible (i.e. they give up).

2) it follows in the wake of events in which the person had no way to exert any control, as distinct from bad or traumatic events where some control or escape may have been possible.

3) it is due to particular ways of thinking or responding that are developed during the time of the uncontrollable events and which are generalized to new and different situations.

Seligman and Maier have demonstrated that the model of Learned Helplessness can be applied to explain a number of specific psychological problems. For instance, depression may in some circumstances be the result of a situation in which one has no control. The "helplessness" is then generalized to other different situations so that one reacts in an unnecessarily passive manner; as depressed.

Despite its share of discussion and controversy, Learned Helplessness has gained credibility within the scientific community as a descriptive model or mechanism to explain certain types of social problems. And because Learned Helplessness deals with uncontrollable events, passivity and failure, it has certain appeal to the victim-making industry which has extrapolated and distorted it to explain all manner of human problems, giving its notions the aura of a scientific basis. For example, *"Women & Risk: How to master your fears and do what you never thought you could do"*[43] is portrayed as a "Guide to Overcoming Learned Helplessness." The author, Nicky Marone, is described as having training in educational psychology, as leading workshops and seminars on Learned Helplessness and as having appeared on television and radio and consulted with "numerous organizations, universities and Fortune 500 companies," leading the reader to the conclusion that she is an expert in the field of Learned Helplessness. However, a closer look at what she writes reveals that it bears virtually no relationship to the behavioural concept of Maier and Seligman. Compare her statements to the criteria of Learned Helplessness:

Criterium	Marone	Learned Helplessness
1) Inappropriate helplessness	- "Learned helplessness ensnares a woman in a tangled web of paralyzing beliefs, emotions, and behaviours. She consistently doubts herself even when she performs at consistently high levels."[44]	This comment about performance "at a high level" conflicts with the aspect of helpless passivity and indicates that the author is not talking about Learned Helplessness.
2) Previous uncontrollable event	"The study of learned helplessness has unearthed many intriguing insights... girls of high ability... are the group most debilitated by confusion; that is, they give up."[45] Later she refers to "the grim realities of learned helplessness... the terrible toll it takes on a woman's life."[46]	But the scientific concept holds that Learned Helplessness is the result of specific learning experiences in situations in which there is no possibility for control. It is not based on personality or gender.
3) Helpless thinking is generalized	"Learned helplessness corrodes self-esteem, blocks ambition... People who suffer from learned helplessness ... exhibit deficiencies in strategic planning, and are often unable to assess the causes of both their failures and their successes."[47]	In contrast, the Learned Helplessness paradigm considers the generalizing of helpless behaviours and does not confuse itself with issues of self-esteem or ambition and does not accommodate successes.

Figure 3

Marone further states that "Learned Helplessness is a debilitating break-down in our belief system that can produce serious behaviour disorders. Fortunately this style of behaviour can be unlearned, but, *left untreated, it can ruin a life that would otherwise be happy and fulfilling.*"[48] Maier and Seligman have shown that Learned Helplessness has a time course, gradually diminishing over a moderate amount of time, and not progressing "if not treated." The writer, in focussing her attention on women, may be right in assuming that many women don't achieve their dreams (as is probably the case with many men), but to attribute this to Learned Helplessness is to distort the theory and confuse the public, and to use science to sell a particular theory, one which targets women as consumers.

But Marone is not alone in using Learned Helplessness to enhance the appearance of opinions and provide the illusion of expert status. Peterson, Maier and Seligman, in surveying some of the misapplications, have criti-cized the attempt to apply the model to "victims" of alcoholism, child abusers, domestic violence, and the effect of the evening news. For instance, alcohol-ism, because of its themes of loss of control and being "powerless over alcohol," has been described as Learned Helplessness. But alcoholism does not meet the criteria of "passivity," for alcoholics generally seem quite active in obtaining their alcohol. Nor does it meet the criteria of originating in an earlier uncontrollable experience, because even the behavioural models of alcoholism emphasize a gradual learning. While placing alcoholism within the Learned Helplessness model is not warranted, it is often again done to lend the aura of science to a problem area for which the Psychology Industry has neither an adequate understanding nor an effective treatment.[49] Simi-larly, Learned Helplessness is inappropriately applied to explain sexual abusers, who hardly seem passive in their behaviour; domestic violence, where the passivity may be to the benefit of the person; or the impact of the evening news where the effects on thinking and beliefs is unknown. Peterson *et al.* are critical of those that attempt to apply the scientific concept to specific, ill-fitting problems because "the danger in treating all applications of learned helplessness as equally compelling is to risk the credibility of the model for which it works best."[50] And this, of course, is exactly why the Psychology Industry seeks to attach itself to this and other scientific concepts — they lend it the credibility it otherwise lacks.

"Post Traumatic Stress Disorder" has been abused in much the same way. In this case, a paradigm first developed to impart understanding to the diverse symptoms exhibited by the veterans of the Vietnam conflict was stretched and blurred so that "trauma" has come to be understood as any subjectively disturbing or upsetting event, whether real or imagined. With this highly diluted definition, the experience of trauma can be identified in anyone and everyone's life and then used as the cause for later complaints and problems which are interpreted as the consequential disorder necessitating psychologi-cal treatment. Whether it is seeing a furry toy shaped like a penis, hearing others' tales of trauma, being criticised in public, or having the delusion of being abducted by a UFO, all are identified as traumas sufficient to produce the disorder. Common sense could discriminate the difference between the battlefield or a violent rape and a scary television movie or a verbal insult, but psychologists, in order to sell themselves and their services, abuse the concept to make it appear that they know the inevitable impact and what to do about it.

The concepts of Learned Helplessness and Post Traumatic Stress Disorder are particularly attractive to the Industry precisely because they are reasonably well researched and have general scientific acceptance. As well, since they both link psychological problems to uncontrollable situations, they have wide appeal in a society obsessed with personal control. Whether it is Post Traumatic Stress Disorder or Learned Helplessness, the concept can be distorted and abused to fit the motif of the Psychology Industry: "you had no control then, but, with treatment, you can gain total control and get what you want." Peterson *et al.* offer a caution to this sales promotion: "an over-riding belief in one's own control presents two problems: it brings increased depression in its wake, and it makes meaning in one's life difficult to find."[51]

Counterfeit data attributed to non-existent studies, numbers misinterpreted to support ideologies or opinions, terms distorted to expand markets and mislead the public; these are some of the things that the Psychology Industry does while claiming to be an objective science. And it is getting away with it for, as Huber notes: "it is in the healing business that the temptations of junk science are the strongest and the controls against it the weakest."[52] There is nothing to stop the Psychology Industry from using its image as a science as a marketing tool to promote the industry. Psychologists take the stand in court rooms and expound their theories as if they are proven facts. In their offices and consultation rooms, they sit in judgment over patients, their lives and their families. They give interviews, hold lectures, present workshops, giving advice about how to feel, what to think, what to do and when to seek professional help. Their subjective ideas and personal beliefs take on the appearance of "facts." Whether they believe it or not, they speak authoritatively, appearing to have answers; they use the scientific mystique to impress, convince, persuade — to sell the Psychology Industry.

Psychologists present themselves as having the special ability to evaluate others, — to diagnose, predict — but how do they apply their supposed science to themselves — to evaluating and judging what they say and do? Do they again use "science" — citing non-existent proof, misusing numbers and blurring concepts — to sell themselves and their services?

PSYCHOTHERAPY EVALUATION

Most therapists, I suspect, have been rather traumatized by the research literature: the lack of hard evidence that any form of therapy really "does any good" in the way that it is supposed to is something to set the seeds of panic sprouting in those who can see no obvious alternative way of making a living. Hence, the attempt by and large has been to explain this kind of evidence away rather than to take it seriously and reflect on its significance.

David Smail[53]

One would assume, considering the yearly use of psychological services by millions of Americans and the many claims made about it, that indisputable evidence exists proving beyond doubt the effectiveness of psychotherapy. But what the Psychology Industry has persuaded people to believe and what has actually been proven are quite different. Most of the information and opinions about therapy's usefulness comes from patients and psychologists rather than from any scientific research.

Early in this century, Freud argued against the use of scientific research to evaluate psychoanalysis, stating that only the patient could accurately assess its effectiveness, a view that was supported and restated more recently by Nehemiah in the *American Handbook of Psychiatry*:

The heart has reasons of which the head knows nothing... For the patient, his immediate knowledge of the effect of analysis is sufficient evidence of its worth, however sceptical the outside observer may be and however lacking the statistics to "prove" its usefulness.

Perhaps its effectiveness can never be shown by scientific methods and possibly, because of the complexity and nature of the analytic process, it is a mistake even to attempt such a demonstration. Perhaps the experience of analysis is like that of beauty, of mysticism, of love — self-evident and world-shaking to him who knows it, but quite incommunicable to another who does not.[54]

However, Allen Wheelis, a psychoanalyst, disputes this saying that "few analyzed persons are critical of psychoanalysis." He notes that if a patient does acknowledge the lack of usefulness, he "will blame himself and exonerate the psychoanalysis. The most common outcome, however, is simply to pretend that the analysis was successful." This opinion was inadvertently supported by the Central Fact-Gathering Committee of the American Psychoanalytic Association which reported that of those who "completed treatment," over 96% "felt benefitted,"[55] a claim which might lead one to consider psychoanalysis at best, to be a long and expensive form of psychological aspirin.[56]

But the client is not the only one to imagine or pretend a cure, for studies consistently show that therapists tend to see more improvement than anyone else, followed closely by their clients. Friends, family and other observers providing independent evaluation are a distant, and often unimpressed, third.

Why would psychologists distort the truth and accentuate the positive, minimizing or ignoring negative results? Of the many reasons, two major ones stand out: 1) paying attention to the negative results might interfere with their established method of practice, creating inconvenience and loss of income, and 2) if they were to look honestly at what they are doing, it would cause them to have doubts about their effectiveness, their worth, their self-image and their career.

Regarding the first, most of the activities of the Psychology Industry follow the same approach both in form and in function. Using a format based on regimented office visits, psychologists irregardless of theoretical orientation strive to establish trust and empathy, uncover the past, make interpretations or suggestions and develop patient insight. If research were not to support this approach, then the changes would disrupt this traditional structure, something to which the Psychology Industry is highly resistant. This rigidity is most evident in the practice of psychoanalysis, where the "fifty-minute" hour is not only held professionally sacred but is used in therapy as a means to interpret patient behaviour. This is in spite of Freud's and Jung's flexible approach to time and Lacan's more recent practice of fitting the time to the therapeutic process.

But a business, even medicine or psychology, is always resistant to changing its method of doing business even if confronted with the necessity to do so. Consider the case of Semmelweis, who noted in the mid 1800's that new mothers who gave birth in a ward served by physicians had almost four times as high a rate of dying from childbed fever as those that were assisted by a midwife. He reasoned that it was due to the doctors' practice not to wash their hands before examining patients or doing deliveries. He insisted that his colleagues and assistants clean their hands in a solution of chlorine of lime, and over a fifteen month period the death rate dropped from 12 percent to 1.2 percent. Subsequently, he was fired from his hospital position, due to his political involvements, and his successor stopped the silly and "unmanly" requirement of hand washing. The death rate rose again to 15 percent but this did not persuade the physicians to change their practice for another forty years (until Lister, understanding the significance of Semmelweis's reasoning, provided additional proof and pressure to reinstate washing.) Despite the importance of Semmelweis's experiment, professional practice won out over scientific evidence, in much the same way that the Psychology Industry now maintains traditional practices ignoring the results which cast doubts on their effectiveness.

Secondly, psychologists have historically been loathe to systematically and objectively evaluate their work, preferring to rely on case studies which are almost always positive in their outcome and which serve to demonstrate the psychologists' ability and effectiveness. As Akner admitted: "Like all therapists, I am constantly looking for signs that the work I'm doing is really helping people."[57] As with the euphemistic "fish stories" told by fishing cronies, these tales of success enhance psychologists' confidence, impress their colleagues and evoke admiration in their clients and the public. Even when they speak of a "failure," it is in the context of how they later resolved the problem, as it were "pulling it out of the fire" or explaining it in terms of the client not yet being ready to change. To admit limitations when colleagues are claiming high success, would put a psychologist in jeopardy, exposing him or her to questions about what they are doing. It is easier to ignore the research literature and to engage in exaggerated positive thinking about one's own work. That is to pretend that one has a high level of positive outcomes, to remember successes and, to handle a failure by blaming the patient, calling him or her "untreatable," "too resistent" or just "not psychologically minded." For example, a psychologist told a prospective client that his form of treatment is always successful in seven to ten sessions, a claim he supported by referring to a book he had authored which contained anecdotal information based on his years of clinical experience. After fourteen sessions the patient reported that the problem for which he sought help was still the same. The psychologist responded by explaining that the estimate was made without knowing that the patient had been sexually abused as a child (the patient still did not know this) which was a serious complication requiring more extensive treatment. In his mind, it was the client's failure both in not responding to treatment and in not reporting the abuse at the beginning. Given this explanation, the client continued seeing the psychologist and eventually accepted a referral to a hypnotherapist for "specialized treatment," never once questioning the overall usefulness of his treatment.

Why would this client continue treatment in the face of unsatisfactory results? And why would many former clients tell how their therapy saved their lives, their careers, their marriages, their families and changed them when there is no visible proof of their claims?

The example above provides one clue. This client had already spent twenty-eight hours (14 two-hour sessions) and a lot of money ($5,600 U.S.), before he expressed his concern that the therapy was not working. Not wanting to appear like a fool for spending all that money and getting nothing, when offerred the explanation of an underlying cause, he was ready and willing to accept it. His dilemma was resolved even if it was at the expense of accepting blame and adopting an image of himself as a victim.

Another reason is that people inevitably learn things about themselves from psychotherapy much as they do from other experiences including evenings with friends and visits to fortune-tellers. It may not be that they get the results they wanted but they do get something: insights, ideas, suggestions, explanations, excuses. So, when evaluating therapy, they can honestly say that there was some benefit even if not in regards to their problems.

As well, as Zilbergeld pointed out, the reason that "clients exaggerate the effectiveness of therapy... has to do with the basic nature of counseling: it is, for most people, a very personal, even intimate, matter... And the therapist is often supportive, understanding, sympathetic... By its very nature, this kind of relationship is hard to criticise... It's hard to say that this kind of relationship or process is useless or harmful, just as it's hard to say that praying is useless even when your prayers aren't answered."[58]

What all of this shows is that rather than being the best suited to evaluate therapy, psychologists and their clients are the most biased and least able to answer to the following:

- Is therapy effective?
- Is it any better than friendship?
- Do higher paid professionals do a better job than minimally trained counsellors?
- Does training and experience improve a therapist's skill?
- Is therapy always helpful and safe?
- Do professionals know more about human nature than the rest of us?
- Would people naturally get worse without professional treatment?

Scientific studies, on the other hand, provide an over-riding answer to all of these questions:

NO!

This is not to say that therapy should be banned. People do have the inalienable right to make choices that affect their own lives, whether good or bad, even to choose psychotherapy.[59] But their choice should be made in the clearer light of evaluative information, not in the dim lighting of an opinion from a professional psychologist or "satisfied customer." Nor is this answer intended to imply that all psychologists are ineffective, or that all therapy is a scam.

Rather this "NO" is a warning and an invitation to look more closely at psychotherapy and see whether it is what the Psychology Industry claims it to be.

When something purports to be "proven effective," one immediately assumes that it has been carefully tested according to scientific procedures. For instance, drugs cannot be put on the market until they have fulfilled the stringent requirements of the FDA both for effectiveness and potential risk. They must be demonstrated to be more effective than placebos and of no serious risk of harm to the user. Can the same be said for psychotherapy; that it is more effective than no treatment or a placebo and poses no serious risk to the patient?

One of the first studies to address this issue was conducted by the psychologist, Hans Eysenck in 1952.[60] He compared the outcome for 7,293 patients who had received eclectic psychotherapy; a style of therapy individualized by a therapist from elements drawn from various schools of psychotherapy. The results indicated that 64% showed improvement; a finding which initially seemed supportive of psychotherapy for it was presumed that these patients would have remained the same or become worse if not treated. However, Eysenck then compared these results with those of 500 patients who had received little or no treatment. This "control group" had made claims to their health insurers for psychoneurotic disability and each individual had taken at least three months off work due to the problems. They had received no psychotherapy having merely been reassured and given some mild sedatives by their physicians. To everyone's dismay he discovered that 72% of them had improved by the second year. Despite the lack of any specific treatment they showed an overall 90% recovery in five years. This led Eysenck to conclude that "roughly two-thirds of a group of neurotic patients will recover or improve to a marked extent within about two years of the onset of their illness, whether they are treated by means of psychotherapy or not." In a subsequent more extensive study in 1965,[61] he concluded psychotherapy was unessential to a patient's recovery: "We have found that neurotic disorders tend to be self-limiting, that psychoanalysis is no more successful than any other method, and that in fact all methods of psychotherapy fail to improve on the recovery rate obtained through ordinary life-experiences and nonspecific treatment." Some have challenged these findings claiming that they were unfair, or not sufficiently controlled to be considered scientific. Whether or not these criticisms have weight, Eysenck's studies served as a gauntlet challenging others to more closely examine the claims of psychotherapy.

Suffice it to say that the invitation to test their claims and to validate the effectiveness of psychotherapy has not been met warmly by psychologists despite their claims that they are a scientific profession.

Some would argue as Kottler does that "there are studies available to substantiate or refute almost any claim one would like to make. The behaviourists have convincing evidence that psychoanalytic treatment is nothing but the haphazard application of such principles of reinforcement and extinction. The analysts can demonstrate that the behaviourists are only dealing with surface symptoms and not getting at the root of problems."[62] Thus, psychologists can argue: "Because the research results indicate a great deal of uncertainty about what to do, my expert judgment can do better in prescribing treatment than these results."[63] Others would agree with Bergin to trust intuition and personal judgment as well as the findings of empirical research:

> The field of psychotherapy is made up of many different kinds of views and findings. With some we may have a fair degree of confidence, with some we may feel the data point us in one direction, but just slightly, and in others we may have to conclude that in the absence of data we are proceeding on what appear to be reasonable or warranted hypotheses or assumptions... In some instances, we can have confidence that our procedures are based on reasonably sound empirical results. In others, we must trust our own judgment and intelligence, recognizing fully what we are doing and the bases for our decisions.[64]

Curiously he omits the possibilities that psychologists are proceeding out of habit or routine ("this is the way we've always done it") without any consideration of effectiveness, or out of economic interest (long-term therapy pays more than brief therapy).

Whatever the arguments are against evaluation, their primary intention is defensive, to protect psychotherapy and the Psychology Industry from the increasing number of studies which draw its value into question. For instance, in a review of therapy factors that account for significant client progress, Lambert calculated the percentage of improvement that could be attributed to each of several variables.[65] He found that "spontaneous remission" (improvement of the problem by itself without any treatment) accounted for 40%, an additional 15% of the change resulted from placebo effects (which he referred to as "expectancy controls," that is that the patient expected to get better no matter what was done), while a further 30% improved as the result of common factors in the relationship such as trust, empathy, insight and warmth. Only 15% of the overall improvement could

Factors for Change
per cent of improvement

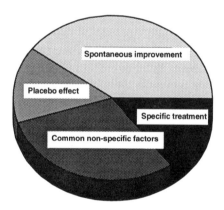

Figure 4

be attributed to any specific psychological intervention or technique. Based on these findings one could conclude that 85% of clients would improve with the help of a good friend and 40% without even that. White found similar results that, regardless of the treatment procedure, 55% of therapeutic effects can be attributable to what he called therapeutic "rituals" which serve as the basis for much of the placebo effect that maximizes positive expectations in all therapies.[66] Many other studies like these have supported the overall conclusion that most of the improvement attributed to psychotherapy is due to the general effects of talking to a warm, kind person and the effect of just naturally getting better anyway.

As well, many others have questioned the whole process of trying to investigate the benefits or effectiveness of psychotherapy, when the term merely serves as a rubric for a disparate group of treatments. Eysenck spoke of this when he described "Psychotherapy" as "a mishmash of theories, a huggermugger of procedures, a gallimaufry of therapies, and a charivari of activities having no proper rationale, and incapable of being tested or evaluated."[67]

Such a concern has lead some to suggest that the 15% or so of change attributed to psychotherapy might be higher with some specific forms of treatment. However, Orlinsky and Howard concluded, in their 1986 study,[68] that there is no consistent evidence that any specific form of therapy produces better results than any other, whether it be individual or group therapy or family counselling, or short compared to long-term treatment; a conclusion again supported by others.[69] Similarly, studies have shown that the length or intensity of treatment has no appreciable effect on the improvement of clients[70] and that, despite loud arguments for long-term therapy, most of the changes occur in the first ten sessions.

It is worth noting here that, despite Orlinsky and Howard's conclusion, the American Psychological Association's Division 12 (Clinical) Task Force on the Promotion and Dissemination of Psychological Procedures[71] constructed a list of 25 "empirically validated treatments:"

- Behaviour therapy for headache and for irritable bowel syndrome.
- Behaviour therapy for female orgasmic dysfunction and male erectile dysfunction.
- Behaviour modification for developmentally disabled individuals.
- Behaviour modification for enuresis and encopresis.
- Behavioural marital therapy.
- Cognitive behaviour therapy for chronic pain.
- Cognitive behaviour therapy for panic disorders with or without agoraphobia.
- Cognitive therapy for depression.
- Cognitive behaviour therapy for generalized anxiety disorder.
- Exposure treatment for post-traumatic stress disorder.
- Exposure and response prevention for obsessive-compulsive disorder.
- Exposure treatment for phobias (simple, social and agoraphobia).
- Family education programs for schizophrenia.
- Group cognitive behavioural therapy for social phobia.
- Interpersonal therapy for bulimia.
- Interpersonal therapy for depression.
- Parent training programs for children with oppositional behaviour.
- Systematic desensitization for simple phobia.
- Token economy programs.

Almost immediately, this created a new aspect of the Industry's business, as books, manuals, and training programs appeared on the market with claims of being "proven effective for improving clinical outcomes."[72]

Whether one agrees with their criteria[73] or not, what is noticeable about this list is the absence of those therapies most often thought of when the term "psychotherapy" is used. It contains primarily behavioural and cognitive-behavioural approaches[74] and then restricts their use to the treatment of specific problems which again are not typically thought of in regard to psychotherapy. Not represented are the "talking-cures" that focus on emotions and memories, those which are most frequently used in the manufacturing of victims and which are used with the majority of Psychology Industry clients.

If, in general, the type, length and intensity of therapy have no significant effect on clients' improvement, one would hope that at least the expertise and training of the therapist does. To look at this, Strupp and Hadley[75] randomly assigned 30 clients to either university professors who had no background in psychology or psychotherapy, or to professionally trained and credentialed psychologists. The presenting problems of these clients were described as neurotic depression or anxiety reactions. The results showed that the professionals were no more effective than the untrained professors, as assessed on a number of measures of clients' functioning. The only slightly significant difference between the two groups was that those who were treated by the professional therapists showed a bit more optimistic view of life, which is consistent with psychotherapy's view of optimism as a criterion of emotional health. It may well be that this belief was communicated to their clients; nevertheless, it failed to show any effect on their symptoms or functioning.

This finding that experience and training have no effect, disturbing as it is to the profession, is not alone in this conclusion.[76] Other studies on the relationship between therapist experience and psychotherapy outcome have similarly concluded that the level of experience of professional therapists is unrelated to their efficacy,[77] that accuracy in professional judgment does not improve with experience, and that paraprofessionals can be just as effective as well-trained professionals.[78] These results fly in the face of the public opinion promoted by the Psychology Industry that specialized training and experience makes better, more capable psychologists (who can then justify higher fees on the basis of their "years of experience.") To counteract these findings which it refused to accept, and with a bias as evident as that underlying the earlier Women and Violence Study, the American Psychological Association has stated that it is "important, perhaps imperative, that psychology begin *to assemble a body of persuasive evidence* bearing on the value of specific educational and training experience."[79] In other words, they are saying: "we believe it works, we need it to look like it works, so let's get numbers to make it look like it works."

Robyn Dawes, in summarizing this area of research writes "that there is no *positive* evidence supporting the efficacy of professional psychology. There are anecdotes, there is plausibility, there are common beliefs, yes — but there is no good evidence."[80, 81, 82]

Critics of this point of view would argue that there is research which shows that therapy has an effect. In fact a study by Smith and Glass[83] is often cited. It looked at the results of 375 studies of psychotherapy outcome and after they had compared and analyzed all of them through a process known as "meta-analysis," Smith and Glass reported that an individual who had undergone psychotherapy had a 2 to 1 chance of being "better" as compared to a person in the control group. Unfortunately "better" was not defined in the same way for all of the studies since individual researchers determined their own meaning of "better." This 66% chance of being better off after therapy may sound impressive even in the light of the ambiguous meaning of "better" until the converse is considered: a 33% chance of being worse off. Is it possible that psychotherapy has this great a risk?

Since the intention of treatment is to provide improvement, most studies have evaluated the positive effects, assuming that, at worst, therapy is benign. However, some have extended their evaluation to include negative change. In 1973, Lieberman, Yalom and Miles studied 170 students in 18 encounter groups with qualified, competent therapists and compared them to 69 students in no group. At the end of therapy, 57% showed positive change, 29% were neutral and 14% showed negative change. Six months after therapy, 46% were still showing positive gains (that is less than half), 32% were neutral, 21% now showed negative change. At first glance, this might suggest that the therapy had a negative or harmful effect. But when compared to the all-important control group, we discover that the change was comparable in both groups, 56 and 52% respectively, leading to the conclusion that "negative change" existed for some members of both groups. Clearly the therapy had not protected its clients from getting worse but it could not, in this case, be held responsible for it.

However, the results of the Cambridge-Sommerville Youth Study, particularly relevant in this victim oriented era, do support that therapy can be held responsible. It evaluated the effectiveness of a project designed to prevent delinquency in underprivileged children. 650 boys between 6 and 10 years of age were randomly divided into two groups with equal chances of delinquency. One group received individual therapy, tutoring and social service; the other, the control group, received no services. The treated boys rated the project as "helpful" and the counsellors rated two-thirds of the group as having benefitted: a positive finding. However, the researcher, Joan McCord, professor of criminal justice at Temple University, went further and followed the boys over time to see if the counselled group did better in terms of criminal behaviour.[84] The results showed little difference between the two groups in terms of the number of crimes, but the counselled group committed significantly *more* serious crimes. A 30 year follow-up showed the same pattern and revealed that, in terms of alcoholism, mental illness, job satisfaction and stress-related diseases, *the treatment group was worse.* McCord summarized the results as " 'More' was 'worse:' " the objective evidence presents a disturbing picture. The program seems not only to have failed to prevent its clients from committing crimes... but also to have produced negative side effects." The therapy appears to have increased criminal behaviour. (One could imagine the effect of a comparable study if it were in the field of medicine; for instance that an AIDS prevention program was found to increase the prevalence of that disease.)

After some pondering, McCord identified three factors which may contribute to the harmful effects of therapy: *encouraged dependency, false optimism, and externalized responsibility,* all of which are encouraged by the Psychology Industry and play a significant role in their approach to business. She suggested that: 1) through the therapy, the psychologists might have fostered a dependency among the boys, rendering them less able or inclined to cope with life's problems on their own after the therapy relationship was terminated, 2) "the supportive attitudes of the counsellors may have filtered reality for the boys, leading them to expect more from life than they could receive," communicating the Psychology Industry's attitude of happiness, and 3) counselling may have taught the boys that they were not reponsible for their behaviour because it was a product of their underprivileged childhood experiences and so the exonerated boys in the traetment group were therefore less troubled by their consiences than those in the non-treatment group.

As one would expect, these conclusions evoked a response from psychologists such as: "McCord's view is literal and simplistic. It lacks an appreciation of the intrapsychic processes that are effected by treatment... the consistently positive subjective reports of the treatment groups about their experiences must have some pervading impact on their lives today."[85] In other words, if they say its so, then it must be so, and you can't question it; a response now echoed by the Psychology Industry about its "victims.'

McCord's study is not alone in its conclusions of harm. Ditman studied the outcomes of 3 groups of alcoholics who had been arrested and charged for alcohol-related offenses. These individuals had been assigned by the court either to AA, to an alcoholism clinic, or to a non-treatment control group. In a follow-up, the researchers found that 44% of the control group were *not* rearrested, compared to 31% of AA group and 32% of those treated in an alcohol clinic;[86] those that received treatment did worse than the untreated. "Not one study" asserts Peele, "has ever found AA or its derivatives to be superior to any other approach, or even to be better than not receiving any help at all... every comparative study of standard treatment programs versus legal proceedings for drunk drivers finds that those who received ordinary judicial sanctions had fewer subsequent accidents and were arrested less."[87]

Such effects as these reported by McCord and Ditman are not rare. Robert Spitzer, of the New York Psychiatric Institute, commented that "negative effects in long-term outpatient treatment are extremely common,"[88] and researchers Truax and Carkhuff stated that "the evidence now available suggests that, on the average, psychotherapy may be harmful as often as helpful, with an average effect comparable to receiving no help."[89]

These studies serve as examples of the *psychiatrogenic* (therapist-caused) or *psychonoxious* (harmful to mind) damages that may result from therapy. For instance, psychologists often assume that the expression of emotion, "getting it all out," is therapeutic and consequently they encourage it as an integral aspect of therapy (i.e. ventilation). However, in a study of 7-year-old boys, those who were rewarded by approval for punching a doll, were far more aggressive when they competed against other children later. Letting or getting it out actually increased the level of hostility, showing that "rewards in therapy (approval) heighten the likelihood of subsequent violence."[90]

Bergin acknowledges this risk when he writes: "it now seems apparent that psychotherapy, as practiced over the last fifty years, has had an average effect that is modestly positive. It is clear, however, that the average group data on which this conclusion is based obscured the existence of a multiplicity of processes occurring in therapy, some of which are known to be either unproductive or harmful."[91] Hans Strupp has estimated that one in ten patients is a psychonoxious victim of psychotherapy.[92]

Adding further weight to that concern, Loftus, Grant, Franklin, Parr, and Brown reported in a letter,[93] the results of a preliminary study investigating a number of "outcome effects" of therapy focussing on repressed memories, and the costs involved:

> In 1990, Washington State permitted individuals to seek treatment under the Crime Victim Act if they claimed previously repressed memory for childhood sexual abuse. From 1991-1995, 670 repressed memory claims were filed. Of these, 325(49%) were allowed.
>
> In the study, a nurse consultant (LP) reviewed 183 of these claims. Of these, 30 were "randomly selected for a preliminary profile." Some of the findings of this analysis are reported here. The sample was almost exclusively female (29/30 = 97%) and Caucasian (29/30 = 97%), with ages ranging from 15 to 67 yrs with a mean of 43 yrs.
>
> The women (and one man) saw primarily Masters level therapists (26/30=87%), although 2 saw a Ph.D., 2 saw an MD, and 6 saw a Master's level therapist in conjunction with an MD. The first memory surfaced during therapy in 26 cases (26/30 = 87%).
>
> All 30 were still in therapy three years after their first memory surfaced. Over half were still in therapy five years after the first memory surfaced (18/30 = 60%).
>
> Prior to memories, only 3 (10%) exhibited suicidal ideation or attempts; after memories, 20 (67%) exhibited suicidal ideation or attempts. Prior to memories, only 2 (7%) had been hospitalized; after memories, 11 (37%) had been hospitalized. Prior to memories, only 1 (3%) had engaged in self-mutilation; after memories 8 (27%) had engaged in self-mutilation.
>
> Virtually all the patients (29/30 = 97%) contended they had been abused in satanic rituals. They claimed their abuse began when they were, on average, 7 months old. Parents and other family members were allegedly involved in the ritual abuse in all cases (29/29); Most remembered birth and infant cannibalism (22/29 = 76%) and consuming body parts (22/29 = 76%); The majority remembered being tortured with spiders (20/29 = 69%). All remembered torture or mutilation (29/29). There were no medical exams corroborating the torture or mutilation.
>
> The sample of (mostly) women was fairly well educated, and most had been employed before entering therapy (25/30 = 83%), many of them in the health-care industry (15/30). Three years into therapy, only 3 of 30 (10%) were still employed. Of the 30, 23 (77%) were married before they entered therapy and got their first memory; within three years of this time, 11/23 (48%) were separated or divorced. Seven (23%) lost custody of minor children; all (30/30) were estranged from their extended families.

> Whereas the average cost of a mental health claim in the Crime Victim Compensation Program that did not involve repressed memory was $2,672, the average cost for the 183 repressed memory claims was dramatically higher: $12,296.

Loftus has clearly stated that this preliminary profile does not "prove" that it was therapy that made these individuals worse. However, in a recent article,[94] she has gone on to state that she views such results as alarming and has made the point that the implications are sufficiently serious to warrant further scientific investigation of the hypothesis that repressed memory therapy is harming patients. And she is not alone in expressing this concern; Lief and Fetkewicz, after completing a study of retractors of abuse accusations, wrote: "As we collect more and more data on the types of therapies involved in recovered-memory therapy, we cannot avoid the conclusion that this is bad therapy. Enormous harm is being done to these patients and to their families. Patients get sicker instead of better, and huge sums of money are spent for years of therapy based on the erroneous assumption that the recovery of memories of sexual abuse in childhood is "a healing process, as Lief and Fetkewicz report in 'Retractors of false memories: the evolution of pseudo-memories' reported in *The Journal of Psychiatry and Law*. (23, 1995, p. 432.)."

If psychotherapy may be dangerous, then why do people still believe that therapy is effective and seek it out in large numbers? The answer may be found in several interacting factors: 1) psychologists have a view of what constitutes a good patient and selectively choose these people, thus hedging their results, 2) "good therapists" are judged by their personal characteristics rather than by their professional abilities, and 3) years of experience and opinion are wrongly equated with expertise and knowledge.

What does a "good patient" look like in the eyes of the therapist? It would seem that there are two essential qualities. The first has come to be known in the industry as the YAVIS; a person who is Young, Attractive, Verbal, Intelligent and Successful. (This is seen in contrast to the HOUND: who is Homely, Old, Unsuccessful, Non-verbal, and Dumb.) Others have described the ideal patient as psychologically minded, reasonably intelligent, anxious, verbal and *not very sick*.[95] Kottler puts it this way: "perhaps it is not the therapist's behaviour that matters much but maybe it is the client who makes all the difference. Those who are trusting and disclosing, who have acute problems, no severe personality disturbances, and who are willing to accept responsibility for their growth, are going to do well in practically any form of therapy with almost any practitioner."[96] In fact Luborsky at the University of Pennsylvania, in examining over 100 evaluation studies, could find no special benefit of analysis or any other method. But what he did note was that "successful" treatment was tied to the patient's mental health at time of treatment; "they (the studies) indicate that the healthier a patient is to begin with, the better the outcome." Thus, in this respect, the good patient is one who doesn't need to be a patient at all and for whom any problem or anxiety is likely to dissipate on its own anyway.

The other patient characteristic repeatedly identified as important is that of *suggestibility* (or *gullibility*).[97] Hans Strupp identified that the best outcomes of treatment are found in those that are most suggestible, who are open to the suggestions of the therapist as to how to think, what to feel, how to act and what to believe.[98] By conforming to the psychologist's theories and belief system, experiencing emotions and memories as suggested by the therapist, the patient is seen to be improving and is assured of this. Thus, the selection of good patients is identical to the selection of good subjects by a stage hypnotist, which is to get interesting, attractive people who are suggestible, able to follow direction, want to comply, and like to be the focus of attention. Then, like the stage performer, the psychologist increases the likelihood of success and the heightens the appearance of power and effectiveness. And from this the reputation will spread!

If half the equation for success is the "good patient" , then the other half is the "good therapist." What makes the "good" therapist? The claims to superior intuitive judgment, clinical insight or therapeutic skills clearly are not true. There is no evidence that psychologists have greater insight into the sources and solutions of psychological problems but, as Dawes[99] points out, it is easy for all of us, including therapists, to fool ourselves about how good we are when we function without facts or when we lack systematic feedback on how well (or poorly) we are doing. For example, a psychologist reported at a conference on hypnosis, that she had a treatment for smoking that was "95% effective," an astounding result considering that most other approaches claim an effectiveness within the 25 — 50% range. When she was asked about her method of evaluation and long-term follow-up she responded, without any apparent awareness of the folly in her method, that she asked the clients when they were leaving her office, whether they were ever going to smoke again. Given that she was an older, grandmotherly woman, the results are not surprising. What may be more surprising is that five percent said "yes," disappointing her and spoiling her otherwise perfect record.

It would seem that two characteristics account for the "good therapist" designation. The first is that the psychologist exudes an aura of warmth, kindness, caring and trust; of being "a genuinely nice person"[100] who pays attention to and sees the world through the client's eyes. How can you not like someone who basically agrees with you and takes your side? The other quality of this good-ness is that of "power." Kottler, in describing what he called *The Compleat Therapist*, writes: "It has become increasingly clear to me that it hardly matters which theory is applied or which techniques are selected in making a therapy hour helpful...What does matter is who the therapist is as a human being — for what every successful healer has had since the beginning of time is charisma and power." He continues: "Perhaps more than any other single ingredient, it is power that gives force to the therapist's personality and gives weight to the words and gestures that emanate from it. It was the incredible power that radiated from the luminaries in our field that permitted them all to have such an impact on their clients... nobody would have listened to them if not for their energy, excitement and interesting characteristics that gave life to their ideas."[101] A similar expression of therapist worship is expressed by Guy in his book *"The Personal Life of the Psychotherapist"* when he writes that, with a truly outstanding therapist, "there is a resultant transcendence which enables these special individuals to accomplish the "impossible thing..." whether in session or on vacation, the fully integrated therapist constantly shares his or her senses of perspective and world view. A personal passion for psychic wholeness is incorporated into nearly every encounter, not because of an uncontrolled drive, but due to a genuine sense of mutuality and caring."[102]

If these self-perceptions of therapists are indicative of the common image of the "good therapist," then it can be seen how therapists presume to act as experts in the absence of demonstrable expertise and to pronounce their effectiveness in the absence of supporting evidence. They don't even attempt a systematic application of scientific principles. Instead, they base their practice on "trained intuition" and expert judgment which presumably allows them to transcend scientific principles and ignore the research findings.[103] In many ways, it becomes an enthralling dance of the patient and therapist, each responding to the moves and sways of the other and each believing that they are getting somewhere together. But when the music stops, the dance is over and therapy is finished, the most likely conclusion is that they aren't much further ahead, that they are about where they began, with both just a little more tired and one a little (or a lot) poorer and the other a little (or a lot) richer.

PLAYING THE NUMBERS RACKET

In the world of evaluation where the best that can be said is that things are beginning to look a "little more optimistic," it is exciting to discover a study that "proves" that an approach of the Psychology Industry is effective. Such enthusiasm was the response to the study by Follette and Cummings[104] which reported the usefulness of psychotherapy in reducing medical utilization. VandenBos[105] summarized the results as they were understood and presented by the Psychology Industry:

> They (Follette and Cummings) found that persons with identifiable emotional distress, although not necessarily diagnosed as having "psychiatric problems," made significantly higher than average use of both in-patient and out-patient medical facilities. When these emotionally distressed individuals received psychotherapy, their medical utilization declined significantly compared to that of a control group of matched emotionally distressed health plan members who did not receive psychotherapy. Significant declines in medical utilization were seen in the period following the completion of the psychological intervention and these remained constant following the termination of psychotherapy. No additional psychotherapy was required to maintain the lowered level of utilization. It would, thus, appear that the costs of providing psychotherapy may be "offset," in part or whole, by cost savings resulting from lowered medical utilization.

This was an exciting finding for several reasons; it successfully demonstrated the effectiveness of psychotherapy in a study balanced by a control group and it provided strength to the economic and business approaches of the Psychology Industry. However, when playing the numbers racket, some numbers are better than others, and some data is sometimes better than all the data. In fact, a number of similar studies have been conducted which claim to show similar significant decreases in subsequent use of medical services follow psychotherapy (as suggested by the right side of Figure 5[106]). But, as Schlesinger, Mumford and Glass[107] point out, "we can not take this conclusion at face value" for several reasons. One is that "most of these studies present the psychotherapy group on what might be called "relative time," that is, the time series is constructed with the zero point at the time when each person in the psychotherapy group entered psychotherapy. But the control group is presented on "absolute time." The distinction is this: One month pretherapy for the psychotherapy group might be January 1, 1975, for one person and August 15th, 1957, for another. In the control group all the people are on the same calendar time. Concern with what might at first seem a minor methodological problem derives from the likelihood that a person who seeks psychotherapy voluntarily does so in response to some felt need."[108]

Effects of Psychotherapy on Medical Utilization
Synthesized average of eleven archival time-series experiments

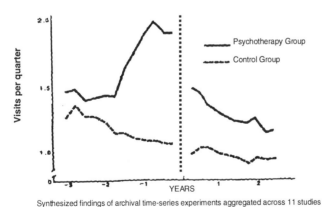

Synthesized findings of archival time-series experiments aggregated across 11 studies

Figure 5

Given that the emotional distress which creates this need might be accompanied by medical symptoms, it is reasonable to suspect that the time of beginning psychotherapy might also be a "peak time of medical utilization," well above the individual's usual level (as indicated on the left side of Figure 5). Thus, it would be expected that the medical utilization would naturally decrease from the more severe level to one closer to the mean. This tendency, called "regression towards the mean" is a statistical way of stating the common expression when things are bad, that "things have got to get better;" that is move towards the average. Figure 5, a compilation of the data from 11 similar studies, shows just these effects: the medical utilization for the psychotherapy group was both far above their average as indicated by the level in years prior to therapy, and well above that of the control group(left half of Fig. 5). Thus, it could have been predicted that the levels would drop (i.e. regress) for the group to a level closer to the norm. And it would also be assumed that this lower level, which is more typical of the person's usual utilization would last with or without psychotherapy. If, at the same time, the person enters psychotherapy, it would be natural, although perhaps completely erroneous, to assume that the change is due to psychotherapy. Even the control (non-psychotherapy) group shows some regression towards the mean, with a smaller reduction. Schlesinger and his colleagues offer the following comment: "Since the tendency of these methodological flaws is to inflate the apparent effect of psychotherapy on medical utilization, it is risky to take the integrated findings of these 11 studies at face value... a conservative conclusion would be that the likely influence of psychotherapy on reduction of medical utilization lies somewhere between 0% and 14%,"[109] far below that implied by VandenBos's earlier statement which claimed dramatic effectiveness and cost savings. Borus and his colleagues in their study of this "offset effect" even found that psychological treatment "boosted the overall care utilization and charges... above those of patients treated solely by their physicians..."[110] In this case, the involvement of psychologists increased the cost (and provided them with income.)

SCIENCE FICTION

> ...a great deal of what passes as attested theory
> is little more than speculation, varying widely in plausibility. [111]

The Psychology Industry with its false explanations of cause, false statements of fact, false reports of cure and false claims of authority, has lent substantial support to the words of Lincoln: "you may fool all the people some of the time; you can even fool some of the people all of the time."

"When I was a student," former APA president Paul Meehl wrote, "there was at least one common factor present in all of the psychology faculty... namely, the general scientific commitment not to be fooled and not to fool anybody else. Some things have happened in the world of clinical practice that worry me in this respect. That skepsis, that passion not to be fooled and not to fool anybody else, does not seem to be as fundamental a part of all psychologists' mental equipment as it was a half a century ago. One mark of a good psychologist is to be critical in evaluating evidence... I have heard of some psychological testimony in court rooms locally in which this critical mentality appears to be largely absent."[112]

Some, psychologists and users alike, fool themselves into believing that they have great understanding into the causes of emotional problems, while others believe they have discovered a new and revolutionary cure. Others grasp hold of the pseudoscience because it seems to explain the unknown and calm the mind. As one psychologist put it: "Science is a way to make people feel more comfortable by allowing them to explain things that they don't understand. In this way it compares to Greek mythology and modern religion."[113]

But time has revealed that a number of known-to-be-effective therapies have turned out to be useless or worse. Biofeedback, a particularly popular therapy of the 70's, for instance, advocated that if one could gain control over the autonomic nervous system, one could master one's state of being, both physically and mentally. It assumed that, since a certain type of brain wave called alpha appears when people are relaxed, learning to "produce" alpha waves would cause people to be relaxed and in control. Without any basic supporting evidence, this presumption was then stretched so that claims were made that biofeedback could cure sexual disorders and deviance, muscle paralysis, migraine headaches, back pain, phobias, and even serve as a means of male contraception.[114]

Wrapped in the aura of science, biofeedback sessions took place in laboratories with white-coated professionals, physiological monitoring and print-outs of brain, heart, muscle and skin functioning. Biofeedback experts claimed that they could cure many of the psychological problems in a shorter period of time and without the unnecessary insight of verbal psychotherapy, persisting with these assertions despite the growing number of scientific studies which failed to offer any evidence to support them. Research had shown unambiguously that biofeedback techniques did not work.[115] Yet the public, open and gullible to anything easy and scientific, thronged to these labs, only to find that the promised cure evaded them. Nirvana was not to be found there. The body and the mind may very well be linked but not in a direct way that allowed the simplistic intervention of biofeedback to work. This science was fiction, its explanations imaginary and its results fantasy. Biofeedback therapy belonged to science fiction; its proponents were novelists not scientists. Much of the equipment was relegated to the museum of fad therapies.

Science fiction, whatever its focus, evokes intrigue by blending the known, the believable and the fantastic. With its starting point being "what is," it then travels beyond these limits into the realm of the "what if." Whether it begins with the submersible and goes 20,000 leagues under the sea, or with a space mission and becomes Star Trek, it merges science with fantasy, fact with fiction.

As a means of manufacturing victims, the Psychology Industry frequently delves into the world of "what if," creating its own science fiction. Take for example the work of John Mack and his followers. Mack, a professor of psychiatry at Harvard University writes:

> I have seen more than a hundred individuals referred for evaluation of abductions or other "anomalous" experiences. Of these, seventy-six (ranging in age from two to fifty-seven; forty-seven females and twenty-nine males, including three boys eight and

under) fulfil my quite strict criteria of an abduction case... I have done between one and eight several-hour modified hypnosis sessions with forty-nine of these individuals, and have evolved a therapeutic approach...[116]

Not an unreasonable statement and one made by a respected psychiatrist from a very reputable institution[117] about physical "abductions" and their emotional consequences. Reasonable that is, until it is realized that he is writing about "alien abductions" in UFO's. Mack is perfectly serious as he weaves together a popular belief in flying saucers, with society's current concern about abductions and violence, and the growing mass of popular and professional articles, books, and workshops on physical and sexual abuse. On his own version of the "slippery slope," Mack begins with the regrettable fact that non-alien abductions do occur and can have psychological consequences. He proceeds by acknowledging that he is exploring at "the margins of accepted reality," and introduces the possibility of the existence of aliens and the pop cultural notions of UFO's and powerful lights in the sky. Then, with the style of a smooth, sleight-of-hand magician, he draws attention away from the "what is" to the "what if," suggesting what might happen to victims while they are "away" and what the later consequences, the "universal properties of the abduction experience" might be. He states that "most often, abductees everywhere are compellingly drawn toward a powerful light, often while they are driving or asleep in their beds. Invariably, they are later unable to account for "lost" periods of time, and they frequently bear physical and psychological scars of their experience. These range from nightmares and anxiety to chronic nervous agitation, depression, and even psychosis, to actual physical scars - punctures and incisions marks, scrapes, burns and sores."[118]

With this theory and with what he calls a "quite strict criteria of an abduction case: conscious recall or recall with the help of hypnosis, of being taken by alien beings into a strange craft, reported with emotion appropriate to the experience being described and no apparent mental condition that could account for the story," he proceeds not only to diagnose and treat abductees but also to make predictive statements about the prevalence (epidemic) of UFO abductions. He writes: "2% of adults in the American population have had a constellation of experiences consistent with an abduction history. Therefore, based on our sample of nearly 6,000 respondents, we believe that one out of every 50 Americans may have had UFO abduction experiences." This would mean approximately 3.7 million people in the United States have been abducted by UFO's at one time or another, a number which he says is dismissed because of society's massive denial.[119]

While Mack acknowledges that indicators may not in fact mean that an abduction has occurred, he makes the statement that "a more serious difficulty in estimating the prevalence of abductions lies in the fact that we do not know what an abduction really is — the extent, for example, to which it represents an event in the physical world or to which it is an unusual subjective experience with physical manifestations. A still greater problem resides in the fact that memory in relation to abduction experiences behaves rather strangely... the memory of an abduction may be outside of consciousness until triggered many years later by another experience or situation that becomes associated with the original event. The experiences in a situation such as this could be counted on the negative side of the ledger before the triggering experience and on the positive side after it."[120]

Follow Mack's thinking for a moment:

1) he combines the social phenomenon of abduction by strangers with the pop belief in UFO's,

2) resulting in the concept of UFO abductions,

3) which can be assessed in individuals by applying a criteria unsupported by any independent research,

4) which leads to the diagnosis, often determined through the use of hypnosis,

5) for which there are "known" psychological and physical consequences,

6) which necessitate specialized treatment by a psychologist.

To lend support to this, he weaves in the already controversial concepts of sexual abuse and repression and the controversial idea that memories reported in therapy or under hypnosis are true. In fact, with regard to memories he states that "thinking of memory too literally as "true" or " false" may restrict what we can learn about human consciousness from the abduction experience."[121] In other words, the experience is true beyond any question of whether the reported memories are true. Nowhere does he, nor could he, provide any independent support or scientific evidence for his science fiction.

For many, the whole notion can be dismissed as a case of science fiction or nonsense. But Mack's reasoning is like that found in the blending of ideas of abuse and impressions about Satanists resulting in Satanic Ritual Abuse, or of incest and monstrous parents resulting in Childhood Sexual Abuse. The process of diagnosis and treatment of these is disturbingly similar to that of John Mack's UFO abductees. In each instance, the psychologist claims to have special abilities to identify people who have been abused, sometimes based on vague criteria applied to what they say, sometimes according to how they look,[122] and sometimes based solely on their wondering if they have been abused, such as the case described in the Introduction. It is then argued, based on clinical case studies rather than empirical studies, that these memories have been hidden from consciousness, through repression. It is assumed that, although the individuals have no conscious memory of the events, the memories have been retained somewhere in the brain (i.e. at the unconscious level) where they continue to create psychic disturbances similar to those described by Mack which result in later problems in living including addictions, relationship difficulties, aggression and violence, passivity and dependence, physical illness, etc. The individual is considered unable to deal with problems in adult life because of injuries done to the child. The only help is psychological treatment to recover memories of the past; to acknowledge, accept and nurture the injured "child within;" and to confront (and avenge) the wrongs and the wrong-doers.

This approach has polarized the experts, creating True Believers,[123] both pro and con. On the one side are many of the psychologists claiming that child abuse is prevalent, that it is the most frequent cause of psychological problems, that it must be identified, and that the perpetrators must be brought out in the open (and often to court). The other side argues that often these memories are false, inadvertently caused by the therapist (iatrogenic), and that the accused are the real victims of a misguiding therapy. Much of the controversy surrounds two topics: memory and denial/repression. Put succinctly, the theory holds that everything that is experienced is stored in memory and that any and all of it can be remembered later. If events in the past, such as those of childhood, can't be remembered, it is assumed to indicate that something bad must have happened and that the memories are being repressed. If one wonders, imagines or thinks that something bad has happened, this is understood as a sign that repression is lessening and that the events are ready to be faced and the memories of bad things worked through.

It is believed by those supporting this approach that memory is historically accurate and in many ways recorded and retained like a video tape. As forensic hypnotist and psychologist Martin Reiser writes when discussing the effectiveness of hypnosis to retrieve memories of a murder: "the mind is like a video tape machine in that everything is recorded, perhaps at a sub-conscious level, and stored in the brain but available for recall under hypnosis."[124] In the 50's, Wilder Penfield, the noted neurosurgeon, demonstrated that if a particular area of the cortex is electrically stimulated during brain surgery, the patient could experience spontaneous flashbacks of old, apparently (though never proven) forgotten memories. It is now argued that Penfield's work proves that all memories are stored in the brain and can be retrieved later and that therapists' questions or hypnotic suggestions have the same power as Penfield's electrical probe but with greater precision, to discover the "right" memories. It is also presumed that the memory system functions from birth in the same way that it does throughout adult life. For example, a respected clinical hypnotherapist claimed to be demonstrating "hypnotic regression" when he suggested to a woman that she go back to the time of her birth. He then asked her to describe her experience immediately after birth. She described the delivery room, the bright lights, the attending staff (identifying some by name), the cold air and the welcoming response of her mother. Based on these "memories," the hypnotist proceeded to affirm her recollections ("That's right! That's good!"), persuading her to accept the event and to see herself as wanted and loved. At no time during or after the session did he caution her that she may be imagining any of this and that it may not be a true record of the events, a reasonable and proper thing to have done considering that there is no research to support the validity of these kinds of memory.

What research does show is that retrospective memory is basically a reconstructive process, that remembrances are put together from partial memory traces and are remembered in such a way as to meet the needs or demands of the moment. That is why everyone has the experience from time to time of remembering some event and then remembering more or less at another time. (If everything was recorded like a tape recorder, then events would be remembered in the same way at all times because the same memory tape would be played each time.) As well, what is remembered is dependent on what is first perceived; that is, what is seen, heard, felt, tasted or smelled. If something is not seen then it can't be remembered later. The woman who described her birth experience didn't know that newborns have a fixed visual focal length and can't see more than 18 inches. She didn't know that she would not have seen, let alone known by name, who was in the delivery room. Without this knowledge, she responded to the hypnotist's leading questions by constructing artificial memories based on information available to her as an adult. As the ability for visual perception changes after birth, so too does the child's ability to think, resulting in further changes in the style and content of memories. "The fact is that no matter how the process of memorizing during infancy is measured, there is clear proof that it is far below the efficiency of that of the older child or adult" stated the Social Science Research Council.[125] "Tests of recognition, memory pictures, rote memory regularly show that human memory has proved to be poor at the earliest level and to increase by a fairly constant rate to a later period." Memories of the past, particularly of childhood, are quite unreliable, since they mix and become confused with fantasies, information gained from other sources and at other times of life, and the suggestions or influences in one's immediate life. As Peter Wolfe writes in challenging the validity of reconstructed memories: "The clinical reconstruction of early childhood experiences deals with the subject's present view about his past, and not with the discovery of archeological artifacts that have been buried."[126]

If adult recollections of childhood are unreliable, perhaps at least children's reports of recent events are more dependable. Again the True Believer phenomenon becomes evident as child therapists/abuse experts make extreme statements such as "Children don't lie about sexual abuse!" and "How would they know about such things (i.e. sexual acts) if it had not been done to them." An interesting study involving anatomically detailed dolls (ADD)[127] sheds some scientific light on these claims. Forty 3-year old children were tested in their paediatrician's office after receiving an annual medical examination. Half the children received a genital examination involving gentle touching of the buttocks and genitals, while the other group did not receive a genital examination. Immediately after each individual check-up, a research assistant, using an ADD, asked the children to show, using the doll, how the doctor had touched their buttocks and genitals (either a leading or misleading question). Results showed that the children were very inaccurate: for those who had a genital examination, 45% denied touching when asked directly, and the accuracy level increased to 57% "when these children manipulated the dolls to demonstrate the genital exam, because some children falsely showed that the doctor had inserted a finger into the anal or genital cavity. Accuracy was also low for children who had not received a genital examination: 42% of their responses included false claims they had been touched when asked "Did he touch you?" and 38% of their responses on the dolls showed that the doctor had touched their genitals or anal region. The children also demonstrated a number of other sexualized behaviours during the interview. Some used other props in a sexual manner on their own bodies or on the dolls.[128] This study highlights the fact that not only are children very inaccurate in reporting sexual touching but also that the rate of false positives (that is , reports of touching in the absence of any) are comparable to the level of false negatives (failure to report what did happen.)

This leads to the other aspect of reports of past sexual abuse, that is the claim that the memory is impaired because the individuals repress or deny the facts. The argument holds that these events of childhood are so traumatic that the mind represses them from consciousness, but continues to retain them in the unconscious, from which they continue to affect and disorder adult life. Freud described repression as one of the primary defense mechanisms which serves to protect the individual by keeping disturbing events from interfering in conscious living. He believed that psychological problems resulted from partial or total failure of this defense process, the breakdown of repression and the leaking through of disturbing material. In contrast, current psychotherapy holds that repression itself is the problem and that mental health comes about from gaining awareness of repressed material (i.e. "facing the facts") and "dealing with it" (of course through therapy).

Repression, however, is a concept that has no research evidence to support it and much of what is purported to be examples of repression can more easily be understood through normal forgetting, selective remembering (i.e. remembering what one wants to remember, a process already identified when it comes to clinical claims of therapeutic effectiveness), or "infantile amnesia," which Sears writes "is apparently a biological trick of an undeveloped memory system, not a Freudian twist of unconscious repression."[129] Despite this lack of supporting evidence, many psychologists interpret the failure to remember childhood as indicative of repressed memories of child abuse, and the wondering about possible abuse as indicative of these memories "slipping through." For example, Bass and Davis write: "If you think that you were abused and your life shows the symptoms, then you probably were." And they continue: "so far no one we've talked to thought she might have been abused and then later discovered she hadn't been."[130] Such circular arguments, another of the Catch-22's of the Psychology Industry's reasoning, defy objective validation in that they argue that if one represses then one doesn't remember, so that if one doesn't remember then one must be repressing memories; and if you think or wonder about abuse (as well as addiction or abduction) then you are a victim and if you don't then you are denying the fact.[131] Once having achieved this level of absurd thinking, the psychologist can lead the patient into the belief of abuse, the pursuit of memories and the creation of their own science fiction.

"Caveat Emptor:" Buyer Beware

> *The aim of science is not to open the door to everlasting wisdom,*
> *but to set a limit on everlasting error.*

Bertolt Brecht, *Life of Galileo*

At the beginning of this century, the discipline of psychology held all the hopes, aspirations and promise of a new-born science. Now, at the end of the century, it is evident that psychology has failed to live up to these. Rather, it epitomizes the self-serving, boastful nature of an adolescent; an entrepreneurial pseudoscience. Despite its popularity, it has not produced the society, free of crime and problems, that it had claimed it would. Psychology has neither provided a better understanding of the psyche, nor created a healthier way of living. In fact, as the number of psychologists has increased in the past three decades so has crime, poverty, homelessness and anxiety increased; in other words, "the world is getting worse."[132] It is clear that the Psychology Industry, put to the test, has failed to prove itself.[133]

So, how is the Psychology Industry still able to maintain the appearance of being scientific? Why do so many people believe that it is based in science? In part it is because beliefs are expressed in scientific jargon and opinions are stated as if they are research findings and empirical facts. Sometimes, this is done in the absence of any research, sometimes through the intentional manipulation of data, sometimes through biased and politically influenced interpretations. Personal interests and egos have distorted the facts and caused psychologists to ignore both the empirical evaluations of their practice and the science that many of them were once taught. In many ways, fact has been replaced with fiction, and knowledge with beliefs. The "science of psychology" has become the "business of psychology," persuading the public that psychologists, both the therapists and the experts, have solutions to their problems.

When *Consumer Reports(CR)* published a report on a "candid, in-depth survey" of its readers regarding their personal benefits of psychotherapy,[134] psychologist Martin Seligman, the consultant to the project, published a companion article in the American Psychological Association's flagship journal, *American Psychologist*.[135] He described the results as sending " *'a message of hope'* for other people dealing with emotional problems,"[136] and as establishing a *"gold standard"* for the evaluation of psychotherapy effectiveness.[137] However, a closer look at the *CR* report and Seligman's paper suggests that this hope may be false and that this "gold standard" may be a counterfeit one reflecting the economic and business motivations of psychologists. Both articles mislead the public by, amongst other things, substituting people who *want* therapy for those who *need* help, and by treating feelings as if they are facts.[138]

Psychotherapy is generally considered to be a treatment option for people experiencing serious emotional problems which significantly interfere with their lives, but such is not the case for the majority of these respondents. What *CR* fails to mention, and which Seligman notes without acknowledging the significance, is that less than half, only 1212 of the 2900 respondents, described their emotional state when they began therapy as "very poor" (426) or "fairly poor" (786). 58.2% felt *very good, quite good,* or *so-so.*[139] (Fig. 6) Seligman views these individuals as "being sick" and not knowing it, referring to them as " 'sub-clinical' in their problems" and falling "one symptom short of a full-blown "disorder.'" However, from a common sense, non-psychologized perspective, these people would be considered normal, "okay" or even in "great shape."

Emotional state when therapy began
A retrospective self-report

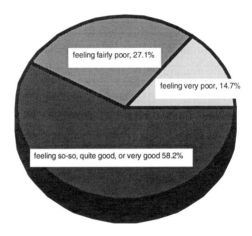

Figure 6

Seligman not only pathologizes them he also confuses what they present as subjective opinion for objective reality. His "gold standard" eliminates the distinction between facts and feelings so that "satisfaction" and "effectiveness" are equated and truth is determined by opinion. Descartes' axiom "I think, therefore I am" is replaced by the Psychology Industry's *"You feel, therefore you are right!"* Despite Seligman's heralding of the *CR* report as an "effectiveness study" providing "empirical validation of the effectiveness of psychotherapy," it would more appropriately be called a "Psychology Industry consumer satisfaction survey," similar to those usually done to rate happiness with cars, toasters or washing machines.

CR, by allowing its opinion survey to be disguised as a scientific tool and transformed into an arbiter of reality, abdicates its role as "an independent, non-profit testing and information organization serving only consumers,"[140] and becomes a marketing extension of the Psychology Industry. In doing so, its publication has become remarkably in line with the promotional intentions of the Industry, and particularly of the American Psychological Association, which are to show that:

- psychotherapy is effective,
- "highly trained" psychologists are more effective than those with lesser or no training (or as Morris calls them "would-be helpers") and
- the constraints on long-term and "eclectic" (i.e. non-specific) therapy, being imposed by managed care, are inappropriate.

As such, the *CR* report is and will be used by the Psychology Industry to promote its services and expand its markets. Already the American Psychological Association has announced that the report will be a part of its "public campaign" to "tell society about the contributions psychologists make," which

> will include a toll-free number that people can call for more information on how psychological services can help them or their family... We (APA) will also send them studies and reports that demonstrate the value of psychological interventions, *such as the November 1995 article in* Consumer Reports, which found that psychotherapy works and that long-term interventions are more effective than shorter ones... That in turn will *increase the value* that people ascribe to these services. In our final message, *we will teach the public* to recognize quality psychological services and protect access to them.[141]

As well, following the release of the CR and Seligman articles, Seligman ran for the presidency of the American Psychological Association and was elected by a large majority. His "platform" was to build on the *CR* study through studies that will "convince all but the most entrenched" that: (1) "long-term therapy works and is worth the cost;" (2) "doctoral-level providers do a better job;" and (3) "clinical judgment and patient choice work better than external case-management systems."[142] Consistent with the Psychology Industry's approach to research, Seligman stated that "the outcome of these three studies is assured;" in other words, that the studies are a political tool to promote the "business" not to support the "science." In this regard, Seligman makes a curious statement: "the evidence as it now stands is *enough to convince the converted*, but is not compelling to the much sterner jury of health-care decision-makers, Congress and the American public."[143] One would have thought that psychology's scientific community would have been more knowledgable and critical than the lay public and business communities.

The *CR* report and Seligman's article, which came out at the same time and used the same proprietary data, were based on the results of a supplement to the 1994 annual survey sent to all 180,000 subscribers.[144] The survey did not ask respondents objective, factual questions such as how much alcohol they drank before going for help as compared to after, or how many fights they had then and are having now with their spouse, or how often they thought of suicide then versus the past month. Instead it asked them how much better they felt and how much they thought therapy had helped them. It was, in the usual style of *CR*, a consumer satisfaction survey that became distorted and translated into "convincing evidence that therapy can make an important difference."[145]

Readers were asked to respond:

> if at any time over the past three years you experienced stress or other emotional problems for which you sought help from any of the following: friends, relatives, or a member of the clergy; a mental-health professional like a psychologist, counsellor, or psychiatrist; your family doctor; or a support group.[146]

Despite the broad invitation, only approximately 7,000 responded to the mental health survey; of these, 4,000 reported seeing a mental health professional, family doctor or attending a support group; the remaining 3,000 had talked to a friend, relative or clergy. For reasons that they would not make public, *CR* chose to ignore the experience of this latter group of 3,000, and to attend only to the 4,000, with particular emphasis on the 2,900 who saw mental health professionals.[147]

Of the 180,000 *CR* Readers surveyed

23,400 (13%) responded	156,600 (87%) didn't
7,000 (3.9%) answered Mental Health Questions	16,400 (9.1%) answered auto only
4,000 (2.2%) sought professional help	3,000 (1.6%) spoke to friends, family, clergy
2,900 (1.6%) saw Mental Health Professional	1,100 (0.6%) saw family doctor/group

Numerous attempts were made by a number of individuals (including the author) to get *CR* to release the summary data for independent analysis or to publish the demographic data collected about the 3000 who sought help from "a friend, relative or clergy." On all occasions, they refused, claiming that this data was proprietary and would not be analyzed or released. Seligman, in private communication, made conflicting comments; on one occasion, saying that he too would like to see the data, and on another assuring the author that there was nothing of substance to be found there.[148]

One is left wondering about Seligman's role and why *CR* will not report on this minimal but important data. If, in fact, those who received professional treatment were either significantly different or currently felt better than those who received lay help, would not both parties want the public to know this, and if not, does not the *CR* have the responsibility to 'consumers' to inform them that paid services may not be better than ones that are free? The questions remain!

Problems exist when all of the conclusions and claims are based on this group of 2900 replies. For one thing, the group consisting of individuals who were mostly middle class, well educated, and with a median age of 46, is not representative of the United States as a whole[149] (and not even of the *CR* readership.) Seligman dismisses this problem by "guessing" that it is however representative of those "who make up the bulk of psychotherapy patients,"[150] never giving further thought as to what this may mean both for the data and about the upper middle class nature of psychotherapy.

Secondly, Seligman admits that the response rate, which he states as 13%, is "rather low absolutely." In fact, the response rate is only 2.2%, far lower than his figure and a rate which *CR* described as "very low." In most cases, such a low return rate would render a study invalid, not warranting any further analysis or comment. (Figures 7 and 8)

"Mental Health" Response Rate
for MH professionnals, family doctors & groups

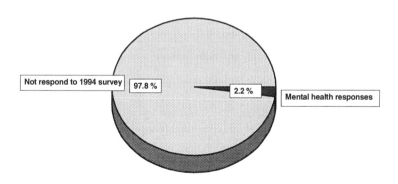

Figure 7

As well, one has cause to suspect that the group is likely biased in favour of those with positive experiences. Seligman considers this to be a possibility when he attempts to explain the remarkably good reports of those who went to AA, by saying that they are favoured by "a preponderance of successes." However, for unexplained reasons, he dismisses a similar possibility for those in psychotherapy. "One is left with the concern that this report may very well be based on a very small, unrepresentative group of "therapy junkies," individuals so committed to therapy as a way of life that they bias the results in this direction."[151]

Proportions of responses to Survey
of 23,400 replies to 1994 survey

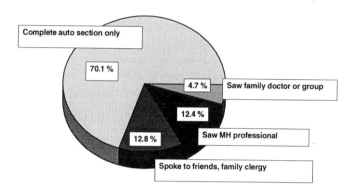

Figure 8

If it is the case, that the group is over weighted with individuals having a "Psychologically-Prone Personality" (to be described in Chapter 6), it is quite reasonable to assume that when asked to express their satisfaction with psychotherapy ("how much do you feel your therapy helped you...?"), they would be the ones most likely to take the time to respond. Seligman would like his colleagues and the public to believe that the bias of such retrospective self-reporting, or "noise" as he calls it, is random and that the results are unbiased. However, as early as 1977, Strupp and Hadley showed that clients, independent of whether they were therapy junkies, evaluate their therapy on a very different basis than do psychologists or third parties such as family, friends, or insurance companies. Also, as mentioned earlier, other studies have shown that patients are second only to their therapists in evaluating their psychological treatment in a favourable light.

CR, and the Psychology Industry, (specifically in this case, Seligman and the American Psychological Association) draw three conclusions from the survey data: 1) therapy is effective; 2) mental health professionals do better than others; and 3) "long-term therapy with a specialist is more effective."[152] The data needed to address these issues is hidden behind CR's non–disclosure rule. Neither CR nor Seligman was willing, when asked, to provide any further information or clarification, let alone actual results. So one can work only with the appallingly sparse data in the actual report and the limited additional information to be found in Seligman's article. As well, there are so many apparent inconsistencies and strange contradictions in Seligman's article that trying to understand and make sense of this is like trying to sort apples and oranges when you can't see them or feel them. Consider the following examples:

- In rebutting the problems of a retrospective study, Seligman acknowledges that asking clients sometime later about their experience with therapy yields less valid results, but in his view, "waiting for the *rosy afterglow* of a newly completed therapy to dissipate, as the *CR* study does, may make for a more sober evaluation."[153] While this argument in favour of a retrospective approach may make sense, it seems not to be consistent with the actual facts of the study as presented by Seligman. For instance, Seligman reveals that of the 487 clients who had "two or more years of therapy," 245 (or 50.3%) are still in therapy at the time of the survey. This not only negates his argument for a period of time in which to gain some objectivity, it also causes concern as to how many people in the other time categories are also still in therapy and reflecting the "glow" of the moment.[154]

- In another case relating directly to the question "Does Therapy Help?" Seligman states that 64% of those receiving 6 months or less of therapy reported that their problems were resolved.[155] However, Seligman's charts (reproduced here as Fig. 9) indicates that only 30% reported that, with respect to their specific problems, treatment "made things a lot

Improvement of Presenting Symptom
Seligman's Figure 2

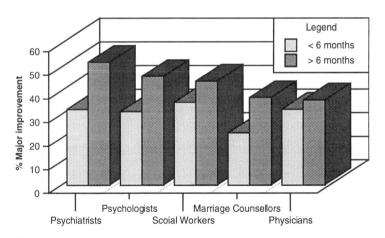

Figure 9

better." One is left wondering (1) how is it possible that 64% reported problem resolution when only 30% said that their problems improved?[156] and, (2) how is it that Seligman failed to identify this inconsistency when he considers the results to be "clear cut" proof of effectiveness? As well, one is left wondering how many other instances of misinformation exist in his article.[157]

Question 1: Does Therapy Help?

Whether it is 30% or 64%, it would seem that for some people their presenting problems changed for the better, but is this proof that therapy works? To adequately answer this question, evidence is needed that shows that (1) the people did not change merely due to the passage of time (remembering that this is a study that looks back over time) or a "regression effect," and (2) therapy does something that *"just* talking to friend, family or clergy"* would not achieve (Seligman's italics).

CR states that 44% of people whose emotional state was "very poor" at the start of treatment, now feel "good"and that 43% who felt "fairly poor" also "improved significantly, though somewhat less." On the basis of this, it concluded that "therapy for mental-health problems can have a substantial effect."[158] Seligman concurs, stating that "the overall improvement rates were strikingly high across the entire spectrum of treatments and disorders in the *CR* study." And he continues: "It means that if you have a patient with a severe disorder now, the chances are quite good that he or she will feel better within three years."[159]

But why assume that, because people's feelings improved while they were seeing a mental health professional, it was therapy which made them better? It would be incorrect to assume that if people are given an antibiotic and their colds go away in a few weeks, that the antibiotic cured the cold. Most people naturally "get over" a cold in a week or two. So too, the "effect of psychotherapy" may simply be due to the passage of time, for Eysenck has shown that, over time, people show comparable improvement with or without treatment. As well, the conclusion that therapy helped overlooks a phenomenon known as regression to the mean which takes into account the high probability that people seek treatment at a time when they feel particularly bad and that, at a later point in time, they are likely to feel better. As Dawes points out, if "people enter therapy when they are extremely unhappy, they are less likely to be as unhappy later, independent of the effects of therapy itself. Hence, this 'regression effect' can create the illusion that the therapy has helped to alleviate their unhappiness, whether it has or not. In fact, even if the therapy has been downright harmful, people are less likely to be as unhappy later as when they entered therapy."[160] This would explain why *CR* and Seligman found the most "robust effect" to be with those who were feeling the worst and, therefore, had the most room to change, with or without therapy; while those who felt better showed less improvement. In fact, when the rate of improvement for all 2,900 respondents is considered, the results are hardly "robust" or even significant; in fact they are downright discouraging.[161] (Fig. 10.[162])

To determine whether therapy was really "effective" for those in the *CR* survey, a comparison group is needed of people with similar problems who did not receive treatment. Such a group did exist but, for unexplained reasons, *CR* chose to ignore those 3,000 respondents who spoke to friends, relatives and the clergy. Although both groups did describe their emotional

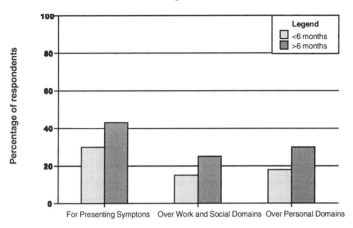

Improvement by "domains"
"Made things a lot better"

Figure 10

state at the time they filled out the survey (#63), which would have given some indication of the effect of time, both *CR* and Seligman declined to reveal whether these groups were similar. Without this, it is impossible to know whether these people similarly improved without professional help.

An alternative way to establish that therapy works, is to demonstrate that a certain treatment method works significantly better with a specific presenting problem. This is the approach that the Clinical Division of the American Psychological Association has adopted in conducting "efficacy studies" and which Seligman supported in his book *What You Can Change & What You Can't.*[163] Although efficacy studies usually involve treatment delivered to selected patients in tightly controlled conditions, the same underlying assumption could be tested with this data. That is, according to efficacy theory, different therapies should work differently for different problems, some working better and some not as well or not at all. However, the survey data apparently revealed "that no specific modality of psychotherapy did any better than any other for any problem."[164] As to whether they did anything at all, the question remains unanswered, for while some respondents report feeling better now as compared to how they remember feeling when they sought therapy, and express some satisfaction about their experiences, there is no clear evidence of treatment effectiveness in this data.

Question 2: Do psychologists (i.e. Mental Health Professionals) do Better?

In the light of the above conclusion, it seems somewhat ridiculous to be entertaining this question. However, if one were, for a moment, to accept Seligman's belief in therapeutic effectiveness, one could consider the issue as to whether trained and licensed psychologists are better therapists. Again, it is regrettable that CR, while they made an initial inquiry of those who sought help from friends, family or clergy, chose to neither survey their experiences nor report on the meagre results that they did accumulate. However, Seligman's article does disclose some information about physicians who, in some ways, can be thought of as comparable to those with little or no mental health training. He states that "for patients who relied solely on family doctors, their overall improvement scores when treated up to six months was 213, and it remained at that level (212) for those treated longer than six months,"[165] as compared with 211 and 232 respectively for the mental health professionals. Figure 11 shows the percent of respondents reporting

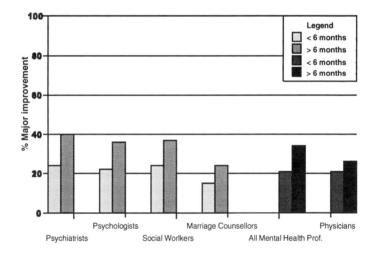

Improvement by Professions
for symptoms, work, social and personal

Figure 11

major symptom improvement in all three domains of life (work, social, and personal). It indicates that physicians do equally well as mental health professionals in the short-term but again not as well in the longer-term, a result which could mistakenly be taken as proof that special training pays off. However, the significance of the apparent long-term difference is reduced when one takes into consideration that many of the long-term mental health patients are still in therapy and might well hold a favourable attitude towards treatment, and that generally family doctors do not see their patients as often as do mental health professionals. In fact, 18% of those who saw physicians complained that their doctor was "too busy to spend time talking with me." It would be unfair to expect similar results when length of time is measured rather than amount of professional contact.

Thus, it would seem that physicians do almost as well as the mental health professionals, suggesting that there may be no significant benefit from "specialized" training and no empirical basis on which to claim superiority.

Question 3: Does Long-term Therapy Make a Difference?

CR asks the question: "When a person needs psychotherapy, how much do they need?"[166] The Psychology Industry answers: *"As much as they want!"* or *"As much as they, or their insurance company, can afford!"* However, such an unrestricted expectation is no longer acceptable on its own. "Research" is needed which will show that longer-term treatment is necessary, makes a difference, and consequently, should be covered by insurance. It is to this end that Seligman addresses much of his attention, managing to conclude that "long-term therapy produced more improvement than short-term therapy. This result was very robust..."[167] In support, he presents the following chart displaying "improvement score" as related to "duration of therapy." (Fig.12) The "im-

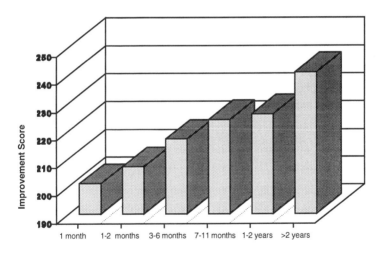

Figure 10

provement score" was obtained by combining the responses to three questions: how much treatment helped with problems that lead to therapy, *satisfaction* with therapist, and how respondents *felt* at the time of the survey compared with when they began treatment. Seligman's chart would suggest a dramatically positive effect of remaining in therapy long-term. But this is a visual illusion. When the graph is redrawn using the same numbers but showing the full extent of the vertical axis (Figure 13), Seligman's "robust" and "dramatic" effect evaporates. As well, if one accepts Seligman's claim

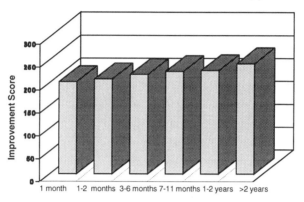

Figure 13

that the first column (i.e. 1 month) approximates "*no treatment,*"[168] *this would mean that over 80% of the improvement, according to Seligman, is* not *due to therapy.* Further, when one considers that many of those at least in the last group (2 years) are still in treatment and subject to a "rosy-glow," one is left with very little support for psychotherapy effectiveness, short or long term. Even, at best, only 13% of the possible improvement can be attributed to long-term treatment.

This raises the question as to whether statistical significance is clinically significant; a reasonable question given that groups can be shown to be significantly different at a numerical level (especially with a sample of this size) while the actual effect is not naturally discernable, as demonstrated in Figure 9. On another occasion, in arguing that respondents whose choice of therapist or duration of care was limited by their insurance coverage did *worse,*

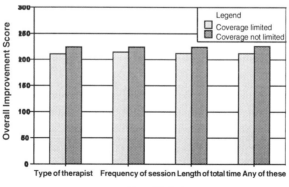

Figure 14

Seligman provided data illustrated in Figure 14. While showing differences that statisticians call significant, these results would hardly seem significant to the person whose overall improvement is 14/300 (212 v. 226) or 4.6% better.

Consumer Reports, as well, expressed concern regarding the strict limits on insurance coverage in light of what it saw as clear benefits of longer term treatment, an opinion it considered to be supported by Figure 15. But this is

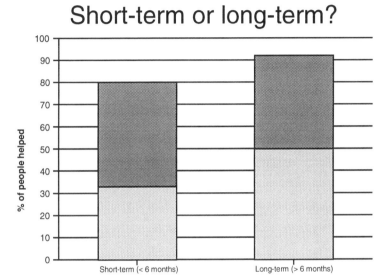

Short-term or long-term?

Figure 15

hardly sufficient proof. What is not known is how many clients stay in therapy long after their symptoms have dissipated, or how much faster they might have shown change if they had received another form of treatment or saved the money and talked to a friend. What is known is that a majority of patients enter therapy with no significant problem, that the long-term patients are "more likely to have psychodynamic treatment"[169] in which change is expected to be gradual over years of therapy, and that the benefits they attribute to treatment included an "enhancement of personal growth," more confidence and self-esteem, a better understanding of themselves, an improved ability to cope with everyday stress, and more enjoyment of life.[170]

While these latter attributes may be desirable, they hardly seem to be the grounds on which to justify psychotherapy or to demand insurance coverage. On the basis of this survey, as reported by *CR* and Seligman, it would appear that psychotherapy is more effective in producing some "satisfied customers" who will speak well of it, than it is in curing specific serious problems. It seems only to make psychologists deserving of the title that Zilbergeld gave to them years ago: "Dr. Feel-Goods."

A House Built on Sand

> *"Clinical services... very effectively delivered... in a higher quality system of care that were nonetheless ineffective. A very impressive structure was built on a very weak foundation."*
>
> Leonard Bickman, Senior Researcher,
> The Fort Bragg Demonstration Project

As well as selling its false abilities to the public, the Psychology Industry has lulled its members into believing in their own inflated skills and effectiveness. A cause for rude awakening was recently published in the form of a report on an extensive project intended to "provide the best possible (psychological) services for children and adolescents without typical limitations."[171]

Cast in such glowing terms as: "a national showcase," "a truly unique opportunity," and "state of the art,"[172] the Fort Bragg Demonstration Project, funded at a cost of $80,000,000 of public funds, was intended to show that "a continuum of mental health and substance abuse services is more *cost-effective* than services delivered in the more typical fragmented system."[173] The Project, which was described by the American Psychological Association's section on Child Clinical Psychology and the Division of Child, Youth and Family Services joint task force as "a model program,"[174] offered in- and out-patient services to the more than 42,000 child and adolescent dependents in the Fort Bragg catchment area for more than five years from June 1990 to September 1995. This group of children were from middle and lower-middle class families and therefore similar to the estimated 68% of the children who are covered by private health insurance.[175]

As such, the Project provided, what psychologist Leonard Bickman, its author, described as "a rare opportunity to examine both costs and clinical outcomes in a careful and comprehensive evaluation of the implementation of an innovative system of care"[176] which psychologists predicted would increase accessibility to treatment, improve results through individualized case management, and reduce overall costs. However, what it found was that, despite better access, greater continuity of care, fewer restrictions on treatment and more client satisfaction, the cost was higher and the clinical results no better than those at the comparison site: not at all what the Psychology Industry had either expected or hoped for!

In summarizing the significance of these results, Bickman and others drew the following conclusions:

- **the notion is clearly false that costs can be controlled by psychologists who determine the type and length of treatment.**

The Psychology Industry argues strenuously against the model that allows others, such as Managed Care Systems, to tell them what treatment they should provide or how long they should do it. Yet, this data shows that what psychologists call their "experienced clinical judgment" was not cost-effective and lead to a higher proportion of children being in treatment longer.

"Six months after starting treatment, 41% at the Demonstration were still receiving services compared to 13% at the Comparison site,"[177] even though, most of the limited change that did occur was evidenced in the first six months with greatly diminishing returns after that time.

- **longer treatment results in higher costs without corresponding significant results.**

Stating that "more is not always better," Bickman attributes these excessive costs to the unlimited access of psychologists to funds. "The Demonstration costs were much higher ($7,777/treated child) than the Comparison ($4,904/treated child)... The costs of treating the average child were higher because of longer time spent in treatment, greater volume of traditional services, heavy use of intermediate services, and higher per-unit costs."[178] Feldman agrees, stating that "the study demonstrates (as was already known full well) that in an unmanaged system of care when services and benefits become rich so do providers."[179] The same view was expressed by the Executive Director for Practice of the American Psychological Association. Newman writes:

"That, when consumers can obtain the benefits of services without having to pay, excess prices or excess consumption occur... Health care cannot be controlled by free enterprise and competition alone. A regulatory framework must be established to provide checks and balances on an industry with ever-increasing private business interests frequently in conflict with public (patient) interests. Without regulatory control, private business interests push towards profit maximization, at times inconsistent with the public interest."[180] Spiegel, in questioning the popular method of treating individuals diagnosed with Multiple Personality Disorder, says: "I would like to say that all of this multiple personality disorder business rarely takes place when financial resources are not available... Its seems to be related to the amount of money the patients have to indulge in this kind of invalidism... Then, when the money starts to run out, the fusion (i.e. integration of the personalities) takes place. That is a sad commentary on the motivation of some therapists."[181] Bickman concurs, suggesting that the experimental model might "be less expensive under a capitated or fixed-price model," where psychologists' fees are limited. Alternatively, one can also suspect that treatment might be shorter in such cases when the psychologist is not paid more for more therapy sessions.

The Seligman and *Consumer Reports* stance that "longer is better"and that the public is suffering when limits are imposed on the length of therapy falters in the face of the data from this study. As Hoagwood, from the National Institute of Mental Health states, referring to this Project, "the belief that simply providing more services will lead to improved outcomes has been shown to be delusional."[182]

- **the assumption that clinical services are in any way effective might very well be erroneous.**

Citing the lack of difference in clinical outcomes between the Demonstration Project and the Comparison site as "the most unanticipated finding," Bickman states that "these results should raise serious doubts about some current clinical beliefs" about the effectiveness of psychological services.[183] He is clear, and well supported by others, that the methodology in the study was not the cause as the Project was highly effective in delivering the best possible services in a continuum of care and yet it failed to show any better results. This leads him and others to "question the assumption that clinical services provided in the community (i.e. outside of the research setting) are effective."[184] This question gains strength in light of the fact that there have been very few studies which have evaluated the effectiveness of treatment in real-world settings, and when these are analyzed, they show an average effect size very close to zero.[185]

Some critics have argued that the Fort Bragg study differs from these in that it shows improvement in both the Demonstration and Comparison groups. To quote Hoagwood: "In fact, 50% of the children improved during the year after intake, as defined by losing a diagnosis, and 84% of the children improved using a summary outcome variable."[186] The problem with this conclusion is that one does not know whether this change would have occurred even if the children had not received any treatment. In the absence of a "Control/No-Treatment group", it is impossible to draw any conclusion of effectiveness since, as Weisz has noted: "individuals who are referred to clinics and are judged appropriate candidates for treatment, but who do not actually receive treatment, tend to show significant improvement over time nonetheless." Those in the study may have gotten better anyway[187] without the expense of psychological services.

- **satisfaction is not a good measure of the effectiveness or value of psychological treatment.**

Despite Seligman's argument for "client satisfaction" as the new measure, the "Gold Standard," for assessing the worth of psychotherapy, this study exemplifies the fact that satisfaction and effectiveness are not related. Those in the Demonstration project were more satisfied but not any better than the rest, causing one to wonder if the 'gold' is merely 'Fool's Gold" used to con the customers.

> *"... the pursuit of truth in some directions is even injurious to happiness, because it compels us to take leave of delusions which were pleasant while they lasted."*
>
> A. E. Housman, Introductory Lectures, 1892.

More is not better! Psychologists are inclined to provide as much service as funds allow even if it is not cost-effective! Satisfied customers are not better off! Psychologists like Bickman even concede that psychological services may not work. He summarizes, with forthright honesty, that "The implications of this are far-reaching because it suggests that services delivered apart from research settings may not be effective regardless of the type of system in which they are placed."[188]

The Ft. Bragg Project was replicated in Stark County, Ohio with similar results at the six month and two year follow-ups, leading Bickman to state that: "although substantial evidence for the efficacy of psychotherapy under laboratory-like conditions exists, there is scant evidence of its effectiveness in real-life community settings. For children and adolescents, the picture is even more disappointing. We have no evidence for the effectiveness of innovative community-based treatments such as home-based care or day treatment."[189] In a major study designed to seek out such evidence, Bickman's colleague, Bhar Weiss, carefully examined the effect of two years of traditional child psychotherapy as it is typically delivered in out-patient settings. What he found was not the expected benefits but rather no effect at all.[190]

What will be the reaction of the Psychology Industry? It is unlikely that these studies will be touted, as the *Consumer Reports* one is, in their public education campaign. It is unlikely that clinicians will reduce or limit their treatment to conserve the scarce resources and limited insurance benefits. It is unlikely that these findings will be referred to by practicing psychologists when they speak of their worth or importance. It is unlikely that they will affect the way psychological services are developed or funded. It is unlikely that they will change the beliefs of those within the Industry for, although the Fort Bragg and the Stark County studies are well-designed, well-implemented, well-analyzed, and produce results that are about as clear-cut as can be imagined,[191] they don't support the current claims of the Psychology Industry. "In the end," as Sechrest and Walsh put it, "what it comes down to is whether professional psychology is going to be guided by its dogma or its data"[192] or, put somewhat differently, whether it will use science to guide its action or misuse science to sell its products.

Seligman's own warning to consumers, though he may now choose to ignore it, seems worthy of repeating:

> Making up your mind about self-improvement courses, psycho-therapy, and medication... is difficult because the industries that champion them are enormous and profitable and try to sell themselves with highly persuasive means: testimonials, case histories, word of mouth, endorsements... all slick forms of advertising.[193]

In the world of the Psychology industry, the concept of "caveat emptor" bears special importance because "science" is a sales pitch. As Frank Farley, a past president of the American Psychological Association, said: "the science side of psychology is in selling ourselves in (the) market."[194]

Endnotes

1. William James. "A Plea for Psychology as a Natural Science" (1892) in *Collected Essays and Reviews* (1920).

2. Bloom, Allan. *The Closing of the American Mind.* New York: Touchstone Books (Simon & Schuster), 1987. p.361.

3. "...in its separation and then divorce from philosophy, and in its embrace of the scientific ethos and methodology, psychology ended up with the nature and structure of individual behaviour (overt and covert) as the object of interest and study. If psychology were to be scientific, it needed a subject matter amenable to scientific study, preferably in a laboratory..." Sarason, Seymour B. *Psychology Misdirected.* New York: The Free Press, 1981. p.94.

4. Revel, Jean-Francois. *The Flight from Truth.* New York: Random House, 1991, p.18.

5. The National Surgical Adjuvant Breast and Bowel Project at the University of Pittsburgh.

6. Canadian Press, September, 21, 1994.

7. Like Galton, Burt was knighted for his work.

8. Burt, C. "Ability and income." *British Journal of Educational Psychology*, 1943, 13, p.200.

9. Burt, C., and Howard, M. "The multifactorial theory of inheritance and its application to intelligence." *British Journal of Statistical Psychology*, 1956, 9, pp.95-131.

10. Eysenck, H. J. and Kamin, Leon. *The Intelligence Controversy.* New York: John Wiley and Son, 1981. p.98.

11. Hearnshaw, L.S. *Cyril Burt: Psychologist.* Ithaca, NY: Cornell University Press, 1979.

12. Psychologist Robert Joynson and sociologist Ronald Fletcher independently wrote that the attacks against Burt were motivated by a mixture of professional and ideological antagonism. Joynson, R.B. *The Burt Affair.* London: Routledge, 1989; Fletcher, R. "Intelligence, equality, character, and education." *Intelligence*, 1991, 15, pp.139-149.

13. McCarthy, Barry and Emily. *Confronting the Victim Role.* New York: Carroll and Graf Publ., 1993. p.26.

14. Ibid. p.69.

15. Ibid. p.144.

16. Sharon Wegscheider-Cruse, author of *Co-Dependency: An Emerging Issue.* Pompano Beach, FL.: Health Communications, Inc.; cited by Anne Wilson Schaef, *When Society Becomes An Addict.* San Francisco: Harper and Row, 1987.

17. Schaef, Anne W. *Beyond Therapy, Beyond Science: A New Model for Healing the Whole Person.* San Francisco: HarperSan Francisco, 1992. p.94.

18. "Fired for being fat, he wins $1 million." *San Francisco Examiner*, September 7, 1995, p.A8.

19. "Body, mind and allergies" *Times-Colonist*, July, 19, 1994, p.C1.

20. Basic Black, CBC Radio, Nov. 11, 1995.

21. Reuters (3/06/94), referencing the University of Southern California, reported in *Cancer Causes and Control Journal*, published by the Harvard School of Public Health.

22. Feinstein, A.R. *Clinical Epidemiology: The Architecture of Clinical Research.* Philadelphia: W.B. Saunders, 1985.

23. Ralph, Diana. *Work and Madness: The Rise of Community Psychiatry.* Montreal: Black Rose Books, 1983. p.76.

24. Canadian Broadcasting Corporation's National News, November 1993.

25. Fekete, John. *Moral Panic: Biopolitics Rising.* Montreal: Robert Davies Publ., 1994.

26. Women's Safety Project first appeared as Appendix A of *Changing The Landscape* (see next note). It was subsequently released as *Private Violence/Public Fear: Rethinking Women's Safety, Final Report* prepared for the Sollicitor General of Canada by Lori Haskell and Melanie Randall, Toronto, March, 1994. (This later report showed unexplained variations in the statistics from those presented in 1993 and is consequently cited as Project "94 at times through this chapter section.)

27. *Changing the Landscape: Ending Violence — Achieving Equality, Final Report of the Canadian Panel on Violence Against Women,* Statistics Canada, November 1993.

28. The tables show a comparison of age and educational characteristics of Canadian women, according to Canadian Census data, and the Womens' Safety Project Sample, reported in 1993 and 1994.

29. 237,250 women are 65 or older out of a total population of 1,986,285 females in Toronto, and 1,839,545 out of 13,842,280 in Canada, according to 1991 census data (StatsCan).

30. 1,083,130 Canadian women have a university degree. Similar data was not available for Toronto, but 1991 Census data showed that 516,935 individuals (male and female) out of 3,893,046 total population, had a degree.

31. For example, Russell, Diana E. H. *Rape in Marriage*. New York: Macmillan Publ., 1982 — gave an overall refusal rate of 50% (p.33). Reena Somers's PhD dissertation, University of Manitoba, 1994, was criticised by opponents for a rate of 63%.

32. *Changing the Landscape*. p.A15.

33. "There really was surprise that someone would even broach this issue. It clearly is a taboo topic." said Eva Ryten, director of research for the Association of Canadian Medical Colleges, when discussing a study indicating that medical schools discriminate against men in the selection of new students. The Canadian Press, October 18, 1994.

34. *Changing the Landscape*. p.A2.

35. This study does not provide information regarding remuneration, an important reinforcer and motivator. It does express appreciation for design input from Diana Russell, who, in her study, paid respondents (the women) a flat fee and the interviews an hourly rate. The latter was explained as having been done to discourage fraudulent data and fabricated interviews. The effect of encouraging longer interviews and possible fabricated material was not explored. (Russell, *Rape in Marriage*. p.32-33)

36. See Fekete. *Moral Panic*. 1994.

37. Italics added in both cases.

38. *Project "94*. p.69.

39. Crime 1 Statistics, Canadian Centre for Justice Statistics, 1993.

40. *Project "94*. p.49.

41. Another example is found in an oft-quoted study sponsored by *Ms.* magazine which stated that 25% of all women have been raped by the time they are in college. However, this figure was based on a question which did not ask women if they had been raped but rather whether they had ever "given in to sexual intercourse when (they) didn't want to because (they) were overwhelmed by a man's continual arguments and pressure." 73 % of these women, who were categorized as rape victims, did not define their experience as "rape." It was Mary Koss, the psychologist conducting the study, who defined it as rape stating that the women themselves didn't recognize what had really happened to them. Katie Roiphe, in her book *The Morning After*, concluded that this spoke more about change in sexual politic than about sexual behaviour or violence. See Koss, Mary, Gidycz, Christine A., and Wisniewski, Nadine. "The Scope of Rape: Incidence and Prevalence of Sexual Aggression and Victimization in a National Sample of Higher Education Students." *Journal of Consulting and Clinical Psychology*, 55(2), 1987, p.162-70; and Roiphe, p.52.

42. Gilbert, Neil. "The phantom epidemic of sexual assault." *The Public Interest*, 1991, 103, p.63.

43. Marone, Nicky. *Women & Risk: How to Master Your Fears and Do What You Never Thought You Could Do*. New York: St. Martin's Press, 1992.

44. Ibid. p. 16.

45. Ibid. p.xii.

46. Ibid. p.xiii.

47. Ibid. p.xiii.

48. Ibid. p. xi. (italics added)

49. Peterson, Christopher, Maier, Seteven F. and Seligman, Martin E.P. *Learned Helplessness: A theory for the age of personal control*. New York: Oxford University Press, 1993. p.233.

50. Ibid. p.228.

51. Ibid, p.16.

52. Huber, Peter. *Galileo's Revenge: Junk science in the courtroom*. New York: HarperCollins Publ., 1991. p.32.

53. Smail, David. *Taking Care: An Alternative to Therapy*. London: J.M. Dent & Sons, Ltd., 1987. p.80.

54. Nemiah, John C. "Classical Psychoanalysis." In *American Handbook of Psychiatry: Volume Five-Treatment*. (2nd Edit.) Daniel X. Freedman and Jarl E. Dyrud (eds.) New York: Basic Books, pp.163-182.

55. Hamburg, David A, et al. "Report of Ad Hoc Committee on Central Fact-Gathering Data of the American Psychoanalytic Association," *Journal of the American Psychoanalytic Association*, Oct. 1967, pp.841-861. Cited in Gross. *The Psychological Society*.1978, p.16.

56. It is important to note that only those who completed analysis are counted. Those that quit (usually as many in number as complete) are not included and probably don't feel better. As well, the report stated that "symptom cure" took place in only 27%.

57. Ackner, Lois F. *How to Survive the Loss of a Parent*. New York: William Morrow and Co., 1993. p.209.

58. Zilbergeld, Bernie. *The Shrinking of America: Myths of Psychological Change*. Boston: Little, Brown and Co., 1983. p.118.

59. "It is an individual's inalienable right to seek therapy, self-enhancement, education, enlightenment, and titillation as long as he or she is willing to pay for it." M.B. Parloff, "Can psychotherapy research guide the policy maker?" *American Psychologist*, 34 (1979), pp.296-306

60. Eysenck, Hans J. "The effects of psychotherapy: An evaluation." *Journal of Consulting Psychology*, 16, 1952, pp.319-324.

61. Eysenck, Hans J. "The effects of psychotherapy." *International Journal of Psychiatry*, 1, 1965, pp.97-168.

62. Kottler, Jeffrey A. *The Compleat Therapist*. San Francisco: Jossey-Bass Publ., 1991. p.10.

63. Dawes, Robyn M. *House of Cards: Psychology and Psychotherapy Built on Myth*. New York: Macmillan, 1994. p.30.

64. Bergin, Allen E. "The Evaluation of Therapeutic Outcome." In S.L. Garfield and A.E. Bergin (eds.) *Handbook of Psychotherapy and Behaviour Change*. (3rd ed.) New York: Wiley, 1986.

65. Lambert, M.J. "Some implications of psychotherapy outcome research for eclectic psychotherapy." *International Journal of Eclectic Psychotherapy*. 1986, 5(1), pp.16-44.

66. White, G.D., and Pollard, J. "Assessing therapeutic competence from therapy session attendance." *Professional Psychology*. 1982, 13, pp.628-633.

67. Eysenck, H.J. "A Mish-mash of Theories." *International Journal of Psychiatry*. 1970, 9, pp.140-146 (p.145).

68. Orlinsky, D.E. and Howard, K.I. "Process outcome in psychotherapy." In S.L. Garfield and A.E. Bergin (eds.) *Handbook of Psychotherapy and Behaviour Change*. (3rd ed.) New York: Wiley, 1986.

69. For example: Barendregt, J.T. "A psychological investigation of the effects of psychoanalysis and psychotherapy." In *Research in Psychodiagnostics*. Paris: Mouton, 1961. Cited in Gross, *The Psychological Society*. p.31; and Frank Jerome D. *Persuasion and Healing: A Comparative Study of Psychotherapy*. (rev. ed) Baltimore, MD: John Hopkins University Press, 1973. (see pp-152-156).

70. For example Lorr, M. and McNair, D.M. "Frequency of treatment and change in psychotherapy." *Journal of Abnormal and Social Psychology*. 64 (1962), pp.281-292.

71. Task Force for the Promotion and Dissemination of Psychological Procedures, American Psychological Association — Division 12. *The Clinical Psychologist*, May 1995.

72. Therapy Works® from The Psychological Corporation is a sophisticated example which c;aims that its "programs have proven effective for improving clinical outcomes of specific disorders."

73. Criteria: "A treatment must be supported by research demonstrating efficacy either by showing it is superior to a pill, psychological placebo or another treatment, or showing that the treatment is equivalent to an already established treatment." *The APA Monitor*, March 1995, p.4.

74. "Cognitive therapy" is a behavioural approach that assumes that thoughts are the true stimuli of actions and that by modifying one's thinking, one can change behaviours and feelings.

75. Strupp, Hans and Hadley, Suzanne. "Specific versus nonspecific factors in psychotherapy." *Archives of General Psychiatry*. 36, 1979, pp.1125-1136 .

76. Stein and Lambert published a study in which they concluded that graduate trained therapists yield modestly better results in outcome than paraprofessionals. Two things should be noted about their "meta-analysis" conclusions: 1) the "effect size" was .2, which is neither

impressive nor able to differentiate the two groups with many para's doing better than the professionals, and in several of the studies they examined the para's as a whole did significantly better than the professionals, and 2) there were a number of "confounding variables;" that is, other reasons why a difference might have been found, such as perceived status of therapist, experience, age, etc. (Stein, D.M. and Lambert, M.J. "Graduate training in psychotherapy: Are therapy outcomes enhanced?" *Journal of Clinical and Consulting Psychology*, 1995, 63(2), pp.182-196.

77. Stein, D.M. and Lambert, M.J. "On the relationship between therapist experience and psychotherapy outcome," *Clinical Psychology Review*, 4, 1984, pp.127-142.

78. See Garb, H. N. "Clinical judgment, clinical training, and professional experience." *Psychological Bulletin*, 105, 1989, pp.387-396.

79. *Report of the Task Force on the Evaluation of Education, Training and Service in Psychology.* Washington, D.C.: American Psychological Association, 1982. (italics added)

80. Dawes. *House of Cards.* p.58.

81. "There is no shred of evidence that psychoanalyzed individuals benefit from the experience." O. Hobart Mowrer, PhD., American Psychological Association President. *Crisis in Psychiatry and Religion.* New York: Van Nostrand, 1961.

82. Morris Parloff, chief of psychotherapy research at the National Institute of Mental Health, after reviewing a large number of studies of psychotherapy, paraphrased the proverbial farmer and said: "The best I can say after years of sniffing about in the morass of outcome research literature is that in my optimistic moods I am confident that there's a pony in there somewhere." M.B. Parloff, "Can psychotherapy research guide the policy maker?" *American Psychologist*, 34, 1979, pp.296-306.

83. Smith, M.L. and Glass, G.V. "Meta-analysis of psychotherapy outcome studies." *American Psychologist.* 32, 1977, pp.752-760.

84. McCord, Joan "Consideration of some effects of a counselling program." In Susan E. Martin, Lee B. Sechrest, and Robin Redner (eds.). *New Directions in the Rehabilitation of Criminal Offenders. Washington, D.C.: National Academy Press, 1981. pp.394-405.*

85. Sobel, S.B. "Throwing the baby out with the bathwater." *American Psychologist*, 1978, 33, pp.290-291.

86. Ditman, K.S., Crawford, G.C. and Forgy, E.W. "A controlled experiment on the use of court probation in the management of the alcohol addict." *American Journal of Psychiatry.* 124 1967, pp.160-163.

87. Peele, Stanton. *Diseasing of America: Addiction Treatment Out of Control.* Lexington, Mass.: Lexington Books, 1989. p.57.

88. Spitzer, R. Cited in Sarason. *Psychology Misdirected.* p.42.

89. Carkhuff, Robert R. *Helping and Human Relations: A primer for lay and professional helpers.* New York: Holt, Rinehart and Winston, 1969.

90. Berkowitz, Leonard. "The Case for Bottling up Rage," *Psychology Today.* July 1978, p.24.

91. Bergin, A.E. "The evaluation of therapeutic outcome." In Bergin, A.E. and Garfield, S.L. (eds.) *Handbook of Psychotherapy and Behaviour Change.* New York: Wiley, 1971. p. 263.

92. Hadley, Suzanne W., and Strupp, Hans F. "Contemporary view of negative effects of psychotherapy." *Archives of General Psychiatry* 33; Nov 1976, pp.1291-1302.

93. Loftus, Elizabeth, Grant, Brian L., Franklin, Gary M., Parr, Loni, and Brown, Rachel. "Crime Victims' Compensation and Repressed Memory." A letter to the Mental Health Subcommittee, Crime Victims Compensation Program, Department of Labor and Industries, State of Washington. (Revised Version 5-1-96) The original letter will never be published.

94. Loftus, E. "Repressed memory accusation." *Journal of Applied Cognitive Psychology.* 1997, 11, *pp. 25-30.*

95. For example: Mahrer, Alvin R. "Some known effects of psychotherapy and reinterpretation." *Psychotherapy: Research, Theory and Practice.* 7(3), 1970, pp.186-191.

96. Kottler. *The Compleat Therapist*, p.18.

97. Dr. Mendel, USC professor of psychiatry, demonstrated this gullibility in an interesting study with his own patients. He created a group of incorrect, horoscope-like interpretations and then made them to his patients. 20 out of the 24 were accepted by the patients who also reported a drop in anxiety as a result. ("The phenomenon of interpretation," *American Journal of Psychoanalysis.* 24(2), 1964, pp.184-90.)

98. Strupp, Hans H. "Needed: A reformulation of the psychotherapeutic influence." *International Journal of Psychiatry*, 10, 1972, pp.114-120.

99. Dawes. *House of Cards*, p.19.

100. Kottler. *The Compleat Therapist.* p.88.

101. Ibid. pp.75-76.

102. Guy, J.D. *The Personal Life of the Psychotherapist.* New York: Wiley, 1987. p.294.

103. Dawes. *House of Cards.* p.4.

104. Follette, W.T., and Cummings, N.A. "Psychiatric services and medical utilization in a prepaid health plan setting." *Medical Care*, 1967, 5, pp.25-35.

105. VandenBos, Gary R. (ed.) *Psychotherapy: Practice, Research, Policy.* London: Sage Publications, 1980, p. 18.

106. Schlesinger, Herbert J., Mumford, Emily, and Glass, Gene V. "Mental health services and medical utilization." In VandenBos, Gary R. (ed.) *Psychotherapy: Practice, Research, Policy.* p.89.

107. Ibid. p.71-102.

108. Ibid. p.88-89.

109. Ibid. p.90.

110. Borus, Jonathan F., Olendzki, Margaret c., Kessler, Larry, Burns, Barbara J., Brandt, Ursula C., Broverman, Carol A., and Henderson, Paul R. "The 'Offset Effect' of mental health treatment on ambulatory medical care utilization and charges." *Archives of General Psychiatry,* 1985, 42, p. 573.

111. Glover, Edward. *The Techniques of Psycho-Analysis.* New York: International University Press, 1958.

112. Meehl, P.E. "Psychology: Does our heterogenous subject matter have any unity?" *Minnesota Psychologist,* Summer 1986. p.4.

113. Kayla Weiner, PhD., internet posting, November 1995.

114. Alan H. Roberts recalls " a special meeting (of the Biofeedback Research Society) devoted to studies ostensibly showing that males could be taught (through biofeedback techniques) to raise the temperature of their testicles high enough to kill sperm and that this process could be used as a form of birth control." In Roberts, A. H. "Biofeedback: Research, training, and clinical roles." *American Psychologist*, 40, 1985, pp.938-941, p.939.

115. Ibid. p.939.

116. Mack, John E. *Abduction: Human Encounters with Aliens.* New York: Charles Scribner's Sons, 1994. pp.2-3.

117. In discussing Mack's abduction ideas, Showalter presents what she calls "Showalter's Law: As the hystories get more bizarre, the experts get more impressive." Showalter, 1997. p.189.

118. Ibid. p.13.

119. Mack, J.E. "Mental health professionals and the Roper Poll." In B. Hopkins, D.M. Jacobs, and R. Westrum, *The UFO Abduction Syndrome: A Report on Unusual Experiences Associated with [sic] UFO Abductions, The Roper Organization's Survey of 5,947 Adult Americans*. Las Vegas: Bigelow Holding Co., 1992, p.15. Researchers at Rutgers University put the number even higher. They surveyed 697 New Jersey residents and found that 3.4 percent had met the criteria, which if the percentage held up across the country would mean that 8.7 million Americans have been abducted. Reported in *Health*, Sept. 1994, 8(5), pp.111-112.

120. Mack. *Abduction.* p.15-16.

121. Ibid. preface.

122. "It's so common that I'll tell you within 10 minutes, I can spot it as a person walks in the door, often before they even realize it." Good Morning America's on-air psychologist on the CNBC program Real Personal, April 27, 1992; after maintaining that "probably one in four women (note the different statistics), one in eight men, have been incested. Cited by Dawes. *House of Cards*. p.8.

123. Hoffer, Eric. *The True Believer: Thoughts on the Nature of Mass Movements.* New York: Harper and Row (Perennial Library), 1966.

124. Reiser, Martin, "Hypnosis as an aid in a homicide investigation." *American Journal of Clinical Hypnosis*, 17(2), Oct. 1974, 84-87 (p.85).

125. Sears, R. R. "Survey of objective studies of psychoanalytic concepts." Social Science Research Council, New York, Bulletin 51, 1943.

126. Wolfe, Peter H. "Psychoanalytic research and infantile sexuality." *International Journal of Psychiatry*. 4(1), July 1967, pp.61-64.

127. Anatomically detailed dolls were initially developed for use with children in play therapy. They often served as a means to discuss health problems and physical disabilities and were employed in hospitals as a way to explain and prepare young patients for surgery. More recently they have been more widely used by psychologists to explore possible sexual and physical abuse by asking children suspected of being abused to use the doll to show what happened.

128. Bruck, Maggie, Ceci, Stephen, and Francouer, Emmett. "Anatomically Detailed Dolls Do Not Facilitate Preschoolers' Reports of Touching: The Abstract Paper" presented at the 1994 Annual Meeting of the Canadian Pediatric Society, St. Johns, Newfoundland.

129. Sears, R.R. 1943.

130. Bass, E. and Davis, L. *The Courage To Heal.* New York: Harper and Row, 1988. p.22

131. A speech given by an AA member to new affiliates provides an example of this same (il)logical style from the addiction field: "If you think you have a problem, or if you think that you are an alcoholic, I assure you that you are. You wouldn't be thinking about it and you wouldn't be here if you weren't an alcoholic." Cited in D. Rudy, *Becoming Alcoholic: Alcoholics Anonymous and the Reality of Alcoholism*. Carbondale, IL: Southern Illinois University Press, 1986.

132. Hillman, James and Ventura, Michael. *We've had a Hundred Years of Psychotherapy and the World is Getting Worse*. San Francisco: HarperCollins, 1992.

133. "When marital therapy began in the 1940's, one unhappy spouse would go to a psychiatrist and complain. That didn't work too well, so the therapy changed. Both spouses went to different psychiatrists, and the psychiatrists met to discuss the problem. By 1960, spouses were seeing the same psychiatrist, but separately. Today they usually see the psychiatrist together, and sometimes even the children are invited. In 1940, the divorce rate was 2.0 per 1,000 population; in 1976, it was 5.4." Delia Ephron, quoted in *Medical Economics*, May 2, 1977, p.198; cited by T. Szasz, in *The Myth of Psychotherapy*. Garden City, New York: Doubleday, 1978, p.196.

134. "Mental health: Does therapy help?" *Consumer Reports*, November, 1995. pp.734-739.

135. Seligman, Martin E. P. "The effectiveness of psychotherapy: The *Consumers Reports* study." *American Psychologist*. 1995, 50(12), 965-974.

136. *Consumer Reports*. p.734.

137. Seligman. "The effectiveness of psychotherapy." p.966.

138. A very limited amount of actual data was available to this author. When *CR* was asked for the actual numbers, they refused on the basis that they owned the results and that it was their policy not to release such information. Given that Seligman had access to the data in preparing his article, he was similarly approached and he declined attributing the restriction to *CR*. Thus, all of the analysis here is based on the very restricted amount of data and comments available in the two published articles.

139. Seligman. "The effectiveness of psychotherapy." p. 968.

140. From the masthead of *Consumer Reports*.

141. Farberman, Rhea K. "Public campaign nears roll-out: Public Communications Report." *The APA Monitor*, January 1966, p.5. (italics added)

142. "1996 President-Elect Candidate Biographical and Issues Statements." Washington, D.C.: American Psychological Association. p.16.

143. Ibid. p.16. (italics added)

144. *Consumer Reports.* Annual Questionnaire, 1994.

145. "Mental Health." *Consumer Reports.* p.734.

146. Survey. *Consumer Reports.* Part 2.

147. The report on physicians: "How is Your Doctor Treating You?" (*Consumer Reports,* February 1995. pp.81-88), was based on a survey of 70,000, a sample over 24 times larger than in this survey.

148. Regarding *Consumer Reports*, Mark Kotkin, the researcher, was asked by the for a copy of the summary data for both groups. It was noted that "It seems that Dr. Seligman has drawn on some of this information in his article; thus, I am assuming it is available." As well, it was asked: "how well did the respondents to this questionnaire match typical *CR* subscribers?" Mr. Kotkin replied that the data belonged to *CR* and "will not be released to anyone requesting it." He also indicated that Seligman did not have access to it BUT prior to preparing his AP article, he did meet with Mark Kotkin and was shown unpublished and unavailable reports on the project. Regarding the respondents, they did differ from the usual *CR* population: they were younger, about twice as many women, and of a higher educational level.

Kotkin and Dr. David Ansley, Science Director at *CR*, were then asked a number of specific questions: "1) Were the 3,000 who chose to speak to a friend, relative or clergy, demographically different than the 4,000 who saw a mental-health professional? 2) Was there a difference in the response to item #63 between these two groups? 3) Why did *CR* decide not to ask the 3,000 similar questions about their experience with friends, relatives and clergy? 4) Why was the issue of 'cost' and 'cost-effectiveness' (ie #20) left out of the analysis and report, when this is a typical topic for *CR* articles? 5) Why was client satisfaction measures interpreted as 'effectiveness'? Dr. Seligman refers to your study as 'an effectiveness study', and *CR* seems to concur when it uses terms such as: 'did much better' (p.734), 'was more effective' (p.736) and 'would be more effective' (p.738). (This stands out in clear contrast to other articles by *CR* which address client responses as measures of 'satisfaction', such as 'How Is Your Doctor Treating You?' (*CR*, February, 1995, pp.81-88.)) In reading both articles, it would seem that *CR* took a 'pro therapy' stance with this article while adopting a more critical, evaluative position in regards to medical care. Am I misreading this or was there a reason for adopting the stance which I perceive?"

Kotkin replied that he could not answer these questions, and directed further communication to Seligman, who replied that he could not release data as it was the property of *CR*, that "there was nothing there of significance."

149. Seligman. "The effectiveness of psychotherapy." p.969.

150. Ibid. p.969.

151. Ibid. p.973. This is Seligman's term for the "true believers" who spend a long time in therapy and are thus, sold on its beneficial effects. *CR* acknowledges that they "may have sampled an unusually large number of people in long-term treatment" (p.734), thus biasing their results.

152. "Mental Health." *Consumer Reports.* p.736.

153. Seligman. "The effectiveness of psychotherapy." p.973. (italics added)

154. Seligman provides only data for this group, and *CR* would not release any further information.

155. On p.971. Seligman reports the "respondents reported not only when they left treatment but why, including leaving because their problem was resolved... less than one month=60%; 1-2 months=66%; 3-6 months= 67%" for an average of 64.3% for those 6 months."

156. The difference is most likely due to the reliance on two different questions (#28 and #30b) to produce these figures. Given that these two questions address the same issue, the results should have been much closer for the study to have validity.

157. The office of the American Psychologist confirmed (on January 29, 1996) that this article was reviewed and approved by other psychologists "in the usual manner," who somehow overlooked or failed to see the errors in favour of presenting "positive" results.

158. "Mental Health." *Consumer Reports.* p.735.

159. Seligman. "The effectiveness of psychotherapy." pp.971-972. This is stated in spite of the fact that "few of the people responding had (a severe problem) such a schizophrenia or manic depression" and were not included in the analysis.

160. Dawes. *House of Cards.* p.44.

161. The numbers were arrived at by collapsing the data and obtaining averages for the information provided in Seligman's Figures 2 (improvement for presenting symptoms), 3 (improvement over work and social domain), and 4 (improvement over personal domains), provided on pp.970 and 971.

162. Seligman identified three areas or domains in which "improvement was measured: for presenting symptoms, over work and social domains (3 factors-ability to relate to others, productivity at work, and coping with everyday stress), and over personal domains (4 factors-enjoying life more, personal growth and insight, self-esteem and confidence, and alleviating low moods.)"

163. Seligman, M. *What You Can Change & What You Can't.* New York: Knopf, 1994.

164. Seligman. "The effectiveness of psychotherapy." p. 969.

165. Ibid. p.969.

166. "Mental Health." *Consumer Reports.* p. 738.

167. Seligman. "The effectiveness of psychotherapy." p.968.

168. Ibid. p. 972.

169. Ibid. p.973.

170. "Mental Health." *Consumers Report.* p. 739.

171. Bickman, Leonard. "A continuum of care: More is not always better." *American Psychologist,* 1996, 51(7), p. 690.

172. DeLeon, Patrick H. and Williams, Janice G. "Evaluation research and public policy formation: Are psychologists collectively willing to accept unpopular findings?" *American Psychologist,* 1997, 52(5), p.551.

173. Bickman L. (1996), p.689. See also: Bickman, L., Guthrie, P.R., Foster, E. M., Lambert, E. W., Summerfelt, W. T., Breda, C. S., and Heflinger, C. A. *Evaluating Managed Mental Health Services: The Fort Bragg Experiment.* New York: Plenum, 1995.

174. Roberts, M. C. "Models for service delivery in children's mental health: Common characteristics." *Journal of Clinical Child Psychology,* 1994, 23, pp.212-219.

175. Bickman, L. 1996, p. 697; citing Cutler, D. M. and Gruber, J. "Does public insurance crowd out private insurance?" (Working Paper No. 5082.) Cambridge, MA; National Bureau of Economic Research, Inc.

176. Ibid. 1996, p.689.

177. Ibid. 1996, p.694.

178. Ibid. 1996, p.694

179. Feldman, Saul. "The Fort Bragg Demonstration and Evaluation." *American Psychologist,* 1997, 52(5), p.560.

180. Newman, Russ. "The case for health-care regulation." *The APA Monitor,* November, 1996, p.39.

181. Borch-Jacobsen, Mikkel. "Sybil - The making of a disease: An interview with Dr. Herbert Spiegel." *The New York Review,* 24, 1997. p p.64

182. Hoagwood, Kimberly. "Interpreting nullity:The Fort Bragg Experiment - A comparative success or failure?" *American Psychologist,* 1997, 52(5), p. 548.

183. Bickman, L. 1996, p. 698.

184. Ibid. 1996, p. 699.

185. Weisz, J. R., Donenberg, G. R., Hans, S. S., and Weisz, B. "Bridging the gap between lab and clinic in child and adolescent psychotherapy." *Journal of Consulting and Clinical Psychology*, 1995, 63, pp. 688-701.

186. Hoagwood, 1997, p.546.

187. Weisz, J. R., Hans, S. S. and Valeri, S. M. "More of what? Issues raised by the Fort Bragg Study." *American Psychologist*, 1997, 52(5), p.544.

188. Bickman, L. "Resolving issues raised by the Fort Bragg Evaluation: New directions for mental health services research." *American Psychologist*, 1997, 52(5), p. 563.

189. Bickman, Leonard, Summerfelt, William Thomas, and Noser, Kelly. "Comparative outcomes of emotionally disturbed children and adolescents in a system of services and usual care." *Psychiatric Services*, Dec. 1997, 48(12), pp.1543-1548.

190. Weiss, Bhar. The effectiveness of traditional child psychotherapy. Unpublished report of the Center for Mental Health Policy, Vanderbilt University, 1997.

191. Sechrest, L. and Walsh, M. "Dogma or data: Bragging rights." American Psychologist, 1997, 52(5), p.536.

192. Ibid. p. 540.

193. Seligman, M. *What You Can Change & What You Can't*. New York: Knopf, 1994. p.8.

194. Farley, Frank. "From the Heart." *American Psychologist*, 51(8), 1996, p.774.

Chapter Five

The Business of Psychology

The demand for psychotherapy keeps pace with the supply, and at times one has the uneasy feeling that the supply may be creating the demand... Psychotherapy is the only form of treatment which, at least to some extent, appears to create the illness it treats.

Jerome Frank

Don't confuse me with the facts. This might very well be one of the slogans of an industry which is not deterred by research that questions the usefulness of its services or results which challenge the effectiveness that it claims. When Neil Jacobson recently wrote: "It is not uncommon for therapists to keep clients in therapy long after it is obvious that little or no progress is being made,"[1] the American Psychological Association President, Robert Resnick, responded "such opinions are, of course, just that. Our rebuttal should be outcomes research and practice patterns. As psychologists like to say, the data will speak for itself."[2]

The data indeed speak, and confirm that psychology's claims are exaggerated, its benefits limited. But the Psychology Industry proceeds undaunted, unaffected by the science it espouses, because it measures its success not by research findings but by satisfied customers, by sales, profit and growth. For the Psychology Industry, science is only one aspect of a marketing strategy, a fact indicated in the admission by Resnick that "the lack of plentiful research on the effectiveness of psychotherapeutic interventions has hampered *our ability to thrive...* but by documenting what we do and having sound data to back our treatment recommendations, we can make *our case for greater access to psychological services.*" Nowhere does he acknowledge the already plentiful research that questions the effectiveness of psychotherapy. Nor does he consider the possibility that new data may not back his call for a greater market share. What he looks for is "designer data" which the Psychology Industry can use to endorse its products and services and support its pursuit of funding. For after all, whatever else psychology may be, it is first and foremost a business.

It is difficult for the public, conditioned to trust and respect professionals, to consider that the Psychology Industry may have a bottom line based on profit and power rather than on its clients' welfare. It is troublesome to think that a business that offers understanding and hope to others can have its attention actually focussed on it own interests. And it is hard to imagine that psychology, which seems relevant and important to so many aspects of life, can be a business whose success has been ensured through insinuating itself into everyone's personal life.

Only one other industry in recent times has shown similar growth and breadth, and diffusion into society: the computer industry. In a matter of a few decades both industries have so effectively mushroomed that their presence is taken for granted and accepted without question, expressed by such thoughts as "what would we do without them?" Society has become reliant on them, allowing a dependency to develop in which the individual has surrendered more and more control of his life to the expert or the technician. But, while both claim to improve life, only one, the computer industry, is easily recognized as an out-for-profit business. The other masquerades as a "helping profession" and will continue to do so until its self-promoting strategies and self-serving solutions are exposed.

As shown in the Introduction, the use of the Psychology Industry services has rapidly grown: 46% of the U.S. population now report having seen a mental health professional at some point in their lives, according to a random telephone survey commissioned by the American Psychological Association in January 1995. While some might consider this to be evidence of a profound national need of epidemic proportions, it can equally, and more accurately, be seen as an indication of the subtle but highly effective marketing techniques used by the Psychology Industry to generate the demand required to meet the ever-increasing supply of psychologists. As Jerome Frank observed:

> Ironically, mental health education, which aims to teach people how to cope more effectively with life, *has instead increased the demand for psychotherapeutic help.* By calling attention to symptoms they might otherwise ignore and by labelling those symptoms as signs of neurosis, mental health education can create unwarranted anxieties, leading those to seek psychotherapy who do not need it. The demand for psychotherapy keeps pace with the supply, and *at times one has the uneasy feeling that the supply may be creating the demand.*

While it is difficult to get an accurate reading of the total number of practising psychologists because of their diversity and the lack of any control over who represents themselves as psychologists or therapists, estimates are that the number has risen twenty-fold since 1970. The following figures give some indication of the growth in one sector of the Industry: licensed psychologists. As Figure 1 indicates, there has been a steady increase in licensed doctoral Psychologists and an even more rapid growth in American Psychological Association members (excluding student and associate members). When these numbers are related to US. Census population data to show the number of Licensed Psychologists per 10,000 population (Figure 2), the

Licensed Psychologists
Data from American Psychological Association

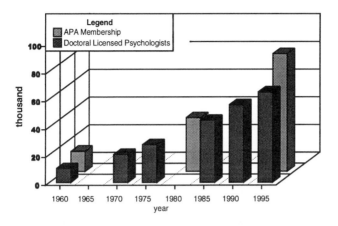

Figure 1

increase in supply is dramatically evident. Current levels of almost 2.5 psychologists per 10,000 Americans, greatly exceed an estimated work force need of 1 psychologist per 10,000.[3] This growth is striking when one considers that three fifths of the states realized at least a 100% increase in licensed psychologists in the 12 years between 1976 and 1988, with three having a 400% increase.[4] In the early 90's, it was seriously suggested that the market was oversaturated and that fewer, not more, psychologists should be trained and licensed.[5]

Supply of Psychologists
Licensed Psychologists / 10,000 pop.

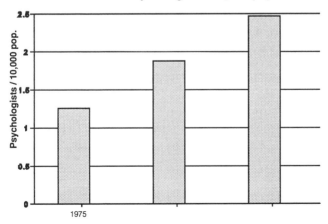

Figure 2

The picture of oversaturation becomes considerably more dramatic when one considers that these licensed Psychologists constitute only one quarter of those who refer to themselves as psychologists and less than five per cent of the estimated total number of psychologists as defined in this book.[6] Using this broader definition, there is at least one psychologist for every 250 people in the U.S.

What becomes immediately apparent is that not only has supply kept up with demand, it has, in fact, exceeded it, creating the need for greater marketing of psychological services and for the development of new "products" and the expansion of the markets for the Psychology Industry.

Figures showing the gross income of the Psychology Industry are impossible to come by, again because of the diversity of therapists. However, when the data of the 1987 National Medical Expenditures Survey, the most recent of its kind, is extrapolated and applied to 1995, 88.2 million outpatient psychotherapy visits were made by Americans for a total cost of 4.7 billion dollars. Considering that approximately half of the Psychology Industry consists of psychologists who cannot receive third-party insurance payments, it is not unreasonable to assume that both of these figures are much larger for the overall Psychology Industry, probably in the region of 175 million visits at a total cost of $9 billion. Of these "separated and divorced persons, females, whites, persons aged 35 to 49 years, and those with more than 15 years of education had a greater likelihood of using psychotherapy;"[7] a group remarkably similar to that of alleged victims. This description was supported by a Canadian study[8] which found that "nice patients," those without a severe problem, young women aged 15 to 44 years, and those from high-income areas, had greater access to and use of out-patient psychiatric/psychotherapy services. Interestingly, about 16% of psychotherapy users in the U.S. were in long-term psychotherapy and used up about two thirds (62%) of the total expenditure (in the Canadian study, 5% used up over 50%). In light of the fact that there is little evidence to support the value of long-term therapy, it is no wonder that managed care plans are moving to curtail this activity, while being opposed by the organized psychology associations.

This utilization is occurring at a time when society is in a period of economic reversal, when there are dramatic changes in the marketplace, when old markets are drying up and new ones have to be established. The existing health care systems no longer have the funds to provide unlimited long-term treatment and individuals have less discretionary money for user-pay therapy. While in 1983, Zilbergeld could write that "virtually everyone can get counselling at a price he can afford to pay," such is no longer the case. Now psychologists of different persuasions vie for the limited health dollars and openly and aggressively compete amongst themselves for clients.

And as the country's attention has shifted somewhat from "health and welfare" to "law and order," so too has that of the Psychology Industry. Where the secret of success for a psychologist once was to develop a professional association with a physician or psychiatrist, it now is to develop a working relationship with law enforcement or the legal profession. Although still using some medical language, it now speaks of "epidemics of violence and crime," "the diseased mind of the criminal" and "toxic parenting."

In light of the economic and social changes in society, the Psychology Industry has had to create a new marketing plan and business approach which this chapter explores by examining the ways that the Psychology Industry is selling itself and the new products and services it has introduced.

Selling the Psychology Industry

...actually, no less than the entire world is a proper catchment for present day psychiatry (and psychology), and psychiatry need not be appalled by the magnitude of the task... Our professional borders are virtually unlimited.

Howard Rome, 1968 President,
American Psychiatric Association[9]

Essential to the success of most industries is their ability to market themselves, for without that there would be no demand for their products or services. Although some naive and altruistic members of the Psychology Industry would like to believe that psychological problems exist in and of themselves and create their own demand for services, such is neither the truth nor the practiced belief of these psychologists. They may criticize others who openly promote their services, or complain about those who exaggerate their effectiveness. Yet, they freely give public lectures or provide interviews to the media on psychological topics, seldom acknowledging that these serve the same promotional function. Whether they psychologically interpret social events (eg. describing the effects of a natural disaster in terms of personal stress), address the "psychologically sick" aspects of an individual's behaviour (e.g. "the carcinogenic properties of trauma") or explain the common nature of a psychological problem (e.g. "we all know what it is to be a victim,") their intentions go beyond providing public information; they are marketing their business, promoting themselves and persuading people to become users.

This selling takes the three-pronged-approach of persuasion, identified in Chapter 2:

- **PSYCHOLOGIZING** - explaining every part of life as a psychological experience which can be handled in "healthy" or "unhealthy" ways and for which an expert or specialist is required to give guidance, direction or approval.
- **PATHOLOGIZING** - turning events, feelings and problems into a variety of disorders requiring professional services without which the individual would supposedly get worse or society would be at greater risk.
- **GENERALIZING** - diffusing the concepts of pathology and increasing the demand for psychological help so that everyone can become a user and demand can keep up with the increasing supply of psychologists.

These three approaches, with variations and combinations, can be seen when psychologists talk to clients or to each other; when they lecture, give interviews, testify in court or appear in the media; in the books and articles they write, and in the representations and petitions that they make to government and funding agencies. Where these methods once were taught informally through apprenticeship called supervised training, they can now be found in guidebooks to developing professional practice and in the marketing packages of psychological associations.[10] As the number of lay and professionally trained psychologists has grown, these techniques have become essential in generating an ever larger market for the Psychology Industry.

PSYCHOLOGIZING

At the moment, we stand very close to being a discipline concerned with relatively superficial problems: the anxieties and fears of otherwise healthy people (how's my self-esteem today?)..."

Frank Farley
APA Presidential Address, 1994

In 1914, *Good Housekeeping* magazine published an article entitled: "Mothercraft: A New Profession for Women" proclaiming that "the amateur mother of yesterday" would be replaced by "the professional mother of tomorrow." No longer were women to rely on their maternal instincts, the wisdom passed down through generations, or the advice and support of family, friends, and other mothers. American mothers were being psychologically persuaded to look for advice to professionals, who at that time were heavily influenced by Freud's theories.[11] Despite the fact that children had been successfully raised for thousands of years, child-rearing began to be considered a psychological task that required expert guidance if it was to be done properly. Not long after the article, John Watson, the behaviourist, applied behavioral theories to child-rearing, giving further strength to the psychologized notion that professionally directed parenting could create a successful child while avoiding the pitfalls leading to problem children. Viewing children as simple stimulus-response machines that could be trained, and considering their brain as "*tabulae rasae*, blank sheets upon which any story could be written depending on the environmental conditions...," Watson claimed that he could take any dozen healthy infants and with proper training "guarantee to take any one at random and train him to become any type of specialist (Watson) might select – doctor, lawyer, artist, merchant-chief and yes, even beggarman and thief, regardless of his talents, penchants, tendencies, abilities, vocations [or] race of his ancestors."[12]

Thus, psychologists, both the Freudians and the Behaviourists, laid claim to child-rearing as one of their areas of expertise as they psychologized life, from "the birth experience" to "the death experience," into a complex array of psychological theories and processes. Taking the words of Smail seriously when he wrote regarding psychology that "*anything people can do for themselves is the waste of an opportunity to make money...,*"[13] the Psychology Industry has undertaken to psychologize all of life by:

- Identifying common events in life, both positive ones, such as giving birth, growing up, or getting married, and negative ones, such as death, divorce or losing a job.
- Turning them into internal psychological phenomena with their own stages and requirements.
- Creating beliefs about the proper way to handle them.
- Establishing cadres of professional experts and specialists to guide the "amateur" public.

Psychologists "really do intend that all of life should be included in their sphere of influence"[14] and, to ensure that no one escapes the purview of the Psychology Industry, they have dissected life into a variety of phases and events, attributing to each some specific psychological importance. Events which once were handled by common experience or passed-down wisdom, and were greeted with joy and happiness or sadness and regret, are now put under sterile psychological management. Millions of intelligent, educated people have been persuaded that there are psychological experts who understand human experience and behaviour better than they do; a belief which has led many into a frantic search for paid professional expertise. And the Psychology Industry has encouraged this belief, declaring itself to have not only wisdom about human existence but also specialized scientific knowledge and skills which far exceed those of the general public. From talk-shows to courtroom commentaries to news bites, psychologists inundate the public with their messages such that the cumulative effect has been to change peoples' beliefs about their own competency and the way they look at life. Intruding not only into the bedrooms of the nation (with therapies for everything from sexual dysfunctions to snoring and sleep disorders) but into the schools, the workplaces, and the courts of the nation, psychologists have embarked on activities of self-promotion both to expand the demand for their services and to set themselves apart as superior. As Dawes noted, this "paternalistic, one-up ethic not only resolves the problems raised by the professionals' ambivalent feelings toward their clients but advances the profession. Practicing psychologists have an ethical mandate to be high status professionals."[15]

Whether it is an aspect of superiority or arrogance, professionalism or parentalism, psychologists consider themselves to be experts in each and every aspect of life, for as George Albee put it: "our social problems are all human problems, and we (psychologists) are the experts on this."[16] Resonating this view and embellishing it, Frank Farley (a recent president of the American Psychological Association) wrote that psychology "may be in the process of re-inventing itself as the primary discipline in the solution of humanity's major problems... Psychology can do much to improve the world."[17]

Although this attitude now pervades society, it is by no means new as evidenced in the attitudes and activities of the Freudian and Behavioural child-rearing experts at the beginning of the century. Each, arguing from his or her own opinion and theory, endeavoured to psychologize parenting, which Evelyn Mills Duvall of the Association of Family Living described as "the last stand of the amateur."[18] The overall effect was not only to intensify parental anxiety rather than to allay it,[19] but also to damage children. As Lousie Ames, Co-Director of the Gesell Institute for Child Development said: "Most of the damage we have seen in child rearing is the fault of the Freudian and neo-Freudians who have dominated the field. They have frightened parents and kept the truth from them. In child care I would say that Freudianism has been the psychological crime."[20] Dr. Spock echoed this conclusion when he studied 21 mothers in Cleveland and found that mothers with more knowledge of Freudian theory had more difficulties, not fewer, in raising their children.[21]

Parenthood is replete with examples of psychologizing and its effects, ranging from how to interpret children's nightmares, to quelling their fears, to administering discipline. For instance, in 1994 a father was charged in London, Ontario, with assault after spanking his five year old daughter in public after a talk and a warning failed to stop her misbehaviour. Section 43 of the Canadian Criminal Code states that "every schoolteacher, parent or person standing in the place of a parent is justified in using force by way of correction toward a pupil or child... if the force does not exceed what is reasonable under the circumstances:" a principle based on previous psychological theories of discipline contingent on behaviour. Despite that, psychological experts spoke up against the father saying that "spanking does not make sense because it fails to address the underlying reason for a child's behaviour. At the same time it spawns a host of adverse reactions, anything from aggression and violence to fear of speaking and acting later in life."[22]

Curiously, in the same newspapers that carried this story were reports of proposed legislation intended to hold parents legally, as well as financially, responsible for the behaviour of their children; this again based on the psychologized assumption that the illegal activities of children were due to incompetent parenting and inadequate discipline. Sometime earlier, Tom Hansen, of Boulder, Colorado, had used this idea to sue his parents for $350,000, charging that his mental health had been impaired by "inadequate parenting." His claim was based on allegations that his father made him dig weeds in the yard when he had caught his son smoking marijuana.[23]

In the psychologized world of child-rearing, the amateur parent is clearly at risk not only of *feeling* guilty but also of being *found* guilty. The only thing that parents can feel confident in is that the standard of today will change tomorrow, the psychological truth of today will be called fiction tomorrow. For it would appear that psychological truth and fact is whatever psychologists choose it to be at any moment (i.e. "most experts agree that..."). "It is obvious that child care fashions are transient. The creation and dissemination of knowledge on how to raise children now appears to be one of the greatest academic hoaxes of our times. Judging from the accumulated evidence, it appears probable that the intelligent, intuitive parent knows as much, or more, about child care as the child educator, the parent-child expert, the psychologist, the social worker or the psychiatrist."[24] Despite this, Westman, a psychiatrist, faculty member at the University of Wisconsin Medical School, and author of *Licensing Parents: Can We Prevent Child Abuse and Neglect,* now proposes a credentialing process. He seriously recommends restricting parenting to individuals who are at least 18, have completed a certified course in parenting and have signed a pledge not to neglect or abuse their children. Otherwise, Westman insists the children that unlicensed parents bring into the world be taken from them, at least until the parents have met the necessary requirements.[25]

Childhood has always been a popular target for psychologizing since it is so amenable to being abstracted into systems of stages and phases each with its own school of experts. There are experts in infant bonding and infant stimulation, in moral, religious, social, psychological, and intellectual development, in early childhood education, for under-achievers and over-achievers, in conduct disorders and shyness, in learning disabilities and cooperative play. The list seems endless as each activity of a child can be analyzed and psychologized. And the child does not even have to have a problem to need the services of the Psychology Industry, for as the American Psychological Association Practice Directorate stated in a practice-related document: "mental health services should serve to promote psychological competence and self-sufficiency rather than focus exclusively on dysfunction and pathology."[26] Children are also a favourite market for psychologists because most parents are prepared to put the perceived "needs" of their children ahead of most other things. When Americans are told that "children suffer from an enormous unmet need for mental health services,"[27] they believe it as indicated by a 1993 opinion poll that found that 73% of Americans consider children's health and education as the number one priority for government funding.

But childhood is not the only arena of life open to expert-making. Psychologizing has taken over every aspect of human existence so that there are psychological experts in death and dying, obesity and eating disorders, being married and being single, sexual pleasure and dysfunction, being fired and being successful, mid-life crisis and growing old, child care and elder care, and so on.

But, nowhere is the entrepreneurial psychologist more evident today than in forensic psychology and the court room. As early as the mid 70's, the American Psychological Association, in its guide to career opportunities for psychologists, expressed the "expectation that in the future forensic psychologists *will roam confidently and competently* far beyond the traditional roles of psychologists..."[28] This prediction has begun to be realized as the crisis in health care has lead to a frantic search by psychologists, relying on income sources that may disappear, for alternative ways to make money, particularly in the free-market economy of the legal system.

A recent article by the Practice Directorate of the American Psychological Association addressing this issue, stated that "diversification is a viable form of self-preservation... Psychologists may still get a steady stream of clients paying out-of-pocket, but not enough to replace third-party payments..." And it continued: "*Forensics offers broad opportunities for psychologists* with the appropriate training. Their expertise can be used for custody evaluations, divorce mediation or expert trial testimony. Practitioners can earn $120-$250 an hour for forensic work..."[29] (For comparison, the 1995 average hourly rate for psychologists was $95.) On another occasion, the American Psychological Association assistant executive director of marketing suggested that "a specialist in adolescent treatment could establish a business relationship with a juvenile court system."[30] Clearly where health care used to be the lucrative arena of choice for psychologists, now it has been replaced by the legal system, as was made explicit at a psychology and the law conference at Villanova Law School where participants agreed that psychology "is poised to grab a more prominent role in law after years on the sidelines."[31] Richard Weiner enunciated the role of psychology "to answer questions raised in law. The goal is to explain human behaviour." But, rather than being dispassionate and objective experts, Stephen Morse made it clear that "lawyers are bottom-line oriented. They won't pursue psychological information unless they perceive it as a benefit to them."[32] Thus, to psychologize law and be a professional expert in that field requires that psychologists not only voice the truth of the moment but also know which truth is wanted, which psychological fact will sell. As a former president of the American Bar Association, stated, "I would go into a lawsuit with an objective uncommited independent expert about as willingly as I would occupy a foxhole with a couple of noncombatant soldiers."[33]

In 1884, a decision of the New York Court of Appeals stated that "twelve jurors of common sense and common experience" would do better on their own than with the help of hired experts, "whose opinions cannot fail to be warped by a desire to promote the cause in which they are enlisted."[34] Despite this, it wasn't long before psychological experts began to appear in court rooms. In the famous trial of Leopold (aged 19) and Loeb (aged 18), who were accused of killing a 13 year old boy in what they thought to be "the perfect crime," psychological evidence formed the major basis of defense. Clarence Darrow, the defence lawyer, stated that: "For the first time in a court of justice, an opportunity was presented to determine the mental condition of persons accused of crime, according to the dictates of science and modern psychiatry, without arbitrary and unscientific limitations imposed by archaic rules of law."

Thus began the long and well-established tradition of psychologists consorting with lawyers to the point where "the pursuit of truth, the whole truth and nothing but the truth has given way to reams of meaningless data, fearful speculation, and fantastic conjecture. Courts resound with elaborate, systematized, jargon-filled, serious-sounding deceptions that fully deserve the contemptuous label used by trial lawyers themselves: junk science."[35] This is no more evident than in highly-public trials where experts for the prosecution are matched by experts for the defense, creating an atmosphere more like tag-team wrestling than the pursuit of truth and justice. In spite of this, psychologizing within the law goes on with the Psychology Industry identifying the field of "law and psychology" as a growth market for psychologists who know how to "play ball." For a psychologist must know that although, as an expert witness, she or he "may not work directly for a contingent fee, the expert is a contingent player anyway... (whose) continued employment today, and reemployment tomorrow, depends criticaly on the strength of the support he can supply... The entrepreneurial expert, in short, is a repeat player, or aspires to be, and such players repeat only if they win."[36]

Huber, in his book *Galileo's Revenge*, noted that "junk science is matched by what might be called liability science, a speculative theory that expects lawyers, judges, and juries to search for causes at the far fringes of science and beyond."[37] He continues: "Sometimes... the cheapest point of control will be at quite some distance from the scene of the accident. The search for the cheapest possible control must inevitably lead out to the edges of scientific knowledge. No one can be certain why the kingdom was lost, and who might most cheaply have avoided the disaster, until the question of missing nails in every single horse's shoe has been examined in depth. Esoteric afflictions like cancer and birth defects, and mundane ones like accidents with cars or Cuisinarts, can always be tracked back and back, into the mist of space and time. Liability science requires no less."[38] And psychologists in sympathy with this and with increasing reliance on the legal system for income and influence, have responded by tracking back and back, searching the fringes of human experience and identifying their own causes; causes which relieve the client of any responsibility and place the blame squarely on someone or something else.

It was out of this that the practice of repressed memory therapy and synthetic victim-making emerged, as people, unhappy with their state or disturbed by their failures, sought relief or remedy, cure or compensation. Psychologists, fearing the loss of their sources of income, responded, recognizing the opportunity to diversify their practice by combining clinical services with forensic work. Through this, they could identify a cause, exercise expert authority, achieve compensation and then enjoy the benefits of funded long-term (or interminable) treatment. Although a conflict of interest is evident to anyone viewing this activity, it is somehow not visible to the many courts and judges who have awarded large settlements, based on psychologized testimony and explicitly including funds for treatment often by the psychologists involved. Consider the recent case in which a California "jury awarded a man more than $1 million after finding that he was fired as manager of an auto parts store because he weighed more than 400 pounds. During the trial, psychologist, Dr. Richard Kamrath, testified that people's weights were determined 80 percent by genes and 20 percent by their environment. The man's lawyer said it was clear to the jury that the man was disabled by his condition, since it was difficult for him to sit, stand and walk in the courtroom. The Superior Court jury in Oakland awarded $776,739 to the man for emotional distress and $258,913 for lost compensation and benefits."[39]

One observer has noted that "verdicts speak to the public at large... and people tend to believe what the courts say, especially when they say it with large amounts of money,"[40] and to this it might be added that the courts, the juries and the public have the tendency to believe what the psychological experts say, especially when their own views have been already psychologized by the Psychology Industry.

Pyschologist Margaret Hagen, in *Whores of the Court*, writes: "When the law welcomes the astrologer into the courtroom as possessing the same status as the astronomer; when the court listens to the priest with the same critical judgment it applies to the testimony of the physicist, then and only then will the testimony of clinical psychologists about the formation and functioning of the human mind in general or in particular individuals make sense as expert testimony. When the concept of expertise is itself debased to nothing more than personal opinion, then the clinicians should take the stand along with the rest of the opinionated. Why not?

Until then, throw them out of the courts."[41]

An amusing variation on this suggestion was proposed recently by a New Mexico State senator:

WIZARDS OF ID

When a psychologist or psychiatrist testifies during a defendant's competency hearing, the psychologist or psychiatrist shall wear a cone-shaped hat that is not less than two feet tall. The surface of the hat shall be imprinted with stars and lightning bolts.

Additionally, the psychologist or psychiatrist shall be required to don a white beard that is not less than eighteen inches in length ad shall punctuate crucial elements of his testimony by stabbing the air with a wand.

Whenever a psychologist or psychiatrist provides expert testimony regarding the defendant's competency, the bailiff shall dim the courtroom lights and administer two strikes to a Chinese gong.

—From an amendment proposed in March 1995 by Duncan Scott, a New Mexico state senator, to a bill addressing the state's licensing guidelines for psychologists and psychiatrists. According to Scott, the proposal was intended to draw attention to the rise of "insanity pleas in criminal trials." The amendment was approved by the state senate but was rejected by the New Mexico House of Representatives.
(*Harper's Magazine*, July, 1995, p.16)

Validators – the 20th Century Witch-prickers

Just as the procedures and records of the witch-hunts of centuries ago were controlled and kept by the inquisitors who had the power to invalidate persons as believers and define them as heretics; so too do psychologists now control the uncovering of abuse and trauma and investigate those accused, defining them as perpetrators.

In discussing the witch-hunts of England, Christina Hole writes: "One of the most terrifying features of the general witchcraft belief was the fact that no one knew for certain who was, or was not, a witch." And she continues: "The most deplorable by-product of the general fear of witches was the professional witch-finder..." [41a] whose pay depended on the number of witches discovered. The witch frenzy provided a lot of work for physicians who were entrusted with locating the often invisible "witch's marks." It also spawned a new profession of "witch-prickers," some of whom were physicians and some of whom were "common prickers." Their practice was to stick a pin into the skin of anyone suspected of being a witch, and based on the degree of pain or bleeding, they were either confirmed as witches or further "examined" by an ordeal of immersion in water, but never acquitted. After the publication of the *Malleus Maleficarum* (*The Hammer of Witches*),[42] the manual for witch-hunters, "a class of men sprang up in Europe who made it the sole business of their lives to discover and burn the witches,"[43] and these lay-prickers along with physicians became the first recognized legal experts. "The parliaments had encouraged the delusion (in witchcraft) both in England and Scotland, and by arming these fellows (prickers) with a sort of authority, had in a manner forced the magistrates and ministers to receive their evidence."[44] Witch-hunting became exceedingly profitable for all involved, except for the witch.

And, just as the power and prestige of the prickers, as diagnosticians and experts, rose with the increasing incidence of witchcraft, so too has the influence and income of psychologists risen with the increasing incidence of reported abuse and assault. Like their predecessors, these 20th Century prickers, gain status and wealth, and build a business on identifying the marks, both visible and invisible, and assembling the evidence. Now, while it is questionable whether any witch ever existed, it is not disputable that abuse, of children and adults, does occur. And it is upon this basis, that the industry of "assessing" and "examining" has been built; some practitioners even referring to themselves as "validators."

In validating the reports of children, play therapy techniques involving anatomically accurate dolls, interviews, and physical examinations are often relied on; while, with adult accusers, clinical interviews, hypnosis, and behavioural lists are generally the basis for determinations and subsequent expert testimony. Despite the prominence these validating psychologists have achieved, their techniques remain highly questionable and unreliable. Research has shown that children provide their adult interviewers with the type of information they think the adult wants, and that, when this is coupled with leading and misleading questions, play therapy, or the use of dolls, the effect is to provide the interviewer with whatever he or she expects to be the answers.[45] As well, the reliance on physical examinations to provide reliable evidence of sexual abuse, evidence which has been used in the conviction of many people,[46] has proven to be so unreliable that the American Medical Association has issued specific guidelines. Krugman observed: "The medical diagnosis of sexual abuse usually cannot be made on the basis of physical findings alone. With the exception of acquired gonorrhea or syphilis, or the presence of forensic evidence of sperm or semen, there are no pathognomic signs of sexual abuse."[47] Similarly, with adults, the use of checklists and "consistent-with-sexual-abuse" reasoning has come under criticism because of the vagueness of the behavioural items which would allow almost anyone to qualify as a victim. Hypnosis, often employed as a memory-enhancement procedure, is also questioned, and in some states the use of hypnosis with a person bars that individual from testifying because of the significant effect of hypnotic suggestion and the unreliability of resulting memories.

Validators have also appeared in recent years among those who treat and assist people with severe developmental disabilities such as autism. Using a method known as "Facilitated Communication" which involves providing physical support as the handicapped individual types out messages on a keyboard, at least five dozen allegations have been made leading to charges of abuse against parents, teachers, and other caregivers.[48] This despite the controlled research in both psychology laboratories and natural settings with a variety of clinical groups which shows that not only are the people with disabilities unable to respond accurately, but that the responses they appear to give are actually those of the assistants, the validators.[49]

One would think that with all of this, there would be limited reliance on validators and that they would have to be specially trained and highly qualified professionals. But such is not the case for many "are self-styled "therapists" who have absolutely no training at all, even in related disciplines... Many of these ill-qualified and incompetent individuals take "courses" in which they are trained by people of questionable qualifications... Some of these therapists have also crept into the sexual abuse field where they serve as not only evaluators but therapists as well. *Sex abuse is a 'growth industry'*."[50] Whether they are self-styled psychologists or professionals with degrees and distinctions, they are members of the Psychology Industry, such as Kee McFarlane, who have found a niche and exploited it to their own advantage.[51]

During the past 15 years the American public has witnessed a series of infamous child abuse cases which have grown out of this industry. The best known of these is the McMartin case, one of the costliest trials in American history. Kee MacFarlane, the now discredited interviewer of the children in that case, testified emotionally before the Congress in September 1984 about powerful conspiracies of sexual predators who appear to be running preschools across the country. She compared the sexual pillage at these facilities to nuclear warfare and called for community disaster planning to combat it. Two weeks after this testimony, Congress doubled its funding of child-protection programmes. Kee MacFarlane's programme was itself the beneficiary of huge federal and state grants.[52]

While validators claim to identify victims, they are, in fact, manufacturing victims; both those that are labelled victims of abuse, and those that are victims of the legal system, the falsely accused. Like the "ecclesiastic epidemiologists of witchcraft" who benefitted from a high rather than low, incidence of this witchcraft, psychologists who seek to identify victims and use statistics to persuade public opinion and public funds that a social problem is worse than previously thought, have a vested interest in inflating the numbers. For instance, Russell[53] contends that 1 out of every 3 females (approximately 45.5 million women) and 1 out of every 6 males (approximately 21 million men) has experienced incest or some other sexual trauma, for a total of 66.6 million Americans; a massive market for validators and the therapists that follow along behind them.

PATHOLOGIZING

In a world in which everything has two meanings, the common one which is understood by most and the psychologized one open only to the understanding of psychologists, it is not surprising that virtually every aspect of life can be interpreted in terms of pathology and sickness. At one time, treating real mental illness was the major responsibility of psychologists, but now it is only a minor activity of the Psychology Industry as it diffuses its therapeutic sensibility and services into every nook and cranny of human existence. Rather than having its work confined to the mental hospital, it would rather "abolish the hospital only to make the whole world a hospital"[54] and everyone a patient. In so doing, the Psychology Industry actively sets about to convince large numbers of people that even minor anxieties and unhappinesses are symptomatic of deeper and more severe problems. For it knows that if people can be persuaded of this, they will become dependent users with no escape since the goal of normality in this case, is unachievable.

The formula for pathologizing, drawing its structure from traditional medical practice, is simply:

- Determine a baseline by defining what is normal.
- Make a diagnosis by identifying and labelling the problem.
- Provide a prescription by recommending psychological treatment.
- State a prognosis by giving the expected outcome with and without treatment.

All four of these elements of pathologizing can be easily recognized in the work and writings of the Psychology Industry. For instance, Zimbardo and Radl, writing about their work with shyness, state:

> our primary concern is to help you to minimize the effects *[the treatment]* of shyness *[diagnosis]* that may keep your children from reaching their full potential as human beings *[prognosis with treatment]*. Even when children are only moderately shy *[implication that shyness is abnormal]*, they still miss out on valuable social experiences. And, when shyness is really severe, living in that psychological prison can ruin a life *[prognosis without treatment]*.[55]

The first step for psychologists in pathologizing is to establish a benchmark, a concept of normality by which peoples' feelings and behaviours can be assessed. But what is this psychological state called "normal'? Ruesch and Bateson argued that normal is whatever doesn't appear in the lives of psychotherapy patients. They believed that "since the (psychologist's) attention is focussed on deviation, and since he has little or no training in normal psychology, he tends to construct a hypothetical norm by averaging the exact opposites of those features he sees in his patients."[56] So, if patients are unhappy, happiness must be normal; if patients are insecure, then, security is normal; if patients are anxious then calmness is normal. Normality, as Freud said, becomes "an ideal fiction."

While this may explain, in part, the popular view of normal as blissful peace and happiness, the Psychology Industry has gone even further in creating this illusion as it seeks to cast its net around all of society. Consider Marone, in her book *Learned Helplessness*, when she states that: "it is fear that begets the most intense feeling of helplessness. Fear of being alone, fear of being attached; fear of failure, fear of success; fear of change, fear of monotony; fear of living, fear of dying; the list is as endless as there are individuals in the world."[57] One can only conclude from this that, if fear leads to helplessness and helplessness is a pathology, then fear is abnormal. But, according to her, fear is experienced by as many people as there are individuals in the world, so everyone has fear: fear is therefore normal and "normal" is therefore abnormal. Such is the Psychology Industry's paradoxical and convoluted logic as it sets an absurd standard for normal and lays the groundwork for turning everyone into a patient. It is the marketing of this form of "normality" that sustains the Psychology Industry and creates victims, as fear, unhappiness, insecurity, sadness, anxiety, failure and so on become synonymous with psychological illness.

DON'T LET THE COST OF THERAPY GET YOU DOWN
You deserve spiritual and psychological health at a reasonable fee. Affordable sliding scale rates.

Are you feeling:
- Fear   • Anger   • Guilt   • Sadness
- Emptiness   • Loneliness   • Despair

Hearing out past pains in a safe, secure place, discharging unexpressed feelings appropriately and nurturing your Inner Deprived Child gives you control over your own personal drama.

A Pathologically-Focussed Advertisement

In promoting such a model of normality, which exists only in psychological fantasy, the Psychology Industry forces people to consider themselves as psychologically disabled, increasing their vulnerability to a psychological diagnosis. Where once people were ashamed of being diagnosed, many are now eager and willing provided that two conditions are met: 1) that the label not only explain but also justify their problems and behaviours, leaving them with little or no sense of guilt or responsibility, and 2) that the label is personally and socially acceptable, which means that it must, at the same time, make them feel special and understood, and be common enough that they will not feel stigmatized.

Psychologists have long believed that labelling a problem is the first step in resolving it. They have argued that it reduces the anxiety about the unknown and focusses the attention on appropriate ways to get better. While this may be true in some cases (perhaps with the labelling and treatment of specific phobias), it carries the risk of false labelling and inappropriate or unnecessary treatment. The schizophrenic can be mis-labelled as a victim of satanic ritual abuse, obstructing appropriate treatment and medication, or the physically injured can be misled and mistreated with a diagnosis of post traumatic stress disorder. However, convinced of the psychologist's expert ability, clients are inclined to accept a diagnosis even when the means used to arrive at it are highly suspect.

One popular and dubious diagnostic approach is that of confusing a problem and a symptom. For example, while it may be true that people abused in childhood may not remember much of their childhood, the reverse, that those who cannot remember their childhood were abused, is an irrational conclusion. It is no more reliable than to say that those that have been abused smile, so that anyone who smiles has been abused. However, based on the false psychologized assumption that "normal people" remember their experiences as children, this means of diagnosing has been widely applied in the manufacturing of victims. As a result, thousands of individuals have been falsely persuaded that their complaints are indicative of deeper unconscious problems which are the result of abuse, incest or trauma. They have been led to believe that they can be helped *only* if they learn the mysteries of psychology which can unlock the Unconscious. Like the primitive witch doctor, the modern psychologist promises to do this in exchange for power and money."[58]

Another flawed diagnostic procedure which traps further tens of thousands in the Psychology Industry web, finds its basis in the absurdity that if one wonders about something then it is true. For example, an AA member speaking to new affiliates is quoted as saying: "If you think you have a problem, or if you think that you are an alcoholic, I assure you that you are. You wouldn't be thinking about it and you wouldn't be here if you weren't an alcoholic."[59] And Bass and Davis, as noted earlier, write; "so far, no one we have talked to thought she might have been abused and then later discovered that she hadn't been. The progression always goes the other way, from suspicion to confirmation. If you think you were abused and your life shows the symptoms, then you probably were."[60] Believe it or not.

Unsupported epidemiological claims have been made for a number of pseudo-diagnoses making them seem both legitimate and sufficiently prevalent to be acceptable. Consider the follow examples:

- 25,000,000 + are alcoholics.[61]
- 80,000,000 suffer from the disease of co-alcoholism and require treatment for being members of families of alcoholics.
- 20,000,000 are addicted to gambling.[62]
- 30,000,000+ women are sufferers of anorexia or bulimia.
- 80,000,000 have eating disorders.
- 75,000,000 (30% of population) are addicted to cigarettes.
- 50,000,000 suffer from depression and anxiety (mostly women).
- 43,000,000, 1/3 of all women, are victims of PMS or PPD(Post Partum Depression).
- 25,000,000 are love or sex addicts.[63]

- 5,600,000 have been abducted by a UFO.[64]
- 22,000,000 suffer from debilitating shyness (social phobia)[65]
- 66,000,000 have experienced incest or some other sexual trauma
- 10,000,000 are "suffering from Borderline Personality Disorder in America today"[66]
- Millions are compulsive shoppers[67]
- 36-48,000,000 are diagnostically addicted to work.[68]
- 1,350,000/year have Post-Traumatic Stress Disorder after car accident[69]
- 12,000,000 (5% of all Americans suffer from a condition called "generalised anxiety disorder"[70]

This brief and incomplete list of possible diagnostic labels accounts for over 561 million Americans, more than twice the nation's population, supporting the Psychology Industry axiom that it is normal to be abnormal and that every person is a potential user.

Traditionally in medicine, diagnosis has served the dual purpose of determining the nature of the problem and of indicating the appropriate treatment.

However, in the Psychology Industry it is generally the case that the diagnosis is adjusted to fit the form of treatment offered by the assessing

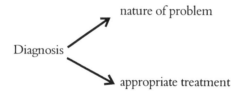

psychologist, and "practice patterns indicate that psychologists most often use the treatments that they prefer, rather than the treatments that are tailored to patient needs."[71]

Preferred Treatment ⟶ Preferred Diagnosis

Consider the following comment; "I was toying with the idea that many of the categories found in the *DSM-III* fit much more readily under the rubric of addiction and codependence, and working with them with the tools of the Twelve-Step program and the deep process work not only was cheaper and easier, it was more effective."[72] What the author, Anne Wilson Schaef, admits is that she takes the wide variety of psychological problems and redefines them as addictions, making her treatment, "deep process work," the most suitable. Similarly, John Mack identifies alleged cases of sexual abuse as actually being UFO abduction disorders, causing them to fall within his area of practice. So often, in the Psychology Industry, the diagnosis is consistent with the treatment offered that one can only presume that the psychologist's area of interest determines the label applied and justifies needed treatment. Such a conclusion was intimated when Frank Pittman III wrote: "psychotherapy involves applying the value system of the therapist to the dilemmas of the clients... his or her value system is more important to you than training, credentials, or even professional degrees."[73] However, sometimes, and probably not infrequently, diagnosis simply becomes a catalogue number for insurance reimbursement, unrelated to assessment or treatment, as Pittman confessed: "I sell them my time and whatever wisdom I have developed. If they expect their insurance to pay for it, I may apply a psychiatric diagnosis to them as well."[74]

Just as the Psychology Industry uses pseudodiagnostic labels to create the market for treatment, so too does it use "fear appeal." The *Dictionary of Marketing and Advertising* defines "fear appeal" as "advertising purporting to develop anxiety within the consumer based on fear that can be overcome by purchasing a particular item or service" as is done in "selling fire insurance by depicting a burnt-out house."[75] For the Psychology Industry, the burnt-out house is replaced by verbal descriptions of the psychological disaster that awaits if one does not purchase psychotherapy. Such is evident in Zimbardo and Radl's earlier statement: "living in that psychological prison can ruin a life," or in that of Marone: "current research shows that this style of behaviour systematically sabotages the very core of an individual's ability to cope with the rigorous demands of living in the world today... The price of helplessness can range from producing minor inconveniences, to obscuring one's vision of major opportunities, to binding one to dangerous or abusive situations."[76] These are the purported inevitable outcomes of severe shyness and learned helplessness if left untreated. Similar statements are made by the Psychology Industry with regards to most types of victims. For example, Suzette Elgin, in promoting her 8-Step Program for treating "the pain of verbal abuse," writes: "Verbal abuse is *literally* dangerous to our health, in the same way that contaminated food and polluted water and toxic waste are dangerous. There's nothing "metaphorical" about this danger; it's real."[77] And in the same vane, Owens, in *Raising Your Child's Inner Self-Esteem: The Authoritative Guide from Infancy through the Teen Years,* claims to "help parents and counsellors accomplish the vital task of building inner self-esteem in children... (by presenting) ways to boost the self-esteem of children who are shy, aggressive, unpopular, learning disabled, or gifted, as well as adopted children, only children, and children of working mothers, divorced parents, step-families, single parents, and same-sex parents."[78] The implication is that children in all of these categories (which includes most children) are at risk if they don't receive help in achieving *"this vital task."* In considering the notion that all children need therapy, David Gelman wrote: "In clinics and private practitioner offices around the country, troubled and troublesome children as young as 3 months old are receiving the benefits of cribside therapy."[79] It would seem that where the common doctrine used to be that children were born into sin, the modern doctrine of the Psychology Industry is that children are born into pathology, and are in need of therapeutic salvation.

But appeal to fear alone would not be effective in selling a product or service, were it not for the complementary emotional image that is portrayed once one makes the purchase. For the home-owner, it is the emotional security and peace of mind that comes from having purchased fire insurance. For the Psychology Industry user, the "emotional appeal" is similar. Harris and Reynolds trying to persuade parents to get therapy for their teenage children, write: "When your teen comes home from a therapy session, you may notice attitudinal changes. Your youngster will be developing *greater self-esteem, improving confidence, and becoming more assertive and expressive.*"[80] And again referring to Marone, she offers, as the therapeutic alternative to helplessness, the mastery-oriented individuals who "create reality and alter the world to fit their conception of it." She adds: "For the benefit of us all, they demonstrate in living color that the world will yield to the creative and focused application of a committed psyche."[81] For victims, the catch phrase is no longer "surviving" but "thriving," no longer is the goal to be "normal" but to achieve the "optimal." It's no longer alright to be just "OK," one has to be "perfect;" for "no matter how free of disease or problems you are and no matter how well you are doing, it's not enough," everyone could do better.[82]

When pathologizing is combined with the psychologized expert role, it makes a potent marketing force and a gold mine for the Psychology Industry. For victim psychology can span both sides of the nation's courtrooms. It is not restricted to the prosecution and the plaintiff, whose psychological diagnoses applied to the victims have become common fare in the arguments of cases ranging from sexual assault to harrassment to motor vehicle accidents. Consider the following in which each and every one of the diagnoses mentioned have been used by psychologists in U.S. and Canadian courtrooms in recent years to present the accused as helpless and blameless victims. (Numbers in paranetheses indicate the *DSM-IV* classification code.)

- Battered Wife Syndrome: a psychologist from London Ontario testified that Karla Homolka participated in the abduction, sexual assault and murder of two teenage girls because she had been battered by her husband Paul Bernardo.
- Premenstrual Syndrome: classified as a "Relational Problem related to a Mental Disorder or General Medical Condition" (V61.9), has been introduced by the defense in a number of cases. A jury in Liverpool England, in December 1994, found a woman not guilty in the killing of her husband after she was diagnosed as suffering from pre-menstrual syndrome.
- Pathological Gambling (312.31): the baseball player Pete Rose claimed an uncontrolable addiction to gambling in his defense.
- Alcoholism (303.90): This was Washington Mayor, Marion Barry's defense against drug charges.
- Other Substance Use Disorders (304.90), Caffeine Intoxication (305.90), Inhalant Abuse (305.90): such diagnoses have been introduced into the defense of a large number of accused including: 1) the

famous "Twinkie defense" (sugar-made-him-do-it) against murderer and former San Fransisco city supervisor Dan White who shot and killed Mayor George Moscone and gay supervisor Harvey Milk, and 2) the case of the Maryland bodybuilder who broke into six homes, stole cash and jewelry and set three on fire. Although found guilty the judge ruled him not criminally responsible because of his excessive use of anabolic steroids which lead to him "suffering from an organic personality disorder."

- Somatoform Disorder (300.81): A university professor was ordered to pay his adult daughter $1500.00 per month until he retires because she is unable to work due to a somatoform disorder that makes her focus on her physical disability.

- Clerambault-Kandinsky Syndrome: John Money, prominent sexologist and psychologist testified that Sol Wachtler, chief judge of New York State, charged with extortion and threatening to kidnap the teenage daughter of his ex-lover, "was manifesting advanced symptoms of CKS, described as involving an irresistible lovesickness or "erotomania."

- Telephone Scatologia (302.90): A psychiatrist argued that Richard Berendzen, forced to resign from the presidency of American University, after being arrested for making obscene phone calls, suffered from this paraphilia.

- Computer Addiction: In Los Angeles, a computer hacker, Kevin Mitnick, plead guilty to theft, after breaking into a corporate computer system and stealing software. The judge saw him as the victim of the insidious disorder of "computer addiction," and sentenced him to treatment for this "new and growing" impulse disorder.

- Attention Deficit/Hyperactivity Disorder (314): Steve Howe, who received a lifetime suspension from baseball for a extensive series of cocaine violations, successfully fought the ban arguing that he was a victim of ADHD, despite the fact that this diagnosis applies to children and Howe was 34 years old.

- Sleepwalking Disorder (307.46): This diagnosis was used successfully in the defense of a Canadian man charged with the double murder of his wife's parents, after he drove 15 miles across Toronto in the middle of the night to commit the act.

- Cultural Psychosis: A defense lawyer in Milwaukee argued that a teenage girl charged with shooting and killing another girl during an argument over a leather coat, suffered from "cultural psychosis" which caused her to think that problems are resolved by gunfire.

- Desensitization by exposure to TV violence: In defense of two young men charged with threatening a bank manager's family and robbing a pub manager at gun-point, a psychologist, Dr. Robert Ley, concluded that the accused were "victims of TV violence and bad group dynamics." He argued that "evidence attests to the fact that exposure (to hundreds of thousands of violent crimes on TV) serves to desensitize individuals, particularly males, to the consequences of crime and violence. This argument was first presented, unsuccessfully, in the trial of a 15 year- old Forida male charged with the murder of an 82 year-old woman. The defense claimed that the violent programmes that he had watched had served as "his instructor, his brainwasher, his hypno-tizer."[83]

- Reactive Attachment Disorder: A Denver woman, Renee Polreis, charged with beating her adopted two-year-old son to death with a wooden spoon attempt to defend herself by arguing that the child actually beat himself to death, the result of a psychological condition. The treating psychologist, Byron Norton, presented the theory that, due to neglect and poor nurturing at infancy in a Russian orphanage, the child suffered from "attachment disorder" which caused difficulty in attaching to caregivers, resulting in a rage during which he inflicted the injuries on himself. He was said to have died from "natural causes." The prosecutors called the definition "pop psychology at best and voodoo at worst," but the Judge ruled to allow the defence.[84]

- Internet Addiction: Sandra Hacker, a 24 year-old Cincinnati mother, was charged with three counts of child endangering. Her children, aged 2, 3 and 5 were taken into custody after they were found locked in a room which was described as having broken glass, debris and children's hand prints in human feces on the walls, while she surfed the Net. In her defence, psychologists likened her computer compul-sion to the addiction to gambling. Kimberly Young, assistant professor of Psychology at the University of Pittsburgh, said "exaggerated com-puter use should be recognized as an addiction."[85]

- A "novel" disorder. Novelist Janet Dailey, whose romance books have sold over 200,000,000 copies, acknowledged plagiarizing a rival nov-elist's work and blamed it on a psychological disorder. "'I recently learned that my essentially random and non-pervasive copying are attributable to a psychological problem that I never suspected I had,' Daily said. 'I have begun treatment for the disorder and have been assured that, with treatment, this behaviour can be prevented in the future.'"[86]

Pathologizing has become a most powerful factor in the marketing of the Psychology Industry as it presents an idealized and unachievable image of 'normal', and then proceeds to label and treat people based on this abstrac-tion. As Zilbergeld remarked: "people who believe that they are entitled to happiness tend to be receptive to almost anything that promises to relieve them of affliction and annoyance..."[87]

But the Psychology Industry doesn't even rely on people having problems to turn them into users, for, in its mind, as the Polsters said: "psychotherapy is too good to be limited to the sick."

GENERALIZING

If "pathologizing" is good for the Psychology Industry then "generalizing" is even better as it produces an ever-increasing size of the psychological pie. In a statement highly predictive of the subsequent growth of the Psychology Industry, Gestalt therapists Erving and Miriam Polster wrote in 1973: "Psychotherapists... have recently glimpsed *the vast opportunities* and the great social need to extend to the community at large *those views* which have evolved from their work with troubled people."[88] But what are "those views" which provide these "vast opportunities" for the Psychology Industry? In most cases, they involve the generalized concepts of *trauma* and *addiction*. If one person suffers from the effects of trauma after a vicious physical attack, or another develops a strong chemical dependency on alcohol, then maybe these terms can be massaged and stretched to apply to many more people, even those who haven't even recognized that they are suffering and troubled. With generalizing, no longer does the Psychology Industry have to be restricted to those individuals with severe psychological problems because now everyone can be found to have their own form of psychological distress.

Where abnormal behaviour was once an indication of problems, now ordinary behaviour is sufficient; where disturbed thinking was once required, now ordinary thoughts qualify; where suffering and distress once existed, these can now be "uncovered" or created. Faced with the psychological illusion that anything less-than-optimal is a sign of problems, people have been rendered vulnerable to the machinations of the Psychology Industry. And what better way to do this than to take a psychological term, popularize it through books, lectures, workshops and the media, and then generally apply it to a whole host of other situations. Referring to this process as "semantic inflation," Szasz noted that it "has resulted in the transformation of the ordinary behaviours of ordinary persons into the extraordinary and awe-inspiring symptoms of mental diseases."[89]

The situation described earlier, in which the predicted trauma of hostages was generalized to compare to others' experience of divorce, a relative's death or a robbery, is but one example. Familiar concepts such as co-dependency, self-esteem, and violence, also illustrate this "take it and run" strategy of the Psychology Industry which taps the "vast opportunities" that the Polsters saw.

"Co-dependency" was first coined to describe women whose lives were so intertwined with those of their alcoholic husbands that they were considered to be indirectly dependent on alcohol. Despite the many difficulties they encounter, their lives were seen to gain focus and meaning as they played the role of rescuer or nurse. But co-dependency is no longer restricted solely to alcoholism, it has been resculpted by the Psychology Industry to apply to any problem associated with any addiction suffered by any family member or anyone close. This re-definition has served to expand the market to include families, friends, business associates and lovers, anyone who might seek help, since "addicts" themselves are unlikely to become willing users. As well, it has opened the flood-gates to allow virtually every facet of life to become an addiction. In fact, Schaef contends that "an addiction is anything we are not willing to give up,"[90] an opinion that is supported by the following partial list of newly invented addictions: sex addicts, love addicts, shopping addicts, religious addicts, food addicts, caffeine addicts, gambling addicts, computer addicts, television addicts, work addicts, speed (i.e. moving fast) addicts, anger addicts, let alone all the legal and illegal chemical addicts including sugar addicts, "chocoholics" and fast food addicts.

Not only has this generalizing of addiction spawned a whole new sector of the Psychology Industry, the recovery movement, with Twelve-Step programmes and treatments for all the varied addictions, it has also given birth to a subsidiary industry that provides treatment for all those addicted to the addicts: those that are co-dependent. As Jeffers jubilantly proclaims: "At last there is a Twelve step program that benefits us all! You may never have had reason to attend any of the Twelve Step programs such as Alcoholics Anonymous (AA)...*But everyone in our society, including you and I, has reason to attend one of the newer Twelve-Step programs – Co-dependents Anonymous (CODA)!*"[91] No longer does one have to be married to an alcoholic, now one can qualify as co-dependent simply by being in any type of relationship. Melody Beattie, the popular author of books on co-dependency, including *Codependent No More* (which has sold over two million copies[92]), confirms this: "Codependency involves our responses and reactions to people around us. It *involves our relationships with other people*, whether they are alcoholics, gamblers, sex addicts, over eaters, *or normal people*. Codependency involves the effects these people have on us and how we, in turn, try to affect them."[93] Further redefined as "a disease of loss of selfhood,"[94] codependency can now be applied to anyone who has ever felt that they have done something they didn't want to do because of someone else; a group that is estimated to consist of 96% of the U.S. population. Accordingly, only the most stubborn or defiant have any protection from co-dependency, and then perhaps their behaviours could be interpreted as reactions to an underlying co-dependency.

In creating this generalized concept of co-dependency, the Psychology Industry blends the original concept from the field of alcoholism, with the passion and promise of religious revivalism, the medical concepts of disease and epidemic (co-dependency is advertised as a national epidemic) and the victim-making process of externalising cause and blame. According to co-dependency authors, it is a result of one or another form of child abuse, either physical, sexual, verbal or neglectful, which, in turn, has lead to the self-ne-glect or self-abuse of co-dependency. Within this circle of logic, everyone becomes both a victim of his or her own dysfunctional family and of the "universal problem of addiction." Schaef asserts in *Co-Dependence: Misunder-stood – Mistreated*: "when we talk about the addictive process, we are talking about civilization as we know it."[95] Harold Rome's prophetic words that "no less than the entire world is a proper catchment" are coming true as millions of people influenced by the Psychology Industry search for psychological answers. One publisher of co-dependency books is reported to have said "A lot of people are looking at why they're not happy"[96] and turning to co-de-pendency as one possible explanation and solution.

Once co-dependency has been psychologized (equating external relationships and internal dependence) and then generalized ("... millions are identifying themselves as codependents,"[97]) it is a natural next step for psychologists to pathologize it, casting it in terms of disease and cure. Consider Ricketson's negative prognosis "As you fall prey to addictions and continually living from a false self, *you will eventually break down under the strain.* Untreated codependency *invariably leads to stress-related complications, physical illness, depression, and death,*"[98] or Bradshaw's statement: "It's crucial to experience *the powerlessness and unmanageability* that results from being codependent ... fortunately, millions are identifying themselves as codependents."[99] These predictions stand in sharp contrast to the positive prognosis Bradshaw gives in his description of a good, non-dependent relationship, one "based on equality, the equality of two self-actualizing spiritual beings who connect at the level of their beingness."[100] Such bizarre statements led Kaminer to note that the definition of co-dependency as "bad and anyone can have it, ... makes this disease look more like a marketing device."[101]

Diagnostic categories are not alone in being susceptible to the generalizing process; terms such as "self-esteem" and "violence" can also be sponged into the overall fabric of society. Self Esteem is a psychological abstraction which most people think they understand but have difficulty defining. It is bantered about by the Psychology Industry to explain everything from good to bad, from mental health to violence and abuse. The psychologist, Nathaniel Branden, author of *The Psychology of Self-Esteem*, wrote: "I cannot think of a single psychological problem – from anxiety and depression, to fear of intimacy or of success, to spouse battery or child molestation – that is not traceable to the problem of poor self-esteem."[102] As such, it can be used both to explain problems and to describe the positive outcomes of psychological treatment. Remember Harris and Reynold's statement: "When your teen comes home from a therapy session, you may notice attitudinal changes. Your youngster will be developing greater self-esteem, improving confidence, and becoming more assertive and expressive."[103]

Through the psychologizing efforts of the Psychology Industry, self-esteem has become over-inflated to the point where it is generally accepted as one of the major causes of personal and social problems, which must be directly addressed and enhanced before people will change or social problems can be solved. As one psychologist wrote: "every theory of mental health considers a positive self-concept to be the cornerstone of a healthy ego."[104]

Such was the belief that led the California State Assembly to set up a task force in 1986 charged with the task of promoting self-esteem.[105] The legislature believed that raising self-esteem would reduce welfare dependency, drug abuse, teen-age pregnancy, and other social ills. Consistent with these commonly held beliefs, the task force intuitively assumed that self-esteem was at the root of both good and bad behaviour and set about to "determine that it is scientifically true." In doing so, it demonstrated the generalized view of self-esteem as it attempted to show the causal connection to child maltreatment, academic achievement, sexual activity of teenagers, unwanted teenage pregnancy, crime and violence, welfare, alcoholism and drug use.

The problem they encountered was that what they "knew" to be true turned out not to be. The editor of the report admitted that "one of the disappointing aspects of every chapter... is how low the association between self-esteem and its consequences are in research..."[106] But contradictory findings or conflicting conclusions have never daunted the Psychology Industry or led it to modify its marketing. So, despite the admission that "there is no basis on which to argue that increasing self-esteem is an effective or efficient means of decreasing child abuse...," the report of the task force went on to state that "policy interventions to reduce child abuse that involve increasing self-esteem should be encouraged and should include interventions at the individual, family, community and societal levels."[107] Thus, psychologically concocted "self-esteem" works well to expand the Psychology Industry's market, creating impressions of the urgent need for psychological services. Never can it be said that facts get in the way of the Psychology Industry's popularized beliefs.

Janet Woititz, author of *Adult Children of Alcoholics*, showed a similar oblivious response when confronted with her research data which showed that children of alcoholics who attended Alateen had a lower self-esteem than those who did not attend. To deal with this, she explained: "Thoughtful analysis of the data and an understanding of the alcoholic family pattern can help explain this result. Denial is a part of the disease both for the alcoholic and his family... This researcher suggests that the non-Alateen group scores significantly higher than the Alateen group scores because the non-Alateen children are still in the process of denial - they deny feeling badly about themselves."[108]

As these examples illustrate, when an abstract psychological concept is generalized such that it becomes part of cultural mythology, it can be applied to all aspects of human life as either cause or consequence, whether it fits or not.

Marketing the Theme of Violence

> *Aggression and violence are prime subjects for "the new seer"... Some psychiatrists and psychologists tend to exploit the public interest in violent crime by offering sensational diagnoses...*
>
> Martin Gross[109]

Violence would, at first glance, seem to be different from psychological concepts such as self-esteem; it is neither abstract nor undefinable, but rather real and brutal. But it is different when used by the Psychology Industry, or when employed in another of its marketing strategies. Violence actually serves as an excellent motif for Psychology Industry promotion, since it plays to one of the major current concerns of society for "law and order" while serving to tap into public funds which, while being reduced in the health sector, are being increased for justice and policing.

Violence can refer to murder, assault, rape and physical abuse, but in this psychologized world, it can also mean "any act that causes the victim to do something she does not want to do, prevents her from doing some things that she wants to do, or causes her to be afraid."[110] Just as low self-esteem can be blamed for failure and disappointment, so too can violence, when defined so broadly, be seen as the cause of problems for which an "other" can be held responsible.

Despite statistics which show a slight decrease in actual crimes,[111] violence, aggression and fear have become popular themes for psychologists to use in their marketing. Ignoring the unfulfilled promises of the 50's to eradicate crime, the Psychology Industry offers "a message of hope," that for instance, "there is overwhelming evidence that (psychologists) can intervene effectively in the lives of young people to reduce or prevent their involvement in violence."[112] This promise is made even though the same report in which this statement was made, acknowledges "the lack of availability of outcome data on many existing youth violence prevention or treatment programs."[113] Again, it would seem that psychologists are numb to their own professional data when they make claims or promote their industry.[114]

The psychologising of violence has lead people to believe that it is due to psychological causes, as demonstrated by the following statements of psychologists which were presented to the Canadian Senate in a debate on Violence in Society:

"...All the boys from quarrelsome families with erratic discipline, but only one-fourth of those from cohesive families with consistent discipline, were convicted of a crime. Interestingly... it was the mothers' behaviour that made the greatest difference in the boys' criminality."

"I have never met a violent juvenile delinquent who was not abused as a child... Secondly, all of the criminals at San Quentin prison who have been studied had violent upbringings as children."

"Thirdly, all assassins, or individuals who have attempted assassinations in the United States during the past 20 years had been victims of child abuse: There is a 100 per cent correlation."

"If you look at the problem of sex murder... you find that they all come from broken families and suffered cruelty and brutality, usually at the hands of a woman, plus acting out, as a child, vandalism, arson, and cruelty to animals. You see the pattern over and over again. There is cruelty to animals, cruelty to kids, and if a woman has beat up on you, then you are more likely to become a sex murderer."[115]

The implication in all of these, is that violence is due to psychological factors and that psychologists are capable of understanding and doing something that can reduce and eventually eliminate the evil of violence. Through fostering a culture of fear and contrasting it with the ideal of security and safety, psychologists create for themselves a niche as experts at the politico-cultural level by advising on issues of prevention and policy making and, at the legal level, by proposing ways of identifying or treating perpetrators. For instance, one psychologist, using "fear appeal" warned that "only one to five per cent of sex offenses are reported" and "the next-door neighbour or community leader may well be an undiscovered paedophile."[116] Meanwhile, the authors of an American Psychological Association task force on Male Violence against Women, who were described as "experts in different aspects of female-directed violence," declared that "one in every three women will experience at least one physical assault by an intimate partner during adulthood," and "34 to 59 per cent of women are sexually assaulted by their husbands."[117] Based on weak to non-existent research,[118] this attitude and expression exacerbates rather than relieves public fear. As well, it conveys the message that members of the Psychology Industry have specialized knowledge about the psychological roots of violence, qualifying them as experts and policy advisers in the field.

Curiously, although this task force report claimed to have "ways to curb violence," most of its recommendations were for further research; enhanced federal data-collection effort, ongoing collection of national data on prevalence and correlates of rape, battering and sexual harassment, more research on the origins of and cultural supports for conceptions of gender that promote violence, and more research on the psychological effects of violence against women. Specifically regarding intervention, the authors recommended "encouraging treatment innovation" (presumably because outcome data fails to show that current programs are effective), "enhancing practitioner knowledge of the history of traumatic victimization, routine screening for histories of victimization and validating women's experiences as part of clinical practice;" and they suggest that sensitivity training be provided to judges[119] and *grants be established* to create innovative techniques to increase arrests, prosecution and conviction rates in domestic violence cases. In other words, although psychologists want the public to view violence in psychological terms and psychologists as experts, they don't really know what to do about violence; the report serves basically as a promotional and marketing tool.

While much of the Psychology Industry's attention is directed towards "controlling violence" and identifying offenders, other psychologists, fully convinced of the intrapsychic nature of violence, such as Judith Becker, president of the Association for the Treatment of Sexual Abusers, *propose increased funding* for the psychological treatment of offenders. In support, Becker referred to Jeffrey Dahlmer, whom she evaluated for his 1992 trial, as "a lonely soul who found sadistic control as his only escape from isolation," whose "cannibalistic compulsions may have been alleviated had he felt safe to seek help when his deviant fantasies began in his adolescence."[120] Despite the lack of data and the view of many psychologists that such serious offenders are untreatable, and in spite of Dahlmer's own claim that none of her ideas made sense to him, Becker and her associates believe that *funds should be provided* to help "offenders explore the origins of their sexual compulsions – which usually involves their own victimization – and explore more appropriate alternatives."[121]

So, whether it is playing the numbers game with statistics, making exaggerated and frightening statements, or claiming unsupportable abilities to treat or prevent violence, the Psychology Industry psychologizes society into believing in its powers. At the same time, it pathologizes those who have survived real violence, turning them into users, for the Psychology Industry has been very effective in persuading people that if they have experienced *any* crime they are psychological victims of traumatic stress; for them the psychological crime has virtually just begun. Psychologists' predictions that, although the incidents may have passed, the psychological effects are ongoing and may be long-term, have given rise to a plethora of government funded "victim-support" services, staffed and directed by psychologists. While some of these people may need assistance and support, the Psychology Industry has succeeded in creating the belief that all those who experience a crime will experience an "emotional backlash." As a director of one Victim Service stated: "The emotional damage is harder to repair than a broken window."[122] However, one elderly woman, whose home was burgled in her absence, when offered professional help to deal with the trauma and fear she was presumed to be experiencing, said that the only help she needed was with the task of cleaning up the mess.

While many might agree with this woman and concede that not all crimes cause psychopathology, most would likely assume that childhood sexual abuse does cause pathology requiring psychological intervention. Bass and Davis attribute almost every psychological disorder and problem to early childhood sexual abuse.[123] But beliefs such as this are the product of Psychology Industry marketing and not supported by research. No one doubts that such abuse can have lasting and malignant effects of both a personal and interpersonal nature. However the assumption that it *always* leads to pathology would seem to be far from accurate. For instance, Nelson[124] found that 65% of the female incest victims in her study regarded the experience as negative, while 9% were uncertain about their feelings and 26% evaluated what had happened to them as positive. As well, Burgess and Hartman found, in a study of the consequences of sex ring exploitation involving the abuse of children by one or more adults, that three quarters of the people studied "demonstrated patterns of negative psychological and social adjustment"[125] the expected outcome. More striking, however, is the complementary finding that 25% of these cruelly mistreated children appeared to be psychologically unharmed.[126] Levitt and Pinnell concluded, in their review of the research literature that "many victims – a sizable minority at least – do not suffer long-range harm. One possible cause of this finding is that father-daughter incest, the most virulent type, is far less common than sibling incest. Another inference is that children are more resilient emotionally than nonprofessionals like Bass and Davis believe."[127] Whatever the reason and whatever the proportion it is which experience harm, it is clear that not all do and that it is an effect of pathologizing that unconditionally defines all these people as victim/users.

If not all victims are harmed by violence, then what about those who only witness it? The Psychology Industry would have society believe that they too are victims, even if they witness it on television or in videos. At the conclusion of the Bernardo trial in Canada, during which videos were shown containing scenes of Bernardo, the accused, raping the two teenage girls, jurors were asked to attend a two day session to deal with their trauma, victims of having had to view the tapes. Interestingly, most refused. In another case, two young men were charged with armed robbery and assault. A psychologist, employed by the defense, could find nothing in either of their backgrounds to explain their criminal behaviour; so he testified that excessive television viewing of violence increased their vulnerability to commit the crime; they were described as "victims of television violence."

Other psychologists have taken a different approach to generalizing violence by altering the concept so that it includes verbal comments, insults and criticism. Suzette Elgin, author of *You Can't Say That To Me*, states that "Physical violence begins, 99 times out of 100, with *verbal violence*"[128] (a claim which she later stated was "not intended as a 'statistic.'"[129]) In the same generalizing vane, Catharine MacKinnon, a legal theorist and antipornography activist, claims that she was raped by a book review. Carlin Romano, the book critic for the Philadelphia Inquirer began his review of MacKinnon's new book *Only Words,* with a hypothetical proposition: "Suppose I decide to rape Catharine MacKinnon before reviewing her book. Because I'm uncertain whether she understands the difference between being raped and being exposed to pornography, I consider it required research for my critique of her manifesto..." The effect according to MacKinnon was that of rape: "He wanted me as a violated woman with her legs spread."[130]

Another example of "definitional ooze" can be found in the report of Secretary of Health and Human Services Donna Shalala that, according to a new government-funded study, "child abuse and neglect nearly doubled in the United States between 1986 and 1993" One odd thing about her claims is that no other sign points to such a dramatic increase in abuse or neglect; fatalities arising from child abuse, for instance, held roughly steady.[131] Further examination reveals that 80% of "the increase" can be accounted for by the inclusion in the criteria of: "endangered children," those who were not actually harmed or neglected but "in danger of being harmed according to the views of community professionals;" and those "emotionally abused," by virtue of "verbal abuse" or "the refusal or delay of psychological care;" or "educational neglect," involving the chronic failure to send a child to school. The apparent explosion of abuse can, more accurately, be attributed to the lava-like spread of the definitions of abuse and neglect.

Thus, it would seem that, according to the Psychology Industry, one can be a psychological victim of violence whether the violence is experienced directly, witnessed, or watched on television or a movie, and regardless of whether it is physical, verbal or even imaginary. But like codependence and "self-esteem," violence, as a concept that appeals to the psychologized and morbid interests of the public, has been applied to a wide variety of situations with the end result being yet a bigger pie for psychologists to slice up.

MAKING GIDGETS AND WIDGETS: A BUSINESS STRATEGY

There seem to be rainy days ahead for psychology not because of what we have done or not done but because of major political and economic changes that seem sure to have profound affect on psychology... Change is in the wind, and (psychologists) have little effect on wind.[132]

This note of concern was voiced by the CEO of the American Psychological Association in regards to the "health care reform initiatives sweeping the country, the continuing evolution of managed care, and other significant market trends affecting the practice of psychology." Ironically, while psychologists seek to establish their expertise and influence in all aspects of life and promote their public prestige, they privately are worried and struggling for their own survival.

Psychology has typically relied on the health care market, whether it has been in the formal health care system, the private mental health clinics, or the private practices dependent on health insurance ("third party') payments. But with the failure of the Clinton health care plan, the severe cut backs both in the size and services of the U.S. government[133] and the federal funding of the Canadian system of universal health care, and drastic reductions in individuals' discretionary monies from which they paid for therapy in the past, the future of psychology would seem to be in jeopardy. As Morris, the treasurer of the Canadian Register of Health Service Providers in Psychology stated: "Psychologists (referring to licensed psychologists) are being excised from institutional practice faster than any other health care professional group – *we are expensive to feed and painless to drown.*"[134] Clearly, despite popular beliefs about the importance and powerfulness of psychologists and efforts by them to prove their relevance and effectiveness, they have been unable to convince decision makers and health care administrators that they are an essential and "valued component of mainstream health care." "Government spending cuts for research, health care and education have gone well beyond the fat and deep into the muscle and bone" wrote CPA Public Affairs Chair, Richard Allon, "*Our discipline is under siege.*"[135] As Morris said when addressing his colleagues: "Like it or not we have got *to do business differently.* This is not a false alarm but a wake up call; at issue is survival... I do endorse entrepreneurship and aggressive marketing..."[136]

Some psychologists have responded to this "crisis" by attempting to demonstrate the cost-effectiveness of psychological insurance benefits, while others have organized to lobby public officials and launch media campaigns to gain support.[137] But at the individual level, as practitioners report that their earnings are decreasing,[138] the search for alternative ways to get paid has begun. Robert Resnick, president of the American Psychological Association, put it this way: "the way to make it when the market is changing is by diversifying, that's what corporations do. *You don't only make widgets; you make some gidgets and some widgets.*"[139]

Although some psychologists may take Resnick's advice and begin making gidgets, others it would seem are just relabelling their widgets as gidgets. Kovacs, concerned about survival, argues, in what seems to be a glimpse of psychologizing-in-action, that psychologists should move out of the mental health business and become "consultants on life-span developmental challenges."[140] To which Herron and Welt commented: "although the same type of patient problems will still be worked with if the patients so desire, the names will be changed to such more palatable alternatives as "unhappiness."... He (Kovacs) is, in effect, attempting to provide himself, and those who use his services, with an alternative that will be more likely to attract paying consumers than by using terms such as "patient" and "psychotherapist."... The approach is a marketing tool that contains economic motivation."[141] In other words, at this point in the life of the Psychology Industry, the repackaging and relabelling of psychological products may be an essential component to maintaining consumer demand.

While the Psychology Industry has been effective in infusing psychology into the human experience and persuading millions of people that they suffer directly or indirectly from psychological problems, it is up to local psychologists to be innovative, entrepreneurial and aggressive; to do business differently.

The Clothes Have No Emperor

In 1993, Jeff Blyskal wrote in *New York*:

Last February, I decided to become a psychotherapist.

I found a comfortable office in the East Fifties for a mere $875 a month. I.S. Furniture Rental was willing to outfit the place in traditional style, with plenty of rich burgundy tones – cherry desks, medical-file cabinets, couch, even oil paintings – for only $335 a month.

The cost of business/appointment cards would come to $70; the phone, installed, would cost $621.81; a month long radio-ad campaign (60-second spots, four times a day) would reach a quarter-million listeners for only $2,000.

So for just $4,000, I could have become a professional healer- with absolutely no training, credentials, or license.[142]

Blyskal didn't hang up his shingle but he could have because, contrary to public opinion, in most states and provinces there is nothing to stop such a scam and there is no enforceable minimal requirement in education or experience for one to call oneself a psychotherapist.[143]

Since the option is open to anyone, the first step in becoming a successful psychologist is to seek ways of implying competence and credibility. Most rely on their academic qualifications and, if possible, use them to achieve licensing or gain restrictive certification. While generally requiring significant effort and commitment, neither an M.D. nor a Ph.D. necessarily ensures any training or ability in psychology or traditional psychotherapy.

Many general medical practitioners, after years of routine practice, have opted to become psychologists out of boredom or frustration with routine medicine. Similarly, a large number of individuals with Ph.D.s in the experimental fields of psychology, in which there are fewer and fewer jobs and lower incomes, have developed clinical and consulting practices. Although both groups are licensed professionals, their licenses in no way are proof of training or competence in psychological treatment. In fact, most licensing boards have no way to determine minimal competence or ability, relying on "self-regulation" by the individual professionals who are expected to restrict their practice to areas in which they are capable. This is an absurd idea at a time when psychologists' jobs and income are being threatened and they are being encouraged to develop alternative services. For most, the doctorate provides the license to "roam freely," declaring new techniques and new expertise as they go.[144]

If the individual in practice has no doctorate and license, then a common way to obtain credentials which increase one's competitiveness in the market is to become "certified." Some certification programs require at least a master's degree, moderate to extensive clinical experience and supervised work; others accept anyone who will pay. Some are established by state laws; others are merely conferred by an association or group of practitioners who

A KIND WORD
AND
A SMILE
$1.00

"I got my basic business education selling lemonade. Later I discovered that my emotional and financial ambitions could best be met in the field of psychology."

augment their own income by giving workshops and nepotistically supervising others. All claim expertise and specialized knowledge of a technique or theory, and all strive in monopolistic fashion to either restrict practice to those who are certified or to distinguish themselves as superior because of their certification. Like licensing, certification provides several advantages to psychologists: it increases their credibility, often creates a critical mass for political lobbying, sometimes provides access to third-party payments and generally lends an enhanced appearance of those who employ them.[145]

However, unlike state licensing, certification is generally unregulated, often open to anyone regardless of education, and allows individuals and groups to set up certification programs for any technique or fad. Perusal of any phone book provides examples such as those below, all of which were used to promote services within the context of treating victims of trauma or addiction: Certified Art Therapist and Certified Expressive Arts Therapist, Registered Clinical Counsellor, Registered Play Therapist, Certified Reality Therapist, Certified Master Rebirther, NLP Master Practitioner[TM], Master Hypnotist and Certified Hypnotherapist, Certified Massage Practitioner, Certified Holotropic BreathWorker[TM], Certified Master Time Line Therapy[TM] Practitioner, and Certified Firewalk Instructor.

A further means of establishing credibility, an approach which has grown with victim-making psychology, is that of personal experience as a victim. "At this point, many people who choose (to work with adult survivors of childhood trauma) are coming to it from their own victimization" according to Marilyn Murray, who is described as a specialist in the field.[146] The opinion, that one is qualified through their own experience, is expressed by many in the Psychology Industry. Ann Jones, author of *Next Time, She'll Be Dead,* says: "I speak from experience. My father was a drunk, a wife beater, and a child abuser."[147] Anne Wilson Schaef, in stating: "my relationship addiction recovery process has been key in its interaction with my professional work and how I came to view my work,"[148] claims the same credential, as does John Bradshaw[149] who has described his approach as having its origins in his own experience, and Andelyn Miller who "feels her personal experience in codependent relationships is her real qualification..."[150]

While to the public's eye, all of these "credentials" may have the same effect, that of persuading one to seek services and trust their psychologists' competence, aggressive, even hostile, competitiveness exists within the Psychology Industry. For instance, Murray added to the above comment by saying "some of the most knowledgeable clinicians are the "front-liners," that is those with other than Ph.D. or M.D. degrees but who have the most direct experience."[151] In her mind, the experience is more important than formal education. Morris, on the other hand, in speaking to licensed psychologists said: "The public is desperate for alternatives to the failed promises of medical men/women and *would-be helpers* (implying those that Murray would favour)"[152] as he encouraged his colleagues to adopt a "GET IN YOUR FACE PSYCHOLOGY" (his capitalization)[153] form of marketing to oppose what he viewed as the "tyranny of acute medicine." It would seem that while the Psychology Industry has been effective in its promotion of psychology, it has not increased the size of the pie sufficiently to meet the needs of all of the purveyors, leading to in-fighting between the various sub-groups of psychologists.[154]

If credentials are not sufficient to ensure success in the Psychology Industry, what else might help? One option, and a short-term means to cope with the problems of oversaturation, has been to specialize in a field or as Robiner terms it, "becoming creative in finding a niche".[155] One such niche is "stress." Psychologists of differing orientations have dealt with stress for half a century. In 1945, Grinker and Spiegel[136] reported on the reactions of WWII combat fliers exposed to the threats and strain of battle and described how the fliers were psychologically treated, outlining possible civilian applications. Stress as a topic was picked up by post-war psychology and applied to a number of new areas including: "life stress events" leading to physical illness,[157] "executive stress" resulting in burnout,[158] and "performance stress" causing academic failure or sexual dysfunction.[159] But in the late 80's and 90's, a new array of specialists emerged, who redefined stress as trauma and claimed to be more capable in identifying and treating the wide variety of problems, old and new, which they now saw as related to earlier life trauma. They received a lot of attention and publicity as they broke from a "here-and-now" approach to problems, and began to advocate the need for patients to regress and mentally return to the earlier time when the trauma occurred or even before it to a time of innocence. Using terms such as Miller's "prisoner of childhood"[160] and Bradshaw's "Inner Child," they began to portray their patients as victims of trauma, who had suffered abuse and were damaged by events outside of their control. The clients' present problems were viewed as only symptomatic of deeper underlying trauma which needed to be uncovered before recovery could take place. Patients were instructed to return in their minds, often with the assistance of hypnosis or guided imagery techniques, to these earlier events and relive them emotionally. At the same time, they were encouraged to discover and nurture their inner child, the person they could have become if it were not for the abuse. It is in this regard that Gloria Steinem once mused whether Marilyn Monroe, if she had not died before the discovery of the inner child, "could have become strong enough to go back and be a parent to her own sad child of the past." She concludes, "we'll never know;" to her the question seemed reasonable.

BREAKING THE SPELL

- Relationship Issues
- Weight Concerns
- Low Self-Esteem
- Depression
- Anxiety
- Disease

What do these have in common? All may be invisible wounds left by emotional abuse. These wounds can be healed. As we awaken from our trancelike spell, we see that what is "normal" may be abusive, and symptoms may be calls to healing. We can break the spell and be free.

An Abuse-focussed Advertisement

Psychologists received an enormous amount of publicity because of these new techniques which often involved hypnosis and hypnoanalysis, regression therapy, or NeuroLinguistic Programming(TM), and the claims they made about the effectiveness of these approaches in finding and resolving trauma. As well, the mass media, through which most beliefs about therapy's effectiveness are taught and encouraged, picked up the topic because it combined the entertaining elements of pathos and promises. This new area of speciality offered the sordid details of abuse and violence and the encouraging news of hope and optimism. From talk shows to tabloids, these psychologists with their new specialities, sold their wares as they described case after case in which individuals had uncovered their trauma, discovered their Inner Child and recovered. The subject matter contained sex and violence, qualities known to draw viewers, but the message was inspiring, and the methods and tales of success went unquestioned often because there was no one willing to challenge them or because the media did not want a debate which might weaken the sensationalism or positive message.[161]

A new field of specialization had been defined which offered practitioners a way to stand out in the market place and to establish a business less affected by the already tightening belt of the health care industry. Thus began the Psychology Industry's current venture into manufacturing victims. Psychologists could now claim to be specialists in the treatment of adults who had been abused as children, victims of sexual abuse, of ritual satanic abuse, and so on. Psychologists' advertisements, even those of licensed psychologists who were now being allowed to aggressively advertise, began to show signs of the "retooling" that was going on within the Psychology Industry.

However, even specialization may not be enough to compete successfully in the Psychology Industry, for many may end up claiming the same specialty. In this case, creating a new one may be the solution for, with a new specialty, there will not be many competitors, at least for a while. And to get full benefit of it, the successful psychologist might consider claiming ownership of it as "intellectual property" and registering it as a product with its own trademark. A number of psychologists have done this with techniques they have developed (eg. NLP, EMDR), thereby restricting others from using the specialty designation unless they obtain training sanctioned by the owner/psychologist. Those who are wise enough, or cunning enough, to do this are able to ride the wave of their success to prestige and profit.

Inventing such a specialty usually means creating a new problem or an innovative treatment. Ries and Trout[162] describe this function as the Second Law of Marketing, "The Law of Category:" "If you can't be first in a category set up a new category you can be first in." In commercial manufacturing, most new products are either a modification or an "improvement" of an existing product or an application of a current product to a new area of use...

Inventing such a specialty usually means creating a new problem or an innovative treatment. In commercial manufacturing, most new products are either a modification or an improvement of an existing product or an application of a current product to a new area of use. The same is true for most of the new specialty creations of the Psychology Industry, in which a new problem is differentiated from an old one or a new technique is cast from existing methods. A variety of fields have opened up in this way and continue to appear at a rapid rate, such as: "Traumatology," a new field treating victims of trauma; "Critical Incidence Stress (CIS) Debriefing," a technical specialty which deals with stress resulting from crime or disasters; and Relationship Addiction, the disease of needing to be needed. As each new problem is dreamt up or psychologized, it is described as a refinement, an improvement, over what was previously understood or done; the Traumatologist "knows" more, the CIS debriefer "does" better and the Relationship Addiction Counsellor "helps" better. When one of these new approaches is created, the next step is usually to establish an Institute, Foundation or Centre to study and promote the area, followed by a book and lecture tour, a series of workshops and training programmes which then certify other psychologists, resulting in a hierarchy or pyramid of specialists.[163]

The April 1995 bombing of the Federal Building in Oklahoma City, provided just such an opportunity for psychologists who called themselves "traumatologists" to demonstrate their wares and promote their specialty. In a programme called "Operation Healing," they undertook to provide trau-matology counselling to the many Oklahomans disturbed by the bombing and to many others around the country who felt affected. Some psychologists worked on-site in Oklahoma City while a nation-wide 800 number was set-up that operated 24-hours a day. An organization called the "Green Cross" was created which would "support not just the Oklahoma Operation but others as well." It was described as "an organization that helps profes-sionals in stricken areas help their neighbours grow healthy... As the Red Cross aids those in crisis, the Green Cross focusses on long-term struggles to recovery." The traumatology organizers then determined that they needed to train others and that a "curriculum" was needed "that would enable them to do the work of healing the traumatized themselves." A "Faculty" was assembled of volunteer psychologists from around the world connected through the use of videos and the Internet. Four training workshops were scheduled, complete with a "Graduation Ceremony" at which time regis-trants would receive their own credential as Registered Traumatologists:[164] the specialization process was complete.

Yvonne McEwan, a Scottish trauma expert who advised the US govern-ment after the Oklahoma City bombing, has openly challenged this new specialty. In an invited address at the 1997 European Trauma Conference in London, she delivered the shocking and unexpected message that profes-sional counselling is largely a waste of time and does more to boost the ego of the counsellor than to help the victim. She declared the profession to be "at best useless and at worst highly destructive to victims..." and accused professional counsellors of "creating a nation of victims in order to boost their flagging careers in the medical profession." As McEwan sees it: "The legal profession and medicine have colluded in the whole fabrication of people undergoing trauma" and "by medicalising what is a non-medical condition and introducing therapy subject matter that is vastly abused, medicine is propping up a lot of dwindling careers." This outspoken critic claims that "the whole disaster scene has become a growth industry since the Bradford fire." She points out that "in Dunblane, for instance, there were far more counsellors than victims."[165]

According to McEwan, many people, including some trauma counsellors, are nodding their heads in agreement.[166] However, despite her dismissive stance, the reactions to it, and people everywhere who shake their heads, quietly wondering about the merits of this "coffee cup therapy,"[167] trauma counselling, largely due to effective and very aggressive marketing strategies.

For example, the American Psychological Association is lobbying federal, state and local governments for disaster-response plans and funding, stating that disaster victims need "more long-term care." Its demands include: licensed clinicians to supervise, a strong research component to identify needs of people affected by the incident, and <u>mandatory</u> provision of mental health services for rescue and relief workers.[168]

According to Ries and Trout, "the most powerful concept in marketing is owning a word in the prospect's mind"[169] and in the minds of many, "trauma" has come to be a psychological word which indicates the need for counselling. Consider the following recent examples:

- The 1996 flooding of the Saguenay/Lac-Saint-Jean region of Quebec lead to a relief program which included the Red Cross paying for a maximum of 20 consultations for psychological assistance, up to $1,000 per evacuee. Similar services were offered to those involved in the Red River flooding in North Dakota and Manitoba in the Spring of 1997.
- Psychologists counselled family members, flight crews coming through New York, rescue personnel and others associated with the TWA crash off Long Island in 1996.
- When a building being demolished in Canberra, Australia exploded rather than imploded resulting in injuries to spectators, a counselling service was set up within hours for the tens of thousands of tourists and locals who had come to watch the afternoon event.

A similar entrepreneurial process can be seen in the development of Critical Incident Stress Debriefing (CISD). Jeff Mitchell, formerly a volunteer firefighter/paramedic and now a psychologist, observed that a large proportion of emergency personnel (firefighters, ambulance/paramedics, and police) experience some reaction – whether emotional, physical or cognitive – to critical incidents, which he defined as those emotional events which, because of their nature or circumstances, cause emotional distress in healthy normal people. While he noted that most of these symptoms were normal and would naturally disappear in a few days or weeks, he believed that, for a very small proportion of workers, they "developed into full-fledged post-traumatic stress disorders." Consequently he designed a structured group discussion, the CIS Debriefing, based on stress education, reassurance that the reactions of the emergency personnel were normal, and an opportunity for emotional ventilation, in which participants could talk about their feelings. The program lead to a number of articles in journals and a book,[170] and numerous workshops and lectures around North America. Workshop registrants became trained CIS Debriefers, a specialty which could be employed in gaining contracts with emergency organizations, school boards, airlines and banks.

Perhaps one of the best examples of entrepreneurship that combines many of the elements previously described is that of John Gray, creator of the *Men are from Mars, Women are from Venus* slogan. For credentials, he proffers a bachelor's degree and an M.A. (in the Science of Creative Intelligence) from Maharishi International University, and a Ph.D. obtained through a correspondence course from Columbia Pacific University in San Rafael, California.

After further tutelage from the Maharishi and experience in operating sex and relationship workshops with his ex-wife, Barbara De Angelis, author of *How to Make Love All the Time,* he unveiled his own "innovative specialty" based on his perception of the differences between the sexes.

Since the release of his 1992 book which has sold a record 6 million copies and been published in 38 languages, earning Gray about $18,000,000, he has written 5 other books for a total sales of 9 million copies. He has also turned his concept into videotapes (3,000,000 in sales), audiotapes (1.3 million sold), and musical CD's (130,000 shipped to date.) As well, he markets seminars (at $35,000), workshops, Mars and Venus vacations, a Broadway appearance which is now "on-the-road" across America, and he hopes for a movie deal and television sitcom.

As for his counseling, Gray has a franchised line of Mars & Venus Counseling Centers run by therapists who have paid $2,500 to be trained in the Mars & Venus 'technique', and a further $1,900, plus $300/month royalties, for the rights to the name and logo.[171]

All of this on a Ph.D. by correspondence and 'chutzpah.'

"Cui bono?" - Who is to Gain?

A question that critical observers might ask is: "Who is to gain from the new services that are created by psychologists?" For whose benefit are they offerred? Is it the client and the community or the psychologist and the Industry? Often this conflict of interest is resolved in favour of the industry's self-promotion. A case in point comes from the new technology of medically assisted reproduction related to problems of infertility. While the development of artificial insemination and embryo implanting has created an array of ethical and moral questions as well as medical, psychological and emotional issues, it has also provided an opportunity for psychology to open a new market and create a new client base of donors.

Matters which might be considered by most to be personal, are, for psychologists, invitations to exercise authority, to expound their peculiar beliefs, to psychologize the experience and to pathologize the inherent difficulties.

As Australian psychologists, Walker and Broderick, show, in a well-documented paper,[172] psychologists are seeking to widen and entrench their role by presenting themselves as experts, able to prescribe the appropriate feelings, thoughts and actions of applicants and to judge who should and shouldn't be allowed to become parents. For instance, Humphrey et al.[173] in describing their screening program, express the belief that infertility has "a deeper psychological meaning" and they screen applicants according to their ability to handle and express this psychologised construct. They write: "we have found evidence of marked variations in (couples') response to an unusual and potentially threatening predicament. Some appeared to have adapted well and could view this means to a child as entirely rational and psychologically acceptable. Others were more defensive and seemed reluctant to explore the deeper meaning of their infertility."[174] It is on this basis, as determined in a single interview with the couple, that these psychologists determine who qualifies for the procedure and who does not.

Psychologists do not stop at claiming to know who qualifies; they go on to claim that they know how the parents should/must act and what will happen if they don't do as they are told. These therapeutic edicts hold that it is better: 1) for people undergoing treatment to talk to family, friends and counselors about their use of donated gametes or embryos; 2) to tell a child of the method of conception and genetic background; and 3) for donors, recipients and children to know one another, regardless of circumstances or personal preferences for privacy. Failure to conform is interpreted as a pathological form of keeping secrets and predicted to create serious psychological problems. The Psychology Industry forecasts that the refusal to inform others, including the child, of the use of "donated material" will result in unhealthy family dynamics, impaired "identity development" and "genealogical bewilderment" in the children who will be "driven to search for, and to seek reconciliation with, their biological ancestors."[175]

Unstoppable, the Psychology Industry spreads its net even wider to draw in the donors as potential clients by stressing that they must also consider the psychological effects on themselves of what some psychologists call "pre-natal adoption." These individuals, often referred to as the 'biological' fathers and mothers, while the recipients are only the 'psychological' or 'social' or 'substitute' fathers and mothers, are told that they must consider such things as "the implications of another couple having your child," and "becoming a parent of children you may never know."[176]

Every aspect of this potentially joyous experience becomes shrouded by the Industry in a cloak of pathology. To quote Daniels and Taylor: "...donor insemination lends itself to secrecy in a way that adoption and assisted fertility techniques such as IVF cannot. This helps support the pretense that the conception, and therefore the family, is "normal,"[177] a view supported by Snowden and Mitchell who entitled one of their papers: "The Artificial Family: A Consideration of Artificial Insemination by Donor."[178] As Walker and Broderick write, "perhaps the only ones who think that a child conceived through donor sperm belongs to an abnormal family are psychologists and social workers such as Daniels and Taylor."[179]

One can wonder how it is that such an esoteric medical area is so psychologized and consequently so regulated. Why is it, as Walker and Broderick ask, easier to donate a kidney than an ova, to receive someone else's heart than it is their sperm? The answer may be in part that the adoption business is diminishing and with it, the role that psychologists have carved for themselves within it, so that they must look for new sources of income. The growing business of assisted reproduction provides such an opportunity as the demand for it increases with the development and refinement of the technology. It is currently estimated that as many as one couple in seven will have trouble conceiving a child.[180] For the Psychology Industry, this represents a significant new market in which psychologists can posture as experts with their claims of specialized knowledge and skills.

When Kenneth Clark, APA President, announced in his 1971 presidential address, the "era of psychotechnology" and described the important role of medications in the future of civilization, it met with strong criticism from psychologists not only because it proposed the drugging of "all power-controlling world leaders" to "assure their positive use of power and reduce or block the possibility of their using power destructively" but also because psychologists viewed themselves as opponents of psychiatrists. Historically, psychologists have criticized psychiatrists for their use of drugs to treat symptoms and control people, while they, on the other hand, have claimed that they treat the actual problem and offer a better psychotherapeutic alternative.

However, as time passes, theories and economies change. The pendulum which not long ago favoured psychological explanations and interventions has begun to swing toward biological theories about the causes of emotional and behavioural problems, and psychologists have begun to express the opinion that they need prescribing privileges in order to be able to treat the "whole person" and to compete in the marketplace. As it now stands, they must refer their clients to psychiatrists or physicians for prescriptions, fearing the possibility of 'losing' the patients. For example, one psychologist wrote that he changed his mind on prescribing when one of his patients informed him "that because she had to see her new psychiatrist for medication, she had decided to undertake her psychotherapy with this practitioner as well.... If psychiatrists place a choke-hold on my patients' access to this therapy, I will devote my energy to gaining the right to provide, independently, the full range of mental health services. *Don't tread on me.*"[181]

Although the proposal for prescribing privileges met with initial hesitation amongst psychologists, it has quickly gained steam so that by 1996, the APA Board of Directors approved model legislation for prescriptive authority, recommended postdoctoral training in psychopharmacology and allocated funds to support efforts to promote state-level prescription privileges for practitioners.[182] The profession that once declared itself as the alternative to psychiatry is now trying to turn itself into a "pseudo-psychiatry" blurring the age-old distinction between medicine and psychology.

Psychoactive drugs are presenting a real threat to the Psychology Industry unless it too can become involved in their prescription. For instance, psychologists have strongly argued that psychotherapy, specifically cognitive-behavioural therapy, is the treatment of choice for depression. But the development and subsequent publicity and popularity of Prozac and its derivatives (e.g. Zoloft), have made it a serious threat. In 1996, Prozac and Zoloft were prescribed to children and adolescents by U.S. physicians more than 580,000 times, more than double that of 1994 and almost ten times that of 1992, even though those drugs cannot be legally marketed for use by children. In 1996, worldwide sales of Prozac alone totalled $2.3 billion US.[183]

But again one can ask: "Who is to gain from this?" Proponents of the scheme argue that the right to prescribe will increase the likelihood that drugs "are appropriately utilized, if used at all, and will ensure that practitioners can address society's pressing needs... in a safe, cost-effective and competent manner."[184]   But why would any of these expectations be true from an industry which already often creates the problems it then seeks to treat with unlimited and unproven therapies?

The costs and the dangers to the public are several. As DeNelsky points out, "there is a powerful seductiveness about medications."[185]   Drugs are easily provided, offer a "quick fix" and give the practitioner the sense that he or she is doing something now. Already concerns exist that drugs are being over-used and, with an increased number of minimally trained prescribers,[186] it is difficult to imagine that this will not escalate. Aided by the forceful push of the pharmaceutical companies which provide large amounts of funding for research, education and travel to conferences supported by them, there is a strong likelihood that psychologists would be doing more prescribing and less of their other therapy. It is equally conceivable that this seductiveness may extend beyond current prescribing practices into the use of drugs to create a happier society free of worry and sadness and their mandatory use to control violent, aggressive, sexual or addictive behaviours deemed unacceptable by society. Already, James Goodwin, a psychologist, has gained international attention for his promotion of Prozac as the treatment of choice for complaints of violence, low self-esteem, chronic irritability, eating problems, hypersexuality and so on. "I have this fantasy of pouring (Prozac) in the water," he states. "If I put out a good product and people are healthier and happier, that's fine by me. I don't mind being Dr. Feelgood."[187]

While Goodwin may be at the extreme, he exemplifies the professions dissatisfaction with its current status and its desire to expand its market, and its "power."

And the Beat Goes On

> An influential group of therapists is promoting a new scare: children who molest other children. Those who question the murky evidence are said to be in denial. But it is the kids, taken from home and given intense therapy, who might be suffering the most.[188]

The Psychology Industry's induced public hysteria about sexual abuse and violence is spawning a new variety of victim (and perpetrator) and creating yet another new specialization: "children who molest."

This diagnostic description, first coined by psychologist, Toni Cavanaugh Johnson in 1988, has been applied to children as young as 2, for "inappropriate " behaviours such as diddling, licking, flashing, mooning, masturbating compulsively, looking up under girls skirts, laying on top of a girl in bed; even using sexual language or asking endless questions about sex. This has lead to brothers, cousins and playmates being diagnosed with "sexual behaviour problems," charged with assault, and removed from their families. And it has led members of the Psychology Industry to promote the inclusion of "juvenile sex offending" into the *Diagnostic and Statistical Manual of Mental Disorders (DSM)*, the catalogue of psychopathologies.

In the early 1990's, *San Diego Union-Tribune* reporter Mark Sauer watched Johnson and social worker Kee MacFarlane presenting their work on children who molest at a professional conference held in San Diego. He was astonished. "First they state that there is no research — that we really don't know anything about normal children's sexual behavior," he recalls. "Then out come the pie charts and graphs and they go on for an hour defining this new abnormality. And everybody is madly taking notes."

It is important to note that "Sauer had reason to be suspicious of MacFarlane and the clinic she worked for, Children's Institute International (CII) in Los Angeles. His newspaper had published some of the only sceptical coverage of the 1980s McMartin Preschool satanic ritual abuse trials. Sauer knew MacFarlane as the woman who headed the team that interrogated nearly 400 children for the prosecution and found 369 to have been victimized in bizarre rituals including anal rape, animal mutilation, and kidnapping through secret tunnels. Except for one, none of the children mentioned abuse until they got to CII. After the jury saw MacFarlane's taped interviews, full of leading, hectoring questions, they voted to acquit the defendants."[189]

But Johnson and MacFarlane are not alone in promoting this new specialization, which in the mid 80's did not exist. The Vermont-based Safer Society Foundation database now lists 50 residential and 396 nonresidential programs that treat "sex offenders" under 12. As well, two studies that provided therapy and evaluated the best treatment approach for hundreds of "sexualized" children under 12 in Vermont, Oklahoma, and Washington were funded at a cost of $1 million. And "at the 1995 Association for the Treatment of Sex Abusers conference, about 80 percent of the exhibition tables featured literature on such programs for children and adolescents."

Such programs have already become structured and Taylorized according to the practice of the Psychology Industry, with "children's group work" and "steps for 'recovery.'" David McWhirter, a social worker and one of the US's most prominent therapists of juvenile offenders is quoted as saying about one 12-year-old: "the boy didn't want to confess guilt, the first stage required for 'recovery.'" Barbara Bonner, chief researcher of one of the million dollar studies admits that such processes are "value driven," and based on what the psychologists "consider to be appropriate and in the best interest of children." This statement is made, as is usual in the Psychology Industry, in the absence of hard facts or known effects. As Bonner admitted: "We will probably never know the harm (of children behaving sexually)... we don't have long term outcomes. They (the children) may turn out to be normal."

In fact, almost everything that Johnson, MacFarlane and other children-who-molest experts think is disturbing or pathological is unremarkable in most cultures and previously was in this society. It would seem that the harm comes not from the events but from the adult's getting upset about it and the experts labelling the children as "sex offenders" and forcing them into treatment.

Despite Bonner's concessions and the concerns expressed by others, psychologists have gone about establishing for themselves this new field of specialization, leading Judith Levine to comment: "So, with little supportive evidence, the new children-who-molest experts have persuaded the child protective systems they work for that "sex-offense-specific" therapy is necessary for any kid with a "sexual behavior problem." They insist this therapy, whose methodologies derive from their own theories, can be practiced only by them or others they have trained."[190]

"This all reminds me of heroic gynecology (during the early 20th century), which regarded the birth process itself as a pathological thing," says Vern Bullough, distinguished professor emeritus at SUNY and author/editor of over 50 books on sexuality. "What we've got now is heroic intervention in childhood sexuality by people who don't know what they are talking about."[191]

Something for Nothing

While the development and promotion of "specialties" are of direct benefit to those that develop them and those that are trained, who can claim specialist status, they also have a pay-off to the Psychology Industry as a whole, as they serve to further psychologize human experience and to identify more users who might otherwise not seek treatment. An information release from the Practice Directorate of the American Psychological Association describing its "Disaster Response Network" (DRN), exposes the pathologizing and promotional aspects:

> The California fires and earthquake. The Midwest floods. Hurricanes Andrew and Iniki. The shooting on the Long Island commuter train and the World Trade Center bombing. These disasters have had a devastating impact on the lives of thousands of Americans. Their losses are, many times, unfathomable: homes, communities, jobs and sometimes, loved ones. As individuals and communities begin to pick up the pieces of their lives, they often times neglect the need for mental health care, something that disaster survivors desperately need at a time when they can least afford it financially. *If left untreated, these needs can develop into chronic problems that are disabling to people in both their professional and personal lives...* The mental health needs of the national disasters have been monumental... In addition to the short-term crisis intervention services the DRN offers survivors, the network *helps them to identify local resources for ongoing psychological assistance.*[192]

Although at first glimpse, this might seem like an altruistic act (the American Psychological Association described it as "APA's centennial gift to the nation"), a look at the American Psychological Association's document for psychologists on "Diversifying Your Sources of Practice Income" reveals an ulterior motive:

Providing public sector services on a pro bono basis is *an effective marketing tool* that may create other professional opportunities involving compensation.[193]

According to the most recent statistics of the American Psychological Association, 72.8% of psychologists provide such pro bono services, perhaps with this in mind.[194]

As well, the move towards specialization has spawned a number of new sub-industries such as those that have grown up around Post Traumatic Stress Disorders and Addictions. There are now specialists in treating the PTSD of the friends and acquaintances of people who have committed suicide;[195] who have lost a pet;[196] who were fired from their job; who experienced a divorce or death;[197] who were raped, assaulted or harassed; who are veterans of WWII and experiencing memories due to the 50th anniversary;[198] or who have experienced gender discrimination.[199] Similarly, there are specialists in the addiction and recovery of those dependent on and thereby victims of love,[200] sex,[201] "urgency",[202] religion,[203] shopping,[204] on-line computing,[205] food,[206] prostitution,[207] and so on.

The invention of a specialty would seem to be restricted only by the limits of one's imagination. The past few years have given rise to a number of other new and imaginative psychological specialities including:

- Certified Shamanic counselling; "Feel like part of you is missing? You're probably right! Trauma of any kind can result in partial soul loss. Shamanic soul retrieval counselling can restore lost parts, facilitating wholeness."

- "Am I Nuts?," a call-in television talk show on America's Talking, a 24-hour all-talk cable TV network which began business in July, 1994. The program features psychologists "helping ordinary people with extraordinary stresses in everyday life."

- "Licensed Volunteer Therapy Dog" – designation awarded animals who complete a series of special obedience courses and pass a test at one of the 35 U.S. chapters of Therapy Dogs International. Licensed dogs were used in the aftermath of the Oklahoma bombing. As Karen Sitterle, a psychologist, was quoted: "The animals gave the children a sense of control. Surrounded by so many adults, the children were the smallest and most helpless people there. Suddenly, they had something smaller and more vulnerable than they were – something they could look after and play with."[208]

- "Llama Therapy" – In Idaho, llamas are used to "teach teenage offenders to develop affection and concern for other creatures," while in South Carolina, llamas are used in the treatment of abused children. In British Columbia, the Llama Therapeutic Group offers stress management. Psychotherapist, George Appenzeller explains that llamas "stick together and take care of each other without giving up their individuality, so you could say they're good role models."[209]

- "Counselling by Phone International" provides professional counselling for hotel guests in distress. "Recognizing the reality that some hotel guests are in distress or even experiencing tragic personal circumstances, Coast Hotels and Resorts is the first hotel chain to offer this new professional services through in-room directories," stated a press announcement by Graeme Benn, Director of Marketing for Coast Hotels.[210, 211]

- Commuting Stress intervention assesses the various aspects of the commuting experience linking causes and consequences of commuting stress and provides intervention which can improve the commuter's affective response.[212]

- Horticultural Therapy – citing studies showing aggression and violence are reduced by 400 per cent in gardens, horticultural therapists (there are over 1000 of them in North America and some universities offer courses in horticultural therapy) believe that plants have a healing psychological effect.[213]

- Juror Stress has been identified as a unique source of stress which can lead to a range of Psychosomatic symptoms including depression, sleep disturbance, stomach distress, headaches and sexual problems according to Thomas Hafemeister, PhD., J.D., senior staff attorney and research associate at the Institute on Mental Disability and the Law at the National Center for State Courts.[214]

- Trade Guns for Therapy – some California psychologists are offering three free hours of therapy in exchange for a gun, with the stipulation that they will help the person continue to go to therapy by providing sliding scale fees or arranging insurance coverage.[215]

- "Compassion Fatigue" – a new syndrome specifically relating to psychologists who are the victims of stress due to the excessive demands that their clients place on them and "from the demands of the changing health-care environment." They are advised to seek treatment from other psychologists with experience in the area.[216]

- "Genetic Sexual Attraction" – a psychological condition/experience in which reunited birth relatives, a mother and son, father and daughter, or siblings, fall in love and become sexually involved. One therapist describes this as a "way of re-enacting the original trauma (of being given up for adoption) in order to reconstruct the relationship."[217]

- "Tickle Healing" In a promotional mailing for workshops, counselling and vacation healing packages in Hawaii, psychologist Paul Carter writes: "Tickle Healing is a simple, direct, outrageous, and respectful pathway back to this center of joyful being. I am convinced that light and deep tickling is one of the most powerful forms of touch there are. The fact that many people hate being tickled or no longer can feel "ticklish" is proof of the power (and the abuse of that power). Tickle Healing is designed in such a way as to allow all people to enjoy tickling again.[218]

- Internet Services. The whirlwind of the Internet has opened a Pandora's Box of psychological services including:

- "One-stop shopping sites for all of the interests of psychological consumers," including workshops, books, tapes and videos.[219]

- Online training in various psychotherapy techniques such as cognitive therapy in which "the program covers all of the basic features of cognitive therapy, and offers a "hands- on" experience in using common treatment procedures."[220]

- Advertising of services such as:

A.V. THERAPY AND EATING DISORDER CENTER
City, California

Psychologist's Name, Ph.D.
Licensed Clinical Psychologist
Director

16 Years Experience, 7 Years Beverly Hills Practice

FREE PHONE CONSULTATION
Specialized care for

Anxiety	Bulimia
Depression	Anorexia
Panic Attacks	Overweight
Marital Issues	Diet Pill
Abuse Victims	Laxative Abuse
Hyperactivity	Children

Effective Short-Term Therapy Groups

- Personal Cognitive Therapy – "The programme has been designed for use by a wide variety of patients, including those with severe levels of depression or anxiety."[221]

- Art Therapy – in which an "art therapist" offers problem-solving sessions as well as session series based on client needs using art-making processes such as painting, drawing and collage to resolve day to day life conflicts and to help clients find right direction in their lives. After an initial consultation, if it is found that short term therapy is counterindicated, clients can be referred to other appropriate long term therapies.[222]

- Individual Psychotherapy – in which the user is offered two options: Option # 1: "Describe the problem that is causing you concern or an issue that you feel needs work. The psychologist will respond within a week and a half with a 45-minute audiocassette. This tape will provide specific therapeutic feedback for the problem or issue you raised." The fee for option 1 is $165.

Option # 2: "The psychologist will set up a private chat room (on the Net) and give you a password that will permit you, and only you, to enter this room. I will then arrange with you to meet me in this room at a specific time on a specific day. This will be a 45-minute session." The fee for option 2 is $135.[223]

- In April 1997, a new cable channel called the Recovery Network debuted in the United States. A video promo explains that topics go "from alcohol to drugs, to depression, sex, obsession, eating disorders, family violence, compulsive gambling and sexual abuse." According to an article in *The New Republic*, this network is "the end of the line, the logical terminus for a culture in love with its own dysfunction: the Recovery Network, a 'round-the-clock' media showcase of addiction and anomie … [a] proudly pathological cable channel..." While "healing" may be the "name," ratings are still the "game." It turns out that not all "victims" are created equal: "The bottom line is that it has to be good television," says the producer, "Some people's stories just aren't very interesting."[224]

- "Going to court can make you sick..." says Karin Huffer, a marriage and family counselor in Las Vegas, who has identified a new disorder, *"legal abuse syndrome,"* "...and it can strike crime victims, witnesses, litigants, attorneys — anyone who has dealt with the American system of laws and courts." Describing it as a variant of post-traumatic stress syndrome, she states that: "While a crash happens quickly, a legal battle can drag on for years, slowly pushing your brain to release the noxious chemicals." Victims of legal abuse syndrome typically jump when a phone or doorbell rings, check obsessively to see if windows and doors are locked and try to avoid anything that reminds them of the legal system. "I've known some who can't even walk into a courthouse," she says. "They'll take a detour just to avoid seeing it." "But even those who have never been to court can fall ill from legal abuse," Huffer states. Anyone who has tried to argue with a government agency, for example, can suffer the frustration and feelings of hopelessness that bring on the disorder. And the cure for legal abuse syndrome? It's complicated, but essentially involves lots of therapy to identify and address the cause of the problem — and lots of crying, according to Huffer.[225]

Once the issues of credibility (credential) and product-line (specialty) are resolved, the next and all important issue facing psychologists is to get publicity. While it is important in science to attempt to give a correct and rational explanation of the facts, such a demand is not there in the marketing of psychological services. When people seek advice or treatment, they often make judgements based not so much on what psychologists can actually do as on what they, and others, claim they can do.

Not long ago, licensed psychologists, social workers and psychiatrists were prohibited from advertising. Even the size of signs and business cards was regulated and controlled. But they argued that this gave other unlicensed psychologists an unfair advantage, and that lawyers already had the right to advertise. Their cause was supported by the Bureau of Competition of the Federal Trade Commission resulting in changes in the Ethical Principles of the professions so that claims of unique services (specialties) are no longer considered unethical unless they are clearly misleading or fraudulent. Although phrased by licensing bodies and professional associations in term of complying with federal regulations, the unacknowledged benefit of this change was to increase the visibility of the Psychology Industry.

No longer are psychologists restricted to contacting referral sources and offering courses or workshops. Neither do they need to be as cautious about participating in media interviews or talk-shows for fear of ethical complaints.[226] Psychologists now have the freedom to openly promote themselves and their services. They can advertise, extol their services and make exorbitant claims about what users can expect, even if their claims contradict research findings.

ARE YOU TROUBLED BY?	WOULD YOU PREFER?
• Pressure & Stress	• Creativity and Energy
• Feeling trapped	• Sense of Freedom
• Low self-esteem	• Self-worth
• Poor relationship	• Ease in Relating
• Resentment	• Acceptance
• Guilt	• Clarity
• Fear	• Confidence

ACT NOW

A High Expectation Advertisement[227]

NOBLE LYING

Do advertisements like this merely portray the psychologizing effect of creating false expectations, or do they constitute lying and fraud?

According to Kottler, the author of numerous books on psychotherapy:

> Telling clients that we can help them is assuredly helpful even if it is not strictly true... By communicating confidence, however false it might feel, we establish hope and motivation in the client. We would lose clients very quickly if after every bungled interpretation... we muttered "Oops, I blew that one." *We would never*

> *get a client to come back if we were completely honest with them...* the client may need to believe in this lie...[228]

Some forms of deception and lying have always been a part of psychological practice, sometimes in the form of suggestive therapies, sometimes in the declarative but unfounded statements of psychologists, and sometimes in the misleading forms of such advertising.

When confronted by moral objections to suggestionists and therapists deceiving their patients, Janet, a contemporary of Freud's and a psychological practitioner and hypnotist responded:

> I am sorry that I cannot share these exalted and beautiful scruples... My belief is that the patient wants a doctor who will cure; that the doctor's professional duty is to give any remedy that will be useful, and to prescribe it in the way in which it will do most good. Now I think that bread pills are medically indicated in certain cases and that they will act far more powerfully if I deck them out with impressive names. When I prescribe such a formidable placebo, I believe that I am fulfilling my professional duty.

He continued;

> We are faced here with one of those conflicts between duties which are continually arising in practical life; and, for my part, I believe that the duty of curing my patient preponderates enormously over the trivial duty of giving him a scientific lecture which he would not understand and would have no use for.[229]

Janet's (and Kottler's) assumption was that patients wanted and needed to be treated as children by paternal and protective, if not always honest, psychologists, and that it is in the best interest of these patients to lie, for "there are some to whom, as a matter of strict moral obligation, we must lie."[230]

Thus deception has become an acceptable practice and a cornerstone of the Psychology Industry,[231] if it can be justified in terms of benefit to the user. For as Kottler wrote: "Certain lies may therefore be necessary, if not therapeutic. If lying to a client, deliberately or unintentionally, is unethical since it promotes deceit and deception, perhaps it is just as unethical to be *completely truthful.*"[232] Whether it is expressed in terms of creating positive expectations which are believed to be essential for a good therapy outcome, or fostering unconditional acceptance and positive regard, or giving unquestioning support to a claim of abuse, the Noble Lie has become acceptable in the Psychology Industry. When Dan Sexton, Director of the National Child Abuse Hot Line, was questioned in this regard, he responded:

> I'm not a law enforcement person, thank God! *I'm a psychology person, so I don't need the evidence.* I come from a very different place, I don't need to see evidence to believe... I don't care what law enforcement's perspective is, that's not my perspective. I'm a mental health professional. I need to find a way to help survivors

heal to the trauma that they had as children and to help support other clinicians who are trying to help survivors and victims of this kind of crime.[233]

And another psychologist and author, when asked about the "facts" he had presented in his best-seller dealing with a case of satanic abuse, replied that it didn't really matter "whether or not they were technically true, that was immaterial;" he didn't want to "nit-pick about facts."[234] For these, and many other psychologists,[235] it doesn't matter whether facts are true or whether what they say is honest, what matters is that the user believes them.

However, Alan Scheflin, a lawyer and law professor, in addressing a conference on hypnosis and psychotherapy, went beyond acknowledging the deception involved in the omission to tell the truth, when he encouraged psychologists to consider the ethical responsibility to intentionally deceive their clients.

> The point I want to make is the assumption that implanting false memories is wrong. I would like to raise the issue of whether we are right to say it is wrong... When we get through the false memory issue perhaps we can start to debate the serious question... that *therapists are in fact social influence purveyors* and it is your job to use those techniques. And hypnosis will lead the way into the social influence literature. An then we can start to talk about *the ethics of using false memories therapeutically.*[236]

Thus, to Scheflin and to the many psychologists who gave him a standing ovation, the end justifies the means even if the means is to mislead, deceive and lie to the user, and to create a false history of her or his life.

Perhaps another reason that Scheflin got such a rousing round of applause on that occasion, was that he was promising psychologists that soon "there will be a point –though there has not been one yet..." when they would find the power that "would make therapists more effective in treating the prob-

lems of the patient."[237] His message was that the power to change people, to create not only good memories but good (albeit false) identities, was soon to be discovered; that although psychologists may feel insecure about their abilities, they need not worry because the techniques to influence, persuade, and change people were being developed. His message was encouraging to the many psychologist who carry on their daily practice of professional deception, creating an image of themselves as confident, self-assured and caring while inwardly feeling anxious, inept and disinterested.

A University of California study of 421 psychologists revealed that psychologists wished to be seen as "irrepressibly superior;" as dependable, capable, conscientious, intelligent, friendly, honest, adaptable, responsible, reasonable, and considerate.[238] That these psychologists are encouraged to practice this deception can be seen in messages that state that image-making is essential for success:

> Therapists who are perceived as confident and credible produce positive results, period. And if they are viewed as being self-congruent and genuine, all the better.[239]
>
> Clients want to grow up and be like their therapists. They want the serenity, the wisdom, the self-control, the confidence they see so effectively demonstrated before their eyes.[240]
>
> It has become increasingly clear to me that it hardly matters which theory is applied or which techniques are selected in making a therapy hour helpful... for what every successful healer has had since the beginning of time is charisma and power.[241]

However, as effective as this deception may be to the public, candid reports of psychologists show them to be lacking in such self-assurance and confidence, and consequently extremely vulnerable to promises of influence and power. Arons and Speigel, in a chapter sub-titled "The Wizard of OZ Exposed," wrote: "When we (psychologists) sit in our consultation rooms, we often try to present *a carefully sculpted image* to our patients... At times, we are much like the Wizard of OZ, trying to make an impressive presentation while hoping that the curtain we hide behind won't be pulled aside to reveal more vulnerable parts of ourselves."[242] In agreement, one female therapist commented: "My clients aren't particularly open-minded. I fear their rejection. Many wouldn't like me if they really knew me, and that wouldn't be very good for my practice."[243]

The Psychology Industry's solution to this dilemma is to deceive; to appear "so sane, so calm, so wise"[244] in order to be effective and to hide any insecurities or inadequacies. Now this wouldn't necessarily be bad, for after all it is a strategy adopted by many business people,[245] if it were not for two potential harms: it obstructs honesty, making it difficult for psychologists to admit their humanness and say "I don't know," and it fosters a "one-up" relationship between psychologists and their clients. Caught in the trap of omniscience, they feel bound to cover uncertainty and natural ignorance with a veneer of extraordinary perception and wisdom, often expressed in terms of "I know something about you that you don't know." And, in response to their insecure feelings, they create a "therapeutic relationship" in which they assume a superior position to the inferior and dependent client: "You may not know it, but you need me." One psychologist unwittingly addressed this when she wrote about her 20 years in therapy:

> While I was in therapy I enjoyed the attention my therapist provided me, which I didn't get from my own distracted parents. I became addicted to this attention, and to keep it, I remained in the role of the dependent one, needing validation and almost by definition feeling insufficient. I pathologized myself to remain in treatment. Negative feelings became symptoms to overcome. Wellness, once a goal, eluded me while I confused it with a utopia of freedom from all negative feelings or distatseful situations. *My dependency needs were gratified rather than processed, for my therapist shared in my illusions.*[246]

And what better, more effective way is there than to portray people as victims; which casts them in the role of weaker and vulnerable users, who must rely on the psychologist for validation, direction and support.

One of the effects of such pretenses and the practice of noble lying is that psychologists are themselves being turned into victims and potential users of the Psychology Industry's own marketing and manufacturing processes. One study of 4000 psychologists reported that 74% had been or were users of the Psychology Industry with an average of four and a half years spent in treatment. But such situations serve to complicate the deceptions and to increase the complexity of the lying. The psychologist in therapy for 20 years also wrote:

> Being in therapy can be gratifying – it certainly was for me – and the profession provides many rationales for that gratification. My favorite rationale for staying in therapy was to view treatment as a means of keeping my unconscious open to communications from that of my patients; this made my own therapy a requirement of practice. But although I used my work as a rationale for staying in treatment, the real reason was that I liked being in therapy...
>
> To counterbalance this dependency (with her therapist), I became a therapist... Now I have become a source of gratification for my own patients... *using my patients to satisfy my own needs to be important...*[247]

And for some yet unexplainable reason, a large majority of the public is gullible to this deception whether it is in the consultation room or court-room, and is inclined to believe whatever is shown on television, heard on the radio, read in books, or told in sessions. Perhaps it is as Smail says, that even though "all promises that we may return to the blissful ease of infancy are false... wishful dreaming renders one vulnerable to commercial promises of its coming true..."[248] Perhaps it is the cultural pressures of Western society to accord an honorific status to professionals, particularly if they can parade as scientists and experts. Whatever the reason, image-making, media coverage and public exposure all serve to establish the psychologist as an "acknowledged expert."

So the business formula for psychologists can be simply put:

1) Establish credentials, through either academic qualifications or certification.

2) Develop a specialty, preferably by creating a new one which allows one to obtain the additional prestige and income associated with training and certifying others.

3) Use noble lying as a means to create false expectations and false explanations.

4) Market through advertising, workshops, lectures, books and media coverage.

Kottler, writing *On Being A Therapist,* candidly said:

> In exchange for spending forty-five minutes listening to someone talk and telling them what we think about what they said, we receive enough money to buy ten books or a whole night on vacation. It is absurd. It would almost seem that even with the hardships of being a therapist, *we have a good thing going.*[249]

Endnotes

1. *The Family Therapy Networker*, March/April 1995.

2. President's Column, *The APA Monitor*, June 1995, p.2.

3. Marwit, S. J. In support of university-affiliated schools of professional psychology. *Professional Psychology: Research and Practice*. 1982, 13, pp 181-190.

4. Robiner, William N. How many psychologists are needed? A call for a national psychology human resource agenda. *Professional Psychology: Research and Practice*. 1991, 22 (6), p.429.

5. Robiner, 1991, pp 427-440.

6. Figure 1 is based on data provided by the American Psychological Association, and Figure 2 is based on data from the 1990 U.S. Census. "All psychologists" includes those who identified themselves as psychologists, social workers, or therapists (#105 Category), and does not include psychiatrists, ministers or unpaid counsellors.

7. Olfson, Mark, and Pincus, Harold A. "Outpatient psychotherapy in the United States." *American Journal of Psychiatry*, 151(9), 1994, p.1281.

8. A study conducted by the Canadian Centre for Health Information Statistics, Ottawa; reported by Alex Richman, the researcher at the American Psychiatric Association annual meeting, in Philadelphia, June 1994.

9. Rome, H.P. "Psychiatry and Foreign Affairs." *American Journal of Psychiatry*, 1968, 125, p.729; and " 'The psychiatrist,' the American Psychiatric Association, and social issues." *American Journal Psychiatry,* 1971, 128, p.686.

10. The American Psychological Association, for instance, recently published "a practitioner's guidebook:" *Business Strategies for a Caring Profession.* (Yenney, Sharon L.; Washington, DC: American Psychological Association, 1994.)

11. Torrey, E. Fuller. *Freudian Fraud: The malignant effect of Freud's theory on American thought and culture.* New York: HarperCollins, 1993. p.129.

12. Watson, *Behaviorism.* p.104.

13. Smail, David. *Taking Care: An Alternative to Therapy.* London: J.M. Dent & Sons, Ltd., 1987. p.40.

14. Zilbergeld, B. *The Shrinking of America: Myths of Psychological Change.* Boston: Little, Brown and Co., 1983. p.91.

15. Dawes. *House of Cards.* p.256.

16. Albee, G.W. "A competency model must replace the defect model." In Bond, L.A. and Rosen, J.C. *Competence and Coping During Adulthood,* 1980. p.95.

17. Farley, Frank. "Thrills:" the President's column, in the *The APA Monitor*, February, 1994, p.3.

18. Duvall, Evelyn Mills. "Growing edges in family life education." *Magazine of Family Living*, 1943, 5, 22-24. Cited in Christopher Lasch, *Haven in a Heartless World: The Family Besieged.* New York: Basic Books, 1977. p.108.

19. Bruche, Hilde. *Don't be Afraid of Your Child*, 1952. Chapter 1.

20. Cited in Torrey. *Freudian Fraud,* p.128.

21. Study cited in Torrey. *Freudian Fraud,* p.222.

22. Stanley Shapiro, director of the Parenting Education Centre in Ontario, quoted in "Spanking: The Discipline Dilemma." *Homemaker's Magazine*, October 1995. p.50.

23. "Son suing his parents opens a Pandora's Box." *Washington Post,* 10/1/1979, B1.

24. Gross. *The Psychological Society.* p.267.

25. Westman, Jack C. *Licensing Parents: Can We Prevent Child Abuse and Neglect.* New York: Insight Books, Plenum Press, 1994.

26. American Psychological Association Practice Directorate. "Children's Mental Health Needs: Reform of the Current System" Document 49022, 1995. p.1.

27. Ibid. p.1.

28. Fenster, C.A. et al. "Careers in Forensic Psychology." In Woods, P.J. *Career Opportunites for Psychologists*. Washington: American Psychological Association, 1976. p.124-125.

29. Scott Sleek. "A varied practice is the key to security." *American Psychological Association Monitor*, March 1995, p.28.

30. Quoted in "Psychologists, lawyers facing similar changes." *The APA Monitor,* 25(2), 1994. p.1.

31. Frank Cavaliere. "Psychology-and-law field well-positioned for growth." *The APA Monitor*, August 1995, p.43.

32. Ibid. p.43.

33. Quoted in "From the People Who Brought You the Twinkie Defense; The Rise of the Expert Witness Industry." *Washington Monthly*, June 1987, p.33.

34. *Ferguson v. Hubbell*, 97, N.Y., pp. 507 and 514 (1884). Cited in Huber. *Galileo's Revenge.* p.13.

35. Ibid. p.2.

36. Ibid. p.18.

37. Ibid. p.3.

38. Ibid. pp. 21-22.

39. "Ex-Pittsburg man managed auto parts store in Berkeley; jury award called 'record breaking'." *San Francisco Examiner*, Sept. 7, 1995.

40. Huber. *Galileo's Revenge.* p.182.

41. Hagen, Margaret A. *Whores of the Court: The Fraud of Psychiatric Testimony and the Rape of American Justice.* New York: Regan Books, HarperCollins Publishers, 1997. p. 301.

41a. Hole, Christina. *Witchcraft in England.* New York: Collier Books, 1966. pp.75 and 89.

42. Sprenger, J. and Kramer, H. *Malleus Maleficarum* (1486) Translated by Montague Summers. London: Pushkin Press, 1948.

43. Mackay, C. *Extraordinary Popular Delusions and the Madness of the Crowds* (1841). New York: Noonday Press, 1962. p.481.

44. Ibid. p.514.

45. See: Lindsay, D.S. Johnson, M.K. and Kwon, P. "Developmental changes in memory source monitoring." *Journal of Experimental Child Psychology,* 1991, 52, pp.297-318; White, S. and Quinn, K.M. "Investigatory independence in child sexual abuse evaluations: Conceptual considerations." *The Bulletin of the American Academy of Psychiatry and the Law,* 1988, 16(3), pp.269-278; Campbell, Terence W. "False allegations of sexual abuse and the persuasiveness of play therapy." In press; and Gabriel, Ronald M. Anatomically correct dolls in the diagnosis of sexual abuse of children." *Journal of the Melanie Klien Society.* 1985, 3(2), pp.40-51.

46. In one case, a new day care teacher cautioned a three year old girl to "keep her privates covered," and warned her that "no one should see your private parts." Accustomed to parental

help with bathroom functions as well as bathing and dressing, the girl remarked, "Mommy and Daddy do." The teacher, promptly took her to a private room for further questioning. Adults have a duty, she felt, to uncover child abuse so that it can be reported and stopped and, from there she called Washington's Child Protective Services agency to report an incident of suspected abuse. Soon a CPS representative arrived to question the child but she denied anything unusual.

The first examination was not conducted by a physician but by a registered male nurse who had no special training with child abuse or with gynaecology. He determined that the girl had been vaginally raped, and the parents were charged. Six years later, after their conviction, an independent physician was able to examine the girl and he determined that the nurse's testimony was wrong: her hymen was fully intact, unstretched, unscarred, unherniated, and undamaged in any way. Trial testimony was that the father had actually inserted his penis into the child's vagina on several occasions to the point of pain, and that the parents together had inserted marbles, candles and scissors. The physician testified in an appeal for retrial that any such activities would certainly have left marks, or at the least destroyed, stretched or scarred the hymen, and that those marks would be seen today. The offense, he testified for the Court of Appeals, could not have occurred. (For more information on this case, contact the Swan Defense Fund, 621 NE 155th, Seattle, Washington 98155.)

47. Krugman, R.D. "The more we learn, the less we know 'with reasonable medical certainty'?" *Child Abuse and Neglect*. 1989, 13, pp.165-166. See also in the same issue: McCann et al. "Perianal findings in prepubertal children for nonabuse: A descriptive study."

48. Margolin, K.N. "How shall facilitated communication be judged? Facilitated communication and the legal system." In H.C. Shane (ed.) *Facilitated Communication: The Clinical and Social Phenomenon*. San Diego, CA: Singular Press, 1994. pp. 227-258.

49. Jacobson, John W., Mulick, James A., and Schwartz, Allen A. "A History of facilitated communication: Science, pseudoscience, and antiscience working group on facilitated communication." *American Psychologist*, 1995, 50(9), pp.750-765.

50. Gardner, Richard A. "The 'Validators' and other examiners." *Issues in Child Abuse Accusations*, 1991, 3(1), p.38-39.

51. A caveat: On September 14, 1995, the California State Senate passed AB 1355, a law which reduces the absolute immunity of juvenile court workers, child protection workers, and other public employees authorized to initiate or conduct investigations or proceedings. The Bill was the recommendation of the San Diego Grand Jury investigation (see below).

52. A Letter from Carol L. Hopkins, Deputy Foreman of the 1991-92 San Diego County Grand Jury which studied the California juvenile dependency system, to The Honourable Henry J. Hyde, Chairman House Judiciary Committee, Washington, D.C. See also: Debbie Nathan and Michael J. Snedeker. *Satan's Silence: Ritual Abuse and the Making of a Modern American Witchhunt*. New York: HarperCollins, 1995.

53. Russell, Diane E. *The Secret Trauma: Incest in the Lives of Girls and Women*. New York: Basic Books, 1986.

54. Lasch, Christopher. *Haven in a Heartless World: The Family Besieged*. New York: Basic Books, 1977. p.136.

55. Zimbardo, Philip G. and Radl, Shirley. *The Shy Child: A Parent's Guide to Overcoming and Preventing Shyness from Infancy to Adulthood*. New York: McGraw-Hill Books Co., 1981. p.26-27.

56. Ruesch, Jurgen and Bateson, Gregory. *Communication: The Social Matrix of Psychiatry*. New York: Norton, 1951. p.71.

57. Marone. *Women and Risk*. p.7.

58. Gross. *The Psychological Society*. p.44.

59. Cited in Rudy, D. *Becoming Alcoholic: Alcoholics Anonymous and the Reality of Alcoholism*. Carbondale, IL: Southern Illinois University Press, 1986.

60. Bass, E and Davis, L. *The Courage To Heal*. New York: Harper and Row, 1988. p.22.

61. G. Douglas Talbott estimated that 22,000,000 Americans were alcoholic in 1984. See Wholey, D. (ed.) *The Courage to Change*. Boston: Houghton-Mifflin, 1984. p.19.

62. According to the National Council on Compulsive Gamblers.

63. "Ten percent of the adult population has a sexual addiction that requires treatment. The extreme figures in the field say that a quarter of the population needs help in some area (of sexual addiction)" states Dr. Edward Armstrong, Executive Director, National Association on Sexual Addiction Problems ("U.S. group helps sex-addict Christian cope with urges" *Toronto Star*, Feb. 16 1989, p.14.)

64. "2% of adults in the American population have had a constellation of experiences consistent with an abduction history. Therefore, based on our sample of nearly 6,000 respondents , we believe that one out of every 50 Americans may have had UFO abduction experiences." Stated by Mack, J.E. "Mental health professionals and the Roper Poll." In B. Hopkins, D.M. Jacobs, and R. Westrum, *The UFO Abduction Syndrome: A Report on Unusual Experiences Associated with [sic] UFO Abductions, The Roper Organization's Survey of 5,947 Adult Americans.* Las Vegas: Bigelow Holding Co, 1992. p.15.

65. Results of a study by Stein, M., Walker, J. and Forde, D., reported in the *American Journal of Psychiatry,* April 1994.

66. Kreisman, Harold J. and Strauss, Hal. *I Hate You – Don't Leave Me.* New York: Avon Books, 1989.

67. "There are no statistics yet on how many people are compulsive shoppers, but undoubtedly they number in the millions... because society encourages shopping, many addicted spenders have not acknowledged their problem – some out of ignorance and some out of denial." Damon, Janet E. *Shopaholics: An 8-week Program to Control Compulsive Shopping.* New York: Avon Books, 1988. p.4.

68. 30 - 40% of working Americans are pathologically addicted to work, resulting not only in their own psychological problems but also affecting their children, "Adult Children of Workaholics;" who end up in therapy with failed marriages, depression or a sense of anger they can't identify, says Psychologist Bryan Robinson. (See Kathleen Ryder, "When parents are addicted to their jobs, they may pass on the legacy." Santa Barbara News/Knight-Ridder News Service, March 22, 1997. p.D1.)

69. "More than 3 million people are involved in serious automobile accidents every year, and up to 45 percent later suffer from PTSD." Blanchard, E. and Hickling, E. J. *After the Crash:Assessment and Treatment of Motor Vehicle Accident Survivors.* APA Books, 1997.

70. According to APA, cited in *Making Us Crazy* (Free Press, New York, $27.50) by Herb Kutchins and Stuart Krik.

71. American Psychological Association past president, Ronald Fox, quoted in "Fox identifies top threats to professional psychology," by Sara Martin in *The APA Monitor*, March 1995. p.44.

72. Schaef. *Beyond Therapy, Beyond Science.* p.94.

73. Pittman III, Frank. "A Buyer's guide to psychotherapy." *Psychology Today*, 1994, Jan/Feb. p.52-53.

74. Ibid. p.50.

75. Rosenberg, Jerry M. *The Dictionary of Marketing and Advertising* . New York: John Wiley and Son, 1995. p.122.

76. Marone. *Women and Risk.* p.xiii.

77. Elgin, Suzette Haden. *You Can't Say That to Me!: Stopping the Pain of Verbal Abuse –An 8-Step Program.* New York: John Wiley & Sons, 1995. pp.2-3.

78. Owens, Karen. *Raising Your Child's Inner Self-Esteem: The Authoritative Guide from Infancy through the Teen Years.* New York: Plenum, 1995.

79. David Gelman, "A is for Apple, P is for Shrink." *Newsweek*, 24/12/90, pp.64-66.

80. Harris, Scott & Reynolds, Edward. *When Growing Up Hurts Too Much.* New York: Lexington Books (Macmillan), 1990. p.70.

81. Marone. *Women and Risk.* p. xiv.

82. From "Beyond Perfect Health," which offered an approach involving seven easy steps, based on the assumption of "an engrained part of therapeutic ideology, is that no matter how free of

disease or problems you are and no matter how well you are doing, it's not enough." Cited by Zilbergeld, *The Shrinking of America.* p.92.

83. "Television Defense," *Washington Post,* Oct. 2, 1977, p.A10.

84. Bowers, Karen. "Little Boy Lost." *Westwood.* (a Denver weekly paper) May 22, 1997; and Miriam Horn, "A dead child, a troubling defense," U.S. News and World Report, July 14, 1997, pp.24-28.

85. "Police say woman who neglected her children was Internet addict." *Associated Press,* June 16, 1997.

86. Wilson, Jeff. "Romance novelist admits plagiarism, apologizes to rival." *Associated Press/Santa Barbara News-Press.* July 30, 1997. p.A4.

87. Zilbergeld. *The Shrinking of America.* p.39.

88. Pollster, Irving and Miriam, *Gestalt Therapy Integrated.* 1973. p.91.

89. Szasz. *The Myth of Psychotherapy.* p.194.

90. Schaef, Anne W. *When Society Becomes an Addict.* San Francisco: Harper & Row, 1987. p.18.

91. Jeffers, Susan. *Dare to Connect.* New York: Ballantine, 1992.

92. See Kaminer, Wendy. *I'm Dysfunctional, You're Dysfunctional: The Recovery Movement and Other Self-Help Fashions.* New York: Vintage Books, 1993. pp. 9-28 for more about "recovery" books.

93. Beattie, Melody. *Codependent No More.* New York: Harper & Row, 1989. p. 26.

94. Jeffers. *Dare to Connect.* p.46.

95. Schaef, Anne W. *Co-Dependence: Misunderstood, Mistreated.* San Francisco: Harper & Row, 1986. p.67.

96. Attributed to Peter Vegso, Health Communications, Inc. Cited by Kaminer, *I'm Dysfunctional, You're Dysfunctional.* p. 12.

97. Bradshaw. *Bradshaw On.* p. 180.

98. Ricketson, Susan Coley. *The Dilemma of Love: Healing Co-dependent Relationships at Different Stages of life.* Deerfield Beach, Fl: Health Communications, 1989. p.13.

99. Bradshaw. *Bradshaw On.* p.180.

100. Ibid. p.47.

101. Kaminer. *I'm Dysfunctional, You're Dysfunctional.* p.10.

102. Branden, N. "In defense of self." *Association of Humanistic Psychology Perspectives,* 8-9/1984, p.12.

103. Harris, Scott & Reynolds, Edward. *When Growing Up Hurts Too Much.* New York: Lexington Books (Macmillan), 1990. p.70.

104. Taylor, S. *Positive Illusions: Creative Self-Deception and the Healthy Mind.* New York: Basic Books, 1989. p.227.

105. For a more thorough review of the task force report, *The Social Importance of Self-Esteem* (1989). See Dawes, *House of Cards.* pp.236-251.

106. Mecca, A.M., Smelser, N.J. and Vasconcellos, J. *The Social Importance of Self-Esteem.* Berkeley: University of California Press, 1989. p.15.

107. Bhatti, B., Derezotes, D., Kim, S.O. and Specht, H. "The association between child maltreatment and self-esteem." In Mecca, A.M., Smelser, N.J. and Vasconcellos, J. *The Social Importance of Self-Esteem.* pp.24-71.

108. Woititz, J.G. "A study of self-esteem in children of alcoholics." PhD dissertation Rutgers University, 1976, pp.53-55.

109. Gross. *The Psychological Society.* p.56.

110. The working definition of Emerge, a Boston counseling program for men who batter. Cited in Jones, Ann. *Next Time, She'll Be Dead: Battering & How to Stop It.* Boston: Beacon Press, 1994.

111. Statistics Canada reported that the rate of violent crimes fell 3 per cent in 1994, while the homicide rate dropped 6 per cent to its lowest level in 25 years.

112. *Violence and Youth: Psychology's Response. Volume I: Summary Report of the American Psychological Association Commission on Violence and Youth.* Washington, D.C.: American Psychological Association, 1993. p.14.

113. Ibid. p.15.

114. It would seem that what the American Psychological Association is really addressing is the increased role (and funding) of psychologists in "developing testable theoretical formulations and scientific methods and measures to evaluate interventions and to identify those with the greatest potential impact" (*Violence and Youth*. p.15) a far cry from actual reduction and prevention.

115. James Q. Wilson and Richard J. Herrnstein in their book, *Crime and Human Nature;* Robert ten Bensel, director, Maternal and Child Health, the University of Minnesota, attributed to Richard Gelles. Both cited by the Honourable Anne C. Cools, Senator, on March 30, 1995, during the 1ˢᵗ Session of the 35th Canadian Parliament, Vol. 135, p.1496.

116. William Coleman, a Vancouver psychologist, quoted when speaking about a sex offender released into the community after serving his prison sentence. *Times Colonist*, August 16, 1995. He continued by saying "People are always looking for the guy in the trench coat who's drooling, and then they gladly send their kids off camping with an uncle."

117. Cited in the section on domestic violence in *No Safe Haven, the Report of the APA Task Force on Male Violence Against Women*, Washington, D.C.: The American Psychological Association, 1994.

118. The Report considered several well-publicised studies which disagreed with their conclusions as "flawed." For instance, the national Family Violence Survey which concluded that men and women are equally likely to report that they've committed violent acts towards their partners at least once, was considered flawed because it failed to discriminate the level of violence. The report claimed that men commit more violent acts. At the same time, the report stated that sexual harassment affects "as many as one out of every two women over the course of their working lives" but failed to consider the issue of severity, accepting a very broad definition of harassment.

119. Such a programme was ordered by the Nevada Supreme Court, citing "near-epidemic proportions of violence against women nationally." All courts were closed for a day (October 18 or 19, 1993) and every judge was ordered to attend a seminar on domestic violence.

120. Becker, Judith, cited in the *The APA Monitor*, January, 1994, 25(1), p.1.

121. Sleet, Scott. Prevention is worth pounds of penalties. *The APA Monitor*, January 1994, 25(1), p.1.

122. Marlene Halisheff, executive director of the Greater Victoria Victim Services, quoted in an article "When crime strikes, volunteers offer comfort," in the *Times Colonist*, Dec 5, 1994, p.1.

123. Bass, E. and Davis, L. *The Courage to Heal.* New York: Harper and Row, 1988.

124. Nelson, J. A. "The impact of incest: Factors in self-evaluation." In L. L. Constantine and F. M. Martinson (eds.) *Children and Sex: New Findings, New Perspectives.* Boston: Little, Brown, 1981. pp.163-174.

125. Burgess, A.W. and Hartman, C. R. "Sex rings, pornography, and prostitution." In S. Ludwig and A. E. Kornberg (eds.) *Child Abuse: A Medical Reference.* New York: Churchill Livingstone, 1992. p.298.

126. Levitt, E. E. and Pinnell, C. M. "Some additional light on the childhood sexual abuse-psychopathology axis." *The International Journal of Clinical and Experimental Hypnosis*, 43(2), April 1995, p.148.

127. Ibid. pp.149-150.

128. Elgin, Suzette Hagen. *You Can't Say That to Me!: Stopping the Pain of Verbal Abuse –An 8-Step Program.* New York: John Wiley & Sons, 1995. p.109.

129. Personal communication received in response to a request to know the source of the statistic, Oct. 12, 1995.

130. Cited in Richard Lacayo's article "Assault by Paragraph." *Time Magazine,* January 17, 1994, p.37.

131. Fatalities for 1986 were 1,014, and for 1993, were 1,216 according to the National Committee to Prevent Child Abuse.

132. Stated by Raymond Fowler, Chief Executive Officer of the APA in his 1994 Report. *American Psychologist,* August 1995, pp.600–601.

133. For example the Veterans Administration is loₒ ng to eliminate 6,000 positions from its health system.

134. Morris, Ted. CRHSPP Treasurer Dr. Ted Mc s awarded OPA Award of Merit: "Calls colleagues to arms in face of growing Psychology 'c s'." *Rapport,* 1995, 3(1), p.13.

135. Allon, Richard. "And now for something comp ₃ly different." *Psynopsis,* Spring 1997, p. 4. Italics added.

136. Morris. 1995. p.13

137. For example, "the National Conversation" of the American Psychological Association Practice Directorate, described in various places such as *Practitioner Update,* 1995, 3(2).

138. In a 1996 mail survey of nearly 1,000 mental-health care providers, 62% of the responding psychologists reported earning less from their full time practice than they did 2 years earlier. "Practitioners report decrease in earnings." *APA Monitor.* March 1997, p.6.

139. Quoting Robert J. Resnick. In "New American Psychological Association president has keen vision for future" in *The APA Monitor,* March 1995, p.7.

140. Kovacs, A. "The uncertain future of professional psychology." *The Independent Practitioner.* 1989, 9, pp.11-18.

141. Herron, William G. and Welt, Sheila Rouslin. *Money Matters: The Fee in Psychotherapy and Psychoanalysis.* New York: The Guilford Press, 1992. p.168.

142. Blyskal, Jeff. "Head Hunt: How to find the right psychotherapist – for the right price." *New York,* January 11, 1993, p.29.

143. Although regulations vary according to jurisdiction, in most states:
• any medical doctor can call himself or herself a psychiatrist, psychologist or psychotherapist without any additional authorization or training,
• the title "psychologist" is protected but the area or method of practice is not,
• generally anyone can practice psychoanalysis, although in some jurisdictions it is still protected as a medical procedure,
• minimum requirements exist to be certified as a social worker, marriage and family therapist, or pastoral counsellor, but anyone cam practice as long as they don't refer to themselves as "certified."

144. As well, some with a Ph.D. (Doctorate in Philosophy) and deserving of the title "doctor," have no academic background in psychology, such as Dr. Jeffrey Masson, author of *Against Therapy* (New York: Atheneum, 1988), whose Ph.D. is in the Sanskrit language and literature.

145. For instance, some Employee Assistance Program (EAP) firms will only hire registered clinical counsellors despite the fact that the certification comes through voluntary membership in an association, does not involve training or supervision and is not regulated by the state. The mutual pay-off is that this requirement provides greater access to jobs for the psychologists and enhances the image of the firm while affording some protection from malpractice law suits.

146. Marilyn Murray is cited in Beigel, Joan Kaye & Earle, Ralph H. *Successful Private Practice in the 1990s: A New Guide for the Mental Health Professional.* New York: Brunner/Mazel Inc., 1990. p.83.

147. Jones, Ann. *Next Time, She'll Be Dead: Battering and How to Stop It.* Boston: Beacon Press, 1994. p.1.

148. Schaef, Anne Wilson. *Beyond Therapy, Beyond Science.* p.91.

149. "John Bradshaw has lived everything he writes about." Jacket cover of *Home Coming: Reclaiming and Championing Your Inner Child.* New York: Bantam Books, 1990.

150. Miller, Angelyn. *The Enabler: When Helping Harms the Ones You Love*. New York: Ballantine, 1988. Also, Beverly Enfel, author of *The Emotionally Abused Woman: Overcoming Destructive Patterns and Reclaiming Yourself*. (Los Angeles: Lowell House, 1990) refers to "the severe emotional abuse (she) received both as a child and as an adult from (her) mother..."

151. Murray, in Beigel and Earle, 1990. p.84.

152. Morris. "Calls colleagues to arms in face of growing psychological crisis." p.13.

153. This approach was adopted by the Canadian Registry of Health Service Providers in Psychology at a 1994 Strategic Planning meeting.

154. Hacking identifies this issue in his exploration into the business of MPD, when he asks "who will finally own the illness: highly qualified clinicians with years of training, or a popular alliance of patients and therapists who welcome a culture of multiples and who cultivate personalities?" He continues: "The movement is certainly capable of splitting. The stakes are high... the economic interests of the grassroots therapists fundamentally diverge, for the first time, from those of the leading psychiatrists and psychologists in the field." (Hacking, Ian. *Rewriting the Soul: Multiple Personality and the Science of Memory*. Princeton, NJ: Princeton University Press, 1995. p.53)

155. Robiner, 1991, p. 432.

156. Grinker, Roy R. and Spiegel, John P. *Men Under Stress*. New York: McGraw-Hill Book Co., 1945.

157. For example, Holmes, T.H. and Rahe, R.H. The Social Readjustment Rating Scale. *Journal of Psychosomatic Research*, 1967, 11, pp.213-218. For more, consult Miller, T.W. (Ed.) *Stressful Life Events*. Madison, Conn: International Universities Press, 1989.

158. For example, Winter, Richard E. (Ed.) *Coping with Executive Stress*. New York: McGraw-Hill Book Co., 1983.

159. For example, Meichenbaum, Donald. *Coping With Stress*. Toronto: John Wiley and Sons, 1983.

160. *Prisoner of Childhood* was the original title of Alice Miller's first book, translated by Ruth Ward. New York: Basic Books, 1981. Reissued as *The Drama of the Gifted Child*. New York: Basic Books, 1982.

161. Zilbergeld provides an illustration of the media's positive bias in describing the experience of Curtiss Anderson, once an editor of *Ladies' Home Journal*. "The Journal had done a series of articles on women who had dieted, lost lots of weight, and gone on to fulfill their dreams: marriage, children, and homes in the suburbs. Anderson decided to do a follow-up, which was approved by chief editor Beatrice Gould, who thought it would show the women 'living happily ever after.' But this is not what was found. According to Anderson, 'Ninety-nine percent had blown right back up to their old weights. They'd lost their husbands, been divorced, and they were angry again.' Anderson thought he had an important story on the meaninglessness of the Journal's stories and diets. But it was never published. Mrs. Gould was appalled. She didn't want to hear about it. 'I don't believe it.' she said. 'I don't believe it's true.'" p.106.

162. Ries, A. & Trout, J. *The 22 Immutable Laws of Marketing*. New York: HarperBusiness, 1993. p. 10

163. Some steps in this procedure are outlined as a way to establish a successful private practice in the 1990's, in the book of the same name by Beigel and Earle.

164. Quoted from Internet communications from Charles Figley, Founding Chair of the Green Cross, July 1995.

165. "Counselling 'does more harm than good'" by David Fletcher, Health Correspondent, *The Daily Telegraph*, London, September 27, 1997

166. Personal Communication, November, 1997.

167. "Coffee-cup therapy" is the term that psychologists use to describe their work as they are "simply talking to survivors as they go about their business" It is also referred to as "stealth pyschology" because they do not identify themselves as mental health professionals. (See Rebecca Clay. "Psychologists help flood victims to cope." *APA Monitor*, July, 1997, p. 23)

168. "Disaster victims need more long-term care, report says." *The APA Monitor*, October, 1997, p.18.

169. Ries & Trout, 1993, p.26.

170. For example, Mitchell, J.T. "Recovery from Rescue." *Response: The Magazine of Rescue and Emergency Management*, Fall 1982, pp.7-10; and Mitchell, J.T. and Resnick, H. *Emergency Response to Crisis*. Bowie, Maryland: Robert J. Brady, 1981.

171. Information is derived from an article by Elizabth Gleick, "Tower of psychobabble." *Time*, June 16, 1997. pp. 69-73.

172. Walker, I, & Broderick, P. "The psychology of assisted reproduction, or psychology assisting its reproduction? Submitted to the Australian Psychologist. 1997; available from Dr. Iain Walker, Psychology Dept., Murdoch University, Murdoch, WA, 6150, Australia.

173. Humphrey, M., Humphrey, H., & Ainsworth, I. "Screening couples for parenthood by donor insemination." Social Sciences and Medicine. 32, 1991. pp.273-278.

174. Humphrey et al. 1991, p.274.

175. Ley, P. "Reproductive technology - What can we learn from the adoption experience? In Swain, P., & Swain, S.(eds.). *To Search For Self*. Sydney: Federation Press, 1992. pp.100-110; Turner, C. "A call for openness in donor insemination." *Politics and the Life Sciences*. 12, 1993, pp.197-199.

176. Western Australia Human Reproductive Technology Council. *Questions and Answers about the Donation of Human Reproductive Material*. Perth, Western Australia: Health Department of Western Australia, 1995.

177. Daniels, K.R., & Taylor, K. "Secrecy and openness in donor insemination. *Politics and Life Sciences*. 12, 1993. p. 158.

178. Snowden, R., & Mitchell, G.D. *The Artificial Family: A Consideration of Artificial Insemination by Donor*. London: Allen and Unwin, 1981.

179.Walker & Broderick. 1997. p.16.

180. Daniels, K., & Stjerna, I. "Infertility: The social work contribution." *Socionomen*. 6, 1993. pp.41-46.

181. Schwarzchild, Michael. "Why I changed my mind on prescribing." *The APA Monitor*. February 1997. p.19.

182. "Helping to secure Rx privileges." *The APA Monitor*. September 1996.

183. According to IMS America Ltd. statistics.

184. DeLeon, Patrick H., & Wiggins, Jack G. Jr. "Prescription privileges for psychologists." *American Psychologist*. 51(3), 1996. p.225 & 228.

185. DeNelsky, G.Y. "The case against prescription privileges for psychologists." *American Psychologist*. 51(3), 1996. p.207.

186. Psychologists are NOT trained in medicine and many have no education in physiology, biology, etc. The training proposed by APA is for 300 hours of didactic instruction (less than 8 full weeks but available in weekend workshops and seminars) and supervised work with 100 patients.

187. "Prozac prophet" The cover story of *Maclean's*. May 23, 1994. p.41.

188. Levine, Judith. " A Question of Abuse." *Mother Jones Magazine* (July-August 1996).

189. Cited by Levine in "A Question of Abuse."

190. More information will be available in Judith Levine's book, *In Search of Innocence: America's Battle Over Children's Sexuality,* scheduled for publication by Houghton-Mifflin in 1998.

191. Again cited by Levine in "A Question of Abuse."

192. A publication of the Practice Directorate of the American Psychological Association describing the "APA Disaster Response Network," p.1 (italics added).

193. A publication of the Practice Directorate of the American Psychological Association on "Diversifying Your Sources of Practice Income," p.1.

194. 72.8% provide pro bono mental health services, and 65.7% provide other services pro bono. From the Profile of All Members: 1993. Prepared by the Office of Demographic, Employment, and Educational Research (ODEER), American Psychological Association Education Directorate.

195. "It is important for all survivors to understand what they are going through, to recognize the symptoms that are part of grieving after suicide, part of Posttraumatic Stress Disorder." From Lukas, C. and Seiden, H.M. *Silent Grief: Living in the Wake of Suicide.* New York: Macmillan Publ. 1987. p.42.

196. For example, Quackenbush, Jamie. *When Your Pet Dies: How to Cope With Your Feelings.* New York: Simon & Schuster, 1985.

197. For example, Akner, Lois F. *How to Survive the Loss of a Parent.* New York: William Morrow & Co., 1993.

198. Beal, Lynne A. "Post-traumatic stress disorder in prisoners of war and combat veterans of the Dieppe raid: A 50-year follow-up." *Canadian Journal of Psychiatry*, 1995, 40, pp.177-184.

199. A woman, Marjorie May, claimed discrimination by the Anglican Church as the reason she was never ordained as a priest. In court, a psychologist stated that she was "suffering from post-traumatic stress disorder, because of her treatment by the church, which left her feeling 'shunned, humiliated and victimized.'" *Times Colonist*, 25/02/95, pp.1 and 6.

200. "Addiction has as much to do with love as it does with drugs. Many of us are addicts, only we don't know it." Stated by Stanton Peele and Archie Brodsky in *Love and Addiction.* New York: Signet, 1975. p. 1. Also, Gloria Steinem applies an addiction model to those she describes as "love junkies" in *Revolution From Within.* Boston: Little, Brown and Co., 1992.

201. For example, Robinson, Barbara L. and Robinson, Rick L. *If My Dad's a Sexaholic, What Does that Make Me?* Minneapolis, Minn.: CompCare Publ. 1992.

202. Tassi, Nina. *Urgency Addiction: How to Slow Down without Sacrificing Success.* New York: Signet, 1991.

203. "No addiction is more toxically shaming and soul-murdering than the religious abuse that flows from the actions of religious addicts." A statement made by John Bradshaw in the Foreword to Father Leo Booth's book, *When God Becomes a Drug: Breaking the Chains of Religious Addiction and Abuse – Attaining Healthy Spirituality.* Los Angeles: Jeremy P. Tarcher, 1992.

2004. For example, Damon, Janet E. *Shopaholics: An 8-week Program to Control Compulsive Shopping.* New York: Avon Books, 1988. Damon is described as "a N.Y. therapist and founder of SHOPAHOLICS LTD., a successful recovery program for compulsive shoppers."

205. O'Neill, Molly. "The Lure and Addiction of Life On Line." *The New York Times,* March 8, 1995.

206. Karen Russell, a recovered over-eater who claims to have lost 300 pounds, presents 1 1/2 day seminars entitled "Reclaiming Your Life" to professionals and individuals concerned with emotional eating. As well, food addicts can call for help to: Overeaters Anonymous World Service Office, P.O. Box 44020, Rio Rancho, NM 87174-4020; 505-891-2664.

207. "Prostitution is not an option for women but an addiction that requires long-range support and encouragement for cure, Samuel S. Janus, Ph.D., said at the annual meeting of the American Psychiatric Association. Eighteen of 22 N.Y. prostitutes who had renounced the trade had returned to prostitution after 5 years; this is a recidivism rate equal to that among narcotics addicts, said Dr. Janus, director of group therapy, N.Y. Medical College." "Prostitution Called an Addiction Requiring Long-Term Treatment," *Clinical Psychiatry News*, 5(June, 1977), p.12. Cited in Szasz, T. *The Myth of Psychotherapy: Mental Healing as Religion, Rhetoric and Repression.* Garden City: Anchor Press/Doubleday, 1978. pp.195-96.

208. Siegel, Micki. "The power of pets." *Good Housekeeping*, November 1995. p.26.

209. "Calming llamas" *The Therapist.* 4(3), 1997. p.7

210. Press release of Coast Hotels, September 4, 1995.

211. One psychologist, a realtor who also counsels "Multiple Personality Gifted Women," developed an innovative marketing and service approach using her pager. This approach won third prize ($500) for an "ingenious and creative way" to use pagers, from the Paging Services

Council. "Since each personality has a different age, I tell them to punch in their callback number and the age they are at the moment. I then know who is paging me by the age they are," said Nadine Noble of Clovis California. (*Chicago Tribune Magazine*, July 19, 1995.)

212. Koslowsky, Meni, Kluger, Avraham N. and Reich, Mordechai. *Commuting Stress: Causes, Effects, and Methods of Coping.* New York: Plenum Publ, 1995.

213. Sibley, Kathleen, "Digging the Therapy of Horticulture." *West Coast Homes and Gardens.* November 1994.

214. Cited in "Juror stress can influence final verdict." *The A.P.A. Monitor*, June, 1995, p.5.

215. For example, the Contra Costa County Psychological Association ran a gun-exchange and public education program Oct.-Dec. 1994. *The APA Monitor*, Feb. 1995, p.37.

216. See Figley, Charles. "Compassion Fatigue," and Edwards, Randall, " 'Compassion Fatigue': when listening hurts." *The APA Monitor*, Sept. 1995, p.34.

217. Tasko, Ann E. "Genetic Attraction -What kind of love?" 5th Annual Canadian Conference on Adoption. February 28 - March 2, 1997.

218. Carter, Paul, Ph.D. Transformational Adventures, a professional mailing, Summer, 1997.

219. For example, Online Psychological Services at: www.onlinepsych.com

220. "Cognitive Therapy: A Multimedia Learning Program," at mindstreet.com.

221. Ibid.

222. "Barbara Ann Levy Business Of Art" Art Therapy Explorations for Women, at levyb@interport.net.

223. Jbcsw@AOL.com. Sea also the "Ask Angie" advice column (http://www.nomius.com/angie.html) where Angie, who claims to have a masters degree in counselling, offers straightforward, common-sense advice on romance, family, computer addiction problems, and even on problems with pets, for no fee. Or "Shrink Link" (http://westnet.westnet.com/shrink/shrink.html), a group of five women psychologists offering professional psychological counselling via e-mail at $20 per question.

224. Shalit, Ruth. "Dysfunction Junction." *The New Republic."* April 14, 1997.

225. Holdings, Reynold. "Sick and Twisted System." *San Francisco Chronicle.* May 18, 1997.

226. With regards to the Americans taken hostage in Iran, one psychologist was taken to task by the American Psychological Association for her remarks on national television about "permanent problems in interpersonal relationships... permanent coordination difficulties ... permanent damages to memory" that they would experience. Cited in Segal, J., 1986. p.2.

227. Advertisement in Common Ground, Nov. / Dec. 1993.

228. Kottler, J. *On Being A Therapist.* p.108.

229. Janet, Pierre. *Psychological Healing: A Historical and Clinical Study.* Vol.II, translated by Eden and Cedar Paul, New York: Macmillan, 1925. p.338.

230. Ibid. p.338.

231. "Thus, does deception become the cornerstone of modern medical psychotherapeutics." Szasz, *The Myth of Psychotherapy.* p.185.

232. Kottler, J. *On Being a Therapist.* p.108.

233. Sexton, D. Gaining insights into the complexity of ritualistic abuse. The Eighth National Conference on Child Abuse and Neglect. 1989, Tape #28.

234. Journalist Bruce Grearson reported during a phone conversation with the author, that this comment was made by Dr. Lawrence Pazder, co-author of *Michelle Remembers.*

235. See Gardner, Richard A. "The 'Validators' and other examiners." *Issues in Child Abuse Accusations,* 1991, 3(1), pp.38-53.

236. Transcribed from the taped recording of the presentation of Alan Scheflin, J.D., LL.M., at the Frontiers of Hypnosis conference: the Fourth National Assembly of the Federation of Canadian Societies of Clinical Hypnosis held at Banff, Canada, May 4-9, 1995. The actual presentation was a requested continuation of Scheflin's Plenary Address, May 8th, 1995.

237. Scheflin, Alan. "Hypnosis 1994 and Beyond." *Hypnos,* 1994, 21(4), p.202.

238. Sharaf, Myron R.,and Levinson, Daniel. "The Quest for omnipotence in professional training." *International Journal of Psychiatry,* 1967, 4(5), pp.426-442. Cited in Gross, p.45.

239. Orlinsky and Howard, 1986. Cited in Kottler, Jeffrey A. *The Compleat Therapist.* San Francisco: Jossey-Bass Publ., 1991. p.88.

240. Kottler. *The Compleat Therapist.* p.71.

241. Ibid. p.75.

242. Arons, Gina and Siegel, Ronald D. "Unexpected encounters: The Wizard of OZ exposed." In Sussman, Michael B. (Ed.) *A Perilous Calling: The Hazards of Psychotherapy Practice.* New York: Wiley Interscience, 1995. p125.

243. Ibid. p.131.

244. Ibid. p.128.

245. According to the Psychology Industry, these people may be victims of another syndrome: *The Imposter Phenomenon.* "The Imposter Phenomenon is a psychological syndrome or pattern. It is based on intense, secret feelings of fraudulence in the face of success and achievement... (The person) doesn't tell anyone his terrible secret, but waits in anxious dread to be discovered. He is certain that the moment of discovery will arrive, and he will face unbearable humiliation and be stripped of his undeserved success forever. At that moment, he will be exposed to the world as a fraud..." Two thirds of the population is reported to suffer from this syndrome according to Joan C. Harvey and Cynthia Katz. *If I'm So Successful, Why Do I Feel Like a Fake?: The Imposter Phenomenon.* New York: St. Martin's Press, 1984. pp.1-2.

246. Seligman, Constance. "The therapist as patient in interminable treatment: A parallel process." In Sussman, Michael B. (Ed.) *A Perilous Calling: The Hazards of Psychotherapy Practice.* New York: Wiley Interscience, 1995. p56.

247. Ibid. p.56.

249. Smail. *Taking Care.* p.128.

249. Kottler. *On Being a Therapist.* p.65.

Chapter 6

The Technology of Victim-Making

Psychotherapy is a service, a business, an industry, yet the mystique of psychotherapy endures beyond all reason. The history and formal assumptions of psychotherapy have clearly been influenced by the economics of psychotherapeutic practice. As a profit-making service industry, psychotherapy warrants an informed customer.

Robert Langs

If psychologists have "a good thing going" with individual therapy, then they have an even greater, absurdly good thing going when they industrialize their service, simplifying the thinking needed and stream-lining their treatments. With the goals of the Psychology Industry being to broaden the market, increase sales and raise income, there has been a trend towards psychological mechanization, in which an "informed customer" is not what the Psychology Industry either wants or treats.

Rather, the Psychology Industry focusses on the vulnerable, the desperate, the lonely, the confused. It targets as its market, those who are neither too "sick" nor too "well," but instead those who may be described as having a "psychologically-prone personality" amenable to simplistic thinking and authoritarian, assembly-line techniques. With the rapid expansion in the industry over the past twenty years, it is not surprising that mechanistic methods of addiction/recovery and trauma/abuse treatment, provided by minimally trained psychologists, have developed.

The "Psychologically-Prone" Personality

Over ten million Americans seek the services of the Psychology Industry each year. Not all become long-term users and manufactured victims. Some have little inclination to the procedure and drop out early; some resist the pressures and take from the experience only what they want; and some detect the coercive nature of the industry and stop. By no means, do all become its willing victims.

But many people do! And those who do seem to be characterized by a *"psychologically-prone personality:"*[1] with which the person is inclined to view life from a psychological perspective, to seek and apply psychological explanations and solutions to life events, and to accept psychologists as the experts in living. They are people who tend to:

- See the world in terms of psychological facts.
- Be emotionally preoccupied and reactive.
- Be predisposed to imagination and fantasy.
- Be open to psychological suggestion and influence.
- Seek direction and guidance in living from a psychological perspective.
- Want simple solutions and answers.
- Attribute authority and control to those they view as psychological experts.

Absorbed in their own world of feelings, and believing that they both should have, and do have the right to feel better, psychologically-prone persons accept psychological explanations of their emotions and adopt psychological suggestions on how to free themselves from these feelings. They see life as a series of internal psychological events to be managed and mastered. They uphold what Thomas Wolfe referred to as "the new alchemical dream." Whereas "the old alchemical dream was changing base metal into gold,... the new alchemical dream is: changing one's personality— remaking, remodelling, elevating and polishing one's very self... observing, studying and doting on it."[4] As the ancient alchemists and magicians were inducted into secret societies, so are those with a psychologically-prone personality inducted into the psychological society with the hope of finding psychological magic.

Probably the most salient feature of psychologically-prone individuals is their suggestibility. It is this openness both to accept and to respond to the suggestions and influences of "psychological authorities" which makes them both suitable and vulnerable to the activities of the Psychology Industry. They can be seduced by the rhetoric of psychology in the books they read and the lectures and workshops they attend. They can be influenced by the subtle communication of the "non-directive" analyst and therapist. And they can be deeply persuaded by the directive guidance and suggestion offered by psychologists in most forms of psychotherapy. As Hans Strupp observed: "all forms of psychotherapy employ suggestion... the patient's suitability for psychotherapy is based on his potential openness to suggestion."[3]

The role of suggestion can be found throughout the history of psychological treatment, from the sleep temples of the ancient Egyptians, to the "magnetic cures" of Mesmer,[4] to the early work of Freud, to the effects of placebos. It is apparent in the fear-appeal claims of the expert, in the artful influences of the psychotherapist, and in the deliberate suggestions of the hypnotist.

Psychologically-prone individuals are vulnerable to the persuasive and exaggerated promises of psychological experts who, in lectures, workshops and writings, identify themes in society, address them in vivid psychological terms and suggest solutions which seem simple and effortlessly achievable.

For instance, Slaby in writing about *"Aftershock,"*[5] which he defines as "delayed effect of trauma, crisis and loss," vividly introduces the topic by saying that "once, almost everyone assumed that aftershock was exclusively contracted during war... But these are the larger-than-life examples, the terrifying horror stories that are the rare exceptions to the rule..." He continues by generalizing the topic to include all sorts of upsets and unpleasant feelings, to which anyone can relate: *"We all* suffer from aftershock, maybe less violently but still at a price we shouldn't have to pay. In fact, aftershock is the disease of today."[6] And he optimistically concludes:

> Together, we have seen the ways to avoid aftershock and the stress that always joins it. What is left?
> Only this: a message for the future, for a world where we can live up to our full potential without fear, without anxiety, without the past to haunt our days.
> Together, we can conquer the 80s disease of aftershock.
> Together, we can make stress work for us. Together, we can welcome the world of crisis, a world of change-for-the-better. For without these crises, there would be no life. And without life, there would be no hope.
>
> Welcome, then, with me, crisis. We may never conquer death, but we can conquer life and make it the best it can be.
> Together we can stop aftershock for good.
> Welcome to a brave— and exciting— new world"[7]

In reading this, the susceptible psychologically-prone person can imagine the horror (and aftershock) of war, and then slide the slippery slope into accepting the suggestion of personal aftershock which Slaby says "we all" experience, and end up believing in the psychological promise of a utopian ("brave, new") world.

While such rhetoric can be persuasive when expressed with authority, two other means of suggestive influence exist for those already in psychological treatment; one being subtle, and almost imperceptible, in form; and the other being directive and hypnotic-like in style.

It is not uncommon for some psychologists to respond to the request for help by giving no advice or encouragement. And caught in this confusing and uncertain situation, psychologically-prone clients, not knowing what to think or do but believing that the therapist has specialized knowledge, search their psychologists' behaviours, moods and remarks for hidden cues, which will influence their thinking and actions. Even the slightest reaction or response can have a great influence, for as Frank noted: "The very subtlety and unobstrusiveness of the therapist's influencing maneuvers, coupled with his explicit disclaimer that he (the psychologist) is exerting any influence, may increase his influencing power."[8] Functioning as "indirect suggestions," these forms of suasion have power over a large number of users, heightening their responsiveness to therapy and extending the influence of psychologists. And because of the inconspicuous quality of the communications, the clients tend to believe that the ideas are their own rather than anything imposed upon them.

Evidence of such subtle influence is available from a number of sources. For instance, people in Freudian analysis have been shown to produce Freudian dreams, while those in Jungian therapy have Jungian dreams, an effect which Calestro explains: "the underlying mechanism apparently involves a process of suggestion in which the patient responds to overt or covert suggestions by the therapists that certain phenomena will occur."[9] Other studies have demonstrated the ability of therapists to influence the values of their patients to come in line with their own. Welkowitz and his colleagues arbitrarily assigned clients to therapists and subsequently found that the values of the therapists resembled those of their own patients more than those seen by other therapists, and that the similarity of values tended to increase over time or length of treatment.[10] Similarly, a study by Rosenthal found a positive relationship between ratings of improvement and the change of clients' moral values towards those of the psychologists, *with respect to sex, aggression and authority*[11] (the "trinity" of victim-making themes). Since such moral conversion is possible, it is no wonder that psychologists with a victim-oriented philosophy can intentionally or inadvertently manufacture victims.

The study of "Hypnosis" has much to contribute to the understanding of the psychologically-prone personality for it is not only susceptible to the indirect cues inherent in psychological treatment, but also the hypnotic-like suggestions of psychologists. The common view of hypnosis popularized by stage hypnotists and tales of Rasputin and Svengali, is that the "power" rests in the hypnotist who can put the subjects into a trance in which they can be made to do things, sometimes against their will. However, hundreds of studies over the past century have shown that hypnotizability is a personality trait, that it varies in the population with individuals being more or less susceptible to hypnotic suggestions, and that this responsiveness can be measured. Initially there was debate whether this personality characteristic indicated a psychological weakness and contributed to problems such as hysteria,[12] or whether it constituted a strength that could be of positive use to the person.[13] Most recent studies, while not agreeing on the specific nature of hypnosis, have generally conceded that hypnotizability may have both beneficial and harmful effects depending on how it is used, and that some individuals may respond minimally or not at all.[14] It has also been recognized that those who are more highly hypnotizable may respond to suggestions whether they are presented as part of an hypnotic experience (i.e. a "trance"), or in the usual conscious state (i.e. that in which therapy occurs). As well, the openness to suggestion, which is synonymous with hypnotizability, has been shown to be positively correlated with psychotherapy outcome.[15]

One of the core characteristics of the state of hypnosis is dissociation,[16] in which perceptions and behaviours seem to occur by themselves and not under the voluntary control of the subject. Dissociation serves to explain why subjects hypnotized on stage can be made to act in such unusual, sometimes bizarre, ways and how pain can be hypnotically controlled. It is also the reason given to explain the correlation or connection between hypnotizability and such victim-related disorders as Multiple Personality and Post Traumatic Stress. In the former, the alternate personalities (or "alters") are considered to be parts of the individual's personality which became dissociated as a result of early trauma or abuse, but which can be accessed (talked to) through hypnosis. In the case of PTSD, memories are assumed to be repressed or dissociated from the person's conscious awareness as a protective response, but are retrievable with hypnosis. In the case of both of these disorders, and others like them, it has been assumed that the dissociative disorder is both an effect of dissociative ability and a cause of heightened hypnotic ability. That is, that the hypnotic ability, which allows one to set apart or dissociate the memories so that they don't interfere with life, is also maintained and strengthened in the process resulting in a greater hypnotizability for those with these problems. For instance, Lynn and Rhue suggest that "imaginative involvement," another aspect of hypnosis, plays a defensive function for abused children in that traumatized children can construct a world of fantasy into which they can retreat as an "adaptive means of coping with negative environmental factors."[17] They theorize that this fantasy-proneness then extends into adult life as an indicator and effect of the early trauma. However, the connection between reported childhood trauma and imaginative involvement of hypnosis is a correlation and it is just as likely that the psychologically-prone person's increased susceptibility to therapist influence results in client characteristics similar to those of the disorder (i.e. an iatrogenic disorder resulting from the treatment), as it is that the disorder causes one to be hypnotically responsive. Consider the following suggestive instructions given by a psychologist to those who have not yet remembered being sexually abused:

> If you sense that you were sexually abused and have no memories of it, it's likely that you were... Spend time *imagining* that you were sexually abused, without worrying about accuracy or having your ideas make sense... When you feel ready, ask yourself... Who would have been likely perpetrators?[18]

If individuals with a psychogically-prone personality are higher in hypnotizabilty and in fantasy-proneness, they are more open to such suggestions of earlier abuse, whether or not it ever occurred, for fantasy-prone individuals are particularly susceptible to distortions in their memory.[19] Bryant reported a study[20] which claimed to investigate the relationship between fantasy-proneness and the age at which reported childhood sexual abuse occurred. The subjects, women who had reported having been sexually abused as children and were attending group therapy at a sexual assault centre, were assessed for their tendency to become imaginatively involved in internal events, and the extent to which fantasy played a role in their adult functioning: both aspects of hypnotic ability. Bryant's study not only confirmed a relationship (i.e. a correlation) between fantasy-proneness and reports of childhood abuse, it also indicated that "reports of abuse at a younger age are associated with higher levels of fantasy proneness." This finding could lead many to the conclusion that trauma plays "a causal role in the development of fantasy-based modes of coping." However, it is equally plausible that individuals who are, by their nature, prone to fantasy, for all of these women were significantly more hypnotizable than the control group, are more likely than those who are less fantasy-prone, to use their imagination to construct memories (pseudomemories) of abusive events at an early age. It should be noted that the female subjects in this study were all involved in an imagery-based treatment program and that the "abuse" was only "reported" and assumed to be true.[21] In this regard, it is also worth noting that research indicates that women experience greater imaginative involvement and creativity (fantasy-proneness) than men;[22] a finding which may explain, in part, why the significant majority of therapy patients and fabricated victims are women.

If psychologically-prone individuals can be identified by their proclivity towards all things psychological and their openness to suggestion as indicated by higher hypnotizability, fantasy-proneness and responsiveness to therapist cues, then what does this mean for the Psychology Industry? The answers may again be found by looking at the world of the stage hypnotist. The success of good stage hypnotists is dependent on their ability to select good subjects. To do this, they first invite volunteers to participate by coming on stage. The reluctant, the sceptical, the uncooperative are screened out as they remain in their seats, while the enthusiastic, eager and cooperative go forward. A series of ambiguous suggestions are then given in which the potential subjects are told that they will never lose control or do things against their will while, all along, the hypnotist is implying or hinting the opposite. The hypnotist then induces a trance and gives a few simple hypnotic suggestions to determine which of the volunteers are the most responsive and trusting. The rest are asked to return to their seats and the hypnotist turns his attention to those remaining on stage: the hypnotically responsive. From the hundreds or more in attendance, there may be only a dozen left as subjects; those who will perform for the audience as they follow the directions and suggestions of the hypnotist.

In many ways psychologists in the Psychology Industry have a similar way of working. From the whole population, only a portion voluntarily participate in treatment, while the rest remain "seated." Of those that seek therapy, many are seen briefly and sent away, while some remain, having the qualities of the psychologically-prone personality that make them amenable to the victim-making efforts of the psychologist.

Many in attendance at a stage hypnosis show wonder why anyone would do what the subjects do. But they fail to recognize that those on stage trust the hypnotist and believe in hypnosis, are open to influence and direction, willingly and easily accept simple suggestions and enjoy the attention that their responsiveness brings. Those with psychologically-prone personalities are much the same; they believe in psychology and what it promises, trust the psychologist, accept suggestions and ideas, and like the attention they receive both in and out of therapy.[23]

Designing Simple Theories

Oh, don't take that too seriously. That's something I dreamed up on a rainy Sunday afternoon.

Freud's response to a question about the logic
of a particular psychoanalytic theorem.[24]

The two key technological components of any manufacturing industry are Design and Production. In the Psychology Industry, "design" involves the construction of theories on which the technologies of treatment rely and about which the experts can lecture and testify. It is at this stage that both the usual and unusual events of life are transformed into psychological blueprints, which supposedly unravel the mysteries of life, making them understandable and open to cure. In some cases, the created theories explain a process; in others, they name the unknown or predict an outcome.

In a society in which truth is most often determined by public opinion and popularity and in which justice is a product of legal machinations, the profession of psychology was to have been an oasis of intellectual freedom and an objective science where all aspects of human life could be explored. But by becoming an industry, psychology surrendered this privilege and became preoccupied with issues of growth and profit, and questions of power and blame. While psychologists have focussed on making their reputations and their fortunes, the Psychology Industry has become a conceptual warehouse of junk science, harmful ideas and malicious influences.[25] It has chosen to create theories for popular use rather than theories based on findings, often reducing them to simple concepts out of which come psychological interventions rather than further investigation and greater understanding. In examining the "American Mind," Allan Bloom observed that the "search for material causes and reduction of higher or more complex phenomena to lower or simpler ones are generally accepted procedures."[26]

And nowhere is this more true than in the Psychology Industry, where discoveries and theories are quickly metamorphized into pop concepts and fad therapies. While the number of examples is numerous, several are particularly relevant to the industry's manufacturing of victims.

"Life Stress Events" is a case in point. In 1967, Holmes and Rahe,[27] in an effort to quantify the effect of recent life changes on physical health, created a list of 43 "life change events", the Social Readjustment Rating Scale of Recent Experiences (SRE). The list contained life changes that were both positive (e.g. promotion and marriage) and negative in nature (e.g. divorce and arrest). Each event was given a Life Change Unit (LCU) which had been determined by having diverse groups of subjects rate the amount of readjustment, from 1 to 100 units required by each event. For a benchmark, "marriage" had been set at 50 units. Subjects responded to each item by indicating whether they had experienced that event during the past two-years. The researchers showed that life events cluster significantly in a two-year period prior to the onset of an illness and that onset can be predicted from the total number of LCU's accumulated. As a research scale, the SRE had achieved some value in that it suggested some connection between life events and physical health or illness, and with it began a whole field of research into the effects of life changes. The scale was altered, refined, and criticised, and the life change approach to studying stress was applauded, questioned, and attacked by others keen to further understand the apparent relationship between life and health.[28] Some complained that the 43 events did not adequately encompass all of the possible events of life, others disputed the LUC's, as to whether they were accurate, were able to be added together, or were too simplistic. Some challenged the life change notion emphasizing that a substantial number of people undergo many severely stressful events without developing illness, and suggested that any reaction depended on the capacity of the person to deal with the event and not with the nature of the event itself. All of the criticism, both constructive and not, was intended to advance and refine the research, and was generally accepted as such, as the study of stressful life events grew.

However, many psychologists in the Psychology Industry, only superficially aware of the ongoing debate and subsequent refinements to the theories, grabbed the Holmes and Rahe scale, which was never meant to be used as a predictive psychological tool,[29] and began to use it in their work with clients and in their lectures and workshops. Executives fired ("outplaced" or "de-hired" are the popular terms of the industry) from their jobs were being given the scale as part of their relocation package. Patients in hospitals were completing the scale to "help them understand the psychological aspects of their disease or illness." And patients in psychologists' private practices were filling out the scale as part of the battery of psychological tests administered before treatment. In some cases, it was being used to predict or explain physical illness. But in many, the majority of cases, it was being misused as a scale to measure overall stress which could then be related to any or all behaviours of the clients. Recent events became the excuse for people's actions as they were described as victims of "the stress they are going through."

Despite the constructive controversy that existed amongst the researchers, and in spite of the number of revisions and changes being made to both the scale and the concept, the Psychology Industry persisted in its misuse of the scale with hundreds of thousands of clients. As one psychologist commented, "the scale is easy to give and score, and its interesting to patients. It doesn't matter whether it is reliable or not, it's simple and it gives us something to talk about."

But not only was Stress something to talk about, the Psychology Industry argued that it was something that must be treated. If stress could make you sick, then, the Psychology Industry reasoned, reversing the process could make you well. Thus, the practice of health psychology was created with the notion that if psychological factors could lead to illness (being a victim) then they could also be the source of "wellness" (being a survivor). While this potential could be seen in everything from arthritis to colitis to dermatitis, two areas drew most of the attention: heart attacks and cancer.

In the late 50's, two American cardiologists, Meyer Friedman and Ray Rosenman, provided an explanation of coronary illness that one might say, hit the jackpot: "we feel that a complex of emotional reactions which we categorize as Type A behavior is *the principal cause* of coronary illness."[30] Type A behaviour is characterized by a chronic sense of time urgency, explosive speech, and extremes in impatience, competitiveness, job involvement, and achievement striving. Type B individuals, on the other hand, are seen as confronting every challenge with placid nonchalance. It is this personality that later came to be identified as the cancer-prone personality, whose passivity and submissiveness made them vulnerable to "the attacks of cancer cells."

Friedman and Rosenman had based their conclusion on a study of their patients, using structured interviews conducted by trained researchers. Their findings and those of other epidemiological studies[31] showed *a strong association* between Type A behavior and coronary disease. *Was it cause or correlation?* The Psychology Industry preferred to consider it as cause, following a form of reasoning which Plous and Piattelli-Palmarini[32] have called "illusory correlation." This "magical thinking" erroneously assumes that a characteristic or symptom is proof of cause; that in a "mechanistic manner the Type A behavior contributed to or caused the heart attack." [33] (See Fig.1)

Based on this assumption, the Psychology Industry developed a number of prevention and treatment procedures intended to identify the sources of stress and Type A behaviour, and modify the individual's behaviour and emotions to reduce the risk. Psychologists, in hospitals and private practices, began to administer the Jenkins' Activity Scale to assess the Type A personality (despite the fact that it was not considered reliable), to teach relaxation techniques to counteract stress, and to use behaviour modification techniques to change Type A behaviours. They taught clients that their behaviour put them at risk and that they were responsible for their own health or heart attack. And they ignored later research which showed that this association has lessened since it was first identified in the 60's so that by the end of the 80's it was questionable and considered far too simplistic.[34] Curiously, some research had even shown that recidivism (the chance of another heart attack) and mortality (the rate of deaths) in people who have experienced a first heart attack is half as strong (reduced by 50%) for Type A's as it is for Type B's.[35]

Parloff once said: "No form of psychotherapy has ever been initiated without a claim that it has unique therapeutic advantages, and no form of psychotherapy has ever been abandoned because of its failure to live up to these claims."[36] Such is true for the psychological treatment of cardiovascular (CV) disease. The Canadian Registry of Health-Service Providers in Psychology recently stated that "the profession of psychology— is now recognised as an authoritative resource with knowledge, skills and techniques which are integral to the process of CV illness prevention."[37] This is stated despite such evidence as that of researchers from Stanford and Duke universities which found no correlation between heart disease and on-the-job stress: "job strain was actually more common in patients with normal coronary arteries than in patients with significant disease."[38]

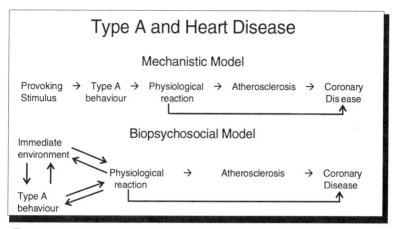

Figure 1

If psychological factors play any role in heart disease and undoubtedly they do; then, they do so in a far more complicated way than the Psychology Industry would have one believe, and in a way far less open to simplistic Psychology Industry interventions.

The employment of "illusionary correlations" by the Psychology Industry also occurred in its efforts to develop cancer as a market. Consider the following:

> A woman is diagnosed by an eminent oncologist as having a terminal form of cancer. She seeks "alternative treatment" from a shaman and on return to her cancer specialist is found to have no signs of the cancer.

And

> A group of women, all diagnosed with metastatic breast cancer (a fatal form of cancer) are divided into two sub-groups. One group receives group therapy including hypnotically guided visualization to imagine their cancer shrinking. The others meet as a group for education about their disease but with no guided imagery. In looking back at the whole group ten years later, all but one have died but the members of the first group had lived significantly longer.

These are just two of the many examples used by the Psychology Industry to support its idea that non-medical (i.e. psychological) treatments of cancer work. In the first case, reported in the *Journal of the American Medical Association*,[39] it was assumed that the rituals of the shaman/healer had a psychological effect; while, in the latter, the patient's own visualization is held to have been somewhat effective in delaying the progress of the disease.[40] From these and other examples, the Psychology Industry again attributes a causal role to psychological factors in the development of illness. And again the "illusionary correlation" must be considered. Perhaps, in the case of the first woman, it was a misdiagnosis or a spontaneous remission. In the second example, all but one of the patients died anyway. Did the "significant" (i.e. one and half years) difference demonstrate living longer or just dying more slowly? And, even if it was the first, was it due to the visualizations or to something else?

The Psychology Industry doesn't care to ask these doubting questions. Rather, it proceeds full steam ahead with "treatment programs for cancer patients." One of the first, and one of the best known, was that of Carl Simonton, a radiologist and his wife Stephanie Matthews-Simonton, a psychologist.[41] Based on a philosophical idea that the "will to live" affects the process of disease, they constructed a programme including meditation and visualization, in which clients pictured in their minds their cancer and then imagined the cancer cells being fought off by the body's natural defenses. They believed that this "imagery work" would strengthen the body's own immune system and help it fight the disease. Patients came to view their cancer as an enemy that affected them because they had given in to it and allowed themselves to become sick. They were victims of their own undoing but, with psychologists' help, they were told that they could "get well again."[42] Simontons' notions spread, resulting in the creation and endorsement (i.e. franchising) of treatment centres around the country, and in other psychologists modifying and adapting their concepts to create their own personalized cancer treatments.[43] However, despite the wide popularity of the approach, evidence of the effectiveness of these programmes was basically limited to anecdotes and stories.

"Whenever the reasons for an illness are unclear, there is a considerable tendency to speak of psychosocial factors as the cause of individual disequilibrium. Illness in which the intervention of such factors is postulated are most likely to have an unknown or insecurely established etiology, and the possibilities of therapeutic intervention are limited or nonexistent."[44] And it is in this void of specific information that psychologists have sought to create their own treatments for people with a wide range of medical conditions.[45] So confident and determined is the Psychology Industry, that one psychologist recently stated that 100% of all medical visits involve a psychologically based health problem.[46]

Research into the unavoidable life event of dying provides another example of the Psychology Industry's simplistic approach to knowledge in order to design psychological technology. In 1981, Kubler-Ross's study of terminally ill patients led her to identify five psychological stages involved in preparing to die[47]:

(1) Denial, involving the refusal to believe it is happening.
(2) Anger, with a sense of "it isn't fair."
(3) Bargaining, or negotiating survival by promising to change.
(4) Depression, with a loss of hope and interest.
(5) Acceptance of the unavoidable; that things can't be changed.

She described these as normal psychological stages and acknowledged that not everyone would go through all of them or always experience them in that order. It was to be a psychological model of dying that would be descriptive and give some understanding of the experience. However, the

Psychology Industry has taken possession of this theory, simplifying, altering and applying it to fit the varied needs of different psychologists and different target groups. Describing the steps as psychological necessities, it has created a constricted technology, a procedure for "psychologically healthy dying," while simultaneously creating an industry that ensures that this constriction will endure; that of bereavement counselling, "grief work" and palliative care. As well, it has taken license with the concept of dying, so that it can refer to any form of "death:" death of hope, an idea, a life style, a marriage. For example, one psychologist has applied it to victims whom he identifies as follows: "If you are a healthy person who experiences a trauma, you will go through each of these six stages in sequence. Problems arise when you get stuck in any one of these stages, or when you miss one. A newly divorced woman who can't get angry at her ex-spouse has not completed the healing cycle. A man who continues to be depressed after losing his job will never get to accept what has happened nor will he find hope for the future. Both situations are fertile ground for aftershock"[48] and for the technology of the Psychology Industry.

But, similar to the life stress events work, research studies of loss present a very different and more complex picture, which expose a number of the myths of coping. Psychologists Camille Wortman and Roxane Cohen Silver,[49] concluded that people have four different coping styles to deal with irrevocable loss. Counter to Psychology Industry claims, the researchers found that almost half of the people who had suffered major traumas did not experience intense anxiety, depression, or grief after the loss. As well, they discovered that, over the years, the roll-with-the-punches people remained well adjusted and healthy, contrary to Psychology Industry predictions. Pennebaker, critical of the Psychology Industry's simplistic approach said: "Not everyone progresses through stages in grieving or coping. In fact, as many as half of all adults may face torture, divorce, the loss of a loved one, or other catastrophe and not exhibit any major sign of depression or anxiety. By definition, then, a substantial number of people may not benefit from attempts to influence their coping strategies."[50]

George Bonanno, a professor of psychology at Washington, D.C.'s Catholic University, supports this view with his empirical data analyzing grieving and bereavement counseling. The goal of his research is to examine the so called grief-work hypothesis; the widely held assumption that venting negative emotions and "telling your story" are necessary for regaining mental health. So far, his experiments have yielded intriguingly counterintuitive results, at least to those who believe in the benefits of letting it all out. Instead of talking out their feelings, Bonanno's studies suggest that grief-stricken people who express intense negative emotions when discussing their loss appear to do worse in the long term, than those that "keep it in," the so-called repressors.

Bonanno is not alone in drawing these conclusions. Wortman and Silver, in their 1989 article "The Myths of Coping With Loss," concluded that there was little evidence that "those who initially show minimal distress following loss are likely to become significantly depressed at a later point." And Dutch researchers Margaret and Wolfgang Stroebe, editors of the *Handbook of Bereavement: Theory, Research, and Intervention* (Cambridge), state: "In our view, bereavement is an issue that needs to be understood from a sound base of theoretically oriented and empirically derived knowledge and not purely on subjective, descriptive accounts."[51]

But psychologists, psychotherapists and grief counsellors are not easily influenced by empirical research. At the 1997 annual meeting of the Association of Death Education and Counselling (ADEC) where Bonanno presented his findings, "attendees enjoyed 'complimentary massages' in one of the conference rooms or visited an odd mourning mini-mall offering books like *Why Are the Casseroles Always Tuna? A Loving Look at the Lighter Side of Grief,* while they shared their own painful stories and talked of 'caring' and 'love.' "[52]

Bonanno's "grief studies" findings come at a time when the "bereavement industry," as Bonanno calls it, is flourishing. The professional field of bereavement counsellors is a growth industry: ADEC now boasts more than 2,000 members.[53]

Where once Kubler-Ross' model gave a glimpse into the unfathomable experience of one's own imminent death and a means by which others, close to the dying person, could understand the vacillations in their moods and thinking, it has now been generalized and trivialized so that the stages apply not to the dying one but to the survivor of the death of a parent, of a child, of a spouse or a friend, even of a poodle or parakeet. Quackenbush, a social worker, for instance, leads survivors through the classic stages of grief to ultimate reconciliation with the loss when a pet dies. His book describes how he "thoughtfully examines the full range of normal emotions (depression, guilt, denial, and anger)" for grieving pet owners.[54] Other psychologists have applied the Kubler-Ross model to a variety of situations in which the word "loss" can be loosely applied: "loss of a job," "loss of an object" (such as in a burglary), or "loss of a friendship" (as in relocating because of work).

And American culture has absorbed these simplistic psychological formulae. For instance, a Girl Scout troop in New York "instituted a 'grief patch' in 1993; troop members could earn this medal by sharing painful feelings with one another, writing stories and poems about death and loss, and meeting with bereavement counsellors." Miss New Jersey 1996 "chose bereavement counselling as her special issue, in response to the loss of her own father. And at the Tiny Hearts Bereavement Group in Ronokonkoma, Long Island, grieving children participate in an 'If Onlys and Farewell Day,' during which they write down guilty or regretful feelings about deceased friends and relatives, tie them to balloons, and release them into the sky."[55]

Sometimes this model maintains its distinction; however, sometimes it becomes enmeshed with another model which has been used and abused freely by the Psychology Industry: that of PTSD. For instance, Matsakis,[56] with "sleight-of-words," changes Kubler-Ross' stages of dying into the stages of grieving, and then places them within her larger and broader approach to the problems of trauma survivors. Psychologizing and generalizing freely, she states that "when you grieve, you experience loss on at least three levels:"

1) over the specific person, object, or aspect of yourself that you have lost, including an organ of the body, a physical or intellectual ability, or a cherished value (eg. faith in a spiritual being, loyalty to government, or the integrity of people),

2) grieving the fact of your powerlessness; for example, you cannot resurrect the dead, replace a body part, or restore your faith, and

3) grieving your mortality; the fact that you are going to die.[57]

Then, she encourages people to identify their losses, beginning with their "financial costs" which resulted from the loss or "trauma and secondary wounding experience." And she directs them to proceed through "the five stages of grief," cautioning that "some other trigger may set you back to an earlier stage."[58]

Again, a theoretical concept, useful to the study of thanatology, had become an industrial mold to be applied willy-nilly to a whole array of issues that the Psychology Industry could identify. One didn't have to be approaching death or even have to be involved with another's death; grief had the semantic elasticity to be applied to almost any event in life.

But if Death and Dying could be made to fit, all the more so could PTSD, because each word in the term could be drawn, stretched, and molded as needed. Once applied to indisputable situations of stress, such as the battlefields of Viet Nam, "trauma" can now be applied to any momentarily upsetting event. Consider this story:

From Monday to Friday, Rosemarie's morning routine never varied. She would get off the bus near her office, stop at the coffee shop on the corner, and order her regular takeout coffee and bran muffin. She would enter her building, buy a paper from the newsstand, and take the elevator up to her office. Before the day's work began, she would eat her muffin and drink her coffee as she skimmed the news. By 9:00, she would be returning early morning calls.

This particular Tuesday was different. Rosemarie was at her desk, eating her muffin and sipping her coffee as she read the neswpaper. She glanced down for a moment at her muffin and discovered a dead cockroach in the uneaten piece. Rosemarie gagged. She ran to the rest room and threw up her breakfast. She was sweating and she had the shakes. Unable to work, she left the office and went home. The coffee shop offered her an apology and reimbursement. But Rosemarie was not interested in any monetary gain; her focus was already beyond lawsuits and retribution.

She became obsessive about disease and cockroaches. She was certain that the cold she had developed was due to the half-cooked bug. She had her aparment exterminated an inordinate number of times, twice each week under a standing arrangement. She became complusively clean, refusing to eat in coffee shops and restaurants. She had recurring nightmares about crawling bugs.

> Six months after the incident, Rosemarie couldn't bring herself to go to the office. She couldn't work and she lost her job. What might have been a repulsive but ultimately insignificant event for someone else had become a highly traumatic life-changing crisis for Rosemarie. She had become a victim of severe aftershock (i.e. PTSD).[59]

Calling it "Kafkaesque," Slaby determines that she experienced trauma because "it was sudden, it was unexpected, it was out of her control, and it changed her life,"[60] and since her problems followed the cockroach incident, it was clear to him that Rosemarie suffered from PTSD. But this has no resemblance to the original meaning of the term, or the experiences of Vietnam soldiers, the original group of PTSD patients. And his assessment ignores all of the immediately apparent alternative explanations: that possibly Rosemarie's life was rigid and her behaviour compulsive, that she may have had pre-existing problems, or that the event may have had secondary gains and compensation.

In discussing the possibility that Sybil's stories and diagnosis of Multiple Personality Disorder were, in some ways, the product of the therapist, Spiegel says: "that is one of the biggest difficulties with working with the concept of causation in psychotherapy. It is the grand illusion that we have inherited from Freud. Freud's concept was that you had to get to the truth, and unless you get the truth no therapeutic effect can take place. So, in the pursuit of the truth we become engaged in story telling and we impose our hypothesis on the patient by the way we ask our questions. Highly suggestible (psychologically-prone) will of course respond in a way that can please the doctors, especially if there is a good rapport between them. That is why I think it is an illusion to believe that we can establish a valid causation for multiple personality, or for almost any kind of psychiatric illness." And he continues by describing a victim-making process consistent with that of Synthetic and Counterfeit victims: "These patients are full of anger and guile. They feel victimized and tend to blame others for their misbehavior. They then find a doctor who can conjoin with them to develop a story of abuse which appears to be a multiple personality disorder, thus giving them a new kind of status in society. They will make use of all this alleged or real abuse which took place in their life, as a way of getting recognition: 'Look, I'm a multiple!' They don't have to do it on their own anymore. Nowadays, they have the collusion of a therapist who is showing them how to do it. And then they can have hospital stays for months to years that the insurance companies pay for."[61]

Psychological Nostrums

Are the emotionally distressed the recipients of the fruits of a true psycho-
logical revolution or the victims of a cheap psychic nostrum?

Martin Gross,
The Psychological Society

Nostrum: (n), [L, neuter singular of noster, ours] 1. a medicine or medical
application, prepared by the person recommending it; esp. a quack remedy,
a patent medicine, 2. a questionable remedy or scheme, a per scheme or
favourite remedy.

The Oxford English Dictionary

Medicine has always had to suffer those within its profession, and the many outside of it, who produce and promote their own ways of getting better. From the witches' brews of ancient times to the travelling medicine shows, from copper bracelets to Kickapoo Indian Oil, society has always had an abundance of secret concoctions and panaceas to cure its ailments. For instance, the discovery of radium by the Curies began the "Mild Radium Therapy" movement, particularly popular among American socialites, and precipitated a lucrative trade in radium-based belts, hearing aids, toothpaste, face cream, and hair tonic. Most popular of all was "Radiothor," a glow-in-the-dark mineral water which carried promises of a cure for more than 150 maladies.[62] The history of medicine reveals an incredible number of such "known-to-be-effective" interventions that turned out to be useless or worse.

Similarly, people have been gullible to promises of easy ways to gain hair or lose weight, so it is hardly surprising that they are open to easy solutions even for personal and interpersonal discomforts, which less affluent societies would regard as trivial. In the first half of this century, one of the most successful psychic nostrums was Couéism. Known otherwise as auto-suggestion, it combined some of the rationale of the modern Psychology Industry with the rituals of ancient times. Emile Coué, a French pharmacist and incidentally a student of hypnosis, instructed persons suffering from nervous disorders to tell themselves repeatedly throughout the day, that "every day and in every way I am getting better and better." For a few decades, his popularity and influence was phenomenal.[63] In an exposition of Couéism, Harry Brooks exhorted: "Say it with faith! You can only rob Induced Autosuggestion of its power in one way — by believing that it is powerless... The greater your faith the more radical and the more rapid will be your results."[64]

Belief in something simple is the sign of a nostrum. Whether it is a magical potion, a miracle tonic, or a psychological formula. The cure-alls of psychologists did not begin nor did they end with Coué's invention. Bergin and Garfield went on record some years ago saying: "it is a matter of concern that so many new therapies that have no empirical support are invented and introduced by licensed practitioners, but even more so by entrepreneurial unlicensed persons. Numerous treatments are also applied by people who have merely attended a workshop or two in a procedure and then considered themselves to be experts. It is also unfortunate that fads continue to dot the landscape of the mental health professionals and that a fair amount of magical thinking regarding the power to change people is associated with such movements."[65]

Whether they are psychic nostrums, therapy movements, or treatment fads, the technologies of the Psychology Industry all have a common theme: "you have to get worse, before you get better!" or in visual terms:

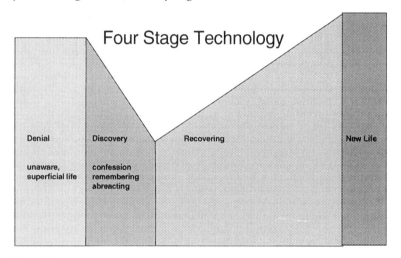

Four Stage Technology

| Denial | Discovery | Recovering | New Life |

| unaware, superficial life | confession remembering abreacting | | |

Figure 2

Both the addiction technologies and the trauma/abuse technologies share this four stage model of manufacturing and maintaining victims. They begin with people who have bad feelings or bad behaviours, and then cause them to feel worse as they begin to identify themselves as victims. Once the identity is established, they start the recovery process with the ultimate goal or promise of a new life and a new identity. The whole process can be considered a technology because it treats all victims identically, as lacking individuality or uniqueness, and therefore puts them all through the same steps and procedures.

Addictions

Despite the current attention to violence and trauma, the *addiction industry* is by far the more established and profitable victim-making business. Twenty-five million Americans alone, are considered to be alcoholics and, when the market is expanded to include all substance abusers and all those addicted to various bad behaviours, the number grows by a further 125 million. When the additional group of all those related to these addicts (the spouses and children, the "adult children," and those who have to relate to an addicted friend or boss) are added, the number of potential victims of addiction soars to 250 million, a number close to the population of the whole nation. Even putting aside Melodie Beatties' claim that everyone could benefit from co-dependence (i.e. addiction to another person) treatment, it would seem that the whole country is, in some way or another, a victim of addiction. It is no wonder that Stanton Peele states that the addiction movement has produced "the multimillion dollar alcohol-as-a-disease treatment industry and now a host of new diseases, such as being the child-of-a-person-with-the-disease-of-alcoholism."[66]

The addiction industry began with the treatment of heroin addicts but really came into its own with Alcoholics Anonymous (AA) and the myriad of offshoots and facsimiles, all of which present the addict and those affected as passive victims rather than as active, responsible agents. AA began as a private fellowship based on the proposition that alcoholics are unable to control their drinking on their own and that only through acceptance and support of the deity and other alcoholics can they achieve sobriety. Due to its success, the movement was gradually co-opted by the medical and psychology industries, resulting in a hybrid theory of addiction as both a bad behaviour and a disease. In 1985, Holden wrote in *Science* describing alcoholism as "the neglected disease in medical education" and stating that "alcoholism, as a chronic disease, offers 'a fantastic vehicle to teach other concepts.'"[67] What Holden didn't say was that "with the attribution of disease, the individual is delivered up to a body of institutional experts – psychiatrists, child guidance counsellors, physicians, alcohol treatment practitioners, social workers – who seek the person's rehabilitation. In becoming technical objects, the deviants give rise to a new group of control agents and agencies whose power is suspect."[68]

But the Psychology Industry had not been neglecting alcoholism nor ignoring it as a prototype for other addictions. Already psychologists had begun taking cuttings from the stem and creating their own variations of addiction as a disease of helplessness requiring identification, education and treatment by psychological experts and addiction specialists. Rather than considering these relationships or behaviours as specific to the individual or due to broader social and political factors, psychologists chose to endorse medicine's disease model, thereby allowing uniform approaches or psychological technologies to be developed and applied. By adopting this notion of addictions as diseases and those addicted as victims, the Psychology Industry encouraged people to believe that the problem is not of their own making and that it is unlikely that they will outgrow the problem, thus legitimizing and excusing the behaviour, increasing the readiness to accept the diagnosis, and sanctioning forced treatment as an alternative to incarceration or job loss.

The growth in addiction treatments has involved casting a wider net to catch more varieties of addictions and to persuade the public of the progressive nature of these "diseases" and the need for early treatment before the behaviours become a problem. From psychologists and private, for-profit treatment centres, the message goes out: that if you think you have a drinking problem, then indeed you do; or if one suspects a child of smoking marijuana, this "is probably only the tip of the iceberg" and parents should make any financial sacrifice necessary to ensure that the child gets treatment for "this could be a matter of life or death."[69] Even highly questionable "addictions" are described in life-threatening terms:

> Compulsive shopping can result in self-loathing, depression, financial ruin and marital breakups, yet often it is not considered a serious addiction... DON'T WAIT FOR DISASTER!

> Shopping addicts spend everything they have — and more — until they find themselves in deep trouble, financially and emotionally.[70]

If the adult, the parent, the child, or the alcoholic, the overeater, the lovesick, the Star Trekkie,[71] the market player,[72] or the TV-watching couch potato, claim they are not addicts, then the Psychology Industry says they are in denial (Stage 1).The approach to dealing with denial is Psychology Industry endorsed coercion or force. The spouse or lover is confronted with the choice of "get help or I'm leaving," the employee with "get help or you're fired," the accused with "get help or go to jail." Peele describes a far more overt form of coercive force:

> CompCare (a prominent hospital chain in America specializing in addiction treatment) trains consultants to work with high school counselling staff, teaching them how to run "interventions"— sessions in which students suspected of drug use are surrounded by family, friends, teachers, and others who insist the child enter treatment immediately. (Intervention protocol recommends that a cab be kept waiting for the moment the student admits his problem so that he can be rushed to a center before he changes his mind.)[73]

Such admissions are the goal of Stage 2. Unlike the early members of AA for whom their alcoholism was obvious to them and everyone else, many of the new "addicts" have to be persuaded to take the First Step of admitting "I am an alcoholic (or a sex addict, a food addict, etc.)" Sometimes this is carried out in the privacy of a psychologist's office where problems are interpreted as "symptomatic" of addiction. At other times, it happens in support

---

"We're all mad here. I'm mad. You're mad."
"How do you know I'm mad?" said Alice.
"You must be," said the Cat, "or you wouldn't be here."

Alice's Adventures in Wonderland

---

groups, as participants share their stories, accepting the new-comers as one of them and offering support as they acknowledge their problem and its dreadful effects on themselves and others they love. For instance, David Rudy investigated AA by sitting in on AA meetings as an observer and described: "When newcomers claim that they cannot remember if they had any blackouts or not, other members use this claim as evidence of the event in question. As one member put it to a newcomer: 'The reason you can't rememberisbecausealcoholfogsyourbrain.'"[74] Together, the psychologist and the group strive to reinforce the self-image of the person as an addict who, in turn, is a vulnerable, dependent and unfortunate victim.

Originally, AA was hostile towards medicine and psychology both for its general ignorance about alcoholism and for its tendency towards being authoritarian and elitist in its approach to treatment. More recently, a rapprochement has been arrived at whereby professional treatment functions as an adjunct to the self-help groups. Psychologists refer clients to the group while the groups encourage individual participation in treatment, serving as a pool of potential clients for psychologists. They share a simple technical model of the recovery process which some have equated with "learning how to be an addict;" acquiring the symptoms, accepting the identity, and admitting the disease. This caused one observer to wonder: "Is it really possible that many alcoholics and addicts have to learn their symptoms in treatment?"[75]

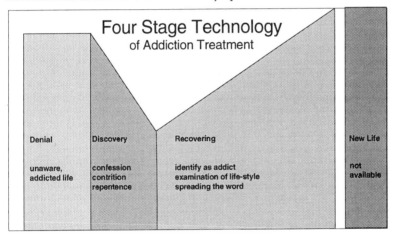

Figure 3

Recovery (Stage 3), however, is a never-ending process for addicts who, after confession and repentance, take on the new identity of a "recovering addict." For AA members, this means "living one day at a time," "improving their conscious contact with God," and spreading the "spiritual awakening" to other alcoholics, remaining aware that they are never free of the problem. For others in programmes founded on the secular psychological religion, they learn to live from one session to the next, while they improve their psychological awareness and promote their psychological awakening to other potential addicts. "All of a sudden, people are pouring back into churches and synagogues with a fervour that hasn't been seen since the 50's. It appears that a great religious revival is sweeping the land— until you examine the situation a little more closely. Then you'll notice the biggest crowds today often arrive in midweek. And instead of filing into the pews, these people head for the basement, where they immediately sit down and begin talking about their deepest secrets, darkest fears and strangest cravings."[76] Of this, Kaminer quips that "never have so many known so much about people for whom they have cared so little."

The addiction industry is a "cash-cow" of the Psychology Industry, which has persuaded the public that addictions are treatable, that more treatment is the answer to treatment failure, that non-addicts also need to be treated and that addiction-like problems need to be identified and treated.

Through labelling addictions as disease, the Psychology Industry has argued, in most cases successfully, that treatment ought to be covered by health insurance, like that of any other illness. The State of Minnesota, for example, has declared alcoholism to be a treatable disease and adopted legislation preventing employees who are unable to perform their jobs because of drunkenness, to be fired. They must be treated at the employer's (or insurer's) expense, even though most of the data shows treatment to be ineffective. A survey of Fortune 500 companies indicated that 79% recognized that substance abuse was a "significant or very significant problem" in their organizations. However, when asked whether the treatment programs did any good: "the overwhelming majority saw few results from these programs. In the survey, 87 percent reported little or no change in absenteeism since the programs began and 90 percent saw little or no change in productivity ratings."[77]

Addiction treatment is probably the only business whose failures lead to more business. Its technology, based on continued recovering, presumes failure and relies on further funds every time an addict relapses and requires further treatment, apparently oblivious to the fact that such recidivism is additional evidence of an ineffective treatment. As well, it is the only business that treats people who aren't in need, for the Psychology Industry actively recruits beyond the boundary of addicts, preaching the message that spouses are codependents and that children are highly susceptible to addiction. "Children of alcoholics deserve and require treatment in and of themselves," stated a founder of the National Association for Children of Alcoholics.[78] It is also interesting to note that psychologist-assisted self-help groups, addressing addictions of all sorts, have become an adjunct treatment for many patients in therapy for non-addictive problems. A recent study showed that in a sample of women attending AA meetings, over half either didn't drink at all or weren't drinking heavily.[79] And Rutter, who specializes in the treatment of women with sexual-boundary issues (those defined as sexually abused, or assaulted, by virtue of having had sex with a therapist, doctor, clergy, teacher, etc.), recommends that his clients attend AA, Al-Anon or Adult Children of Alcoholic groups because "the psychological dynamics of chemical dependency bear many similarities to those of sexual-boundary violations, and the two are often intertwined."[80]

And finally, the Psychology Industry has discovered that this technology can be applied to an endless host of new problems. Consider the following, from an article in a hospital magazine: "Obesity is an incurable disease... We don't know its etiology. We can however, put a patient into remission for a lifetime through our weight-loss program...We try to make our patients aware that obesity is a disease, that it is incurable, and that they *will need maintenance assistance for the rest of their lives.*"[81] In accordance with this strategy, John Leo whimsically wrote that in "this golden age of exoneration... Almost nobody can really be held accountable... Bonnie and Clyde came along too soon. Nowadays they could settle for a year at the Betty Ford Clinic as victims of compulsive bank-robbing addiction."[82]

A review of the myriad of existing programs designed to treat the many varieties of addictions indicates that most are based on the simplistic technology of AA; they follow, with some minor variations, its Twelve Step program and, despite the many celebrity claims to the opposite, lack any evidence of effectiveness at anything other than bestowing a lot of money on psychologists.

HI AND LOIS

Trauma/Abuse

While the addiction industry has been a significant contributor to the Psychology Industry for some time, the *trauma/abuse industry* is a relative new-comer. Prior to the 80's, trauma was generally associated with stress and treated as a medically-related issue through health-promotion programs, or as an anxiety problem addressed through traditional psychotherapy or behavioural and relaxation techniques. However, at the turn of the decade, two

T/A Technology

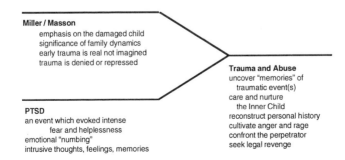

Figure 4

new ventures of the Psychology Industry combined to create a rampant third enterprise: the treatment technology for Trauma and Abuse. While Alice Miller and Jeffrey Masson championed the notion that the psychological problems of adults were due to bad parenting and/or abuse, those involved in counselling Vietnam veterans developed and promoted the concept of Post Traumatic Stress Disorder to explain the repeated intrusion of distressing recollections and the numbing of feelings and emotions. Together these two forces provided the basis on which the Trauma/Abuse industry would create its technology.

Miller, a Swiss psychoanalyst, presented the view that everyone's needs as children have not been met and have often been exploited for the adults' own ends, and that society "takes the side of the adult and blames the child for what has been done to him or her." Based on this belief, Miller concluded that:

- The way we are treated as small children is the way we treat ourselves the rest of our life.
- The child is always innocent.
- The child represses the trauma and idealizes the abuser.
- This repression leads to neuroses, psychoses, psychosomatic disorders and delinquency.
- Repression leads to feelings of guilt,
  - or is turned into "madness,"
  - or is felt in the body as pain the cause of which is concealed,
  - or is acted out in unacceptable ("bad") behaviours.
- Therapy can be successful only if the memories and feelings are uncovered.
- Fantasies serve to conceal truth but unconsciously convey childhood experience in symbolic ways.
- Past abuse/crime can not be understood or excused as perpetrator's blindness or unfulfilled needs.
- Victims' reports can bring awareness and a sense of responsibility to society.[83]

Miller was vehemently critical of Freud and of Miller's psychoanalytic and psychotherapeutic colleagues for what she considered to be a cover-up of the widespread social problem of child abuse.[84] Masson supported her claim when he printed letters between Freud and his friend, Wilhelm Fleiss, which Masson claimed revealed that Freud changed his theory to aid his friend, who had been guilty of abuse. Initially, Freud had theorized that the complaints of his patients could be attributed to incestuous actions of the parents. Later, he altered this theory, believing that the patients had fantasized the relationships as part of natural childhood development during what he termed the Oedipal stage.[85] Miller, Masson and others took the stance that Freud's revisioning was intended to protect Fleiss and to conceal the larger social problem of child abuse.[86]

The Miller/Masson theory was quickly accepted by a large number of psychologists who saw it as a way to explain, via a single cause, a wide range of problems. The family came to be viewed as "dysfunctional," with the effect on the children of, as Bradshaw termed it, "soul-murder."[87] But the application of their theory had an initial obstacle; many clients found it hard to believe and accept.

Post Traumatic Stress Disorder (PTSD) served to overcome that problem by casting the abuse theory within a broader, more palatable, trauma context. As Dolan writes, in discussing the "advantages of using a PTSD diagnosis:"

> A PTSD diagnosis is helpful for survivors of sexual abuse because the definition has a normalizing effect for clients ... when symptoms of childhood sexual abuse are explained as initially reasonable, and in many cases valuable, efforts to survive extreme psychological stress, they become less stigmatizing in clients' eyes... Seeing themselves in the same group as victims of natural disasters, airplane and car accidents, and random criminal assaults can be helpful in overcoming a tendency to blame themselves rather than the perpetrator.[88]

"Once this diagnosis developed," Blume writes, "therapists independently began applying it to survivors of incest. Many have extended this application to other traumatized children: those who were physically, verbally, or sexually abused; those whose families were contaminated by alcoholism; those who witnessed the battering of a parent."[89] And the list goes on, including psychiatrists in training,[90] those exposed to toxic substances,[91] potential aids patients,[92] and those who have survived a heart attack.[93] Contrary to Dolan's view of "normalizing," the application of PTSD has resulted in everything being pathologized until the only way to be is to be "abnormal."

However, many people thus diagnosed still had no idea that they had been sexually abused and did not experience the intrusive repetitive flashbacks or memories of the traumatic event associated with PTSD. But the Psychology Industry managed to pathologize them by insisting that the absence of traumatic memories was, in itself, an indication that the diagnosis was accurate. Bass and Davis, in *Courage to Heal*, the text for women learning to view themselves as sexually abused, state that "the fact that people experience amnesia for traumatic events is — or should be — beyond dispute."[94] For them and others in the Psychology Industry, this lack of memory was explainable through the psychological notions of "repression," the unconscious denial of events due to intensely negative affect, "dissociation," the defensive walling off of traumatic experiences from ordinary consciousness (as in Multiple Personality Disorder, or as it is now called, Dissociative Identity Disorder.)[95] According to Blume, "indeed, so few incest survivors in my experience have identified themselves as abused in the beginning of therapy that I have concluded that *perhaps half of all incest survivors do not remember* that the abuse occurred."[96]

This merger of the Miller/Masson theory and PTSD theory provides a number of advantages for the Psychology Industry:

• It provides a simple theory that is easy for psychologists to understand.

- It creates a technology that can be applied to a diverse group of problems including alcoholism, addictions, eating disorders, sexual problems, anxieties and phobias, depression, multiple personality disorder, and schizophrenia.
- It is amenable to everyone; patient and psychologist alike.
- It requires no previous training in psychology or psychiatry. For instance Bass and Davis state emphatically that "none of what is presented (in their book) is based on psychological theories."[97]
- It needs no knowledge of psychological assessment or psychiatric diagnosis. Traditional diagnostic categories are ignored in favour of the all-inclusive labels of Abuse and PTSD.

As McHugh notes, a patient's belief in trauma, abuse or incest "makes psychotherapy easy at first. Therapists and patients can say 'We have found the secret.' The fact that patients and families steadily become more confused, incoherent and chaotic is then believed to be an expression of the original incest." But what really is happening, he says, is that "conflicts are being generated by false memories. We have found something to make therapy easy."[98]

While concepts have been stretched and broadened, treatment has been technologically narrowed so that it has become a *"One-Size-Fits-All"* approach. This approach is taught in seminars and workshops across the country and incorporated in books and manuals. It is based on the oral tradition of unsubstantiated and unproven anecdotes. And with a religious and moralistic zeal, psychologists who promote it have become more aggressive, invasive and coercive in their approach, some even claiming this right through having been "anointed" by God.[99]

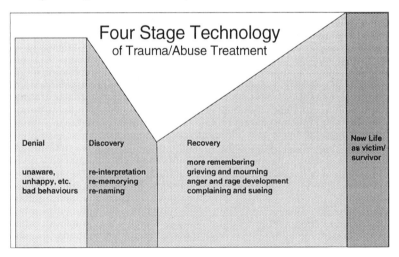

Figure 5

Although psychological technicians have described this approach in differing numbers of stages from three to eight,[100] the process remains basically the same when it is applied to clients:

I)   Establishing an Identity as a Victim.

II)   Restructuring memory, thinking and feeling.

III)   Acting and reacting.

The success of the Psychology Industry technology relies on the ability of psychologists to develop a victim identity in clients and to this end it relies on cognitive illusions and distortions. The first can be illustrated by the simple example of syllogistic logic:

> *Adult survivors of Child Abuse can't remember their early childhood;*
> *You can't remember your early childhood,*
> *Therefore, you must be a survivor of Child Abuse.*

This form of magical thinking, another example of the "illusory correlation," gives the mistaken impression that unrelated variables are somehow connected, or that a symptom is proof of a cause. That the Psychology Industry has adopted this syllogistic thinking is evident both in the "bait-and-switch" and "mis-information" tactics of many psychologists and in the checklists used to identify trauma and abuse.

Williams has described how psychologists can adopt the "bait-and-switch" tactics of retail sales practice in which customers are "baited" by advertisements of items at a low price and then "switched" to other items at higher prices.[101] He explained how the Psychology Industry can bait clients by appearing to respond to their expectations of symptom reduction and emotional relief, and then, once hooked into treatment, they tell them that their problems are more complex and of a deeper nature than they realized. In turn, they are "switched" to the therapist's particular brand of treatment, a modality that differs substantially from what the clients expected and which often takes much longer and, of course, costs much more.[102] This observation is particularly pertinent to the victim-making industry in which all problems are thought to originate from trauma and abuse. The schizophrenic man who thought that he might be a victim of abuse is a case in point. Instead of conducting a broad assessment and undertaking a systematic approach to diagnosing with consideration of possible alternatives, the psychologist merely applied her brand of therapy, drawing him into long term treatment for satanic ritual abuse.

Cognitive memory researchers, knowing that such suggestions about the past have power even without hypnosis, have repeatedly demonstrated the *"misinformation effect"* in which individuals who are intentionally misled about events, often integrate the inaccurate information into their accounts of the events. Studies have shown that this effect can influence all sorts of real memories including those involving personal behaviour and experience, violent crimes, and childhood trauma,[103] causing people to believe that they were victims of false events.

The association between a symptom and a problem often leads psychologists to the "invalid conclusion that those with the characteristic will have the problem."[104] For instance, the following are some of the items in Blume's "The Incest Survivors' Aftereffect Checklist," which she prefaces with "Do you find many characteristics of yourself on this list? If so, you could be a survivor of incest." This list is described by "Survivors United Network" as a "standard diagnostic tool for clinicians and counsellors" which helps "to identify incest survivors."

1. Fear of being alone in the dark, of sleeping alone.

2. Swallowing or gagging sensitivity.

4. Gastrointestinal problems; gynaecological disorders; headaches; arthritis or joint pain.

8. Phobias.

16. Trust issues: inability to trust; total trust; trusting indiscriminately.

23. Blocking out some period of early years (especially 1— 12) or a specific person or place.[105]

Similarly, Whitfield has provided a survey which he claims "reflects woundedness." Respondents are asked to respond "never," "seldom," "occasionally," "often," or "usually," and he notes that "If you answered 'Occasionally,' 'Often,' or 'Usually' to any of these questions, this book may be helpful to you (i.e. you are wounded). If you answered mostly 'never,' you may not be aware of some of your feelings (i.e. you are in denial or emotionally numb, and therefore wounded.)" For example:

21. Have you tried counselling or psychotherapy, yet still feel that "something" is wrong or missing?

24. Do you feel a lack of fulfilment in life, both personally and in your work?

27. Do you have a tendency toward having chronic fatigue, aches and pains?

30. Have you ever wondered if you might have been mistreated, abused or neglected as a child?[106]

And Jan Marie has constructed a list of 31 items which she claims are indicative of sexual abuse and incest, including symptoms such as "...a dislike for tapioca pudding, mashed potatoes and runny eggs."[107] Suzette Elgin offers a slightly different list for "victims of verbal abuse," described as those to whom the following have been said:

Can't you do anything right?

I can't believe you would feed that junk you your child!

What is this? And don't tell me it's a casserole, I already know that.

If you really cared about me, you wouldn't behave this way.

Of these she writes that

... frequent and repeated use of unanswerable questions, scalding accusations, sarcasm, insinuations, and even icy silence is more than simply unpleasant; it is abusive, destructive, and frequently leads to escalating arguments and physical violence... Life is a torture chamber, where the verbal abuser is the Torturer, getting wicked sadistic pleasure from the pain of the victim; where the verbal victim is the Torture Victim, defenseless and doomed to suffer; and where, if the victim finds any pleasure in life at all, it is the twisted pleasure of the masochist, who seeks out pain. In the reality created by this metaphor, words are whips and knives and fists; conversations are interrogations and ordeals; relationships are bondage from which the only solution is escape; homes and workplaces are prisons; and hope is folly. It is no wonder people get sick, in such an environment!"[108]

Whether through clinical experience and intuition, or psychological quizzes and checklists, people are given the professional opinion, the suggestion, that their symptoms, personality or memories are indicative of abuse or trauma. A refusal to accept the diagnosis, like Whitfield's interpretation of "never" responses in his questionnaire, is interpreted as denial, and those rejecting it are told that: "Often people are unwilling to accept *this fact* at first. They want to deny it. You're not alone." On the other hand, when someone neither denies nor accepts the notion, but expresses some reservation about the truth of it, the message is given: "If you wonder about it, you were." It becomes a Catch-22, where all reactions lead back to the same conclusion, that the individuals are victims of trauma and abuse.

NON SEQUITUR *by WILEY MILLER*

Having named or diagnosed the problem as trauma and abuse, the Psychology Industry proceeds to strengthen and solidify the victim identity by applying the technology of guided imagery and hypnosis to rehearse, recover, or construct memories of the traumatic event. So common is this that Ganaway has described the thriving trauma/abuse industry as "memory mills with an almost assembly-line mentality."[109] In fact, the focus on false memories has by now received so much attention that most people assume that manufacturing memories is at the core of manufacturing victims. While manipulating memories is a dominant and sometimes essential feature, equally important are the efforts to influence feelings and actions/reactions. It should be noted that, while psychologists vehemently, and sometimes viciously, debate the accuracy and validity of these new memories, it would be a serious presumptive error to think that all pre-existing memories are true, simply because they existed before treatment began. Memory is generally susceptible to interference and influence.

Certainly not all trauma/abuse treatment involves recovering memories; many clients arrive with memories, which can be influenced and altered by the Psychology Industry. The first task in therapy is to review these already existing memories and reinterpret them. The staring look of a stranger is no longer merely uncomfortable; it is unrecognized abuse. The embarrassing comment of a father, the touch of a baby-sitter, or the roughness of a physician's medical examination — all of these and many more can be transformed and identified as traumatic. Much of what the Psychology Industry does involves working with memories, giving them new meaning, new character, new emotions, and new importance. With the goal of reviewing and revising an existing memory, a typical hypnotic session might involve the following (in this case, the memory being addressed is an uncomfortable stare from a stranger. Note the suggestive assumptions that more was seen and felt than was at first remembered):

> While you rest right there in that chair, I want you to let your mind drift back, back in time, back to the time when that stranger stared at you and you felt uncomfortable. You can remember that. You can see him, see him almost as if he is right here, right now. And just look at him, listen to him and just listen to yourself, to your feelings and your thoughts.
>
> And for a moment, just watch him there. Look at that stare. Look at his eyes and notice what you see. They're not just looking at you are they? Look closely and see what else you can see. If those eyes could talk what would they say? And you don't see just his eyes. You can see his whole body, so just for a moment look at his body and notice what it is doing, what it is saying by what it is doing. Notice his shoulders, his hands, the way he stands there, his body. Just watch. Is he moving?
>
> And then, without letting your eyes off of him, listen. Listen to his voice. What does he say or not say? What would his voice be saying if it was talking out loud. Listen to what he is saying inside his head. It is so quiet that you can hear his thoughts if you really listen, can't you?
>
> And then, notice your feelings. What are you feeling? Pay attention to that feeling and let it grow so that you can feel it more clearly. Let yourself feel it all over your body. What else do you notice about that feeling? What does it want you to do? What would you feel if you did the opposite? Look under that feeling and see what other feeling is there? What else do you feel that you may not have been aware of. That's right, there is more, there are other feelings, different feelings, stronger feelings. Would it be all right to allow yourself to feel those feelings now? You are perfectly safe here and it is safe to have these feelings now.[110]

When such memories are less available or when the psychologist, as in Gondolf's case, is not satisfied and wants something more dramatic to work with, it may be necessary to resort to other suggestive means. For instance, Maltz, as mentioned earlier, directs people who can't remember to "spend some time *imagining that you were sexually abused*, without worry about accuracy or having your ideas make sense."

"I can't believe *that*," said Alice.
"Can't you?" the Queen said in a pitying tone.
"Try again; draw a long breath, and shut your eyes."

Lewis Carroll, *Through the Looking Glass*

Others give clients the instruction to "ground the experience or event in as much knowledge as you have and then let yourself *imagine what actually might have happened*."[111] Others rely on even more obviously coercive tactics. Cory Hammond, a well-known psychologist and past president of the American Society of Clinical Hypnosis, in lecturing to a training session for several hundred licensed psychotherapists on how to use hypnosis to retrieve memories of ritual abuse, said that after inducing hypnosis, he will typically say to a person: *"You know, I know a secret about you."*[112] Such a pronouncement presupposes abuse and directs the patient to find out the secret: when, how and by whom the abuse occurred.

Some psychologists, believing that these repressed memories are easily accessible through hypnosis, will simply ask the person what happened, who hurt them, how they were hurt. They accept the Psychology Industry theory that traumatic memories are stored differently than other memories; sealed away, compartmentalized and preserved in their original form, waiting for the safe moment to be accessed or opened. Others practice a hypnotically induced "age-regression," in which clients are led to believe that they are actually being taken back in time to their childhood. A typical hypnotic session intended to uncover abuse memories might include the following excerpts (note the repetition and subtle changes in the suggestions):

> As you sit there right now, right there in that chair, you can be aware of the feel of the chair and of the sound of my voice. At the same time you may notice that your mind drifts occasionally; sometimes to other sounds, sometimes to other feelings; some-times back into the back of your mind to other thoughts and other memories. That's perfectly natural. We all do that. We can be sitting in a meeting and find that although we seem to be listening, in fact, at times our mind is drifting. We know where we are and at the same time it is almost as if we can be some other place. Part of us is here and part of us can go some other place and yet we never lose track of where we are. You know what that is like. And right now as you sit right here, I would like you to consider the possibility that your mind could drift. It could drift back to yesterday; what you did, where you were, maybe even what you had for supper. That's right! It's all there. And in just the same way, memories rest at the back of your mind about what you did last week, last year, even years ago. Good memories and not so good. Happy memories and not so happy. And right now I would like you to let your mind just drift, and as you drift

> back into that chair, you can allow your mind to drift back, back into the back of your mind, back in time, back to other times and just let that other part of you remember what it already knows...

Frequently a mythical entity called by various names, such as "the Inner Child," the "Child Within," "the True Self," "the Unconscious" or "the Guide"[113] is called upon to assist in either "finding" the memories or in uncovering the traumatic feelings imbedded in them. Based on pseudo-philosophical theories of "the innocent child," this Inner Child is presumed to be the pure and undamaged being who existed before the trauma and who continues to reside somewhere inside the person's unconscious, trapped by a cruel external world but desperately wanting to come out and be known, nurtured and protected. "To find the Inner Child is part of every human being's journey toward wholeness" writes Bradshaw.[114]

Either in guided imagery, relaxation or hypnosis, this "homonculus" is called upon to tell its story, to describe its emotions, to identify its damage and to explain how and by whom it was abused. Since almost everyone has had the experience at one time or another of feeling childlike (e.g. playful, wild, scared, etc.), it is not difficult for a psychologist to persuade someone that a child or a childlike personality exists within, and that through such techniques as meditation or hypnosis, this child can be contacted and talked to.[115] Consider this example, adapted from a video-tape of a forensic hypnosis session:

> I'd like you to consider for a moment the fact that inside of you is a part of you that is like a parent. It is always telling you what you have to do. It may be telling you to go to work, or to pay a bill, or to phone somebody that you would rather not talk to. You know that feeling, that part.
>
> And at the same time, there is a part of you, a much younger part that likes to play, to have fun, to ride a bicycle. And sometimes that part is very brave and sometimes it gets scared. Sometimes it wants to laugh and sometimes it wants to cry but it doesn't want anybody to know about its crying. And you know that part. And it knows a lot of things.
>
> And I wonder if that part, that little boy/girl would be willing to talk to me for a little while? Would it feel safe enough to tell me what it knows that maybe you don't even know yet?

Still other psychologists count on "body memories" as the means to access memories of infantile abuse. It is generally accepted that young children lack the cognitive abilities for their minds to store memories. But victim-making psychologists believe that the body is able to store these memories even when the mind is unable to.[116] Smith reports that, in her survey of 38 psychologists specializing in sexual abuse recovery, 59% claimed that their clients experienced body memories and 95% of the therapists said it was common for memories to surface via body memories,[117] this despite the lack of any research evidence to support the theory.[118] Operating from this belief, many psychologists do "body work" in which they touch, massage or move the body while they pay attention to any reactions, memories or feelings that come to the client. Or they do "somatic bridging" in hypnosis, by asking clients to notice a feeling in the body and then let their minds follow that feeling back in time to another occasion when that feeling was stronger. One woman, who said that she felt physically uncomfortable sitting in the chair, "followed that body feeling back in time," eventually describing the pain in her bottom which was interpreted as an early act of anal penetration. Another woman whose reported experience of "blurry vision" and loss of the ability to read, was taken as proof that she was in the infant state, eventually felt a sense of suffocation which was seen as indicative of an episode of early infant molestation by her father.[119]

Thus, through the combination of biased interpretation, coercive suggestions, and recovered memories, many psychologically-prone people are persuaded that they have been victims of trauma or abuse.[120] Herman claims that "the traumatized person is often relieved simply to learn the true name of her condition. By ascertaining her diagnosis, she begins the process of mastery."[121] And for those who say: "This process is really dumb," or "This theory is too simplistic," or "Who says your way is the right way?," Chopich and Paul have a response; they describe these people as "clients who resist doing their inner work, who resist learning with and taking responsibility for their Child."[122] They declare them to be in danger of becoming the neglectful abusers of their Inner Children and probable perpetrators of future abuse against others.

While establishing the victim identity is the primary goal of this stage in manufacturing victims, an additional important factor is the creation of an environment that facilitates being a victim. Variously described as "developing a therapeutic alliance," "building a working relationship," or "creating safety," it refers to forming a way of relating in which the psychologist implicitly agrees not to challenge the "victim," while the client, in turn, accepts the role of relying, depending on, and accepting the direction and suggestion of the psychologist. The alliance is one in which there is an agreement to share the same ideas, the same beliefs, and the same understanding of the problem and process. To enhance this influence, ostensibly to "protect" the victim, the psychologist may recommend that any contact with family and friends be avoided unless they agree not to challenge the victim's beliefs or the reconstructed story,[123] and that alternative support be sought from self-help groups consisting of similarly victimized people; thereby isolating the victim and increasing the dependency on the Psychology Industry.

Adopting the victim identity and label, through memories, interpretation and naming, is only the beginning; it takes work and practice to learn the intricacies of being a victim, for as one of Hammond's patients said: "I don't have that many memories. I'm new at this diagnosis."[124] The key elements of the second stage in manufacturing are: recovering or re-experiencing more memories, reconstructing history, identifying loss and experiencing grief, and learning to feel and express anger and rage.[125]

"Memory Work," as it is called by the Psychology Industry, is not only necessary to encourage clients to believe, it is essential to reinforce the victim state. Herman describes it as "ambitious work. It requires some slackening of ordinary life demands, some 'tolerance for the state of being ill.' "[126] "The denial of an incest history must be broken through," Blume declares, "in order for healing to begin; one cannot recover from what one does not acknowledge and "breaking the secret" helps the survivor to acknowledge that she was unfairly harmed and is not a bad person... the more totally the previously buried traumas are uncovered and worked through, the deeper the recovery."[127] Herman agrees: "A narrative that does not include the traumatic imagery and bodily sensations is barren and incomplete."[128] In the Psychology Industry, there is a general consensus that memories, however they are arrived at, are requisite and the worse, the better.

To assist, psychologists rely on techniques that include hypnosis and age regression, relaxation and guided imagery (in which the images are believed to come from an inner world of facts), hearing and reading other victims stories (which "trigger" or inspire new memories), looking at family photos (for emotions which confirm abuse), and body work. The role of the psychologist is "to affirm a position of moral solidarity with the survivor," never questioning or doubting anything the person says. One victim is quoted as telling a psychologist: "Keep encouraging people to talk even if it's painful to watch them. It takes a long time to believe. *The more I talk about it, the more I have confidence that it happened*, the more I can integrate it. Constant reassurance is very important..."[129] Through repeated requests to remember "the story" and tell all of the details, and with unconditional and unquestioning acceptance by the psychologist, the greater becomes the certainty and the more hardened the memory, right or wrong. Johnson, in her research in memory, has found that the more that imaginary memories are like real sensory perceptions, the more subjects will actually confuse imagination with perception and think that they actually saw something that they had only seen in their imagination. And the more often they picture it in their minds, the more confident they become of the certainty of the event.[130]

Support groups serve an important role at this stage by applying their social influence and group pressure to affect memory production. According to a psychologist who works extensively with victims:

> The cohesion that develops in a trauma-focussed group enables participants to embark upon the tasks of remembrance and mourning. The group provides a powerful stimulus for the recovery of traumatic memories (or the fabrication of new ones). As each group member reconstructs her own narrative, the details of her story almost inevitably evoke new recollections in each of the listeners. In the incest survivor groups, *virtually every member who has defined a goal of recovering memories has been able to do so*. Women who feel stymied by amnesia are encouraged to tell as much of their story as they do remember. Invariably the group offers a fresh emotional perspective that provides a bridge to new memories.[131]

As well, the group's belief system can cause existing memories to be re-interpreted and rehearsed. Over thirty years ago, social psychologists identified the phenomenon of "group-think" which leads group members to conform to the ideas of the majority. As Hilgard describes it: "the mere assertion of majority opinion, without any effort to persuade, may lead *susceptible individuals* to agree with the majority even on a matter of fact on which individual judgment would lead to opposite conclusions."[132] Thus, the support groups, despite their label as "self-help," are vehicles of persuasion and conformity, and are central to the Psychology Industry's business of manufacturing victims.

For clients to become firmly set in their identity as victims, any prior sense of identity and trust must be shattered and replaced by a constructed life history of trauma, a story shadowed by fear and abuse. This "new past" will often be radically different from the one previously held, for "if you maintained the fantasy that your childhood was 'happy,' then you have to grieve for the childhood you thought you had," state Bass and Davis. "You must give up the idea that your parents had your best interests at heart... If you have any loving feelings toward your abuser, you must reconcile that love with the fact that he abused you... You may grieve over the fact that you don't have an extended family for your children, that you'll never receive an inheritance, that you don't have family roots." This revised history becomes the foundation for the victim's identity and future; a costly future as Nisbet predicts, for "without roots, human beings are condemned to a form of isolation in time that easily becomes self-destructive."[133]

Since this reconstructed story is inevitably sad, the perceiving and telling of the story invariably "plunges the victim into profound grief," which psychologists refuse to see for its destructive effect but rather as leading to "the necessity of mourning... in the resolution of traumatic life events." According to Herman, "failure to complete *the normal process of grieving* perpetuates the traumatic reaction" for which the "potential for pathological grief and severe, persistent depression is extremely high." And Blume adds further emphasis: "trauma theory addresses only part of the problem. Bereavement is necessary to address the other aspect of family trauma: the emotional loss suffered by the child... She grieves lost hopes, lost safety, lost innocence... Like the cognitive after-effects (of PTSD), grief is a normal and natural consequence of abuses such as incest."[134]

In the Psychology Industry's technical guidebook, grieving leads directly to anger: the next step in victim-fabrication. As Kubler-Ross noted, one aspect of grieving involves anger and, for the Psychology Industry, anger is extremely important; the feeling must be developed and targeted at the perceived perpetrator, the family or at anyone else deemed to have been complicit in the "crime." Clients are instructed that "to move... toward anger is one of the first steps towards healing,"[135] for "anger is the backbone of healing."[136] They are encouraged by psychologists to cultivate their rage:

A little like priming the pump, you can do things that will get your anger started. Then, once you get the hang of it, it'll begin to flow on its own... You may dream of murder or castration. It can be pleasurable to fantasize such scenes in vivid detail. Wanting revenge is a natural impulse, a sane response. Let yourself imagine it to your heart's content... Suing your abuser and turning him in to the authorities are just two of the avenues open... Another woman, abused by her grandfather, went to his deathbed and, in front of all the other relatives, angrily con-

> fronted him right there in the hospital... Create an anger ritual
> (burn an effigy on the beach)...Visualize punching and kicking
> the abuser when you do aerobics...You can be creative with your
> anger...You can heal with anger.[137]

Anger and rage lead into the third stage of the process, that of "empow-erment" through seeking public recognition and retribution as a victim. According to Herman, "the remedy for injustice also requires action."[138] Whether it is described as fighting back, getting even or seeking revenge, one major goal of feeling angry is to force others to confront the person's victim-status. The Psychology Industry offers three options: confrontation, law suits and social action. Since, by this time in the process, both the victim and the psychologist are convinced of the truth of the trauma, there is little hesitation about acting on the story as fact. Many are encouraged to confront their abuser as a means to gain this empowerment or control. They are told to "Go in, say what you need to say, and get out." Such condoned confron-tations involve such things as:

> A woman went to her grandfather's funeral and told each person
> at the grave site what he had done to her. In Santa Cruz,
> California, volunteers from Women Against Rape go with rape
> survivors to confront the rapist in his workplace. There they are,
> ten or twenty women surrounding a man, giving tangible sup-
> port to the survivor, as she names what he has done to her. This
> makes for *a dramatic and effective confrontation.*[139]

Another venue encouraged by the Psychology Industry for confrontation is the courts. "A lawsuit offers a survivor an opportunity to speak the truth about what happened, to break the silence. She is able to confront the person who abused her in a public forum, to seek *monetary compensation for therapy expenses*, lost income, and emotional distress, and to ensure that the abuser is confronted, in some way, with the effects of what he or she did."[140] Although psychologists claim that, "knowledge is power," what they actually mean is "accusations render others powerless, entangled in a web of legal process and psychological absurdities;" as illustrated by the Levy case (Chapter 2). Her-man endorses such legal action as a means of healing: "By making a public complaint or accusation, the survivor defies the perpetrator's attempt to silence and isolate her, and she opens the possibility of finding new allies... the survivor may come to understand her own legal battle as a contribution to a larger struggle, in which her actions may benefit others as well as herself."[141] While the overt and promoted benefits are incarcerated villains, vindicated victims and a revisioning of the legal system, the covert benefits are the further psychologizing of both the law and society and an expanded market for psychologists to plie their wares. As Bass and Davis admit, "what lawsuits are best able to do is to get money,"[142] and two of the major recipients of these funds are the lawyer and the psychologist who encourage and support the suit.

And the nation's courts of law have been psychologized to facilitate this "healing." Accused of being perpetrators and participants in "revictimization," the courts have modified the pursuit of truth to create a legal world where incest and sexual abuse no longer need to involve even touching let alone intercourse or lack of consent, and where the victim's interpretation of the perpetrator's design holds weight over the overt, expressed intention. The role of psychologists has become elevated so that it is they, and they alone, not the judge or the jury, who can interpret what a look or a comment meant, and what was in the mind of not only the perpetrator but also the victim. They do it for clients and they can do it for the courts. While Freud has fallen into disrepute, the courts and the law-makers have been persuaded by the Psychology Industry to imbed some of his concepts into law, blurring legal concepts such as "fact" and "consent" with vague notions of "recovered memories," and "transference." Just as "memories" have been used to "validate" trauma and incest, so too has "transference" been used to establish abuse. One of the advocates of this trend is Peter Rutter, a Jungian analyst, consultant and expert witness on "boundary issues," who views some of these psychologically determined laws "as wonderful because they use the language of transference. The concept of transference is actually recognized in most of the statutes as a very real element that undermines the notion of free consent."[143] According to Rutter, and the Psychology Industry, no longer can a woman function as a fully responsible and independent adult in any relationship with her lawyer, doctor, therapist, clergy, teacher, mentor, or other males, because "the man holds in trust the intimate, wounded, vulnerable, or undeveloped parts of the woman."[144] By this standard, women are considered to be naive, innocent and powerless, unable to assume the right and power to be responsible or self-determined. Although the stated goal of the Psychology Industry in manufacturing victims is "empowerment," its true effect is that of "disempowerment" — turning people into victims and women into children.

Rutter offers as an example of such a "victim," Beth, a psychotherapist in her forties, who became involved with her psychologist, and then much later regretted it. He quotes her as saying;

> I went to my third session with Dr. Adams with my raincoat on and nothing but underwear underneath. When it was time to go I took off my coat and rubbed up against him. He was kind of passive about it, but I could tell that he was going to let it keep happening. It just escalated from there... He looked good to me by contrast with my family. I could see he was attracted to me, and I wanted to make myself important to him. I was always looking for something else, and he was part of something else.[145]

In Rutter's eyes, this woman was a victim of rape. Her power to seduce or control this man was taken away from her and any pleasure she might have had was denied, erased from any existing memory she had of her own experience. By his reinterpretation of what happened, she was rendered childlike, powerless and not responsible for her actions; she was a victim of one of the Psychology Industry's most clearly authoritarian and offensively patriarchal creations, "therapy abuse."

The Psychology Industry operates a powerful technical process of victim-making. Sometimes the evoked emotionality of the users is mistaken for authenticity, and the emphatic statements of the psychologists for expertise, however, what their actions reflect is a simplistic process that ignores the individuality of people, the intricacies of thoughts and feelings, and the mysteries of the darker sides of life. Ganaway's image of the assembly-line seems fitting and raises other questions about the workers on the line.

Tailored (Taylored) Technicians

> *There is a serious dilemma occurring in our vocation and in our practice of helping people with their personal problems. The question is: are we training technicians or professionals?*

> Rollo May

The public's opinions and tastes are susceptible to commercial marketing whether it takes the form of direct advertising or involves indirect methods through association with events and individuals. For instance, the sale of Reese's Pieces, a chocolate and peanut butter candy, soared after the young boy in the movie ET was shown eating them. Similarly the public attitude about psychologists has been influenced by both direct and indirect advertising initiated by the industry. The American Psychological Association recently began a three quarter of a million dollar advertising campaign to create and shape public opinion about psychological services; they called it "educating the public." Although their specific goal was to stress the qualifications and expertise of licensed psychologists, setting them above others, the more likely effect will be to enhance the prestige of all psychologists regardless of their training or licensing. The public is more susceptible to overall impressions than specific facts, to labels more than descriptions of content, and is more likely to consider as the same, all those who call themselves psychologists or imply that they are. Studies, including APA's own recent survey, have shown that most people don't know the difference between psychiatrists, psychologists, psychotherapists and counsellors, and that they presume they are all generally qualified, if for no other reason than they say they are. But are they?

A serious investigation of this question would suggest that psychologists, regardless of what credentials they may or may not have, are NOT well trained, are often as badly off as their clients, apply their own values and ideas whether they are appropriate or not, don't know or acknowledge their own limitations, and get by either because they are just "nice people" or because they know how to play the role of "an authority and expert.'

Although the American Psychological Association claims that there is "value added when a mental health professional has at least a doctoral degree," this view expresses a bias which is neither supported by public opinion nor by empirical research. In response to the recent American Psychological Association survey, only 29 percent thought that a doctorate should be the minimum degree for treating depression, substance abuse or schizophrenia; 71% did not share APA's view. And Dawes, in reviewing the literature on therapist effectiveness, concluded that "there is no positive evidence supporting the efficacy of professional psychology."[146] If this is so, then one would wonder why the American Psychological Association argues differently, that psychology is "a recognized and valued component of mainstream health care."[147] The reason lies in society's move towards "Taylored" mental health.

As described in Chapter 3, Taylor, an early industrial psychologist, engineered the reorganization of industry, dividing work previously requiring skilled labour into its component parts so that workers no longer had knowledge or control over the whole manufacturing process, but rather, performed limited smaller tasks as part of a fixed and rigid process. Many of the effects of this Taylorism can now be seen within the Psychology Industry:

1. Just as unskilled workers were trained to perform specific tasks, breaking down the power of the guilds, so too have unskilled people been trained to carry out limited and narrowly defined psychological tasks. Where the psychology guilds of "the Four Professions" used to defend the view that breadth of knowledge and skill was essential to functioning as psychologists, now individuals are being trained, in government recognized courses and privately run workshops, to do abuse counselling, addiction counselling, crisis work, rape counselling and so on. No longer does one have to have extensive academic training or professional experience to be a child care worker or child protection officer, a psychometrist, behaviour therapist or intake worker. And if one can find a niche, one can be a Recovered Memory therapist, a Satanic Ritual Abuse therapist, a Relocation counsellor, a Victim Services worker, an Assertiveness trainer, a Traumatologist; and the list goes on.

2. As Taylorism increased the dependency of workers and the power of management, resulting in workers being unable to leave the Company and go into business for themselves, similarly these new Psychology Industry technicians are limited to their defined task and have nowhere else that they can go. While some, like intake workers or psychometrists, depend on their places within a health service organization, others rely on a continuing supply of clients who need their service. Abuse workers need abused individuals, relocation counsellors need fired employees, and assertiveness trainers need passive people. They lack the skills and freedom to leave their positions and do something else.

3. The economic effect of Taylorism was to lower the cost of labour. Unskilled people could be easily and economically trained, replacing the more expensive skilled workers. And the same possibility greatly concerns the licensed psychologists and psychiatrists who see their earning power being threatened and reduced as aggressive psychological entrepreneurs compete for their business by offering similar services at lower rates. Consumers can now get therapy from abuse or addiction "specialists"

for much less than it would cost them to see a licensed psychologist. Even HMO's, Managed Care facilities and school boards, seeing this a means of lowering health care costs, have hired these workers and/or invited psychologists, who previously billed for services, to put in "bids" for referrals and business.

4.   And Taylorism removed the workers' ability to influence production, making each worker, in Taylor's words, "a mere automaton, a wooden man."[148] Critical thinking and a sense of responsibility for the final product was done away with, as the ability to carry-out repetitive behaviour was valued over skill and intelligence. Probably no where is this effect currently more evident within the Psychology Industry than in the simplistic, repetitive "steps" of the various recovery movements. Just as General Motors and Chrysler copied the assembly-line process of Ford, so have the various recovery therapies copied the "Twelve Steps" production process of AA, turning out victims as fast as Ford does cars. "The American treatment of alcoholism follows a standard formula that appears impervious to emerging research evidence (which shows no evidence of effectiveness), and has not changed significantly for at least two decades."[149] The process is structured and rigid and there is little room for variation, improvement, or innovation. The recovery process and that of most psychological services have become Taylored rather than tailored to the needs of the individual.

Although many traditional psychologists resist the loss of their monopolistic power and protest the reduction in their earning potential, the door has been opened that allows those with limited skills, limited training and even limited ability to be psychologists. In previous times, a "specialist" was someone with specialized skills that came from added training *after* broad general training; and the public came to expect and presume that these specialists offered more because they had both the general and the advanced, specific knowledge. However, "Taylored psychology specialists" are different. They have a limited focus without the general training; they know less not more. As Rollo May suspected, they are technicians disguised as professionals. Trained to see only through the blindered eyes of their particular focus, they are often unable to grasp the "larger picture" or to consider alternative diagnoses or treatments. Clients' problems are fitted to their limited skills, redefined according to their area of practice, and "labelled" with their particular approach in mind. Spiegel is even more outspoken when he says "...the role of therapists in this whole phenomenon of multiple personality and victimization is more intriguing than the patients themselves. The therapists, with some exceptions, have become unconscious con artists. They are taking highly malleable, suggestible persons and molding them into acting out a thesis that they are putting upon them."[150]

Consider the following testimon offered before a Hearing into "Violence and Abuse within the Family: The Neglected Issues," sponsored by a Canadian Senator:

In various legal contexts where abuse was the issue, evidence would be offered (in court) such as: the child was shy in the presence of the father, and that is indicative of child abuse. The child bed wet. The child's marks in school fell, or the marks rose; if they fell it was fear, if they rose it was because the school was an escape from the abuse. Either way, that was evidence of abuse.

It becomes obvious that no matter what was observed, it was consistent with abuse. So you ask: "What is inconsistent with abuse?," and the answer always is: "Well, nothing is inconsistent with abuse." In fact, since most abused victims do not show any aftermath, the lack of symptoms itself is consistent with abuse. This is truly like falling into some kind of rabbit hole, like Alice in Wonderland. These "child abuse experts" all share several things in common: first, they know nothing about science: they have no appreciation for concepts like "control groups," to make sure that suspected differences are objectively real and statistically significant: they have no idea at all that to learn something about a group, you have to study the "not" group. Someone who only studies horses would tell you that the next creature with four legs is a horse because that's the only creature with four legs they have studied. And as a result, a lot of dogs will get saddled up in error."[151]

Even some licensing boards have fallen prey to this trend by issuing licenses for limited scopes of practice to individuals with less training. They expect these licensees to "self-regulate," in other words, to restrict themselves from going beyond their skills; an amazingly foolish assumption by people who claim to understand human nature.[152]

Who are these "Taylored" psychologists, these limited experts, these mental health technicians? Williams, a psychologist, argues that some of them are the bait-and-switch operators who feed off of the public's assumptions and misperceptions about psychologists, hooking them into treatment based on false expectations and then switching them over to the Psychology Industry technology.

Jay Schadler, a journalist, after watching hypnotists and recovered memory specialists at work, thinks that "some...may be as sick as their patients,"[153] perhaps drawn into the business because of their own problems.

Alan Gold, a lawyer, who has been cross-examining psychologists in court for twenty years, thinks that some may lack the intelligence necessary to succeed in other fields. According to "Gold's Law," "the "softer" the area of alleged expertise, the easier it is for dumbness to survive." Citing Syke's book, *Dumbing Down Our Kids: Why American Children Feel Good About Themselves But Can't Read, Write or Add*, he continues: "Dumbness does not last long in some industries, for example aircraft construction, where its mistakes crash and burn." However, in the Psychology Industry, mistakes go unnoticed, failures are forgotten, and "feeling good" is considered more important than thinking straight; all reasons Gold sees for "why a growing population of high school educated 'dummies' gravitate to therapy as a 'profession.' "[154] He offers hundreds of case studies and court transcripts to support his theory.

While the Psychology Industry would vehemently deny such a theory, Schadler is likely among the growing number outside the industry who might agree with Gold. His televised interview of a psychologist who uses hypnosis to uncover memories of SRA, illustrates well the basis of Gold's theory. In the excerpt below, Schadler is shown on screen, talking with a psychologist ("DR."), while a videotape is simultaneously being shown of "DR." doing hypnosis with a client, "Vanessa." She had initially sought help for depression and eating disorders, but with "DR's" hypnotherapy, she had begun to "remember" episodes of sexual abuse which evolved into vivid recollections of satanic rituals:

SCHADLER (describing the situation to viewers): Her therapist presses ahead using an assortment of mysterious code words.

"DR." (to "Vanessa" in hypnosis): "Priority level."

SCHADLER: (voice-over) He's looking for a response.

"DR.": "Priority level."

SCHADLER (asks "Dr."): For example , what kind of reaction?

"DR.": If their eyes roll up and their eyes flutter, and then an alter personality comes out behaving like a robot.

SCHADLER: Then you know you're on the trail to ritual abuse.

"DR.": Well, I don't know of any other way to account for it.

"DR." (speaking to "Vanessa"): *Hello, Satan? Hello, Satan.*

"VANESSA": Hi,

"DR.": Hi, how are you?

"VANESSA": Pretty good.

SCHADLER (to the "DR."): You called up a lot of personalities—

"DR.": Yeah.

SCHADLER:— on "Vanessa."

"DR.": Yeah.

SCHADLER: You called up Satan.

"DR.": Right

SCHADLER: He's pretty easy to talk to?

"DR.": *Vanessa's Satan seems like a pretty friendly guy to me.*[155]

Undoubtedly, these comments left Schadler and many of the thousands of viewers dumbstruck over this therapist's "dumbness." And his demonstration gives further support for Gold's contention that psychologists know and understand less, not more.

This leaves one wondering, if some are "slick," and some are "sick" and some are "dumb," how are these Taylored psychologists able to function and, in doing so, persuade people of their importance and authority.

The work of Carkhuff sheds some light on the first issue.[156] In his research with Berenson and Truax, he found that the "core" ingredients that made effective professional helpers were empathy, respect and genuineness; that is, those features found in good friendships. They understood these qualities to exist at differing levels in counsellors, which would either facilitate (called Levels 4 and 5) or limit (Levels 1 and 2) their ability to help. And, taking a somewhat more optimistic position than Schadler and Gold, Carkhuff believed that these qualities could be developed or improved through technical skill-training. Although this research and writing was carried out in the late 60's, their work remains relevant in light of the previously cited research suggesting that education, training and experience do not improve the outcome of psychotherapy. In fact, and in support of the Taylorised approach to psychology, Carkhuff took the position that graduate academic training and education impeded effective counselling, and that individuals with little to no training in psychology, but with training in specific counselling skills, could be good helpers.

Although psychological technicians seem to be the way of the future for the Psychology Industry, the public continues to view psychologists as experts, setting them apart as authorities. Much could be written about psychologists playing this role of authority. The inducement towards impostering can be found in the professionally promoted notion that psychologists have superior knowledge, and in their own words, that they "are experts in living." Kottler in his book, *On Being A Therapist*, writes: "Therapists have become the contemporary equivalent of the oracle perched on a mountaintop; clients are the pilgrims who journey in search of enlightenment. Mistrusting their own inner voices and lacking self-direction, clients look to their gurus for guidance and see them as embodiments of power to worship."[157] And from his book, *The Compleat Therapist*: "It has become clear... that it hardly matters which theory is applied or which techniques are selected in making a therapy hour helpful... What does matter is who the therapist is as a human being—for what every successful healer has had since the beginning of time is charisma and power."[158]

Probably nothing describes the psychologist, the "Taylored technician," and the whole of the Psychology Industry better than the words of T.S. Eliot:

> *Half of the harm that is done in this world*
> *Is due to people who want to feel important*
> *They don't mean to do harm— but the harm does not interest them.*
> *Or they do not see it, or they justify it*
> *Because they are absorbed in the endless struggle*
> *To think well of themselves.*[159]

Endnotes

1. This term is not meant to suggest a clinical entity or syndrome (which might then be seen as fair game for another psychological technique) but rather is used to identify that portion of the population most amenable to the approaches and methods of the Psychology Industry and thus, the target group of the industry.

2. Thomas Wolfe, "The 'Me' decade." *New York*, 8/23/76, p.30.

3. Strupp, Hans, H. "Needed: A reformulation of the psychotherapeutic influence." *International Journal of Psychiatry*, 26, March, 1972, pp.270-278.

4. In 1785, Benjamin Franklin headed a Royal Commission for the King of France, responsible for investigating Mesmerism. Their conclusion was that mesmeric effects were due to *suggestion* rather than magnetic fluids.

5. Slaby, Andrew E. *Aftershock: Surviving the Delayed Effects of Trauma, Crisis and Loss.* New York: Villard Books, 1989.

6. Ibid. pp.4-5.

7. Ibid. p.217 (the last page of the book).

8. Frank. *Persuasion and Healing.* (1973), p. 216.

9. Calestro, Kenneth M. "Psychotherapy, faith healing and suggestion." *International Journal of Psychiatry*, 10, 1972, pp.83-113. See, also, Whitman, Roy M. "Which dreams does the patient tell:" *Archives of General Psychiatry*, 8, 1963, pp.277-282.

10. Welkowitx, J., Cohen, J. and Ortmeyer, D. "Value system similarity: Investigation of patient-therapist dyads." *Journal of Consulting Psychology*, 31, 1967, pp.48-55.

11. Rosenthal, D. "Changes in some moral values following psychotherapy." *Journal of Consulting Psychology*, 19, 1955, pp.431-436.

12. For example, Jean Marie Charcot, a French neurologist, believed that hypnosis was very similar to hysteria and that both were the result of a diseased nervous system.

13. For example, Hippolyte-Marie Bernheim, a French physician, who wrote *Hypnotism and Suggestion in Psychotherapy.*

14. Like many personality traits, hypnotizability appears to conform to a "normal distribution" or bell curve.

15. For more information about hypnosis, see Fromm, Erika, and Shor, Ronald E. *Hypnosis: Developments in Reserach and New Perspectives.* New York: Aldine Pubishing, 1972 (revised 1979); Bowers, Kenneth S. *Hypnosis for the Seriously Curious.* New York: W.W. Norton, 1976; Lynn, Stephen Jay, and Rhue, Judith W. (eds.) *Theories of Hypnosis: Current Models and Perspectives.* New York: The Guilford Press, 1991.

16. See Hilgard, E. R. *Divided Consciousness: Multiple Controls in Human Thought and Action.* (expanded edition) New York: Wiley, 1986.

17. Lynn, S. J. & Rhue, J.W. "Fantasy-proneness: Hypnosis, developmental antecedents, and psychopathology." *American Psychologist*, 43, 1988, pp.35-44.

18. Maltz, Wendy. *The Sexual Healing Journey: A Guide for Survivors of Sexual Abuse.* San Francisco: HarperCollins, 1992.

19. See Zelig, M. and Beidleman, W. "The investigative use of hypnosis: A word of caution." *International Journal of Clinical and Experimental Hypnosis*, 29. 1981, pp.401-412.

20. Bryant, Richard A. "Fantasy-proneness, reported childhood abuse, and the relevance of reported abuse onset." *International Journal of Clinical and Experimental Hypnosis*, 43, 1995, pp.184-193.

21. Curiously, three participants who reported being abused before the age of three, were dropped from the study "because memories of such an early age cannot be regarded as reliable." The author stresses that their omission "does not imply that these reports were false," the implication being that the remaining are true.

22. Bowers, K.S. "Sex and susceptibility as moderator variables in the relationship of creativity and hypnotic susceptibility." *Journal of Abnormal Psychology*, 78, 1971, pp.93-100.

23. The *Consumers Report* survey discussed in Chapter 4 which gave psychotherapy such a high consumer satisfaction rating likely targeted as a sample the psychologically-prone.

24. Kardiner, Abram. *My Analysis with Freud.* New York: Norton, 1977. p.75.

25. Saul Bellow in his Foreword to Allan Bloom's *The Closing of the American Mind.* New York: Touchstone Books (Simon and Schuster), 1987.

26. Bloom. *The Closing of the American Mind.* p. 360.

27. Holmes, T. H., and Rahe, R. H. The Social Readjustment Rating Scale. *Journal of Psychosomatic Research.* 1967, 11, pp.213-218.

28. For reviews, see: Miller, Thomas W. (Ed.) *Stressful Life Events.* Madison, Conn: International Universities Press, Inc., Stress and Health Series, Monograph 4, 1989; Stone, G.C., Cohen, F, and Adler, N.E. *Health Psychology— A Handbook.* San Francisco: Jossey-Bass Publishers, 1979, pp.77-111; Dohrenwend Barbara S., and Dohrenwend, Bruce P. "Some issues in research on

stressful life events." In Millon, Theodore, Green, Catherine, and Meagher, Robert (Eds.) *Handbook of Clinical Health Psychology*. New York: Plenum Press, 1982, pp.91-102; and Dohrenwend, Barbara S., Krasnoff, Lawrence, Askenasy, Alexander R., and Dohrenwend, Bruce P. "The psychiatric epidemiology research interview life events scale." In Goldberger Leo, and Breznitz, Shlomo (eds.). *Handbook of Stress: Theoretical and Clinical Aspects*. New York: The Free Press, 1982. pp.332-363.

29. It is interesting that psychologists refer to their psychological tests as "tools," consistent with the industrial approach of the Psychology Industry.

30. Friedman, M, and Rosenman, R. H. *Type A Behavior and Your Heart*. New York: Knopf, 1974.

31. Rosenman, R. H. and Chesney, M. A. "Type A behavior and coronary heart disease." In C. D. Spielberger, I. G. Sarason, and P. B. Defares, (eds.) *Stress and Anxiety*, Vol. 9. Washington, D.C.: Hemisphere, 1985. pp.207-229; G.D. Jenkins, Rosenman, R.H., and Zysanski, S. J. Prediction of clinical coronary heart disease by a test for coronary-prone behavior patterns. *New England Journal of Medecine*. 1974, 290, pp.1271-1275.

32. Plous, Scott. *The Psychology of Judgment and Decision-Making*. New York: McGraw, 1993. pp.162-167; and Piattelli-Palmarini, Massimo. *Inevitable Illusions: How Mistakes of Reason Rule Our Mind*. New York: John Wiley and Son, 1994. pp.120-123. Piattelli-Palmarini describes this as one of "the seven deadly sins." Also, Dawes, Robyn. *Rational Choice in an Uncertain World* (San Francisco: Collins, 1988); Sutherland, Stuart. *Irrationality: Why We Don't Think Straight*. (New Brunswick, NJ: Rutgers University Press, 1994; Schick, Theodore, and Vaughn, Lewis. *How to Think about Weird Things: Critical Thinking for a New Age*. (Mountain View, CA: Mayfield Publ., 1994) ; and Katzer, Jeffrey, et al. *Evaluating Information: A Guide for Users of Social Science Research*. (New York: McGraw, 1991.)

33. Dantzer, Robert. *The Psychosomatic Delusion: Why the Mind is Not the source of All Our Ills*. New York: The Free Press, 1993 (Originally published in French, 1989). p.153.

34. Matthew, K. A. "Coronary heart disease and Type A behaviors: Update on an alternative to the Booth-Kewley and Friedman (1987) quantitative review." *Psychological Bulletin*, 1988, 104. pp.373-380.

35. Ragland, D. R. and Brand, R. J. "Type A behavior and mortality from coronary heart disease." *New England Journal of Medicine*. 1988, 318, pp.66-69.

36. Parloff, Morris. Cited in Gross. *The Psychological Society*. p.30.

37. *Rapport*, 2 (1), April 1994. p.8.

38. A study by Mark Hlatky and others, published in *Circulation*, August 1995.

39. Kirkpatrick, R. A. "Witchcraft and lupus erythematosus." *Journal of the American Medical Association*, 1985, 245, p.1937.

40. Spiegel, David. *Living Beyond Limits: New Hope and Help for Facing Life-Threatening Illness*. New York: Times Books (Random House), 1993.

41. This idea had existed in psychology prior to the Simontons, including the work of Lawrence LeShan; *You Can Fight for Your Life: Emotional Factors in the Causation of Cancer* (1977); *Cancer As A Turning Point: A Handbook for People with Cancer, Their Families and Health Professionals* (New York: Dutton, 1990).

42. *Getting Well Again* was the title and thesis of the Simontons' first book. (Simonton, O. Carl, Matthews-Simonton, Stephanie, and Creighton, James L. *Getting Well Again: The New Bestseller about the Simontons' Life-saving Self-awareness Techniques*. Los Angeles: Jeremy P. Tarcher, 1978.)

43. For example, Bernie Siegel, author of *Love, Medicine and Miracles: Lessons learned about Self-Healing from a Surgeon's Experience with Exceptional Patients*. (San Fransisco: HarperCollins, 1990) and *Peace, Love and Healing: Bodymind Communications and the Path to Self-Healing: An Exploration*. (San Fransisco: HarperCollins, 1990.)

44. Dantzer. *The Psychomatic Delusion*. p.22.

45. For example; Kelly, Sean F., and Kelly, Reid J. *Imagine Yourself Well: Better Health through Self-Hypnosis*. New York: Plenum Publ., 1995.

46. Cynthia Bellar, a clinical and health professor at the University of Florida Health Science Center. Cited in the *The APA Monitor*, October 1995, p.18.

47. Kubler-Ross, Elizabeth. *On Death and Dying*. New York: Alfred Knopf, 1981.

48. Slaby, Andrew E. *Aftershock: Surviving the Delayed Effects of Trauma, Crisis and Loss*. New York: Villard Books, p.26.

49. Wortman and Silver. *Journal of Consulting and Clinical Psychology*, Vol.57 (1989) pp.349-357.

50. Pennebaker, James W. *Opening Up: The Healing Power of Confiding in Others*. New York: William Morrow & Co., 1990. p.97.

51. Stroebe, Margaret and Wolfgang. *Handbook of Bereavement: Theory, Research, and Intervention*. Cambridge: Cambridge Press, 1993.

52. "Good Grief! The Case for Repression." by Emily Nussbaum, *Lingua Franca*, Oct.1997. pp.48-51.

53. Ibid. p.49.

54. Ibid. p.49.

55. Quackenbush, Jamie. *When Your Pet Dies: How to Cope With Your Feelings*. N.Y.: Simon & Schuster, 1985. Quotes were taken from the jacket cover.

56. Matsakis, Aphrodite. *I Can't Get Over It: A Handbook for Trauma Survivors*. Oakland, CA: New Harbinger Press, 1992.

57. Ibid. pp.196-197.

58. Ibid. p.201.

59. Slaby. *Aftershock*. p.22. Citing Scrignar, C. B. *Post-Traumatic Stress Disorder*.

60. *Ibid*. p.23.

61. Borch-Jacobsen, Mikkel. "Sybil - The making of a disease: An interview with Dr. Herbert Spiegel." *The New York Review*, 24, 1997. p.62.

62. Huber. *Galileo's Revenge*. p.34.

63. See Weatherhead, L.D. *Psychology, Religion and Healing*. New York: Abingdon Press, 1952 (revised edition). pp.122-128.

64. Brooks, Harry. *The Practice of Autosuggestion by the Method of Emile Coue*. (1922) Cited in Szasz. *The Myth of Psychotherapy*. p.187.

65. Bergin, Allen and Garfield, Sol L. (eds.) *Handbook of Psychotherapy and Behavioral Change: An Empirical Analysis*. New York: J. Wiley, 1971 (4th ed. 1993) p.827.

66. Peele. *Diseasing of America*. p.4.

67. Holden, C. "The neglected disease in medical education." *Science*, 1985, 229, pp.741-742.

68. Conrad, Peter, and Schneider, Joseph W. *Deviance and Medicalization: From Badness to Sickness*. St. Louis, Missouri: C.V. Mosby, 1980. p.viii.

69. A publication of Straight Inc. Cited by Peele. *Diseasing of America*, p.51.

70. Damon, Janet E. *Shopaholics: An 8-week Program to Control Compulsive Shopping*. New York: Avon Books, 1988. p. 3 and jacket cover.

71. *Star Trek* fans are like drug addicts who suffer withdrawal symptoms if deprived of their favourite television show, a British study suggest. Psychologist Sandy Wolfson is quoted as saying: "My research found that about five to ten percent of fans met the psychological criteria of addiction."

72. Psychologist Marvin Steinberg says "the stock-market frenzy of the last few years has brought out unhealthy tendencies. Some people may now have an addiction to the market every bit as dangerous as compulsive gambling at casinos or racetracks." *The Canadian Press*, June 6, 1997.

73. Peele. *Diseasing of America.*, p.51.

74. Rudy, D. *Becoming Alcoholic: Alcoholics Anonymous and the Reality of Alcoholism*. Carbondale, IL: Southern Illinois University Press, 1986.

75. Peele. *Diseasing of America*. p.91.

76. "Unite and Conquer." *Newsweek*, Feb. 5, 1990, p.50.

77. M. Freudenheim, "Business and Health: Acknowleding substance abuse." *New York Times*, 13/12/1988, p.D2.

78. Peele. *Diseasing of America.* p.52.

79. An unpublished study by the Addiction Research Foundation of Ontario, Toronto, Canada; by sociologist Sandra Aylward, 1994.

80. Rutter, Peter. *Sex in The Forbidden Zone: When Men in Power— Therapists, Doctors, Clergy, Teachers, and Others— Betray Women's Trust.* New York: Fawcett Crest, 1989. p.197.

81. *Caring*, Fall 1985.

82. "The Its-Not-My-Fault Syndrome." *US News and World Report*, 18 June 1990, p.16.

83. Miller, Alice. *Thou Shalt Not Be Aware: Society's Betrayal of the Child*. (Trans. by Hildegarde and Hunter Hannum). New York: Farrar, Strauss, Giroux, 1984. pp.316-317.

84. Miller, Alice. *Banished Knowledge: Facing Childhood Injuries.* Trans. by Leile Vennewitz. New York: Doubleday, 1990. See pp.181-189.

85. This view is at odds with Freud's personal explanation of the events as described in his autobiography: "Under the pressure of the technical procedure which I used at the time, the majority of my patients reproduced from their childhood scenes in which they were sexually seduced by some grown-up person. With female patients that part of seducer was almost always assigned to their father. I believed these stories, and consequently supposed that I had discovered the roots of the subsequent neurosis in these experiences of sexual seduction in childhood. My confidence was strengthened by a few cases in which relations of this kind with a father, uncle or elder brother had continued up to an age at which memory was to be trusted. If the reader feels inclined to shake his head at my credulity, I cannot altogether blame him; though I may plead that this was at a time when I was intentionally keeping my critical faculty in abeyance so as to preserve an unprejudiced and receptive attitude towards the many novelties which were coming to my notice every day. When, however, I was at last obliged to recognize that these scenes of seduction had never taken place, and that they were only phantasies which my patients had made up or which I myself had perhaps forced upon them, I was for some time completely at a loss. My confidence alike in my technique and in its results suffered a severe blow..." Freud, Sigmund. *An Autobiographical Study*. James Strachey (trans.) London: Leonard and Virginia Woolf, The Institute of Psycho-Analysis, 1936. pp.60-61.

86. Some have even stated that it was done to help Freud deny his own abuse at the hands of his father, and have argued that his later cocaine use is evidence of this. See Sylvia Fraser. "False Memory." *Saturday Night,* March 1994, pp. 19-21 and 56-59.

87. Bradshaw, John. *The Family—A Revolutionary Way of Self-Discovery.* Deerfield Beach, Florida: Health Communications, Inc., 1987.

88. Dolan, Yvonne M. *Resolving Sexual Abuse: Solution-Focused Therapy and Ericksonian Hypnosis for Adult Survivors.* New York: W.W. Norton and Co., 1991. p. 5.

89. Blume, E. Sue. *Secret Survivors: Uncovering Incest and Its Aftereffects in Women.* New York: John Wiley and Son, 1990. p.78.

90. "Psychiatric Residents Show Signs of Post-Traumatic Stress." *Psychiatric News*, August 6, 1993. pp. 7 and 20. In a national survey of 212 residents, 26% of the psychiatric residents reported PTSD symptoms, with women having a higher overall rate (20%) than men (9%). Curiously the emergency medicine residents did not meet the criteria for PTSD.

91. Scrignar, C. B. *Post-Traumatic Stress Disorder: Diagnosis, Treatment and Legal Issues*. New York: Bruno Press, 1988. pp.66-73.

92. Ibid. pp.74-78.

93. In *The Heart Attack Prevention Recovery Handbook* (Vancouver: Hatley and Marks, 1995), Glen Elliot suggests that "if you survived a heart attack... you may find your memory and concentration impaired from stress, related to a 'post-traumatic stress disorder,' commonly called burn-out syndrome."

94. Bass and Davis, *Courage to Heal: A Guide for Women Survivors of Child Sexual Abuse.* New York: Harper and Row, 1988. Reprinted by HarperPerennial, 1994. p.513.

95. For more, see: Herman. *Trauma and Recovery.* p.45; Bessel A. van der Kolk. *Psychological Trauma.* Washington, D.C.: American Psychiatric Press, 1987; Goodwin, Jean. "Credibility problems in Multiple Personality Disorder patients and abused children." In *Childhood Antecedents of Multiple Personality Disorder,* Richard Kluft (ed.). Washington, D.C.: American Psychiatric Press, 1985.

96. Blume. *Secret Survivors.* p.81.

97. Bass and Davis, *Courage to Heal.* p.14.

98. Cited in "Lies of the Mind." *Time,* November 29, 1993, p.57.

99. For example, Friesen, James G. *Uncovering the Mystery of MPD— Its Shocking Origins... Its Surprising Cure.* San Bernardino, CA.: Here's Life Publishers, 1991.

100. Herman, Judith Lewis. *Trauma and Recovery: The Aftermath of Violence— From Domestic Abuse to Political Terror.* New York: Basic Books, 1992 (has three stages); Crowder, Adrienne. *Opening the Door: A Treatment Model for Therapy With Male Survivors of Sexual Abuse.* Ottawa, Ont.: National Clearinghouse on Family Violence, 1993 (identifies 4 stages); Brown, D. B., and Fromm, E. *Hypnotherapy and Hypnoanalysis.* Hillsdale, NJ: Lawrence Erlbaum, 1986 (identify five stages); and Putnam, F.W. *Diagnosis and Treatment of Multiple Personality Disorder.* New York: Guilford Press, 1989, and Whitfield, Charles L. *Healing the Child Within: Discovery and Recovery for Adult Children of Dysfunctional Families.* Deerfield Beach, Florida: Health Communications, Inc., 1987 (describes eight stages in recovery).

101. Williams, M. H. "The bait-and-switch tactic in psychotherapy." *Psychotherapy.* 1985, 22, pp.110-113.

102. Ibid. p.111.

103. For example, regarding personal behaviour and experience, see Haugaard, J. J., Reppucci, N. D., Laurd, J., & Nauful, T. "Children's definitions of the truth and their competency as witnesses in legal proceedings." *Law and Human Behavior,* 1991, 15, pp.253-272; Abelson, R. P., Loftus, E. F., & Greenwald, A. G. "Attempts to improve the accuracy of self-reports of voting." J. M. Tanur (ed.) *Questions about Survey Questions: Meaning, Memory, Expression, and Social Interactions in Surveys.* New York: Russell Sage, 1992. pp.138-153; regarding violent crime, see Pynoos, R. S., & Nader, K. "Children's memory and proximity to violence." *Journal of American Academy of Children and Adolescent Psychiatry,* 1989, 28, pp.236-241; and regarding childhood trauma, see Loftus, E. F. "The reality of repressed memories." *American Psychologist,* 1993, 48. pp.518-537; and Garry, Maryanne and Loftus, E. F." Pseudomemories without hypnosis." *International Journal of Clinical and Experimental Hypnosis,* 1994, 42 (4), pp.363-378.

104. Dawes. *House of Cards.* p.125.

105. Blume. *Secret Survivors.* pp. xviii-xx.

106. Whitfield. *Healing the Child Within.* p.3-4.

107. Marie, Jan. 31 Symptoms of Physical, Emotional and Sexual Trauma. Cited by Smith, Susan E. "Body memories: And other pseudo-scientific notions of 'survivor psychology.' " *Issues in Child Abuse Accusations,* 5 (4), 1993, pp.220-234.

108. Elgin, Suzette Haden. *You Can't Say That to Me!: Stopping the Pain of Verbal Abuse—An 8-Step Program.* New York: John Wiley & Sons, 1995. back cover and p.186.

109. Cited in "Lies of the Mind." *Time,* November 29, 1993. p.57.

110. Provided by a psychologist highly qualified in the field of hypnosis for memory recall.

111. Bass and Davis. *Courage to Heal.* p.154.

112. "Devilish Deeds." ABC News Primetime Live, January 7, 1993. (Transcript #279)

113. The terminology of John Bradshaw, Charles Whitfield, Alice Miller, many hypnotists, and Sue Blume, respectively.

114. Bradshaw, John. *Bradshaw On: Healing the Shame that Binds You.* Deerfield Beach, Florida: Health Communications, 1988.

115. Some psychologists, like Dolan (Dolan, Yvonne. *Resolving Sexual Abuse: Solution-focused Therapy and Ericksonian Hypnosis for Adult Survivors.* New York: W.W. Norton and Co., 1991. pp.144-148), rely on "ideomotor signalling," to communicate with this unconscious entity. In

hypnosis, they ask questions that can be answered yes or no (i.e. leading or suggestive questions) and ask that the "unconscious" answer by moving one of two fingers previously identified as "YES" and "NO." These psychologists presume that non-verbal answers are more accurate because they don't involving verbalizing and are less susceptible to conscious interference. There is no support for this theory.

116. See Bass and Davis. *Courage to Heal*. 1988; Blume. *Secret Survivors*. 1990; Frederickson, Renee. *Repressed Memories—A Journey to Recovery from Sexual Abuse*. New York: A Fireside/Parkside Book, Simon and Schuster, 1992.

117. Smith, Susan. *Survivor Psychology: The Dark Side of a Mental Health Mission.*Boca Raton, FL: Upton Books, 1995. p.19.

118. Smith cites Bill Lawren as calling the molecular memory theory one of the ten "greatest hoaxes of the 1980's." p.26.

119. Described on "I Can't Hide My Painful Secrets Anymore." The Sally Jessy Raphael Show, October 22, 1992. (Transcript #1078)

120. Lee Coleman, in "Creating 'memories' of sexual abuse." *Issues of Child Abuse Allegations*, 1992, 4 (4), pp.169-176, provides an "analysis of a case of alleged recovered memories of sexual abuse... to illustrate how such mental images can be created in therapy."

121. Herman. *Trauma and Recovery*. p.158.

122. Chopich, Erika J., and Paul, Margaret. *Healing Your Aloneness: Finding Love and Wholeness Through Your Inner Child*. San Francisco: HarperCollins, 1990. p.114.

123. In *Sullivan v. Cheshire*, the Illinois court judge concluded that a jury could decide that the psychologist's conduct, especially his instruction to his patient to break contact with her parents if they disagreed with her memory, could be a basis for a liability action.

124. Stated on ABC News Primetime Live, January 7, 1993.

125. Since Freud and Breuer conceived their model of trauma, abreaction/catharsis has been a major component of most psychological treatment approaches to trauma. Abreaction grew out of their notion that problems were the result of an inability to react fully at the time of the trauma, and that "putting the affect into words" dissipated the emotion attached to the memory. Breuer, J. & Freud, S. Studies in hysteria: On the psychical mechanisms of hysterical phenomena: Preliminary communication. In Strachey, J. (ed. and trans.) *Standard Edition of the Complete Psychological Works of Sigmund Freud*. London: Hogarth Press, 1955. Vol.2, pp. 3-17 (Original work published 1893.)

126. Herman. *Trauma and Recovery*. p.176.

127. Blume. *Secret Survivors*. p.106.

128. Herman, p.177; concurring with McCann, L. and Pearlman, L. *Psychological Trauma and the Adult Survivor: Theory, Therapy and Transformation*. New York: Brunner/Mazel, 1990.

129. Herman. *Trauma and Recovery*. p.179.

130. "Strong emotions can blur the source of memory," by Beth Azar in *The APA Monitor*, October 1995, p.31.

131. Herman. *Trauma and Recovery*. p.224. (Parenthetical comment and italics added.)

132. Hilgard, Ernest. *Introduction to Psychology*. (3rd ed.) New York: Harcourt, Brace and World, Inc., 1962. p.556. This phenomenon was identified with regards to the "Bay of Pigs" invasion. Despite the fact that most of Kennedy's cabinet had strong reservations about the plan, none of them expressed them and instead, agreed with the majority as they perceived it.

133. Nisbet, Robert. *History of The Idea of Progress*. New York: Basic Books, 1979. p.323.

134. Blume. *Secret Survivors*. pp.78-79.

135. Ibid. p.130.

136. Bass and Davis. *Courage to Heal*. p.122.

137. Ibid. p.124.

138. Herman. *Trauma and Recovery*. p.178.

139. Bass and Davis. *Courage to Heal* (1994). p.150.

140. Ibid. p.318.

141. Herman. *Trauma and Recovery*. p.210.

142. Bass and Davis quoting Mary R. Williams. *Courage to Heal* (1994), p.319.

143. Interviewed November 22, 1995.

144. Rutter, Peter. *Sex in the Forbidden Zone: When Men in Power - Therapists, Doctors, Clergy, Teachers and Others - Betray Women's Trust*. New York: Falcon Crest, 1989. p.28.

145. Ibid. p.88.

146. Dawes. *House of Cards*. p.58.

147. *American Psychological Association Practitioner Update*, 3(2), June 1995, p.2.

148. Taylor, F. W. *The Principles of Scientific Management*. New York: Norton, 1967, p.125.

149. Peele. *Diseasing of America*. p.76.

150. Borch-Jacobsen, 1997. p.64.

151. Edited transcript of remarks by Alan D. Gold, Barrister, before The Honourable Senator Anne C. Cools. June 10, 1995, in Toronto, Canada.

152. For example, The College of Psychologists of Ontario which formerly licensed only psychologists with an approved doctorate, recently instituted a second level license for "Psychological Associates." These individuals did not need a doctorate; only a master degree with work experience. Although their licenses are "limited," there are no requirements for them to inform the public and they are expected to control or limit themselves.

153. Primetime #279, p.3.

154. Personal communication, November, 1995.

155. Primetime, #279, p.3.

156. Carkhuff, Robert R. *Helping and Human Relations: A Primer for Lay and Professional Helpers, Volume I*. New York: Holt, Rinehart and Winston, Inc., 1969. (See Appendix 4.)

157. Kottler. *On Being A Therapist*. p.17.

158. Kottler. *The Compleat Therapist*. p.75.

159. T. S. Eliot. *The Cocktail Party. New York: Harcourt, Brace and World, 1950, p.111.*

Chapter 7

Taking Back Our Private Lives

*We need to **take back our private lives**, to retrieve them from the intrusive interest of the market and of the social discipline (norms) so that we can live them in privacy, as diversely, eccentrically, and if the occasion demands it, as unhappily as we like. It is indeed a particular privilege of the grown-up to live a private life however he or she likes.*

David Smail

From the outset of this book, it has been made clear that real victims do exist. They may be the victims of natural events like earthquakes, land slides, hurricanes and famines; or of accidents, from a car accident, to the Chernobyl explosion or the release of toxic gases at Bophal; or of conflict and war, including the Holocaust and other ethnic cleansings and tribal genocides; or of cruel men and women, such as the Bundys, Dahlmers, Bernardos and Wests.

As with anything that is real, from silk to pearls to paintings, there is always the copy, the synthetic and the counterfeit, the product made to look like the real thing. In this case, just as there are real victims, so too are there Fabricated Victims: the Synthetic ones persuaded by false ideas, false interpretations, false memories and false diagnoses; the Counterfeit ones who make up stories and feign problems; and the Contrived ones who suffer from a physical cause which the Psychology Industry claims is due to, or treatable by, psychological means.

These Fabricated Victims are, by and large, the products of the current Psychology Industry, a conglomerate consisting of licensed psychologists, psychiatrists, and social workers, the mental health consultants, and all the lay and self-determined therapists, counsellors, helpers and healers. From its beginning a century ago, the profession of psychology has kept one foot (or both feet) firmly planted in business. From some of its earliest ventures into detecting defective aliens, the psychology of advertising and persuasion, and the control of unproductive workers and soldiers, it has sought to benefit by proving itself useful to society. It has repeatedly made the claim that it can help to bring about a better world by understanding and controlling human nature. And it has successfully persuaded the public, courts, social service agencies and aspects of bigger business, that it can achieve individual and social well-being. Only briefly, during a period in history when governmental authority was being challenged, did psychology depart from its theme of "control" and entertain the notion of individual freedom and responsibility. With the demise of the counter-culture, the Psychology Industry returned to its previous mechanistic view of the individual and embarked on its current endeavour. As its new theme, it has chosen to identify and promote the issues of trauma, abuse and addiction as the causes of the malaise and of illness. To this end, it has not only distorted the meaning of the terms to fit everything from serious physical assault, to unwanted comments, gestures, and looks; it has distorted personal histories and scientific data. It has lied about the numbers, the studies and the meaning of the findings, in order to mislead the public and inflate its own importance. While a small proportion of psychologists are adhering to scientific principles, most who claim to be scientists are using the label as a means of advertising and persuasion. By calling psychology a science, they imply that the industry is objective in its methods and findings, that its theories are based on the natural laws of human behaviour, and that its methods are proven effective and safe. But its own findings, which are hidden from the public and which render "informed consent" invalid, disagree with its own claims. Its treatments and therapies are basically found to be ineffective or no better than non-treatment. And, when a method, such as recovered memory therapy, is found to be harmful, these findings are given over to debate, while the method continues to be practiced uncontrolled. Science is not being used to evaluate the industry, it is being used as a term to persuade people to buy what the Psychology Industry sells. And once they become users, these psychologically-prone masses are discouraged of any tendency to think, wonder or question. Their individuality is squelched, as they become shaped by the industry's defective theories and destructive technologies. While scientific theories are created as ideas to be tested, challenged and refined, or dismissed, the theories of the Psychology Industry exist as totems which reduce people to whining, weak, passive and vulnerable children, more intent on nurturing their Inner Child than on strengthening their resolve as adults. In the Psychology Industry, "truth" becomes relative; beliefs are not to be challenged; "memories" are to be "validated;" "victims" are to be propped up and supported; and the damaging effects on individuals, families, communities and society as a whole are to be ignored. The Psychology Industry has found that the best people to carry out this work on the large scale are not the intellectual elite or the well trained, but rather the assembly-line workers, its Taylored technicians, the "automatons."

Realizing this, one must wonder what are the overall effects, and what should and can be done. The effects are several and significant. They touch the soul of the individual, the essence of relationships and the heart of what it means to be a civilized society.

At the conclusion of WWII, psychology promised that, with its scientific knowledge and particular understanding of human nature, it would produce a safer and better world. However, what has resulted is a two-dimensional, mechanistic world in which lives have lost their colour and texture, and people follow fruitless psychological plans which promise happiness and success. People have lost the ability to live their own lives in whatever weird, eccentric, dull or reckless way they want, as the Psychology Industry structures each stage of life and creates steps for overcoming problems and pain. Their individuality has been erased by psychological processes which have lead to homogeneity and regimentation.[1]

With its technical approach to life, the Psychology Industry stresses thriving and optimal living, causing people to focus on what they aren't rather than on who they are. Life has become black and white, good and bad; people have learned to sulk and blame. Ernest Becker realized this problem when he wrote:

> All the analysis (therapy) in the world doesn't allow the person to find out who he is and why he is here on earth. Why he has to die, and how he can make his life a triumph. It is when psychology pretends to do this, when it offers itself as a full explanation of human unhappiness, that it becomes a fraud that makes an impasse from which he cannot escape.[2]

By casting people as victims, by contending that "man's inhumanity to man" evidenced in violence and greed can be controlled by psychological means, and that shame, unhappiness, pain, guilt and sorrow, even death, can be overcome, it demonstrates both its naivete and its dishonesty. The Psychology Industry robs people of their chance to learn from mistakes, cope with betrayal, take risks, meet obligations and comfort each other. As Bollas and Sundelson write: "... the telling aim of the health industry complex is to suppress individual freedom and to create a nation of 'normopaths' or 'normotics' – the abnormally normal – for whom psychological conflict is viewed at worst, as endangering or, at least, as vulgar. In the end, such anxieties reflect a fear and loathing of freedom itself."[3]

The Psychology Industry has cast a long shadow over life and human relationships. While psychologists say "trust me," they question and often discourage one's trust and reliance on family and friends. With concepts such as "emotional abuse," "verbal assault," and "co-dependency," they create the notion that the only safe relationship is the therapeutic one. But what they offer is artificial empathy, cultivated warmth and phony genuineness, which foster a dependency in which they can persuade people to see life the way they see it, and live life in a psychologically ordered fashion. Years ago, psychotherapy was described as "the purchase of friendship." What people need is not more but vastly fewer psychologists; men, women and children need less interference in their lives and more truly genuine relationships, which, however imperfect these may be, are reciprocal rather than purchased. As Smail comments: "There will no doubt always be a place for... kindness, encouragement and comfort, but it is surely too much to expect a professionalized, and hence interest saturated, therapy industry somehow to replace or take over the function of an ethics of human conduct."[4]

People must learn to question the "good intentions" and altruistic appearance of the Psychology Industry. It is first and foremost a business, intent on selling its services and expanding its market. As such, psychologists are selling the public "a bill of goods," making promises about happiness, health and safety which they cannot fulfill. Psychologists are in the business of posing as experts in living, claiming for themselves the ability to divine right from wrong, and cause from effect. The Psychology Industry has persuaded society that the "good life" is possible with the guidance and assistance of psychologists, and it has intimidated gullible people into surrendering their independence and their money. It has ignored the caution of Reinhold Niebuhr, the theological philospher, that "Goodness, armed with power is corrupted."[5] Instead, it persists in malicious benevolence, insisting that people must live by expert advice.

These effects on individuals, relationships and social institutions, constitute the most egregious harms inflicted by the Psychology Industry. They threaten the fabric of society and the principles upon which it relies. But the Psychology Industry is harmful also in other, more sweepingly pervasive ways. As Langs said: "Therapy, as currently practiced, is neither a science nor subject to exact standards. Yet the intervention of a therapist have consequences every bit as enduring as those of a surgeon."[6]

The story of Semmelweis provides a lesson which the Psychology Industry has failed to learn. Despite the evidence which showed Semmelweis's simple idea of hand-washing to be correct, his medical colleagues chose to ignore the data, preferring their own traditional ways of doing things.

Like Semmelweis's colleagues, the Psychology Industry shows a lack of interest and commitment to research findings as a basis of practice. Despite mounting evidence that practices such as recovered memory therapy are both invalid and harmful, the Psychology Industry and its professional organizations take no effective action to control the practice and protect the client. This is in sharp contrast to professional medicine in which the systematic investigation of possible new drugs and treatments has come to play a significant role in determining their use, and in which practitioners who ignore these evaluative results are judged as harming their patients and can face charges of incompetence.[7]

Rather, the Psychology Industry expresses concern that "psychology's image is faltering in the public eye" and puts its attention to "revising the ethical code to be more definitive about psychologists who undermine the public's trust in the discipline... (because) while the current code encourages psychologists to not bring disrespect on the profession, there are no enforceable standards that address the issue."[8] The perceived harm of greatest concern to the Psychology Industry is not that done to its thousands and thousands of damaged users, but rather, the threat to its public image which "will end up having to recreate the trust this country puts in psychotherapy."[9]

The Psychology Industry is not concerned, and would prefer to overlook the damage not only to users but also to society as a whole. Most people, when they consider the Psychology Industry and the work of psychologists, think of it on the level of the individual. They imagine individuals being counselled about behaviours, feelings, and relationships. They believe that these people are victims who really have been abused, injured and damaged. They hear psychologists talk and testify about individual cases. What is missed entirely is the larger social effect of the industry, how the Psychology Industry is manipulating everyone to accept its victim stereotypes and how it is using its persuasion to enforce conformity.

Instead of freeing people to live fuller and richer lives, the Psychology Industry is creating evermore constricted and conforming ones. As Hoffer observed: "people raised in the atmosphere of a mass movement are fashioned into incomplete and dependent human beings."[10] Smail adds that

> it is indeed a particular privilege of the grown-up to live a private life however he or she likes. It is, furthermore, the business of the psychotherapist, if asked, as far as possible to help people to do precisely that, and not to try to push them into conformity with some standardized conception of 'mental health.' Rather than being, as they unwittingly too often are, representatives of a form of social discipline, psychotherapists could better become the reticent and unheroic assistants of people whose private struggles are nobody's business but their own...[11]

But the Psychology Industry does not accept or even acknowledge this responsibility. Instead, it allows itself to be a willing, cooperative agent of social policy, with its activities and research dependent on current social policy and governmental/institutional funding. By doing so, it diminishes its capacity to step back and question the always present and unspoken assumptions that underlie the present form of society; "an undergirding that drastically limits the universe of alternatives that social policymakers can consider."[12] It is this willingness to ignore alternatives in favour of current social policies (eg. violence against women) and to avoid challenging the views of policymakers, which has diminished the profession and rendered it an industry. Instead of probing human nature and, thereby, coming to some understanding of why the social order has come to be the way it is and how to build a better one, psychologists have colluded to maintain the present one in which they have gained power and become part of the elite. Despite psychologists' apparent willingness to describe themselves as "social influence purveyors," they fail to see that in being such, they, themselves, become pawns in a larger game of manufacturing dependent, conforming and disciplined people, the real victims of the Psychology Industry. Justice Brandeis wrote a long time ago that "experience should teach us to be most on guard to protect liberty when the government's purposes are beneficent;" to this can be added the Psychology Industry's purposes.[13]

The last twenty years have seen an exponential growth in the Psychology Industry and predictions have been made that there will a further 64% increase in the number of psychologists in the next ten years,[14] leading one

320 / Dr. Tana Dineen

to worry, as Boring did, that soon "there will be more psychologists than people in this country." These psychologists, in the hope of furthering their own interests, have cooperated with big business, the military and government. And yet they still seem to believe that they are acting as reformers in a humanitarian sense, as they simultaneously trap millions of people in a psychological system which causes them to go backwards into the future. Undermining the courage and determination of the Forefathers of America, the Psychology Industry has turned the New World into a nation of weak and whining dependent children. Perhaps never before has Abraham Lincoln's warning been more accurate:

> At what point, then, is the approach of danger to be expected? I answer, if it ever reach us it must spring up amongst us; it cannot come from abroad. If destruction be our lot, we must ourselves be its author and finisher. As a nation of freemen, we must live throughout all time, or die by suicide.

With this caution in mind, what can be done?

A solution should not be expected to come from within an industry which is intent on self-protection, self-preservation and self-interest. Beyond acknowledging the "black eye" it has received due to the public disgrace of recovered memory therapy, most psychologists and professional organizations have done nothing to stop so pernicious an abuse.[15] They remain mute, impotent or divided in opinion about the Psychology Industry's assertions about violence, abuse, addiction, stress, trauma, and so on, which manufacture victims and rent apart relationships, families, and institutions. By their silence and their failure to take either an ethical or scientific stand on the matter, they have entirely failed in their mandate to protect the public. What they have done instead is create the impression of giving it serious but silent thought and, as a way to distract attention, gone after those whom they identify to be "bad psychologists." In particular they have targeted those "on the fringe" who use crystals or dabble in past lives and those who have "dual relationships," such as sex (or even friendship) with a client.

By declaring zero tolerance around this latter issue, they appear to be taking a firm approach to self-regulation. By publicly identifying and scapegoating those individual psychologists found guilty of "falling in love," seducing, being seduced by, or even inadvertently touching or looking at a client "the wrong way," they are diverting public attention away from the magnitude of the damage inflicted on people by the whole Psychology Industry. Rather than looking at the real casualties of the industry's sanctioned ploys of false interpreting, remembering and naming, they choose to create yet another variety of fabricated victims, those who are unequivocal victims of "therapist abuse." In so doing, they have developed another facet of the Psychology Industry, devoted to servicing these people as users.[16]

Meanwhile, they ignore the ethical standards they claim to uphold; "*do no harm*" is a point forgotten when these professional organizations address complaints of damage from false interpreting, remembering and naming. The practice of victim-making is so widespread throughout the Psychology Industry, that it is difficult to garner any support to stop the practice. Psychologists do not want to lose their freedom to do their own type of therapy whatever that might be, whether there is any support for its effectiveness or not. This has recently been most noticeable as psychologists have protested the moves of Managed Care to limit their practice to brief forms of therapy, a restriction which they argue is unfair despite the massive evidence which shows that prolonging therapy is not useful. Clearly, the industry cannot be trusted to regulate itself and to deal with its own serious problems, let alone to evaluate its overall role in society. Of significance in this regard is APA President Seligman's statement that the American Psychological Association "must convince the public and Congress of our effectiveness. A public education campaign has begun. But we need it to do more than just burnish our image. We need it to undergird our image with undeniable facts."[17]

What is needed are some short-term initiatives to control the damaging effects of an out-of-control industry, and some long-term goals to curb its influence. In the immediate future, action must be taken to:

•make psychologists legally responsible for their activities. Controversy currently exists within and around the Psychology Industry regarding recovered memories, their validity and harmful risks. While opponents stress the high probability of false memories and false allegations, and the damage done to those who are falsely accused, proponents emphasize the frequent corroboration of memories either by conviction or admission of guilt, and point to the damage to clients and to society.

What is evidenced in this heated argument is the Psychology Industry's intention to *use* therapy patients in a social cause that is based on popularized opinions. Some have even made "social action" a recognized part of treatment, recommended for full recovery.[18] In doing so, psychologists have expanded their mandate beyond helping clients, and into a patriarchal role of policing and protecting society. This goes against previous practice in which the one exception to the privacy and sanctity of the therapist/patient communication which existed was the obligation to report when the client was "considered to be at risk to self or others." Now the Psychology Industry has independently changed that to include "when others are a risk to others" however that might be defined.

What is needed is to reaffirm the responsibility and liability of psychologists for what they do in providing treatment and not be drawn into the Psychology Industry's larger goal to be social influencers. Psychologists need to be held accountable for the therapy methods they use, and if they are controversial or experimental (i.e. unproven) they must be identified as such at the outset, with all clients being warned of the risk of potential harm, the significant possibility that interpretations and memories will be inaccurate, and made aware of the psychologist's stance regarding social and legal actions. Society and the law understand the role of "accomplice" and such a concept must be applied to therapists involved in malicious or wrongful accusations and actions.[19]

•**cut insurance coverage for psychology**, thus removing the third party payments[20] that have allowed many Fabricated Victims unlimited access to psychological services and which provide the Psychology Industry with a major source of income.

Currently the whole matter of insured psychological services is under examination. While Canadian governments, both federal and provincial, are reviewing and restricting insured services, the shift towards HMO's and Managed Care in the United States has created considerable uncertainty regarding the future of third party payments. Given the moves to limit sessions, to create indexes which relate diagnoses to methods of treatment and number of sessions, and to open psychological service positions to competitive bidding, all indications are that the previous funding systems were losing money for insurers. While these new restrictions, which are being opposed by many psychologists, will shorten the "free ride," they may have a paradoxical effect. To compensate for the reduced income per client, the Psychology Industry may very well work to increase the overall number of victims, with each having the possibility of receiving treatment funding from alternative sources such as those provided through the courts, businesses, and professional liability insurers.

An immediate solution is to staunch the flow by ceasing to insure psychological services related to "there-and-then" issues, and to support only established treatments that address immediate problems without dwelling on the etiology or imaginable "causes."[21] Some moves in this direction are already taking place.[22] In approximately 40 states, plans are being made to put into law an act, "the Truth and Responsibility in Mental Health Practices Act." As well, an esteemed group of psychologists wrote to the U.S. Congress suggesting that all relevant sections of health care codes specify that:

> No tax or tax exempt monies may be used for any form of health care treatment, including any form of psychotherapy, that has not been proven safe and effective by rigorous, valid and reliable scientific investigation and accepted as safe and effective by a substantial majority of the relevant scientific community.[23]

While this may be a step forward, the Psychology Industry, given its abysmal track-record in self-regulation, should not be made responsible to oversee this activity, for it would enjoy a clear benefit in approving techniques even if the positive findings are based on limited or flawed research. The Psychology Industry's actions must be closely watched for recently it has begun to employ a clever ploy of applying "here-and-now" problem-oriented techniques to issues from the past, thereby using an approved method in an inappropriate way.[24] There is the distinct possibility that this proposed Act could have the unintended effect of creating a new sub-industry for psychology. In fact, as this book goes to print, a number of manuals have begun to hit the professional market promoting "proven" therapies, and a committee is in the midst of creating a "treatment and statistical manual" similar to the *DSM* specifically codifying "proven" psychological treatments.

Another newly developing tactic of licensed psychologists is their lobbying for the right to prescribe psycho-active drugs;[25] this is by a profession which historically has fought the use of such drugs by psychiatry, and has argued that psychotherapy is "just as effective."

• **cease to recognize psychologists as experts in court**, removing the status which allows beliefs, opinions and industrial myths to be expressed as "facts" and "specialized knowledge," implying expertise.

In the place of established facts, the Psychology Industry substitutes "professional opinions," "clinical experience" or "expert intuition" since it lacks proof or hard data. Despite this, the Psychology Industry has insidiously persuaded the courts to accept as experts, psychologists, who are self-proclaimed[26] or supported by colleagues of a "like-mind." Rather than disqualifying them or avoiding psychological experts completely, the courts generally allow the opposing side to provide its own expert(s), so that the eventual outcome is determined by whose expert is more persuasive rather than what is the truth.

Bogus psychology experts, often supported by their professional organization, mislead the courts on a daily basis, deluding judges and juries into believing that their procedures and opinions are uncontroversial and based on responsible, scientific research.[27] In fact, this activity has become so rampant that the proposed "Truth and Responsibility in Mental Health Practices Act" requires "all psychotherapists and social scientists to *tell the truth* in American courts of law.[28] One can only hold in contempt a profession for which this must be mandated when all other citizens have always accepted this as their ethical and legal responsibility.

Junk psychology is a serious threat to the integrity of the legal system, and, with irresponsible and unethical testimony by psychologists reaching epidemic proportion, the only solution is to disallow any involvement of psychologists posing as experts.

• **stop the public sanctioning of the Psychology Industry**, through such things as court-ordered treatment, mandated treatment for addictions and work-performance problems, and compensation for psychological stress and damage.

In an effort to appear humane, courts have moved towards referring for psychological treatment, those who have been convicted of a crime in which "psychological problems" played a factor. As well, in some jurisdictions, laws mandate that employers provide treatment for employees with psychological problems, such as alcohol and substance abuse, or sexual disorders. While these treatments generally lack any proof of their long-term effectiveness, they have become legally sanctioned, publicly endorsed and accepted, and used as a means to avoid discipline or punishment. Similarly, workers' compensation programmes now include provisions for job-related stress.

All of these serve to encourage the adoption of the victim identity and provide the secondary gains to maintain it; an effect which the Psychology Industry ignores in favour of having its services recognized and sanctioned.

• **demand "truth in advertising"** by requiring that claims of knowledge and skill be substantiated. While the public continues to be swayed by "an aura of honesty and infallibility" and presumes that psychologists not only know the truth but also speak it, such is neither generally the case nor even a professional requirement.

Psychologists of all varieties are now allowed to advertise their wares, describing them as they wish as long as they avoid committing outright fraud. For instance, the NLP practitioners described earlier, who treated allergies, claimed a 99% success rate, without any supporting data other than their own impressions. Many others make similar, nonsensical claims or promote their particular form of treatment as more effective than others.

Whether privately in therapy sessions, or publicly in advertisements and seminars, psychologists must be held accountable for their claims which may mislead the public. No longer should the image of professionalism be allowed to protect the Psychology Industry from the laws and regulations applied to other commercial operations. Users deserve the same protection from consumer fraud and product harm with psychological services that they are entitled to from the auto or appliance industries.

•**reduce the emphasis on, and funding of, psychological programmes** in favour of addressing broad social needs such as poverty, education and basic health.

In the early 80's, Zilbergeld wrote that "millions of people today seek therapy for personal and interpersonal discomforts that less affluent societies would regard as trivial." But North America is no longer as affluent and can no longer afford the luxuries it once enjoyed. Psychological programmes are, by and large, an extravagant distraction from the real problems that affect people's well-being. They are the pseudo-treatments which contribute to the income of the Psychology Industry, while doing little to treat society's ills. Meanwhile, the more significant psychological factors of poverty, nutrition, employment and education are ignored or negatively affected as society's attention gets diverted to trivialized versions of violence and the self-indulgent whining of those already better off. Rather than hire psychologists to go into the schools to teach self-esteem, it would make more sense to teach the students skills that they can use to build their own self-respect. Rather than employ psychologists to teach parenting to the poor, it would do better to help provide food, housing and parenting relief to families. Rather than make biopolitical knee-jerk responses to violence, as defined or identified by the Psychology Industry, it would do better to consider the boredom, frustration and lack of meaning underlying the real violence found amongst the youth.[29] Rather than promote illusive but expensive mental health, it would be better to attend to the needs of the seriously mentally ill who have been abandoned in the streets and alleys.[30]

While these immediate steps are necessary to curb the damaging effects, they are merely "stop-gap" manoeuvres. There are broader issues that must be addressed. The long-term goals can best be understood in the context of the following which is said to have been Carl Jung's favourite story:

The water of life, wishing to make itself known on the face of the earth, bubbled up in an artesian well and flowed without effort or limit. People came to drink of the magic water and were nourished by it, since it was so clean and pure and invigorating. But humankind was not content to leave things in this Edenic state. Gradually they began to fence the well, charge admission, claim ownership of the property around it, make elaborate laws as to who could come to the well, put locks on the gates. Soon the well was property of the powerful and the elite. The water was angry and offended; it stopped flowing and began to bubble up in another place. The people who owned the property around the first well were so engrossed in their power systems and ownership that they did not notice that the water had vanished. They continued selling the nonexistent water, and few people noticed that the true power was gone. But some dissatisfied people searched with great courage and found the new artesian well. Soon that well was under the control of the property owners, and the same fate overtook it. The spring took itself to yet another place - and this has been going on throughout recorded history.[31]

This is a sad but essentially encouraging tale of human egotism, greed and foolishness, characteristics of which the Psychology Industry suffers in large proportions. The encouragement comes not from the Psychology Industry but rather, from the strength of human nature to survive in spite of psychologists.

For the past fifty years, psychologists have been building fences, charging fees, making laws and padlocking their "turf;" all in an attempt to claim their role as "keepers" of psychological knowledge and to establish themselves as the licensed or certified dispensers of psychological wisdom and healing. Where they can, they have subverted basic truth into egocentric possessions; and where they can't, they have manufactured truths to expand their activities and to maximize their profits.

Most people assume that licensing exists to protect the public but, in fact, it only serves to protect the privileged group in society who possess the credentials. Rollo May wrote recently about the early days of licensing and his thoughts in retrospect. He described the time in the mid 50's , the "dangerous years," when a conservative wing of the American Medical Association threatened to outlaw all non-medical psychotherapists and to take ownership of psychotherapy. For 6 or 8 years, May lived in intense anxiety that his practice would be outlawed. Eventually, he and his colleagues concluded that "the best step for us as psychologists would be to clarify all the different branches of psychotherapy" and they organized a conference on the training, practice and safeguards of psychotherapy. "From that moment on, the fact that psychotherapy was conducted by psychologists... was then accepted in the various legislatures around the country." May went on to describe a conversation he had at that time, with Carl Rogers; "expecting his (Rogers') enthusiastic help, I was taken aback by his stating the he was not sure whether it would be good or not to have psychologists licensed... During the following years, I kept thinking of Carl Rogers' doubts about our campaign for licensing. I think he foresaw that we psychologists could be as rigid as any other group, and this certainly has been demonstrated... "[32]

Rogers' hesitation should have been heeded, licensing should never have happened. Instead of resisting the threat, psychologists took on the very nature of those that threatened them. They claimed joint ownership of psychotherapy, only extending the menacing monopoly so that now it included them. And they licensed themselves to appear similar to those medical doctors that had earlier threatened their existence. They became rigid and controlling, deriving their identity from their licenses, titles and credentials. And they have used these licenses to give themselves the authority to decide who and what is normal and abnormal, good and bad, healthy and "sick." It is these symbols of authority, these totems of arrogance, that must be eliminated in order for society to survive.

For society, the real danger to be found in the Psychology Industry is not in false memories or false allegations. It is in the false thinking and false living which are the primary effects of the Psychology Industry. The Psychology Industry may abandon long-term therapy for shorter forms of insured psychotherapy. It may denounce recovered memory therapy in much the same way that a large corporation jettisons a subsidiary that either loses money or causes internal problems. But society must not be fooled by these actions. The real danger of the Psychology Industry is that it is crafting people and manufacturing victims who substitute a glib patter about caring and nurturing their inner being for true self-knowledge. To draw from one of Pete Seeger's songs, "they're all made out of ticky-tacky, and they all look just the same."

Whether in recovered-memory therapy or short-term cognitive therapy, psychologists treat the core beliefs about oneself, both past and present, as playthings, which they toy with and manipulate. They seek to impose their view as to how people should think and feel and act, generally ignoring the implications of their opinions and coercive techniques, and the conformity and mediocrity that they are imposing. Something as common and profound as anxiety is considered by psychologists as an emotion to be reduced, rather than as a possible sign of some significant threat in the person's outer world or an effect of broader social factors. The Delphic injunction to *"Know Thyself"* referred neither to memories of the past nor to a psychologically healthy self-image. It required that individuals know their character, their strengthens and limitations, their needs and gifts, their desire for truth and their tendency towards self-deception. But it is deception and self-deception, rather than these aspects of self-knowledge, which the Psychology Industry fosters.

Most psychologists, if they looked back a hundred years, would hold Galton's theory and beliefs about intelligence and eugenics with disdain, yet they fail to recognize the same kind of rigidity and ego-centrism in their own theories. They go about their work seemingly unaware that their own self-interests and privileged positions in society have more influence on their thoughts and actions than does their research. They have pursued and achieved social influence and economic gain, but they are blind to the fact that, in doing so, they have become dependent on institutions, industries and governments for this income and status. Psychology has abdicated its fundamental intellectual and moral responsibility for simple honesty, intellectual autonomy, critical self-scrutiny and humane respect. Instead it promotes cognitive distortions, self-aggrandizement and social prejudice.

To stop this, it will be necessary to recognize that "the well has run dry," that the power has gone, that the practice and profession of psychology is bankrupt. It does not have enough assets and resources to meet its obligations. Ultimately, the initiative should be taken to remove the licenses and certifications which serve to support and maintain an unworthy profession. For it is only in removing these symbols of authority, these vestments of power and influence, that society will be able to take back its right to psychological freedom, where people are accepted or judged by their families, friends and peers, and not by self-ordained experts. It will then begin to reacquire the human traits of tolerance, understanding, and concern. If people take back their basic right to think for themselves, to exercise their "common sense" in finding solutions to their own problems, they can stop falling prey to the "illusory fantasies" of professional experts and bureaucrats. And if the courts stop relying on the prejudiced and conflicted opinions of experts, they can take back their responsibility to make decisions based on facts.

There is too much dissatisfaction with psychology; with its actions, institutions and professional organizations. Those within the Psychology Industry, as well as those outside, have cautioned it, criticised it, warned it; and yet, it remains unchanged, going about business in its customary way.[33] The Psychology Industry can neither reform itself from within nor should it be allowed to try. It should be stopped from doing what it is doing to people, from manufacturing victims. And while the Psychology Industry is being dismantled, people can boycott psychological treatment, protest the influence of the Psychology Industry and resist being manufactured into victims. And they can wonder what would happen if philosophy took back the issues of "soul" (psyche) and "meaning," science took back the study of the body and behaviour, friendship took back its place as the source of consolation and encouragement, and everyone, fabricated victims included, took back their own private lives.

Endnotes

1. This was Alexis de Tocqueville's fear which he expressed in the 1800's in Vol. 2 of *Democracy in America*.

2. Ernest Becker. *The Denial of Death*. New York: The Free Press, 1973.

3. Bollas, Christopher and Sundelson, David. *The New Informant: The Betrayal of Confidentiality in Psychoanalysis and Psychotherapy*. Northvale, N.J.: Jason Aronson Inc., 1995, p.105. "Normopath," a defensive movement toward an extreme in normality was created by Joyce McDougall (*A Plea for a Measure of Abnormality*. New York: International Universities Press, 1980.) and "Normotic" by Christopher Bollas (*The Shadow of the Object*. New York: Columbia University Press, 1987.)

4. Smail. *Taking Care*. p.142.

5. Niebuhr, Reinhold. *Beyond Tragedy: Essays on the Christian Interpretation of History*. North Stratford, NH: Ayer Co., 1977 (first published, 1938.)

6. Langs, Robert. *Rating Your Psychotherapist: Everything You Need to Know to Find the Therapist Who's Right for You - From Getting Referrals to Ending Treatment.* New York: Ballantine Books, 1989. p.5.

7. Dawes. *House of Cards.* p.14.

8. American Psychological Association's Past President Ron Fox, as quoted in "Psychology's image is faltering in the public eye." *The APA Monitor,* October 1995, p.6.

9. Paul McHugh, professor and director of the Department of Psychiatry and Behavioral Sciences at the John Hopkins University School of Medicine, quoted in *Times*, Nov. 29, 1993.

10. Hoffer. *The True Believer.* p.118.

11. Smail. *Taking Care.* p.129-130.

12. Sarason. *Psychology Misguided.* p.176.

13. Justice Brandeis, *Olmstead vs United States* 277 U.S. 438,479 (1928) (dissenting opinion).

14. Wiggins, Jack G. Jr. "Would you want your child to be a psychologist?" *American Psychologist*, June 1994, p.486.

15. Some shifts have begun to appear. For instance, a report commissioned by the Royal College of Psychiatrists concluded that no recovered memories of child abuse have ever been proven and that the techniques employed to unearth 'memories' are 'potentially dangerous methods of persuasion'. However, since the findings caused deep divisions within the profession, the College decided to delay publication of the full report, preferring to confine itself initially to issuing guidelines warning members about the dangers of recovered memory techniques. (Fiona Barton, "Memory Therapy Is Damned by Experts," *Mail on Sunday.* June 29, 1997.) The American Psychological Association Task Force addressing the reliability of recovered memory was hotly divided between the clinical and research members and no conclusion was forthcoming. It has in fact been an organization of private citizens, the False Memory Syndrome Foundation (F.M.S.F., 3401 Market Street, Suite 130, Philadelphia, PA, 19104-3315) which has compiled research data, submitted amicus curae briefs, and provided a source of hope to the many individuals who have been harmed by recovered memory therapy.

16. For example, the Council of the College of Psychologists of Ontario, ignoring the obvious conflict of interest, approved a regulation making it mandatory that all members furnish proof of insurance coverage for therapy for victims of therapist abuse to "the equivalent fee for 100 hours of psychotherapy." ("The Bulletin," 21(1), August 1994) And, as well, the Psychology Industry is creating a niche for itself in the offering of expert professional testimony in cases of professional complaints, civil suits and criminal trials generated by charges based on beliefs emanating from within the industry.

17. "1996 President-Elect Candidate Biographical and Issues Statements." Washington, D.C.: American Psychological Association. p.17.

18. For instance, "finding a social mission," Herman. *Trauma and Recovery.* p.207 ff.

19. In courts across the U.S. and Canada, lawsuits have begun to be heard against psychologists. For example, in the case of Sullivan vs Cheshier, a psychologist was successful sued by the parents of his patient for having imposed a false memory in her, and for having instructed her to break contact with her parents if they dissented from her memory. (See Loftus, E. "Memories of childhood trauma or traumas of childhood memory," American Psychological Association Annual Meeting, New York, August 1995.)

Similarly, in 1995, psychiatrist, Dr. Diane Humenansky, was sued by two former patients for, amongst other thing, the creation of false memories. In one case, *Humanne vs Humenansky*, where the plaintiff "claimed that Humenansky convinced her that she and her family were members of a satanic cult and that she had over 100 'alter' personalities," the jury awarded the former patient $2.6 million. In the other case (*Carlson vs Humenansky*) a similar finding resulted in an award of $2.5 million; representing "the two largest amounts ever awarded from a psychiatrist on trial." ("Psychiatry in the Courtroom." *Law & Politics*, March 1996, pp.34 - 39.) By the end of 1997, similar lawsuits were leading to even larger settlements. In a Texas case (Carl vs Keraga) the amount was $5.8 million and in an Illinois case (Burgus vs Braun) the amount was $10.6 million.

There is a noticable trend in these legal actions toward expansion beyond suing therapists to include victim-accusers. The British House of Lords opened the way for people wrongly accused of crimes - including men falsely accused of rape - to sue their accusers for damages. One of the judges, Lord Keith, stated: "To deny any remedy to a person whose liberty has been interfered with as a result of unfounded and malicious accusations... would constitute a serious denial of justice." (*The Guardian Weekly*, July 23, 1995, 153(4), p.9) In the U.S., George Franklin, who was incarcerated for murder based on the repressed memory testimony of his daughter, is suing his accusers to clear his name and recover his life savings. He is suing his daughter for $1 and the other defendants (including psychologists) for unlimited damages.

There are indications that lawsuits may be expanded further to include licensing boards and other organizations that credential or approve psychologists. For example, in 1997 George Bergen and his sons launched a suit against not only two former Winnipeg therapists, Colin Ross and Tammy Schultz, but also the Manitoba Government, the University of Manitoba and the College of Physicians & Surgeons of Manitoba. They claim that these organizations permitted and encouraged the therapists to practice a form of fraudulent psychotherapy which caused injury to the Bergen family and to other families in Manitoba.

20. Such as Employee Assistance Programs, "victim-support" and mental health insurance coverage.

22. This is, in many ways, what behavioural forms of therapy used to do, as they paid attention to immediate rather than historical causes, and sought ways to either intervene in the "stimulus" or modify the "effect."

22. In response to threats being rumoured about severe cut-backs in insurance coverage, and with an embarrassed awareness that there is little to no evidence that most therapies work, the clinical division of the American Psychological Association created a "schedule of proven therapies" which it felt should be covered by insurance.

23. "The Barden Letter," p.3 For more information or a copy of the letter and proposed act, write the National Association for Consumer Protection in Mental Health Practices, 937 Brunswick Circle, Schaumburg, IL. 60193, or visit the *Manufacturing Victims* web-site at http://scholefieldhouse.com/mv/. The State of Indiana has passed the informed consent portion of the Act (98-0 in the House and 58-0 in the Senate).

24. For example, cognitive-behavioural therapy, approved by the American Psychological Association, has more recently been applied to the treatment of incest, and early childhood abuse.

25. The May 1996 issue of *The APA Monitor* addresses the "active interest and controversy" of prescription privileges.

26. Again the professional organizations act in a blind fashion to this, their response being that psychologists are expected to regulate themselves and restrict their activities and practice to their areas of competence.

27. The courts determine the trustworthiness of expert testimony on the basis of the "Frye test." In 1923, the case of Frye vs United States (*Frye vs United States*, 54 App. D.C. 46, 293 F.1013 (D.C. Cir. 1923) provided a means by which the admissibility of expert testimony, was to be judged:

"Just when a scientific principle or discovery crosses the line between the experimental and demonstrable stages is difficult to define. Somewhere in this twilight zone the evidential force of the principle must be recognized, and while the courts will go a long way in admitting expert testimony deduced from a well-recognized scientific principles or discovery, *the thing from which the deduction is made must be sufficiently established to have gained general acceptance in the particular field in which it belongs.*"(Ibid., p.1014, italics added) *(Frye vs United States.* 54 App. D.C. 46, 293 F.1013 (D.C. Cir. 1923.) However this ruling never assumed that such a "field" could or would become a self-endorsing and self-serving industry.

28. An Overview of the *STATE* version of the *Truth and Responsibility In Mental Health Practices Act* (draft 1/14/1995) p.2

29. Both US and Canadian statistics showed a slight reduction in overall violence in 1994, except amongst the youth. However some of the increase in youth crimes is due to the reclassification

of 16 and 17 year olds as "youth" rather than "adult," and the zero tolerance policies "that almost guarantee a schoolyard bully ends up in court." "Three years ago, they weren't arresting kids for those crimes. Now we are and the numbers are up" says Rosemary Gartner, University of Toronto sociologist. (Canadian Press, May 19, 1995.)

30. In this regard, see Isaac, Rael Jean, and Arnat, Virginia C. *Madness in the Streets*. New York: The Free Press, 1990.

31. This story of Carl Jung's was recounted in Johnson, Robert A. *Owning Your Own Shadow*. San Francisco: Harper, 1991. pp.vii-viii.

32. May, Rollo. Foreword. In Freedheim, Donald K. (ed.) *History of Psychotherapy*. Washington, D.C.: American Psychological Association, 1992. pp.xx-xxvii.

33. For examples, see: Rollo May (1992); Sarason, Seymour B. *Psychology Misdirected*. New York: The Free Press, 1981: Christopher Lasch, *The Culture of Narcissism: American Life in an Age of Diminishing Expectations*. New York: W. W. Norton and Co., 1979: Gross, Martin L. *The Psychological Society: The Impact-and the Failure-of Psychiatry, Psychotherapy, Psychoanalysis and the Psychological Revolution*. New York: Random House, 1978; Zilbergeld, Bernie. *The Shrinking of America: Myths of Psychological Change*. Boston: Little, Brown and Co., 1983; Nisbet, Robert. *History of The Idea of Progress*. New York: Basic Books, 1979.

Suggested Readings

Brown, E. Richard. *Rockefeller Medicine Men: Medicine & Capitalism in America*. Berkeley, CA: University of California Press, 1979.

Campbell, Terence W. *Beware the Talking Cure: Psychotherapy may be Hazardous to Your Mental Health*. Boca Raton, FL: Upton Books, 1994.

Ceci, Stephen J. and Bruck, Maggie. *Jeopardy in the Courtroom: A Scientific Analysis of Children's Testimony*. Washington, D. C.: American Psychological Association, 1995.

Dantzer, Robert. *The Psychosomatic Delusion: Why the Mind is Not the Source of All Our Ills*. New York: The Free Press, 1993.

Dawes, Robyn M. *House of Cards: Psychology and Psychotherapy Built on Myth*. New York: MacMillan, 1994.

Des Pres, Terrence. *The Survivor*. New York: Oxford University Press, 1976.

Fekete, John. *Moral Panic: Biopolitics Rising*. Montreal: Robert Davies Publ., 1994.

Frank, J. D. and Frank, J. B. *Persuasion and Healing: A Comparative Study of Psychotherapy*. (3rd ed.) Baltimore: John Hopkins University Press, 1991.

Freedheim, Donald K. (ed.). *History of Psychotherapy: A Century of Change*. Washington, D. C.: American Psychological Association, 1992

Freyd, Pamela, and Goldstein, Eleanor. *Smiling through Tears*. Boca Raton, FL: Upton Books, 1997..

Goodyear-Smith, Felicity. *First Do No Harm: The Sexual Abuse Industry*. Auckland, New Zealand: Benton-Gay Publishing, 1993.

Gross, Paul R. & Levitt, Norman. *Higher Superstition: The Academic Left and Its Quarrels with Science*. Baltimore: The Johns Hopkins University Press, 1994.

Gross, Martin L. *The Psychological Society: The Impact - and the Failure - of Psychiatry, Psychotherapy, Psychoanalysis and the Psychological Revolution*. New York: Random House, 1978.

Hacking, Ian. *Rewriting the Soul: Multiple Personality and the Sciences of Memory*. Princeton, N.J.: Princeton University Press, 1995

Hagen, Margaret A. *Whores of the Court: The Fraud of Psychiatric Testimony and the Rape of American Justice*. New York: Regan Books, HarperCollins Publishers, 1997.

Herman, Ellen. *The Romance of American Psychology: Political Culture in the Age of Experts*. Berkeley, CA: University of California Press, 1995.

Hillman, James and Ventura, Michael. *We've had a Hundred Years of Psychotherapy and the World is Getting Worse*. San Francisco: HarperCollins, 1992.

Hoffer, Eric. *The True Believer*. New York: Harper and Row, 1951.

Huber, Peter W. *Galileo's Revenge: Junk Science In The Courtroom*. New York: HarperCollins, Publ. 1991.

Hughes, Robert. *The Culture of Complaint*. New York: Oxford University Press, 1993.

Kaminer, Wendy. *I'm Dysfunctional, You're Dysfunctional.* New York: Vintage Books/Random House, 1993.

Lasch, Christopher. *Haven in a Heartless World: The Family Besieged.* New York: Basic Books, 1977.

Lasch, Christopher, *The Culture of Narcissism: American Life in an Age of Diminishing Expectations.* New York: W. W. Norton and Co., 1979.

Loftus, E. F. and Ketcham, K. *The Myth of Repressed Memory.* New York: St. Martin's Press, 1994.

Masson, Jeffrey Moussaieff. *Against Therapy: Emotional Tyranny and the Myth of Psychological Healing.* New York: Atheneum, 1988.

May, Rollo. *Psychology and the Human Dilemma.* New York: W. W. Norton. 1967.

Nisbet, Robert. *History of the Idea of Progress.* New York: Basic Books, 1979.

Ofshe, Richard and Watters, Ethan. *Making Monsters: False Memories, Psychotherapy, and Sexual Hysteria.* New York: Charles Scribner's Sons, 1994.

Oppenheim, Janet. *"Shattered Nerves:" Doctors, Patients, and Depression in Victorian England.* Oxford: Oxford University Press, 1991.

Peele, Stanton. *Diseasing of America: Addiction Treatment Out of Control.* Lexington, Mass.: Lexington Books, 1989.

Plous, Scott. *Psychology of Judgement and Decision Making.* New York: McGraw, 1993.

Ralph, Diana. *Work and Madness: The Rise of Community Psychiatry.* Montreal: Black Rose Books, 1983.

Revel, Jean-Francois. *The Flight from Truth.* New York: Random House, 1991.

Roiphe, Katie. *The Morning After: Sex, Fear and Feminism on Campus,* Boston: Little, Brown and Co., 1993.

Sarason, Seymour B. *Psychology Misdirected.* New York: The Free Press, 1981.

Schultz, Duane. P. *A History of Modern Psychology.* New York: Academic Press, 1969.

Showalter, Elaine. *Hystories: Hysterical Epidemics and Modern Media.* New York: Columbia University Press, 1997.

Smail, David. *Taking Care: An Alternative to Therapy.* London: J. M. Dent and Sons, 1987.

Smith, Susan. *Survivor Psychology: The Dark Side of A Mental Health Mission.* Boca Raton, FL: Upton Books, 1995.

Sykes, Charles. *A Nation of Victims: The Decay of the American Society.* New York: St. Martin's Press, 1992.

Sykes, Charles. *Dumbing Down Our Kids: Why American Children Feel Good About Themselves But Can't Read, Write Or Add.* New York: St. Martin's Press, 1995.

Szasz, Thomas. *The Myth of Psychotherapy, Mental Healing as Religion, Rhetoric, and Repression.* Garden City, N. J.: Anchor Press/Doubleday, 1978.

Szasz, Thomas. *The Manufacture of Madness: A Comparative Study of the Inquisition and the Mental health Movement.* New York: Harper and Row, 1970.

Torrey, E. Fuller. *Witchdoctors and Psychiatrists.* New York: Harper & Row, 1986. (revised and reprinted as *The Mind Game: Witchdoctors and Psychiatrists.* New York: Aronson, 1994.)

Torrey, E. Fuller. *Freudian Fraud: The Malignant Effect of Freud's Theory on American Thought and Culture.* New York: HarperCollin, 1993.

Yapko, Michael D. *Suggestions of Abuse: True and False Memories of Childhood Sexual Trauma.* New York: Simon & Schuster, 1994.

Zilbergeld, Bernie. *The Shrinking of America: Myths of Psychological Change.* Boston: Little, Brown and Co., 1983.

Ziskin, Jay. *Coping with Psychiatric and Psychological Testimony. (Volumes 1-5).* Los Angeles: Law and Psychology Press, 1995.

Index

Dr. Tana Dineen

Dr. Dineen is a licensed psychologist in Ontario and British Columbia, Canada. She was drawn to the study of psychology in 1965. She holds an Honours Bachelor of Science degree (1969) from McGill University, and a Masters (1971) and Doctoral Degree (1975) from the University of Saskatchewan. She is a Full Member of the American Psychological Association and the Canadian Psychological Association.

Early in her career, while establishing a system for monitoring and assessing diagnostic and treatment services, she became concerned that the personal beliefs of mental health "experts" could contaminate their work with patients. At the University of Saskatchewan she investigated psychiatric decision making and identified how the beliefs of individual psychiatrists, as to the causes of problems, influenced how they diagnosed and treated their patients.

While maintaining this research interest, she taught in the Department of Special Education, University of Saskatchewan, and established a service for identification, assessment and consultation regarding learning disabilities in rural schools.

For four years, starting in 1977, she worked as Treatment Director of a large Ontario psychiatric facility, establishing specialized programs, including an assessment ward for the investigation of complex diagnostic questions and an intensive treatment ward for young Schizophrenics, which won an American Psychiatric Association prize for innovative programming. During that time, Dr. Dineen came to recognize the limitations of what psychologists had to offer in the treatment of the seriously mentally ill and to be concerned that psychologists were as prone as psychiatrists to being swept along by their personal interests and beliefs.

In 1981 she established a private psychotherapy practice in Toronto and served as a consulting and supervising psychologist at a treatment centre for children with medical and language problems, and a community agency for individuals of all ages with developmental handicaps, such as cognitive delays and autism.

Dr. Dineen's experience is not limited to clinical problems. For several decades she has been concerned about issues of responsible professionalism and has donated a significant proportion of her time to conflict resolution issues, traveling extensively in volatile regions, throughout South and Central America and writing prolifically on issues such as *"Blaming The Boys: A Feminist Fallacy,"* and *"Enemy Making: The Psychology of Propaganda."*

Through her wide-ranging career, Dr. Dineen has become progressively more concerned about the role psychologists are playing in people's lives and in society. By 1993, she had come to realize that psychology was not the caring profession that people thought it to be but rather an "industry" in which she saw many of her colleagues creating "consumers" and manufacturing "victims." She closed her clinical practice and moved to Victoria, B.C. where she researched and wrote the book *'Manufacturing Victims: What the Psychology Industry is Doing to People.'*

Dr. Dineen has been an invited speaker at conferences of judges, lawyers, police officers, ethicists, criminologists, psychologists and philosophers. As well she has been a guest on numerous radio and television shows across North America.